A COMPARATIVE SEMITIC LEXICON OF THE PHOENICIAN AND PUNIC LANGUAGES

SOCIETY OF BIBLICAL LITERATURE
DISSERTATION SERIES

edited by
Howard C. Kee
and
Douglas A. Knight

Number 32

A COMPARATIVE SEMITIC LEXICON OF THE PHOENICIAN AND PUNIC LANGUAGES

by
Richard S. Tomback

A COMPARATIVE SEMITIC LEXICON OF THE PHOENICIAN AND PUNIC LANGUAGES

by
Richard S. Tomback

WIPF & STOCK · Eugene, Oregon

Wipf and Stock Publishers
199 W 8th Ave, Suite 3
Eugene, OR 97401

A Comparative Semitic Lexicon of the Phoenician and Punic Languages
By Tomback, Richard S.

ISBN 13: 978-1-5326-9091-4
Publication date 5/7/2019
Previously published by Scholars Press, 1978

For David and Deborah

ACKNOWLEDGMENTS

I would like to acknowledge my indebtedness and gratitude to my teachers and friends who have helped me in the preparation of this study. My greatest debt is to Professor Baruch A. Levine for his learned instruction in class and for his encouragement, guidance, and invaluable suggestions during the course of my studies and the preparation of my dissertation.

I should also like to thank my other professors for their advice and inspiration: Professor Stephan J. Lieberman in Akkadian and Sumerian, Professor Lois Giffen in Arabic, Professor Moshe Held in Hebrew, and Professor Michael Bernstein in Aramaic and Syriac.

A great debt of thanks is also due my two friends and colleagues, Dr. Pauline Albenda and Mr. Abraham Dacher, for their constant advice and encouragement throughout the years of my research.

At this time I would also like to express my thanks to my family, to my wife Simone, my parents, Mr. and Mrs. Harry Tomback, and my aunt, Mrs. Florence Blum, for their unflagging faith in me and for their constant encouragement and patience during the many years of sacrifice they made during my studies.

A special debt of gratitude is due to my principal, Mr. Joshua Lichtenstein, for his cooperation in the persuance of my research. Professor Douglas A. Knight, editor of the Society of Biblical Literature Dissertation Series, kindly read my manuscript and offered many helpful suggestions. To my typist, Joann Burnich of Scholars Press, I owe a special thanks. She typed the long and very difficult manuscript with great accuracy and saved me from many errors which otherwise I would have overlooked.

R.S.T.

September 1977

TABLE OF CONTENTS

INTRODUCTION

The past ninety years have seen the appearance of several investigations on the Canaanite-Phoenician branch of Semitic languages. Since the initial publication of the *Corpus Inscriptionum Semiticarum* in 1881, of the Academie des Inscriptions et Belles Lettres, various scholars have issued voluminous collections of texts, editing and interpreting the ever-massing materials as they were discovered.

Of particular significance have been such studies as *A Text-Book of North-Semitic Inscriptions*, written by G. A. Cooke in 1903, Mark Lidzbarski's *Ephemeris für semitische Epigraphik*, issued in three volumes and appearing between 1902 and 1915, and his *Handbuch der nordsemitischen Epigraphik*, issued in 1898. In 1917, under the general heading Punica, various collections of inscriptions were gathered by J. B. Chabot and published in the *Journal asiatique*. More recently, the work of H. Donner and W. Röllig, *Kanaanäische und aramäische Inschriften*, has appeared. This last work, issued in three volumes between 1966 and 1969, contains a representative selection of Phoenician, Punic and Neo-Punic texts together with a commentary and glossary.

In 1936 the grammar of Zellig Harris appeared (*A Grammar of the Phoenician Language*). This work remained standard until 1951 when there appeared the grammar by Johannes Friedrich (*Phönizisch-punische Grammatik*, second edition, Rome, 1970). In it, Friedrich analyzed the epigraphic evidence obtained from new discoveries. Of great significance for Semitic studies was the publication by Ch.-F. Jean and J. Hoftijzer of the *Dictionnaire des inscriptions sémitiques de l'ouest*. This last book provides extensive listings of lexicographical material in the area of Phoenician and Punic studies as well as related materials from other Northwest Semitic dialects.

In most of the works cited above, the lexicon of Phoenician-Punic has received some attention. Harris in particular has dealt with some comparative Semitic phenomena, and has also cited several important phonological changes found in those inscriptions which he utilized in the preparation of his important grammar.

Yet, during this entire period of discovery and study, no work has appeared that is exclusively concerned with the lexicon of Phoenician or its related dialects, Punic and Neo-Punic.

I believe that the need for an organized study of the Phoenician lexicon is especially important today in order to bring together a systematized, coherent body of materials to which the scholar can refer when analyzing the epigraphic remains belonging to this particular branch of the Canaanite languages. A major parallel achievement designed to bring together the lexica of one branch of the Semitic languages has been the important research project concerned with the Akkadian language under the auspices of the Oriental Institute of the University of Chicago and the *Akkadisches Handwörterbuch* produced by W. von Soden and published by Otto Harrassowitz, Wiesbaden.

In the new study presented here, the materials found in Part I of the *Corpus Inscriptionum Semiticarum*, *Répertoire d'épigraphie sémitique* and the *Kanaanäische und aramäische Inschriften* have been carefully reconsidered. Many professional journals in which epigraphic remains and materials related to this study are found have also been consulted. I have made use of primary publications of inscriptions whenever available as well as various other studies involving cultic phenomena, government and other sub-topics which do not relate directly to the languages considered and their morphology or phonology.

The manner in which the comparative data of my lexicon are arranged is based upon the biblical lexica, such as the *Hebrew and English Lexicon of the Old Testament* by F. Brown, S. R. Driver, and C. A. Briggs, and the *Lexicon in Veteris Testamenti Libros* by L. Koehler and W. Baumgartner. The Phoenician or Punic entry is presented first and then followed by other languages, viz. Hebrew (Biblical and Neo-Hebrew), Akkadian, Ugaritic, Ancient Aramaic, Biblical Aramaic, Mandaic, Syriac, Egyptian, Epigraphic South Arabic, Jewish Aramaic, Neo-Syriac, Nabatean, Palmaryne, Geez, Amharic, Amarna Akkadian (West-Semitic glosses), Ammonite, Moabite, Sumerian, Samaritan Aramaic, Tegriña, Soqotri, Meḥri, Shauri, Proto-Sinaitic,

Christian Palestinian Aramaic, Empire Aramaic, Thamudic, Saftaitic, Latin, and Greek.

I have also decided to list all words in Hebrew alphabetical order rather than arrange them under their appropriate stem, since the derivation of a word was not always certain.

A sample entry from this lexicon would be as follows:

Entry. Comparative Semitic (or other) data. Possible spellings. Meaning one, meaning two (if any). Part of speech.

1 a) Line from inscription
"Translation"
(Source, text found in, line and page)

Bibliography.

All comparative material has been selected in order to provide greater insight into the development of the Phoenician or Punic lexeme and to consider with further understanding any semantic changes which may have occurred within the Semitic language family. A listing for the mere presentation of a "naked" Semitic root has been studiously avoided. Where an entry is doubtful, it has been indicated by brackets. Uncertain translations are indicated with question marks. When two readings of a given line are possible, both possibilities are given.

In the comparative evidence I have capitalized all consonants (except initial *'alif* and *'ayin*), while full vowels and half vowels are presented in small letters. All Hebrew and Aramaic entries are presented without spirantization.

When necessary, each entry lists the variant spellings and specifies the particular dialect in which they occur.

After each completed entry, a bibliography of relevant discussions is included. At the conclusion of the lexicon I have appended a three-part bibliography as follows: Part A contains materials assembled by other scholars to the year 1971, which are considered relevant to our study; Part B cites additional books referred to by the author; Part C lists important articles utilized in the study.

ABBREVIATIONS

A. BIBLIOGRAPHIC ABBREVIATIONS

AJSL	*American Journal of Semitic Languages*
AIPHOS	*Annuaire de l'Institut de philologie et d'histoire orientales et slaves.*
Albright	W. F. Albright, *Yahweh and the Gods of Canaan.* Garden City, 1969
Albright-Fs	*Near Eastern Studies in Honor of William Foxwell Albright.* Baltimore, 1971
Amadasi	M. G. Guzzo Amadasi, *Le iscrizioni fenicie e puniche delle colonie in occidente* (Studi Semitici 28). Rome, 1967
ANET	J. B. Pritchard, *Ancient Near Eastern Texts Relating to the Old Testament.* Third edition. Princeton, 1969
Aruch	*Aruch Completum*
ARM	*Archives royales de Mari*
B. Metz.	*Talmud Babli- Tractate Baba Metziah*
BAC	*Bulletin archéologique du Comité des travaux historiques et scientifiques*
BASOR	*Bulletin of the American Schools of Oriental Research*
Benz	F. L. Benz, *Personal Names in the Phoenician and Punic Inscriptions* (Studia Pohl 8). Rome, 1972
Berthier/Charlier	A. Berthier and R. Charlier, *Le sanctuaire punique d'El-Hofra à Constantine.* Paris, 1952-55
Bib	*Biblica*
BMB	*Bulletin du Musée de Beyrouth*
BMQ	*British Museum Quarterly*
Branden	A. van den Branden, *Grammaire phénicienne.* Beirut, 1969
CB	*Cahiers de Byrsa*
CBQ	*Catholic Biblical Quarterly*
CIS	*Corpus Inscriptionum Semiticarum.* Paris, 1881-
ClassFol	*Classical Folia*
CRAI	*Comptes rendus des séances de l'Academie des inscriptions et belles-lettres*
CRST	Loren R. Fisher, *The Claremont Ras Shamra Tablets* (Analecta Orientalia 48). Rome, 1972

CT	*Cuneiform Texts*, published by the British Museum
Dahood I	M. Dahood, *Psalms I* (Anchor Bible vol. 16). Garden City, 1966
Dahood III	M. Dahood, *Psalms III* (Anchor Bible vol. 17). Garden City, 1970
de Vaux	R. de Vaux, *Studies in Old Testament Sacrifice*. Cardiff, 1964
DISO	Ch.-F. Jean and J. Hoftijzer, *Dictionnaire des inscriptions sêmitiques de l'ouest*. Leiden, 1965
Driver-Fs	D. W. Thomas and W. D. McHardy, *Hebrew and Semitic Studies Presented to G. R. Driver*. Oxford, 1963
Driver, Sam.	S. R. Driver, *Notes on the Hebrew Text and the Topography of the Books of Samuel*. Second edition. Oxford, 1913
Dunand/Duru	M. Dunand and R. Duru, *Oumm el-Amed*. Paris, 1962
EI	*Eretz Israel. Archaeological, Historical and Geographical Studies*
EHO	F. M. Cross and D. N. Freedman, *Early Hebrew Orthography* (American Oriental Society 36). New Haven, 1952
EncMiq	*Encyclopedia Miqrait* (Hebrew). Jerusalem, 1965-
ESE	M. Lidzbarski, *Ephemeris für semitische Epigraphik* I-III. Giessen, 1900-15
Fitzmyer	J. A. Fitzmyer, *The Aramaic Inscriptions of Sefîre*. Rome, 1967
Gaster-Fs	*The Gaster Festschrift*, Journal of the Ancient Near East Society of Columbia University, 1973
Gibson	John C. L. Gibson, *Textbook of Syrian Semitic Inscriptions*. Vol. I. Oxford, 1971
Harris	Zellig S. Harris, *A Grammar of the Phoenician Language* (American Oriental Society 8). New Haven, 1936
HTR	*Harvard Theological Review*
HUCA	*Hebrew Union College Annual*
JA	*Journal asiatique*, Series 11
JAOS	*Journal of the American Oriental Society*
JBL	*Journal of Biblical Literature*
JCS	*Journal of Cuneiform Studies*

JEA	*Journal of Egyptian Archaeology*
JKF	*Jahrbuch für Kleinasiatische Forschung*
JNSL	*Journal of North-West Semitic Languages*
JPOS	*Journal of the Palestine Oriental Society*
JQR	*Jewish Quarterly Review*
JSS	*Journal of Semitic Studies*
KAI	H. Donner and W. Röllig, *Kanaanäische und aramäische Inschriften.* Mit einem Beitrag von O. Rössler. Wiesbaden, I 1966, II 1968, III 1969
KAR	*Karthago-Revue d'archaeologie africaine*
Leš	*Lešōnenu*
Levine	B. A. Levine, *In the Presence of the Lord.* Leiden, 1974
Leslau	*Lexique Soqotri.* Paris, 1938
LibAnt	*Libya Antiqua*
LS	*Lāšōn WeHaSSefer* I-III. Jerusalem, 1954-55
M. Sanh.	*Mishnah, Tractate Sanhedrin*
Muséon	*Le Muséon. Revue d'études orientales*
MUSJ	*Mélanges de l'Université Saint-Joseph*
NE	M. Lidzbarski, *Handbuch der nordsemitischen Epigraphik.* Weimar, 1898
NSI	G. A. Cooke, *A Text-Book of North-Semitic Inscriptions.* Oxford, 1903
OrAnt	*Oriens antiquus*
Or	*Orientalia, Nova Series*
PPG	J. Friedrich and W. Röllig, *Phönizisch-punische Grammatik* (Analecta Orientalia 46). Rome, 1970
RB	*Revue biblique*
RES	*Répertoire d'epigraphie sémitique*
RPA	*Ricerche Puniche ad Antas* (Studi Semitici 30). Rome, 1969
RSO	*Rivista degli Studi Orientali*
Sainte-Marie	E. Sainte-Marie, *Mission à Carthage.* Paris, 1884
Sem	*Semitica*
Slouszch	Naḥum Slouszch, *Otzar HaKKitōbōt HaPPiniqiyōt* ["Thesaurus of Phoenician Inscriptions"]. Tel Aviv, 1942

Speiser	E. A. Speiser, *Genesis* (Anchor Bible, Vol. I). Garden City, 1964
TrabPre	*Trabajos de Prehistoria*
Tur-Sinai	N. H. Tur-Sinai, *The Book of Job. A New Commentary.* Jerusalem, 1967
VT	*Vetus Testamentum*
ZA	*Zeitschrift für Assyriologie*
ZAW	*Zeitschrift für die alttestamentliche Wissenschaft*

B. GENERAL ABBREVIATIONS

adj.	adjective
adv.	adverb
Akk.	Akkadian
Amar.Akk.	Amarna Akkadian (West Semitic)
Amh.	Amharic
Amm.	Ammonite
Anc.Aram.	Ancient Aramaic
B.Aram.	Biblical Aramaic
B.Heb.	Biblical Hebrew
Chr.Pal.Aram.	Christian Palestinian Aramaic
col.	column
coll.	collective
conj.	conjunction
C.S.	Common Semitic
C.W.S.	Common West Semitic
dem.	demonstrative
Eg.	Egyptian
Emp.Aram.	Empire Aramaic
ESArab.	Epigraphic South Arabic
f.	feminine
Gk.	Greek
Heb.	Hebrew
Hith.	Hithqattel
ins.	inscription
J.Aram.	Jewish Aramaic
Lat.	Latin
L.W.	Loan Word

m.	masculine
Meh.	Meḥri
Moab.	Moabite
n.	noun
N	Niqtal
Nab.	Nabatean
N.Heb.	Neo-Hebrew
N.Pu.	Neo-Punic
N.Syr.	Neo-Syriac
num.	numeral
obv.	obverse
Palm.	Palmaryne
part.	participle
pers.pr.	personal pronoun
Ph.	Phoenician
pr.	pronoun
pl.	plural
p.p.	past participle
Pu.	Punic
P.S.	Proto-Sinaitic
Q	Qittel
Q.Aram.	Qumran Aramaic
Q.Heb.	Qumran Hebrew
Qu.	Quttal
rt.	root
rel.	relative
rel.pr.	relative pronoun
rev.	reverse
Sam.Aram.	Samaritan Aramaic
sing.	singular
Soq.	Soqotri
subst.	substantive
Sum.	Sumerian
Te.	Tegriña
Ug.	Ugaritic
vb.	verb
Y	Yiqtil

C. SCRIPTURAL ABBREVIATIONS

Gen.	Genesis
Ex.	Exodus
Lev.	Leviticus
Num.	Numbers
Dt.	Deuteronomy
Josh.	Joshua
Jud.	Judges
Sam.	Samuel
Is.	Isaiah
Ez.	Ezekiel
Ps.	Psalms
Prov.	Proverbs
Ecc.	Ecclesiastes
Dan.	Daniel
Neh.	Nehemiah

D. SYMBOLS

ī/ō, ā	long vowels
e	short vowels
ṀL̇K̇	unclear or broken, restorable letter(s)
[ ]	letter(s) uncertain; conjectured where possible
< >	letter(s) omitted by scribe or engraver
{ }	letter(s) to be omitted
*	prior to a lexical form = assumed root or lexeme

E. TRANSLITERATION TABLE

ʾ B G D Ḏ H W Z Ḥ H̱ Ṭ Ẓ Y K L

M N S ʿ Ǵ P Ṣ Ḍ Q R Š Ś T Ṯ

This transliteration system is used for all Semitic, Sumerian, Egyptian, Latin and Greek entries in the lexicon.

⊃

'*B*

C.S. Ph., Pu., N.Pu. '*B* (N.Pu. '*B*)
1. "father" n.m. (in royal inscriptions)
2. "father".

1 a) '*RN Z P'L* [']*TB'L BN 'ḤRM MLK GBL L'ḤRM 'BH*
"the sarcophagus which [']*TB'L* son of '*ḤRM* king of *GBL* made for '*ḤRM* his father"
(Ph. Byblos: KAI/I p. 1, ins. #1, line 1)

b) *BT 'BY*
"the house of my father"
(Ph. Zinjirli: KAI/I p. 4, ins. #24, line 5)

c) *W'NK LMY KT 'B*
"and I, however, to some I was a father"
(Ph. Zinjirli: KAI/I p. 4, ins. #24, line 10)

d) *P'LN B'L LDNNYM L'B WL'M*
"*B'L* made me as a father and a mother to the *DNNYM*"
(Ph. Karatepe: KAI/I p. 5, ins. #26, line A I,3)

e) [*MM*]*LKT L'BYTY ZR*
"[a rul]er (who was) an enemy to my fathers"
(Ph. Byblos: MUSJ 45 [1969] p. 262, line 6)

2 a) *L'BY LPRSY*
"to his father, to *PRSY*"
(Ph. Kition: KAI/I p. 8, ins. #34, line 1)

b) '*Š N*[*DR*] '*BY'* [ ] *BN ḤMLKT*
"that which is father [ ] son of *ḤMLKT* vo[wed]"
(Pu. Carthage: Slouschz p. 350, ins. #580, lines B 2-3)

c) *PHL' L'B'NHM*
"they made for their father"
(N.Pu. Tunisia: KAI/I p. 26, ins. #142, line 4)

d) *TYN' L' 'BWY'*
"his father erected it for him"
(N.Pu. Masculula: JA Series 11 vol. 7 [1916] p. 454, ins. #3, line 4)

Bibl. DISO 1; EHO 14; Harris 73; ANET 653-54, 661; NE 232; PPG 35, 40, 47, 110, 114; GP 14, 16, 19, 26-27, 50; Benz 256-57; MUSJ 45 (1969) 272; JA Series 11 vol. 7 (1916) 454.

'BD Heb. *'āBaD* "to perish, be lost"; Ug. *'BD*; Akk. *'aBāTu*; Moab. *'BD*; Anc.Aram. *'BD*; Emp. Aram. *'BD*; J.Aram. *'aBaD*; Syriac *'eBaD*; Mandaic *'aBD*, *'aWD*, *'aUD*; Geez *'aBaDa* "to lose one's mind"; Amh. *'aBBaDa* "to be mad"; Nab. *'BD*. 1. "to destroy" vb. (Q)

a) *WY'BD H[ ] Z'*
"and destroy this [ ]"
(Ph. Cyprus: KAI/I p. 7, ins. #30, line 3)

Bibl. DISO 1-2; KAI/II 48.

'BN Heb. *'eBeN* "stone"; Ug. *'aBN*; Akk. *'aBNu*; ESArab. *'BN*; Anc.Aram. *'BN*; Emp.Aram. *'BN*; J.Aram. *'aBNa'*; Syriac *'aBNa'*; Mandaic *'aBNa'*; Soq. *'oBeN*; Ph., Pu., N.Pu. *'BN* (N.Pu. *HBN*, *'BN*). 1. "stone used as an altar or funeral monument" n.f.

a) *'Š BTKT 'BN*
"which is in the midst of a (semi-precious) stone"
(Ph. Byblos: KAI/I p. 2, ins. #10, line 5)

b) *MZBḤ 'BN*
"a stone altar"
(Pu. Carthage: KAI/I p. 17, ins. #77, line 1)

c) *'BN 'Š NDR MTNB'L BN Y'R*
"the stone (altar) which *MTNB'L* son of *Y'R* vowed"
(Pu. Constantine: Berthier/Charlier p. 87, ins. #106, lines 1-2)

d) *ṬN' HBN ST LSWL' BN ḤMLKT*
"this (grave) stone was erected to *SWL'* son of *ḤMLKT*"
(N.Pu. Maktar: KAI/I p. 28, ins. #151, lines 1-2)

e) *Ṭ'N' 'BN Z LB'ḶŠM' BN M'SQL''*
"this (grave) stone was erected to *B'ḶŠM'* son of *M'SQL''*"
(N.Pu. Tunisia: KAI/I p. 25, ins. #133, lines 1-2)

f) *ṬN' 'BN Z*
"this (grave) stone was erected"
(N.Pu. Tunisia: KAI/I p. 25, ins. #134, line 1)

Bibl. NE 205-6; DISO 2; Harris 73; PPG 153; Branden 31; Berthier/Charlier 87; ANET 656; KAI/II 12, 94, 115, 135, 146.

'BST Heb. *'eBūS* "manger, bowl"; Akk. *'aBūSu* "storeroom"; Ug. *'iBSN* "bowl" n.m.

a) *'BST Z 'Š NDR*
"this bowl (is that) which...vowed"
(Pu. Malta: Amadasi p. 39, ins. #31, line 2)

Bibl. Amadasi 39; CRST 39-40, 52-53.

'BT Akk. *'aBBūTu* "intercessor"; Arabic *'aBaT* "father"; Syriac *'aBaHaTa'* "fatherhood, father". 1. "intercessor" n.f.

a) *W'P B'BT P'LN KL MLK*
"and moreover, every king made me as (an) intercessor" (or "as a father")
(Ph. Karatepe: KAI/I p. 5, ins. #26, line A I,12)

Bibl. DISO 3.

'GD N.Heb. *'āGaD* "to bind together"; J.Aram. *'aGaD*; Mandaic *'GD*, *'aGD*. 1. "to gather together" vb.

a) *HWN YM L'GD LM MLḤM*
"the wealth (?) of the sea (?), the sailors did gather together for themselves"
(Ph. Byblos: MUSJ 45 [1969] p. 262, line 2)

Bibl. MUSJ 45 (1969) 271.

'GNN Heb. *'aGGāN* "bowl, basin"; Akk. *'aGaNNu*; Ug. *'GN*; Eg. *YKN*; J.Aram. *'aGGāNa'*; Syriac *'aGaNa'*; Arabic *'iJāNaTuN* "type of vessel for washing"; Geez *'ayGaN* "basin"; Amh. *GaN* "jar".

a) *[BṢ]PR 'GNN*
"[for a bi]rd (prepared) in a *'GNN* bowl (?)"
(Pu. Marseilles: KAI/I p. 15, ins. #69, line 11)

Bibl. DISO 3; Slouszch 146; KAI/II 83; ANET 656; Harris 73; Amadasi 179; Gibson 52.

'DLN etymology unknown. 1. "with" prep.

a) *KY 'Y 'DLN* KSP 'Y 'DLN ḤRṢ*
"for there is not in it (?) silver (and) there is not in it (?) gold"
(Ph. Sidon: KAI/I p. 2, ins. #13, lines 4-5)

*The reading of Dalet is uncertain. The reading of a Resh would give us the infinitive absolute of the vb. *'RY*. Hence this line could be translated "for there is not gathered in it (the sarcophagus) silver (and) there is not gathered in it gold."

Bibl. ZDMG 62 (1908) 154; AJSL 46 (1929) 59; DISO 58; Harris 74; NSI 29; Slouszch 16-17; ANET 662; KAI/II 17; Gaster-Fs 144, esp. note 58; JQR 16 (1904) 283.

'DM Heb. *'āDāM* "man, mankind"; Ug. *'aDM*; ESArab. *'DM* "serf"; Arabic *'aDaMiiuNa* "human beings".
1. "man" n.m.

a) *WKL 'DM 'L YPTḤ 'YT MŠKB Z*
"and any man, may he not open this resting place"
(Ph. Sidon: KAI/I p. 3, ins. #14, line 4)

b) *'Š YŠT' 'DM LLKT DRK*
"where a man was afraid to walk on the road"
(Ph. Karatepe: KAI/I p. 5, ins. #26, lines A II,4-5)

c) *W'L KL ZBḤ 'Š 'DM LZBḤ*
"and for all sacrifices which a man would be wont to sacrifice"
(Pu. Marseilles: KAI/I p. 15, ins. #69, line 14)

d) *WBY PY 'DM BŠMY*
"and without the word of a man (speaking) in my name"
(Pu. Carthage: KAI/I p. 17, ins. #79, lines 8-10)

e) *L'DM H' L'DRB'L*
"for that man, for *'DRB'L*"
(N.Pu. Leptis Magna: KAI/I p. 22, ins. #119, line 5)

Bibl. DISO 4; ANET 653, 656, 662; NE 208; Amadasi 169; Harris 74; PPG 104, 149; Branden 63; Benz 260; KAI/II 19, 36, 83, 97, 124; Bib 44 [1963] 292; Albright 122.

'DN I See under *'DN* II for etymology.
1. "lordly" adj. 2. "royalty" n.m.

1 a) *WYṬN' 'NK BT 'DNY*
"and I erected my lordly house(s)"
(Ph. Karatepe: KAI/I p. 5, ins. #26, lines A I,9-10)

2 a) *WP'L 'NK LŠRŠ 'DNY N'M*
"and I acted kindly to the root(s) of my royalty"
(Ph. Karatepe: KAI/I p. 5, ins. #26, line A I,10)

Bibl. DISO 5; ANET 653; KAI/II 36.

'DN II — Heb. *'āDōN* "lord"; Ug. *'aDN* "lord, father"; Mandaic *'aDuNai* "a name given to the sun"; Ph., Pu., N.Pu. *'DN* (Pu. *'DN, 'N, DN, 'DDN*; N.Pu. *'D'N, 'DN, ḤDN*). 1. in divine titles "lord" n.m. 2. in royal titles.

1 a) *P'LT 'NK 'BD'ŠMN BNH BN 'S'' L'DNN*
"I *'BD'ŠMN* the builder, son of *'S''*, made for our lord"
(Ph. Sidon: KAI/I p. 2, ins. #12, lines 1-3)

b) *L'DN LŠDRB'*
"for the lord, for *ŠDRB'*"
(Pu. Carthage: KAI/I p. 17, ins. #77, line 1)

c) *LḤDN LB'L ḤMN*
"for the lord, for *B'L ḤMN*"
(Pu. Constantine: Slouszch p. 224, ins. #232, line 1)

d) *L'DDN LB'L ḤMN*
"for the lord, for *B'L ḤMN*"
(Pu. Carthage: CIS I, ins. #3086, line 1)

e) *L'DN NB'L ḤBN*
"for the lord, for *B'L ḤMN*"
(Pu. Sousse: KAI/I p. 19, ins. #94, lines 1-2)

f) *L'DN LB'L ḤMN*
"for the lord, for *B'L ḤMN*"
(N.Pu. Constantine: KAI/I p. 30, ins. #164, line 1)

g) *L'DN B'LMN*
"for the lord, *B'L ḤMN*"
(N.Pu. Guelma: KAI/I p. 30, ins. #167, line 1)

h) *L'D'N B'LM'N*
"for the lord *B'L ḤMN*"
(N.Pu. Masculula: JA Series 11 vol. 7 [1916] p. 461, line 1)

i) *L'NY B'L 'MN*
"for his lord *B'L ḤMN*"
(Pu. Constantine: Berthier/Charlier p. 42, ins. #43, lines 3-4)

2 a) *BŠT 180 L'DN MLKM*
"in the one hundred and eightieth year of the Lords of Kingdoms"
(Ph. Umm el-Awamid: KAI/I p. 3, ins. #18, lines 4-5)

b) *'DNN B'LR[M]*
"our lord *B'LR[M]*"
(Ph. Idalion: KAI I p. 8, ins. #39, line 2)

c) *BMYP'L 'DN 'ŠMNḤLṢ*
"in the employ (?) of lord *'ŠMNḤLṢ*"
(Ph. Carthage: CIS I, ins. #5522, lines 2-3)

Bibl. DISO 5; Harris 74; NE 208; AJSL 57 (1940) 71-74; ZDMG 79 (1963) 145-49; PPG 110; Berthier/Charlier 42; ZAW 74 (1962) 66-68; KAI/II 16, 26, 48, 94, 106, 153, 155; Benz 260-61; JAOS 74 (1954) 228; VT 12 (1962) 149; JCS 15 (1961) 43.

'DR I

B.Heb. *N'eDaR* "to be powerful" (Ex. 15:11); Q.Heb. *'DYRYM* "mighty, evil"; Ug. *'aDR* "mighty". 1. "to empower" vb. (Q)

a) *'Š 'DR 'WRK MLK DNNYM*
"whom *'WRK* king of the *DNMYM* empowered"
(Ph. Karatepe: KAI/I p. 5, ins. #26, line A I,2)

Bibl. ANET 653; KAI/II 36; DISO 5-6; Benz 261-62; Harris 74-75.

'DR II

[Akk. *uDDuRu* "to annoy"]. 1. "cause annoyance" vb. (Q)

a) *W'DR 'LY MLK D[N]NYM*
"and the king of the *D[N]NYM* caused me annoyance (?)"
(Ph. Zinjirli: KAI/I p. 4, ins. #24, line 7)

Bibl. KAI/II 30; ANET 654; DISO 5-6; Benz 261-62.

'DR III

Heb. *'aDīR* "glorious, mighty"; Ug. *'aDR*; J.Aram. *'aDiRa'*. 1. "mighty" adj. m. 2. "mighty" n.m. 3. as an epithet 4. "noble" (of men) 5. "glorious" adj.

1 a) *WYSGRNM H'LNM HQDŠM 'T MMLK<T> 'DR*
"may the holy gods deliver them up to a mighty ruler"
(Ph. Sidon: KAI/I p. 3, ins. #14, line 9)

b) *BMTKT MLKM 'DRM*
"in the midst of mighty kings"
(Ph. Zinjirli: KAI/I p. 5, ins. #24, lines 5-6)

c) *W'Z 'DR 'L KL MLK*
"and awesome strength over all kings"
(Ph. Karatepe: KAI/I p. 5, ins. #26, line A III,4)

2 a) *BŠT 26 LPTLMYS 'DN MLKM H'DR*
"in the twenty-sixth year of *PTLMYS*, the Lord of Kingdoms, the mighty (one)"
(Ph. Ma'ṣub: KAI/I p. 4, ins. #19, lines 5-6)

3 a) *L'DR LB'L ḤMN*
"to the Mighty (one), to *B'L ḤMN*"
(Pu. Carthage: CIS I, ins. #1976)

b) *L'LṄ L'DR LB'L 'DR*
"to the god, the Mighty (one), to *B'L 'DR*"
(Pu. Constantine: Berthier/Charlier p. 15, ins. #5, line 1)

c) *LRBBTN LTNT 'DRT*
"for our lady, for *TNT* the Mighty"
(Pu. Ibiza: KAI/I p. 16, ins. #72, line B 3)

4 a) *'DR' 'LPQY*
"the nobles of *'LPQY*"
(N.Pu. Leptis Magna: KAI/I p. 22, ins. #119, line 4)

b) *'Š LPNY 'DR' 'LPQY W'M 'LPQ[Y]*
"that which is before the nobles of *'LPQY* and the people of *'LPQ[Y]*"
(N.Pu. Leptis Magna: KAI/I p. 24, ins. #126, line 7)

5 a) *'RṢT DGN H'DRT*
"the glorious corn lands"
(Ph. Sidon: KAI/I p. 3, ins. #14, line 19)

b) *'ṬRT 'DR'T L' WL'M'*
"glorious cornice (work), for him and for his people" (?)
(N.Pu. Maktar: KAI/I p. 27, ins. #145, line 3)

Bibl. Benz 261-62; NE 209; DISO 5-6; LS I 74; Harris 74-75; KAI/II 19, 27, 31, 36, 88, 124, 131, 141; ANET 653-54, 662; Benz 144; PPG 154; VT 17 (1967) 1-7.

'DR IV — Akk. *'aDāRu* "to fear a deity, to respect an oath". 1. "to fear" vb.

a) *WBRBM Y'DR*
"may they greatly fear"
(Ph. Karatepe: KAI/I p. 5, ins. #26, line A III,10)

Bibl. ANET 653; KAI/II 36; DISO 5-6; Benz 261-62; Harris 74-75.

'DT — Ug. *'aDT* "lady"; N.Heb. *'aDōNā*. 1. "lady" n.f.

a) *LB'LT GBL 'DTW*
"for the Mistress of *GBL*, his lady"
(Ph. Byblos: KAI/I p. 1, ins. #7, lines 3-4)

b) *[LB]'LT GBL 'DTW*
"[for the Mis]tress of *GBL*, his lady"
(Ph. Byblos: KAI/I p. 1, ins. #6, line 2)

c) *MTT L'ŠTRT 'DTY*
"(as) a gift to *'ŠTRT*, her lady"
(Ph. Carchemish: KAI/I p. 7, ins. #29, line 2)

Bibl. DISO 5; KAI/II 8-9, 47; Harris 74; EHO 15; JAOS 67 (1947) 157 note 41, 74 (1954) 238 note 39; PPG 22; Slouszch 9.

'W — Heb. *'ō* "or"; Ug. *'W*; Akk. *'aW*; Anc.Aram. *'W*; Emp.Aram. *'W*; J.Aram. *'ō*; Syriac *'ō*; Nab. *'W*; Palm. *'W*; B.Aram. *'ō*; Arabic *'aW*. 1. "or" conj.

a) *'LT 'W M[N]ḤT*
"holocaust(s) or off[erin]g(s)"
(N.Pu. Henschir Medina: KAI/I p. 29, ins. #159, line 8)

Bibl. KAI/II 148.

'ZR — meaning and etymology unknown. 1. "cursed" adj. m. (Perhaps related to B.Heb. *ZāR* "hated"; Akk. *ZēRu*; Soq. *ZRY* "to hate")

a) *BN MSK YMM 'ZRM*
"the son of limited cursed days (?)"
(Ph. Sidon: KAI/I p. 3, ins. #14, line 3)

Bibl. DISO 7; Harris 75; NE 211; ANET 662; KAI/II 19; Slouszch 19-20; Albright-Fs 260 esp. note 30.

'ZRM Ug. *'uZR* "type of sacrifice." 1. type of sacrifice, n.m. Pu. *'ZRM* (N.Pu. *'ŠRM*)

a) *MLK 'DM 'ZRM 'Š 'Š* NDR*
"a *MLK 'DM 'ZRM* sacrifice which... vowed"
(Ph. Constantine: Berthier/Charlier p. 37, ins. #37, lines 2-3)

*I am of the assumption that the second *'Š* is not the demonstrative adj. *Z* but a dittography of the rel. pr. *'Š*.

b) *MLK B'L 'ZRM 'Š NDR*
"a *MLK B'L 'ZRM* sacrifice which... vowed"
(Ph. Sousse: KAI/I p. 19, ins. #98, lines 2-3)

c) *'ŠRṀ 'ŠT*
"this *'ŠRṀ* sacrifice"
(N.Pu. Guelma: KAI/I p. 30, ins. #167, line 3)

Bibl. Berthier/Charlier 38; Harris 75; KAI/II 106, 155; DISO 7; Slouszch 73, 213; LS I 106-7, note 3.

'ZRT meaning and etymology unknown. 1. "clan" (?) n.f.

a) *'Š NDR 'BD'ŠMN Š'ZRT 'BD'ŠMN*
"that which *'BD'ŠMN* of the clan (?) of *'BD'ŠMN* vowed"
(Pu. Carthage: CIS I, ins. #3712, line 4)

b) *WB'ZRT ŠL'*
"and from his clan (?)"
(Pu. Dougga: KAI/I p. 19, ins. #100, line 5)

c) *'ZRTM*
"his clan (?)"
(Pu. Constantine: Berthier/Charlier p. 142, ins. #223, line 3)

d) *[BR]ḤT H'DMM HMT WBRḤT 'ZRTNM*
"[by means of the spi]rits of these men and the spirits of their clans (?)"
(Pu. Carthage: CIS I, ins. #5510, line 2)

Bibl. Harris 75; DISO 8; Berthier/Charlier 143; PPG 48, 113; KAI/II 107; Slouszch 212.

'*Ḥ* C.S. n.m. Ph., N.Pu. '*Ḥ* (N.Pu. *Ḥ*) 1. "brother"

a) *WLMY KT 'Ḥ*
"to some I was a brother"
(Ph. Zinjirli: KAI/I p. 4, ins. #24, line 11)

b) *WKN 'Ḥ Š'L*
"and there was my brother *Š'L*"
(Ph. Zinjirli: KAI/I p. 4, ins. #24, lines 3-4)

c) *LQN'M WL'ḤY'*
"for *QN'M* and for his brothers"
(N.Pu. Leptis Magna: NE p. 434, line 2)

d) *ḤYMY ḤNB'L*
"his brother, *ḤNB'L*"
(N.Pu. Guelma: JA Series 11 vol. 8 [1916] p. 494, ins. #11, lines 2-3)

e) *BN' ḤYM*
"his brother's sons"
(N.Pu. Guelma: JA Series 11 vol. 8 [1916] p. 493, ins. #10, line 6)

Bibl. ANET 654; KAI/II 31; DISO 8-9; Harris 75; NE 211; EHO 16; JA Series 11 vol. 8 (1916) 494; PPG 109, 114; Branden 15, 19; Benz 263-64.

'*ḤD* C.S. n.m. Pu. '*ḤD* (N.Pu. *ḤD*, '*D*, *D*). 1. "one"

a) *KSP 'ŠRT B'ḤD*
"ten silver (shekels) for each"
(Pu. Marseilles: KAI/I p. 15, ins. #69, line 3)

b) *'RBM WḤD*
"forty-one"
(N.Pu. Henschir Guergour: KAI/I p. 27, ins. #143, line 4)

c) *'SRM W'D*
"twenty-one"
(N.Pu. Henschir Moded: KAI/I p. 29, ins. #158, line 3)

d) *ŠŠM WD*
"sixty-one"
(N.Pu. Guelma: JA Series 11 vol. 8 [1910] p. 488, ins. #4, line 4)

Bibl. ANET 656; DISO 9; Harris 76; PPG 13, 119, 121; Branden 37, 39; JA Series 11 vol. 8 (1910) 489.

'ḤDY for etymology see under *LḤDY*. 1. "together" adv.

a) *WP'L SDLM 'ḤDY*
"and the makers of sandals, together"
(Pu. Carthage: CRAI [1968] p. 117, line 6)

'ḤR Heb. *'aḤaR* "after"; Ug. *'ḤR*; Akk. *'aḪaRRu*; Emp.Aram. *'ḤR*; B.Aram. *'aḤaR*; Syriac *LeḤōRe*; J.Aram. *'aḤōRe*; Mandaic *'ḤuRia'*, *'ḤuRia'*. 1. "after" adv.

a) *'ḤR 'Š P'L*
"after he made"
(N.Pu. Cherchel: NE p. 438, line 2)

'ḤRY B.Heb. *'aḤaRiT* "remainder, end"; N.Heb. *'aḤaRiT* "end, future"; Ug. *'aḪRYT*. 1. "remainder" n.m.

a) *'ḤRY HŠ'R*
"the remainder of the flesh"
(Pu. Marseilles: KAI/I p. 15, ins. #69, line 4)

b) *KL 'ḤRY [HMQDŠ]Ṁ*
"all the remainder of [the [sanctuari]es"
(Ph. Ma'ṣub: KAI/I p. 4, ins. #19, lines 9-10)

Bibl. Amadasi 169; Harris 76; KAI/II 27, 83; DISO 10; NE 212; ANET 656; Slouszch 95, 144; PPG 98, 125, 130.

'ḤT I C.S. 1. "sister" n.f.

a) *'MR L'ḤTY 'ṘŠT 'MṘ 'ḤTḲ BŠ'*
"say to my sister *'RŠT*, thus says your sister *BŠ'*"
(Ph. Saqqara: KAI/I p. 12, ins. #50, line 2)

b) *ṮYN' L'ḤT 'MM*
"set up for his mother's sister"
(N.Pu. Leptis Magna: KAI/I p. 23, ins. #123, line 2)

Bibl. Harris 75-76; Benz 265; PPG 114; DISO 8-9; KAI/II 67, 130.

'ḤT II C.S. 1. "one" n.f.

a) *B'ḤT<T> 'RB'M ŠT*
"in the forty-first year"
(Pu. Constantine: Berthier/Charlier p. 51, ins. #56, lines 3-4)

b) *BŠT 'SRM W'ḤT*
"in the twenty-first year"
(N.Pu. Dschebel Massoudj: KAI/I p. 26, ins. #14, line 3)

c) *P'M'T 'SR W'ḤT*
"for the eleventh time"
(N.Pu. Leptis Magna: KAI/I p. 22, ins. #120, line 1)

Bibl. DISO 9; PPG 120; KAI/II 116, 126, 138; Berthier/Charlier 55; JAOS 74 (1954) 228-29.

'ṬWMṬ' meaning and etymology doubtful; perhaps related to: B.Heb. *'āṬaM* "to shut, stop" (as lips); N.Heb. *ṬuMṬuM* "a person whose genitals are hidden or underdeveloped"; Akk. *ṬuMMuMu* "deaf, hollow"; Syriac *ṬaM* "solid, close"; Arabic *ṬaMMa* "to cover, wrap up". 1. "sexual underdevelopment" n.m.

a) *B'GL 'Š QRNY LMBMḤSR B'ṬWMṬ'*
"for a calf whose horns are wanting on account of (its) sexual underdevelopment (?)"
(Ph. Marseilles: KAI/I p. 15, ins. #69, line 5)

Bibl. DISO 11; ANET 656-57; Harris 76; Slouszch 144; KAI/II 83; Amadasi 178.

'Y I B.Heb. *'Y* "island"; Eg. *'W*; ESArab. *'WY*. 1. "island" n.m.

a) *L'DN LB'ŠMM B'YNṢM*
"to the lord, to *B'L ŠMM* on the Island of Hawks (?)"
(Pu. Sardinia: KAI/I p. 14, ins. #64, line 1)

b) *'Š NDR 'ZRB'L BN B'LḤN' BN B'LYTN 'Š B'M 'YTNM*
"that which *'ZRB'L* son of *B'LḤN'* son of *B'LYTN* who is among the people of the Island of Jackals (?) vowed"
(Pu. Carthage: KAI/I p. 19, ins. #99, line 5)

c) *'Š B'M YBŠM*
"who is among the people of the Island of Spice(s) (?)"
(Pu. Carthage: Slouszch p. 286, ins. #402, lines 3-4)

d) [*BN*] *'DRB'L BYR'Š*
"[son of] *'DRB'L* (who is) on the Island of Earthquakes"
(Ph. Carthage: Slouszch p. 278, ins. #379, lines 3-4)

Bibl. Harris 76; NE 213-14; DISO 11; Or 37 (1968) 434; KAI/II 79, 107; Slouszch 278, 286; Syria 48 (1971) 399.

'Y II Heb. *'ī(y)* "no, not"; Akk. *'ai*. 1. "not, not" adv. 2. in combinations

1 a) *K 'Y ŠM BN MNM*
"for there is nothing placed in it"
(Ph. Sidon: KAI/I p. 3, ins. #14, line 5)

b) *'Y MPT WR'Š*
"there is no dignitary (?) or leader"
(Ph. Cyprus: KAI/I p. 7, ins. #30, line 1)

c) *K 'Y 'Ṙ LN KSP*
"for there is not gathered in it silver" (also see *'DLN*)
(Ph. Sidon: KAI/I p. 2, ins. #13, line 4)

2 a) *BY PY 'NK*
"without my word"
(Pu. Carthage: KAI/I p. 17, ins. #79, line 8)

b) [*K*]*L MŠ'T 'Š 'YBL ŠT BPS Z*
"[eve]ry payment which is not set down on this tablet"
(Pu. Marseilles: KAI/I p. 15, ins. #69, line 18)

c) *'BL LPTḤ*
"do not open"
(Ph. Avignon: KAI/I p. 16, ins. #70, line 4)

Bibl. Amadasi 182, 184; NE 213; ANET 656, 662; KAI/II 17, 19, 48, 83, 87, 97; PPG 125, 161; DISO 11; Brandon 114, 129-30; Slouszch 16-17, 21; Gibson 38.

'YBL Heb. *'aBāL* "verily"; Ug. *BL* "surely". 1. "only" adv. 2. emphatic particle

1 a) *'YBL 'M 'T 'BTM*
"(but) only with his forefathers"
(N.Pu. Leptis Magna: KAI/I p. 22, ins. #119, line 7)

2 a) *W'M 'BL TŠT ŠM 'TK*
"and if you place my name with yours"
(Ph. Byblos: KAI/I p. 2, ins. #10, line 13)

Bibl. KAI/II 12, 124.

'YL Heb. *'aYYāL* "stag"; Ug. *'YL*; Akk. *'aYYāLu*; Syriac *'aYLa* ; Arabic *'iYYāLuN*; Geez *HaYeL*. 1. "stag" n.m.

a) *'M B'YL*
"or for a stag"
(Pu. Marseilles: KAI/I p. 15, ins. #69, line 5)

Bibl. DISO 12; KAI/II 83; Slouszch 144; JBL 56 (1937) 142; Amadasi 178.

'YR N.Heb. *'iYYāR* name of the second month; Akk. *'aYYaRu*; Syriac *'iYaR*; Arabic *'iYāR*. 1. name of a month n.

a) *TŠ' LYRḤ 'YR*
"the ninth of the month of *'YR*"
(Pu. Constantine: Berthier/Charlier p. 57, ins. #61, line 3)

Bibl. Berthier/Charlier 58.

'YT Heb. *'T* "sign of the determined object"; Q.Heb. *T*; Moab. *'T*; Geez *KiYā*; Emp.Aram. *WT*; B.Aram. *YT*; J.Aram. *YaT*; Syriac *YaT*; Palm. *YT*; Arabic *'iyyā*; Ph., Pu. *'YT* (Pu. *T*; N.Pu. *T*, *'T*). 1. sign of the determined object. 2. with the pronominal suffix

1 a) *WQR' 'NK 'T RBTY*
"and I invoked my lady"
(Ph. Byblos: KAI/I p. 2, ins. #10, lines 2-3)

b) *'L YPTḤ 'YT MŠKB Z*
"may he not open this resting place"
(Ph. Sidon: KAI/I p. 2, ins. #14, line 4)

c) *YTN LN 'DN MLKM 'YT D'R WYPY*
"the Lord of Kingdoms gave us *D'R* and *YPY*"
(Ph. Sidon: KAI/I p. 3, ins. #14, lines 18-19)

d) *T MQDŠ Z BN' B'L' TBGG*
"this sanctuary the citizens of *TBGG* built"
(Pu. Dougga: KAI/I p. 20, ins. #101, line 1)

e) *ŠM' 'T QLM*
"he heard his voice"
(Pu. Constantine: Berthier/ Charlier p. 84, ins. #103, line 9)

f) *'YT HMṬBḤ Z*
"this slaughtering place"
(Pu. Carthage: KAI/I p. 17, ins. #80, line 1)

g) *WT 'RPT ST*
"and this portico"
(N.Pu. Leptis Magna: KAI/I p. 25, ins. #129, line 2)

h) *W'T BD'ŠTRT BN YPŠ*
"and *BD'ŠTRT* son of *YPŠ*"
(N.Pu. Bir Bou-Rekba: KAI/I p. 26, ins. #137, line 7)

2 a) *ŠM' QL' BRK 'T'*
"he heard her voice (and) blessed her"
(Pu. Carthage: Slouszch p. 247, ins. #289, line 3)

b) *W'LNM ŠMŠ* (?) *'DL 'TY* (reading of *ŠMŠ* uncertain)
"and the divine Sun (?) justified (?) me"
(Pu. Carthage: Slouszch p. 180, ins. #155, line 5)

Bibl. DISO 229; ANET 656, 662; Harris 76; NE 230; PPG 13, 37, 128-29; Branden 118; Slouszch 247; KAI/II 12, 19, 98, 110, 132, 136; Muséon 76 (1963) 195-200; Fitzmyer 69.

'KL C.S. 1. "to eat" vb.

a) *KM 'Š 'KLT ZQN*
"as a fire consumes a beard"
(Ph. Zinjirli: KAI/I p. 4, ins. #24, lines 6-7)

b) *'Š 'KLT YD*
"a fire consumes a hand"
(Ph. Zinjirli: KAI/I p. 4, ins. #24, line 7)

Bibl. KAI/II 31; ANET 654; DISO 12-13.

'L I C.S. 1. "to" prep.

1 a) *'L 'BDŠMŠ*
"to (?) *'BDŠMŠ*" (or "I am [?] *'BDŠMŠ*")
(Ph. Abydos: KAI/I p. 11, ins. #49, line 29)

b) *'L 'RŠT BT 'ŠṀNY[TN]*
"to *'RŠT* daughter of *'ŠṀNY[TN]*"
(Ph. Saqqara: KAI/I p. 12, ins. #50, line 1)

2 a) *'L 'LT HMQDŠM 'L*
"into these sanctuaries"
(N.Pu. Bir Bou-Rekba: KAI/I p. 26, ins. #137, lines 4-5)

Bibl. KAI/II 65, 67, 136; DISO 13; Slouszch 210.

'L II C.S. 1. "god, deity" n.m. 2. "temple (with *BT*)" n.m. 3. with specific identification. 4. designating a specific cultic functionary. 5. qualifying silver. 6. designating a cultic object. 7. designating a specific priestly group (?). 8. "worshiper" n.m. (?). 9. "household god" n.m. 10. as a proper name of a deity. Ph., Pu., N.Pu. *'L* (N.Pu. *ʿL*)

1 a) *MPḤRT 'L GBL QDSM*
"the assembly of the gods of *GBL*, the holy ones)
(Ph. Byblos: KAI/I p. 1, ins. #4, lines 4-5)

b) *LPN 'L GBL QḊŠṀ*
"before the gods of *GBL*, the holy ones"
(Ph. Byblos: KAI/I p. 1, ins. #4, line 7)

c) *'YT HBT Z BN L'LY*
"this temple he built for his god"
(Ph. Sidon: KAI/I p. 3, ins. #15, line 2)

d) *L'LM Z YKN GR'ŠTRT*
"for this god *GR'ŠTRT* prepared" (or "for these [?] gods")
(Pu. Carthage: Slouszch p. 178, ins. #145, line 1)

2 a) *ḤṢR BT 'LM*
"the temple court"
(Ph. Piraeus: KAI/I p. 13, ins. #60, line 2)

3 a) *L'LM N'MM*
"for the kind gods"
(N.Pu. Constantine: KAI/I, p. 30, ins. #162, line 3)

b) *'ŠMNṢLḤ RB KHNM 'LM NRGL*
"*'ŠMNṢLḤ* chief priest of the god *NRGL*"
(Ph. Piraeus: KAI/I p. 13, ins. #59, line 2)

c) *LRBTY L'LM 'DRT 'S 'LM 'ŠTRT*
"to my lady, to the divine, mighty *'S*, the divine *'ŠTRT*"
(Ph. Memphis: KAI/I p. 11, ins. #48, line 2)

d) *W'LNM ŠMŠ* (reading of *ŠMŠ* uncertain)
"and the divine sun"
(Pu. Carthage: Slouszch p. 180, ins. #155, line 5)

e) *'L QN 'RṢ*
"*'L*, the creator of the earth"
(Ph. Karatepe: KAI/I p. 5, ins. #26, line A III,18)

f) *L'L[NM] 'R'P'M*
"to the gods, the shades"
(N.Pu. Leptis Magna: KAI/I p. 22, ins. #117, line 1)

g) *L'LṄ L'DR LB'L 'DR*
"to the god, to the Mighty, to *B'L* the Mighty"
(Pu. Constantine: Berthier/Charlier p. 15, ins. #5, line 1)

h) *L'DN L'LN HQDŠ B'L ḤMN*
"to the lord, to the holy god, *B'L ḤMN*"
(Pu. Constantine: KAI/I p. 20, ins. #104, line 1)

4 a) *GRMLQRT BN BDMLQRT MQM 'LM*
"*GRMLQRT* son of *BDMLQRT*, the awakener of the god(s)"
(Pu. Carthage: Slouszch p. 186, ins. #163, lines 2-3)

b) *'BDMLQRT HŠPT RB KHNM MQM 'LM*
"*'BDMLQRT*, the magistrate, chief priest, awakener of the god(s)"
(Pu. Carthage: Slouszch p. 197, ins. #190, lines 3-4)

5 a) *BKSP 'LM*
"of the finest silver" (or "silver of the god")
(Ph. Piraeus: KAI/I p. 13, ins. #60, line 6)

6 a) *M'Š 'LM ŠP'R ST*
"this divine (?) statue (fashioned from) pottery (?)"
(N.Pu. Ras el-Haddigia: KAI/I p. 22, ins. #118, line 1)

7 a) *MRZḤ 'LM*
"priestly guild (?)"
(Pu. Marseilles: KAI/I p. 15, ins. #69, line 16)

8 a) *'Š 'LM 'Š LMLQRT*
"the worshiper (?) of (the god) *MLQRT*"
(Ph. Beirut: NSI p. 36, no. 5, lines 1-3)

9 a) *'L BT*
"household god" (or "god of the dynasty")
(Pu. Constantine: Berthier/Charlier p. 27, ins. #25, line 1)

10 a) *WKL BN 'LM*
"and all the sons of *'L*"
(Ph. Arslan Tash: BASOR 197 [1970] rev. line 11)

b) *L'DN L'L QN 'RṢ*
"for the lord, for *'L*, the creator of earth"
(N.Pu. Leptis Magna: KAI/I p. 25, ins. #129, line 1)

Bibl. JBL 75 (1956) 255-57; JBL 76 (1957) 91; Harris 77; Benz 266-68; VT 12 (1962) 190-94; DISO 13; Berthier/Charlier 5; Slouszch 182, 218; NE 214-15; HTR 55 (1962) 232-50; Branden 19, 32; PPG 115, 154; KAI/II 6, 15, 16, 36, 64, 67, 72-73, 114, 122-23, 152; Albright 165-66; ANET 653; JSS 1 (1956) 25-37.

'L III Heb. *'eLLe*; B.Heb. *'el*; ESArab. *'LN*; B.Aram. *'iLLeN*, *'eLLe*; J.Aram. *'iLLeN*; Syriac *HāLeN*; Palm. *'LN*; Mandaic *'LYN*, *H'aLiN*; Geez *'aL*, *'eLLū*; Arabic *'ūLā*; Shauri *'eLyeNu*; Ph., Pu., N.Pu. *'L* (N.Pu. *'L'*). 1. "these" dem. pr. n.

a) *MPLT HBTM 'L*
"the ruins of these temples"
(Ph. Byblos: KAI/I p. 1, ins. #4, lines 2-4)

b) *BMQDŠM 'L*
"in these sanctuaries"
(Pu. Carthage: KAI/I p. 17, ins. #81, line 2)

c) *HMQDŠM 'L*
"these sanctuaries"
(N.Pu. Bir Bou-Rekba: KAI/I p. 26, ins. #137, lines 4-5)

d) *'BNM 'L'*
"these stones"
(N.Pu. Bordj Hellal: KAI/I p. 26, ins. #139, line 2)

Bibl. Harris 77; DISO 70-71; KAI/II 6, 98, 136, 138; PPG 24, 50-51; Branden 9, 58.

'L IV — Heb. *'aL* "not, do not"; Ug. *'aL*; Akk. *'uL*; Anc.Aram. *'L*; B.Aram. *'aL* (Dan. 2:24); Emp.Aram. *'L*; ESArab. *'L*; Geez *'L*; Soq. *'aL*. 1. "do not" adv. of negation.

a) *'L 'L TPTḤ 'LTY*
"do not, do not open my sarcophagus (?)"
(Ph. Sidon: KAI/I p. 13, ins. #13, lines 3-4)

b) *W'L TRGZN*
"and do not disturb me"
(Ph. Sidon: KAI/I p. 7, ins. #13, line 4)

c) *W'L Y'MSN BMŠKB Z*
"and may he not carry me from this resting place"
(Ph. Sidon: KAI/I p. 3, ins. #14, line 21)

d) *W'L YBQŠ BN MNM*
"may he not seek anything within it"
(Ph. Sidon: KAI/I p. 3, ins. #14, lines 4-5)

e) *W'L YKN LM BN WZR'*
"may they have no son and offspring"
(Ph. Sidon: KAI/I p. 3, ins. #14, line 8)

Bibl. ANET 662; KAI/II 17, 19; Harris 77; PPG 125, 161; Branden 114, 130; Slouszch 16, 21, 23.

'L V — B.Heb. *'aYiL* "leader, chief" (Job 41:17). 1. "chief" n.m.

a) *'Š BN H'LM ML'K MLK'ŠTRT*
"which the chiefs, the envoys of *MLK'ŠTRT* built"
(Ph. Ma'ṣub: KAI/I p. 4, ins. #19, lines 2-3)

Bibl. DISO 12; Harris 77; Slouszch 27; KAI/II 27; CRST 45, note 7.

'L VI — Heb. *'iLLū* "if, though" (Ecc. 6:6); Emp.Aram. *HNLW*; J.Aram. *'iyLū*; Syriac *'eLū*. 1. "if" conj.

a) *W'L MLK BMLKM*
"and if any king"
(Ph. Byblos: KAI/I p. 1, ins. #1, line 2)

Bibl. DISO 13; JAOS 45 (1945) 272; Slouszch 3; KAI/II 2; PPG 130.

'LM Heb. *'iLLeM* "to be dumb, unable to speak". 1. "exorciser" n.m.

a) *BD'ŠTRT 'LM HGLM*
"*BD'ŠTRT* the exorciser (?) of the *GLM* spirit (?)"
(Pu. Carthage: CIS I, ins. #3427, line 3)

Bibl. DISO 214.

'LMT Heb. *'aLMāNā*; Ug. *'aLMNT*; Akk. *'aLMaTTu*; J.Aram. *'aRMaLTa'*; Syriac *'aRMaLTa'*; Mandaic *'aRMaLTa'*; Arabic *'aRMaLaTuN*. 1. "widow" n.f.

a) *YTM BN 'LMT*
"an orphan, son of a widow"
(Ph. Sidon: KAI/I p. 3, ins. #14, line 3)

b) *YTM BN 'LMT 'NK*
"an orphan, the son of a widow am I"
(Ph. Sidon: KAI/I p. 3, ins. #14, line 13)

Bibl. DISO 15; Harris 78; KAI/II 19; Slouszch 20; ANET 662; PPG 101; Branden 10.

'LP I Heb. *'eLeP* "cattle"; Ug. *'aLP* "heifer"; Akk. *'aLPu*; Emp.Aram. *'LP'*; Arabic *'aLFuN*; Soq. *'aLF*. 1. "ox" n.m.

a) *WMY BL ḤZ PN 'LP*
"and whoever had never seen the face of an ox"
(Ph. Zinjirli: KAI/I p. 4, ins. #24, line 11)

b) *B'L 'LPM*
"the possessor of oxen"
(Ph. Karatepe: KAI/I p. 5, ins. #26, line A III,8)

c) *B'LP KLL 'M ṢW'T*
"in the case of an ox: for a whole offering or *ṢW'T* offering"
(Pu. Marseilles: KAI/I p. 15, ins. #69, line 3)

Bibl. KAI/II 31, 36, 83; ANET 653-54, 656; Harris 78; Slouszch 141; Benz 268; DISO 15; Amadasi 169.

'LP II B.Heb. *'aLLūP* "chief"; Ug. *'uLP*.
1. "chief" n.m.
a) *NDR 'Š NDR B'LŠLK 'LP BN 'BDŠD'*
"the vow which *B'LŠLK* the chief (?) son of *'BDŠD'* vowed"
(Pu. Constantine: Berthier/Charlier p. 76, ins. #88, lines 2-3)

Bibl. Berthier/Charlier 76.

'LP III C.S. (except Akk.) 1. "one thousand" num.
a) *KSP 'LP*
"one thousand (shekels) of silver"
(Pu. Carthage: CRAI [1968] p. 117, line 7)

Bibl. CRAI (1968) 131-32.

'LT I Ug. *'iLT* "goddess"; Akk. *'iLTu*.
1. "goddess" n.f.
a) *BDMLQRT [BN 'ŠM]NḤLṢ KHN 'LT*
"*BDMLQRT* [son of *'ŠM*]*NḤLṢ*, priest of the goddess" (or "priest of *'LT*")
(Pu. Carthage: Slouszch p. 254, ins. #308, lines 3-4)

b) *BN YTNMLK R[B] KHN 'LT*
"...son of *YTNMLK* chi[ef] priest of the goddess"
(Pu. Carthage: Slouszch p. 315, ins. #492, lines 3-4)

c) *RBT ḤWT 'LT*
"O lady *ḤWT*, goddess"
(Pu. Carthage: KAI/I p. 18, ins. #89, line 1)

d) *LHRBT L'LT*
"for the lady, for the goddess" (or "for *'LT*")
(N.Pu. Sulci: Amadasi p. 130, ins. #5, line 3)

Bibl. DISO 13; MUSJ 45 (1969) 312; Amadasi 131; JAOS 74 (1954) 229; KAI/II 102, 157; Slouszch 200, 316; Harris 77; ZAW 51 (1933) 86; Benz 268-69; PPG 115; LS I 56.

'LT II — B.Heb. *'āLā* "oath, curse"; Akk. *i'Lu* "written agreement", *'a'āLu* "to bind together"; Arabic *'iLLuN* "something inviolable or sacred". 1. "covenant" n.f. 2. "oath".

1 a) *K{R}RT LN 'LT 'LM*
"the Eternal one has made a covenant with us"
(Ph. Arslan Tash: BASOR 197 [1970] p. 44, rev. lines 8-10)

2 a) *B'LT B'L [']DN 'RṢ*
"with the oath of *B'L*, the [l]ord of the earth"
(Ph. Arslan Tash: BASOR 197 [1970] p. 44, rev. lines 14-15)

Bibl. BASOR 197 (1970) 44-45; KAI/II 43; DISO 14; ANET 658; LS I 58-60.

'M I — Heb. *'iM*, *HeN* "if"; Ug. *HM*; ESArab *HM*; Syriac *'eN*; B.Aram. *HeN*; J.Aram. *'iyN*; Arabic *'iN*; [Akk. *ŠuMMa*]. 1. "if" conj. 2. "whether, or"

1 a) *'M NḤL TNḤL*
"if you would cast lots"
(Ph. Byblos: KAI/I p. 1, ins. #3, lines 3-4)

b) *'M MLK BMLKM*
"if any king"
(Ph. Karatepe: KAI/I p. 5, ins. #26, line A III,12)

2 a) *'M 'DM 'Š 'DM*
"or a man who is only a man"
(Ph. Karatepe: KAI/I p. 5, ins. #26, lines A III,12-13)

b) *'M BḤMDT YS' 'M BŠN'T WBR' YS'*
"whether with good intention he removes (it) or with hatred and with evil (intention) he removes...."
(Ph. Karatepe: KAI/I p. 5, ins. #26, line A III,17)

c) *'M ṢW'T 'M ŠLM KLL*
"or a *ṢW'T* offering or a *ŠLM* of the *KLL* offering"
(Pu. Marseilles: KAI/I p. 15, ins. #69, line 3)

Bibl. Harris 78; DISO 16; ANET 653, 656; Amadasi 169; PPG 130, 162-63; Branden 122-23, 132; KAI/II 5, 36, 83; JAOS 81 (1961) 33.

'M II C.S. 1. "mother" n.f. 2. in divine epithets 3. "metropolis"

1 a) *'M MLK 'ZB'L*
"the mother of king *ZB L*"
(Ph. Byblos: KAI/I p. 2, ins. #11, line 1)

b) *'MY 'M'ŠTRT*
"my mother *'M'ŠTRT*"
(Ph. Sidon: KAI/I p. 3, ins. #14, line 14)

c) *W'T 'MNM ḤN'ŠTRT*
"and their mother *ḤN'ŠTRT*"
(Ph. Memphis: Slouszch p. 52, ins. #35, line 3)

2 a) *LRBT L'M'*
"to the lady, to the mother (?)"
(or "to *'M'*")
(Ph. Carthage: KAI/I p. 18, ins. #83, line 1)

b) *L'M LRBT LTNT PN B'L*
"to the mother, to the lady, to *TNT PN B'L*"
(Pu. Carthage: Slouszch p. 173, ins. #151, lines 2-3)

c) *L'M RBT PN B'L*
"to the mother, to the lady *PN B'L*"
(Pu. Carthage: Slouszch p. 171, ins. #149, lines 4-5)

3 a) *LṢR 'M* ṢDNM*
"to *ṢR* the metropolis of the *ṢDNM*"
(Ph. Tyre: Slouszch p. 34, ins. #17, line 1)

*N.Heb. *'eM* as a reference to the land of Israel, see Jerusalem Talmud *Mō'eD QāṬāN*, col. C, Arabic *'uMMuN* as in the expression *'uMMu 'al QuRa* as reference to the city of Mecca.

b) *LṢDN 'M KKB*
"to *ṢDN* the metropolis of *KKB*"
(Ph. Sidon: Slouszch p. 32, ins. #14, line 1)

c) *LL'DK' 'M BKN'N*
"to *L'DK'* the metropolis in *KN'N*"
(Ph. Laodica: Slouszch p. 46, ins. #30, line 1)

Bibl. Benz 269; Harris 78; NE 219; DISO 15-16; PPG 48, 112; Slouszch 32-33, 34-35, 46-47, 53, 172; KAI/II 15-16, 19, 64, 100; HUCA 18 (1944) 439-40; Gaster-Fs 74-89.

'ML B.Heb. *'āMaL* "to languish, be feeble". 1. "to enfeeble" vb. (piel)

a) *WL'KR WLŠBT Y'ML YD*[']
"and to ban (?) and to put an end to [that] which enfeebles (his) hand"
(Pu. Carthage: CIS I, ins. #5510, line 3)

Bibl. DISO 17.

'MR I Heb. *'āMaR* "to say"; Ug. *'MR* "to see"; Akk. *'āMaRu*; Anc.Aram. *'MR* "to say"; Emp.Aram. *'MR*; J.Aram. *'aMaR*; Syriac *'eMaR*; Mandaic *'aMR*; Nab. *'MR*; Palm. *'MR*; ESArab. *'MR* "to command"; Arabic *'aMaRa*; Geez *'aMMaRa* "to show"; Soq. *'MoR* "to say". 1. "to say" vb.

a) *DBR MLK 'ŠMN'ZR MLK ṢDNM L'MR*
"thus spake king *'SMN'ZR*, king of the *ṢDNM* saying"
(Ph. Sidon: KAI/I p. 3, ins. #14, line 2)

b) *'MR L'ḤTY*
"say to my sister"
(Ph. Saqqara: KAI/I p. 12, ins. #50, line 2)

c) *WY'MR 'P'L SML ZR*
"and he would say, 'Let me fashion a hated image'"
(Ph. Karatepe: KAI/I p. 25, ins. #26, lines C III,17-18)

Bibl. KAI/II 19, 36, 67; DISO 17-18; Harris 78; Slouszch 19; ANET 662; PPG 62, 71.

(Etymological relationship between Ug., Akk. and Geez verbal forms to other entries doubtful)

'MR II Ug. *'iMR* "lamb"; Akk. *'iMMeRu*; Anc.Aram. *'MR*; B.Aram. *'iMMaR*; Emp.Aram. *'MR*; J.Aram. *'iMRa'*; Syriac *'eMRa'*; Mandaic *'MBRa'*; Arabic *'iMMaRuN*. 1. "lamb" n.f.

a) *B'MR 'M BGD*
"for a lamb, or for a goat"
(Pu. Marseilles: KAI/I p. 15, ins. #69, line 9)

b) *LḤNQT 'MR*
"O stranglers of lamb(s)"
(Ph. Arslan Tash: KAI/I p. 6, ins. #27, lines 4-5)

Bibl. BASOR 197 (1970) 44-45; DISO 18; ANET 658; LS I 92, note 1; Amadasi 169; KAI/II 43, 83; Harris 78; Slouszch 145; Speiser 367.

'MT Heb. *'āMā* "maidservant"; Ug. *'MT*; Akk. *'aMTu*; Emp.Aram. *'MH*; J.Aram. *'aMTa'*; Syriac *'aMTa'*; Mandaic *'aMTa'*, *'aMuTa'*; ESArab. *'MT*; Geez *'aMaT*; Arabic *'aMTuN*. 1. "maidservant" n.f. 2. designating a specific cultic functionary.

1 a) *'MTB'L BT PṬ'S 'MT '[ ]*
"*'MTB'L* daughter of *PṬ'S*, the maidservant of '[ ]"
(Ph. Carchemish: KAI/I p. 7, ins. #29, line 1)

b) *'MTNM 'ZYB'L*
"their maidservant *'ZYB'L*"
(Pu. Carthage: Slouszch p. 317, ins. #496, lines 3-4)

2 a) *'BB'L BT GDN'M[T] 'MT 'LM*
"*'BB'L* daughter of *GDN'M[T]* maidservant of the gods"
(Pu. Carthage: Slouszch p. 230, ins. #243, lines 2-3)

Bibl. KAI/II 47; Benz 270; Harris 79; Slouszch 230, 317; DISO 16.

'N I Heb. *'eN* "non existence"; Moab. *'N*; Akk. *iāNu*. 1. without adv.

a) *B'N ṢDN*
"without payment (?)"
(Pu. Carthage: CIS I, ins. #5522, line 9)

Bibl. DISO 335-36

'N II B.Heb. *'oNi* "fleet, ships"; Ug. *'NY*; Amar.Akk. *'aNaYi*; Akk. *uNūTu* "vessel"; Arabic *'iNāuN*; Eg. *WY'*. 1. "fleet" n.m. (reading uncertain)

a) *ṘB[ ] 'N[Y] HLK[ ] QR[ ]*
"the captain (?) of the fleet (?) travelling (?) to QR (?)"
(Pu. Carthage: Slouszch p. 244, ins. #280, line 3)

Bibl. Slouszch 244.

'NḤN Heb. *'aNaḤNu* "we"; B.Heb. *NaḤNu*; Akk. *NiNu*; Geez *NeḤNa*; B.Aram. *'aNaḤNa'*; Q.Aram. *'NHNH*; Arabic *NaḤNu*. 1. "we" first person pl. pr.

a) *W'NḤN 'Š BNN*
"and it is we who built"
(Ph. Sidon: KAI/I p. 3, ins. #14, line 17)

Bibl. KAI/II 19; Harris 79; DISO 18; PPG 46.

'NK B.Heb. *'āNōKi*; Ug. *'aNK*; Akk. *'aNāKu*; Amar.Akk. *'aNūKi*; Anc.Aram. *'NK*; Moab. *'NK*; Eg. *'NK*; Ph., Pu., N.Pu. *'NK* (Ph. *'LK*, *'L*, *'NKY*; Pu. *'NKY*). 1. "I" pers.pr. 2. used as an enclitic

1 a) *'NK YḤWMLK MLK GBL*
"I am *YḤWMLK* king of *GBL*"
(Ph. Byblos: KAI/I p. 2, ins. #10, line 1)

b) *'NKY B'LSKR*
"I am *B'LSKR*"
(Ph. Abydos: KAI/I p. 11, ins. #49, line 6)

c) *'L 'BDŠMŠ*
"I am *'BDŠMŠ*" (or "to [?] *'BDŠMŠ*")
(Ph. Abydos: KAI/I p. 11, ins. #49, line 29)

d) *'LK YḤLB'L*
"I am *YḤLB'L*"
(Ph. Abydos: KAI/I p. 11, ins. #49, line 15)

e) *'K 'RŠ*
"I am *'RŠ*"
(Ph. Abydos: KAI/I p. 11, ins. #49, line 39)

f) *'NKY MṢLḤ*
"I am *MṢLḤ*"
(Pu. Carthage: KAI/I p. 18, ins. #89, line 2)

2 a) *WBYMTY 'NK*
"but in my days"
(Ph. Karatepe: KAI/I p. 5, ins. #26, line A II,5)

b) *BY PY 'NK*
"without my word"
(Pu. Carthage: KAI/I p. 17, ins. #79, line 8)

c) *'Š NDRT 'NK*
"which I vowed"
(N.Pu. Constantine: ZDMG 13 [1863] p. 654, lines 3-4)

Bibl. Harris 79; NE 222; DISO 19; ANET 653, 656, 662; PPG 41, 45, 46; ZDMG 13 (1863) 657-68; Branden 8, 46-47; KAI KAI/II 12, 19, 36, 65, 97, 102.

*'*SP* Heb. *'āSaP* "to gather up"; Akk. *eSēPu*; Ug. *'aSP*; Syriac *'aWSeP* "to add, increase"; J.Aram. *'aSaP* "to gather in"; Nab. *'WSP* "added". 1. "to be gathered" vb.

a) *WT 'KHNYM 'Š 'L MRM KL' N'SP L'*
"and the bases which are raised are totally gathered together to it" (N.Pu. Cherchel: KAI/I p. 29, ins. #161, line 6)

Bibl. KAI/II 150.

'SR B.Heb. *'āSaR* "to tie, bind"; Akk. *eSēRu* "to collect"; Syriac *'eSaR* "to tie"; B.Aram. *'eSuR* "bond". 1. "to harness" vb. (Gen. 46:29)

a) *B'L 'SR MRKBTY*
"*B'L* has harnessed his chariot" (Ph. Arslan Tash: BASOR 209 [1973] p. 18, obv. lines 1-2)

Bibl. ZA 39 (1931) 291.

'P Heb. *'aP* "even, also"; Ug. *'aP*; Emp.Aram. *'P*; Syriac *'aP*; B.Aram. *'aP*; J.Aram. *'aP*; Palm. *'P*; Mandaic *'aP*. 1. "moreover, even" conj.

a) *W'P B'BT P'LN KL MLK*
"and moreover, every king made mas as (an) intercessor" (or "as a father") (Ph. Karatepe: KAI/I p. 5, ins. #26, line A I,12)

b) *'M 'P YḤMD 'YT HQRT Z*
"even if he should desire (good for) this city" (Ph. Karatepe: KAI/I p. 5, ins. #26, lines A III,14-15)

c) *'P 'NK ŠLM*
"even (as) I am well" (Ph. Saqqara: KAI/I p. 12, ins. #50, line 2)

d) *'P 'M 'DMM YDBRNK*
"yea, even if men impel you" (or "speak with you") (Ph. Sidon: KAI/I p. 3, ins. #14, line 6)

Bibl. ANET 653, 662; Harris 80; DISO 21; PPG 130; Branden 121-22; KAI/II 19, 31, 36, 37.

**'PY* Heb. *'āPā* "to bake"; Akk. *ePū*; Ug. *'PY*; Arabic *MiFaN* "oven"; J.Aram. *'aPe*; Mandaic *'aP'*; Syriac *'ePa'*; ESArab. *'aFYM* "anything baked". 1. "to bake" vb. (reading uncertain) 2. "baker" n.m.

1 a) *L'ṖM 2 'Š 'P*
"for the two bakers who baked" (Ph. Kition: Or 37 [1968] p. 305, line A 10)

2 a) *L'ṖM 2 'Š 'P*
"for the two bakers who baked"
(Ph. Kition: Or 37 [1968] p. 305, line A 10)

Bibl. Or 37 (1968) 314, esp. note 5.

'PS B.Heb. *'ePeS* "non existence, only end"; N.Heb. *'ePeS* "ankle"; Ug. *'aPS* "end, tip".
1. "only" adv.

a) *'PS ŠM 'ZTWD YKN L'LM*
"only the name of *'ZTWD* will remain forever"
(Ph. Karatepe: KAI/I p. 5, ins. #25, lines A IV,1-2)

Bibl. DISO 22; ANET 655; KAI/II 36; PPG 124; Branden 123.

'ṢL Heb. *'eṢeL* "in conjunction to, proximity to".
1. "from beside" prep. 2. "in proximity to".
Ph. *'ṢL* (N.Pu. *'Ṣ'L*)

a) *B'ṢL HMŠK[B]*
"from beside the resting pla[ce]"
(Ph. Byblos: KAI/I p. 2, ins. #9, line B 2)

b) *W'L KL KTMM 'Ṣ'L 'QMT*
"and upon all the *KTMM* (in) proximity (?) to the *QMT*"
(N.Pu. Guelaat Bou-Sba: KAI/I p. 30, ins. #165, line 4)

Bibl. KAI/II 11, 154; DISO 22; OrAnt 4 (1965) 63.

'RB' C.S. 1. "four" num.

a) *HŠ L'RBTNM*
"woe for the four of them"
(N.Pu. Tripolitania: LibAnt 1 [1964] p. 57, line 5)

Bibl. LibAnt 1 (1964) 59.

'RB'M C.S. Pu., N.Pu. *'RB'M* (N.Pu. *'RBM*).
1. "forty" num.

a) *B'Ḥ T{T} 'RB'M ŠT LMLKY*
"in the forty-first year of his rule"
(Pu. Constantine: KAI/I p. 21, ins. #110, lines 3-4)

b) *M'TM W'RB'M*
"two hundred and forty"
(N.Pu. Dschebel Massoudj: KAI/I p. 26, ins. #141, line 5)

c) *''W' Š'NT 'RBM WḤD*
"who lived forty-one years"
(N.Pu. Henschir Guergour: KAI/I p. 27, ins. #143, lines 3-4)

Bibl. DISO 23; Harris 196; KAI/II 116, 139-40.

'RG I [Heb. *'āRaG* "to weave"; J.Aram. *'aRaG*].
1. "sharpener" n.m.

a) *'RŠ BN 'KBR 'RG 'MLQḤ*
"*'RŠ* son of *'KBR*, sharpener (?) of the tongs (?)"
(Pu. Carthage: Slouszch p. 243, ins. #279, lines 3-4)

Bibl. Slouszch 243-44; DISO 23; Harris 80.

'RG II Heb. *'āRaG* "to weave"; J.Aram. *'aRaG*.
1. "weaver" n.m.

a) *HNB'L 'RG*
"*HNB'L*, the weaver"
(Pu. Carthage: CIS I, ins. #5703, line 3)

Bibl. DISO 23.

'RW Heb. *'aRi* "lion"; Emp.Aram. *'RY'*, *'RYH*; Akk. *'aRMu* "gazelle", *'aRu* "eagle"; J.Aram. *'aRYa'*; Syriac *'aRYa'*; Mandaic *'aRYa'*; Palm. *'RY'*; ESArab. *'aRW* "ibex"; Geez *'aRWe* "wild animal"; Arabic *'aRWa(y)* "ibex"; Meh. *'aRRiyy* "tom-cat".

a) *W'RWM ŠNM*
"and the two lion (images) (?)"
(Ph. Kition: KAI/I p. 7, ins. #32, line 3)

Bibl. DISO 22; KAI/II 50; Harris 80; Slouszch 70; NE 226; Bib 49 (1968) 356-57.

'RY I Heb. *'uR* "fire"; Te. *'aRWa* "to blaze"; Arabic *'aRā(y)* "to burn". 1. "ashes" n.m.

a) *'RYT MGN BN Ḥ[L]Ṣ*
"the ashes (?) of *MGN* son of *ḤLṢ*"
(Pu. Almunecar: Muséon 83 [1970] p. 225, lines 1-2)

b) *QBR BD'ŠT[R]T W'RḤ*
"the grave of *BD'ŠT[R]T* and his ashes (?)"
(Pu. Carthage: Slouszch p. 186, ins. #162, lines 1-2)

Bibl. ESE II 177; Slouszch 186; Harris 81; DISO 24, 81; Muséon 83 (1970) 254-55.

*'*RY* II Heb. '*āRā* "to gather (fruit)"; Akk. '*aRū* "to prune". 1. "to gather" vb.

a) *KY 'Y 'Ṙ LN KSP 'Y 'Ṙ LN ḤRṢ* "for there is not gathered in it silver (and) there is not gathered in it gold" (Ph. Sidon: KAI/I p. 2, ins. #13, line 4)

Bibl. PPG 24, 71, 82, 85 (also see under '*DLN*).

'*RK* I Heb. '*āRaK* "to be long"; Ug. '*RK*; Akk. '*aRāKu*; Anc.Aram. '*RK*; Emp.Aram. '*RK*; ESArab. '*RK* "to be lasting"; J.Aram. '*aRiK* "to be long"; Syriac '*eRaK* "to be prolonged"; Mandaic '*aRK*, '*RK*; Arabic '*aRaKa* "to be late". 1. "to lengthen" vb. 2. "long" adj.

1 a) *WT'RK YMW WŠNTW 'L GBL* "and may she lengthen his days and his years over *GBL*" (Ph. Byblos: KAI/I p. 2, ins. #10, line 9)

b) *Y'RK B'L ŠMM* "may *B'L ŠMM*...lengthen" (Ph. Byblos: KAI/I p. 1, ins. #4, line 3)

c) *T'RK B'LT GBL YMT ŠPṬB'L WŠNTW* "may the mistress of *GBL* lengthen the days and years of *ŠPṬB'L*" (Ph. Byblos: KAI/I p. 1, ins. #7, lines 4-5)

2 a) '*BN* '*RKT* "a long stone" (Pu. Carthage: KAI/I p. 17, ins. #78, line 5)

Bibl. ANET 656; DISO 24; Harris 81; JSS 17 (1972) 82; KAI/II 6, 9, 12, 96.

'*RK* II Heb. '*oReK* "length"; Ug. '*uRK*; B.Aram. '*aRKā* "prolonging" (Dan. 4:24). 1. "length" n.m. 2. used as an epithet.

1 a) '*RK YMM WRB ŠNT* "length of days and many years" (Ph. Karatepe: KAI/I p. 5, ins. #26, lines A III,5-6)

b) *YTN LH RKB'L 'RK ḤY* "may *RKB'L* grant him long life" (Ph. Zinjirli: KAI/I p. 5, ins. #25, lines 5-7)

2 a) *LRBT L'ŠTRT 'RK ḤYM*
"to the lady, to *'ŠTRT* (who is) of long life (?)"
(Pu. Eryx: CIS I, ins. #135, line 1)

Bibl. KAI/II 35-36; ANET 653; DISO 24; Harris 81, 100; JSS 17 (1972) 83; Amadasi 54; Slouszch 134.

'RN Heb. *'āRōN* "ark, coffin"; Akk. *'aRāNu*; Emp.Aram. *'RWN, 'RN*; Syriac *'āRūNa'*; Mandaic *'aRuaNa'*; J.Aram. *'aRōNa'*; Nab. *'RN'*; Ug. *'aRN* "chest"; Arabic *'uRuNuN* "large bread basket", *'iRāNuN* "stretcher". 1. "sarcophagus" n.m. 2. "chest"

1 a) *'RN Z P'L [']TB'L BN 'ḤRM MLK GBL*
"the sarcophagus which [']*TB'L* son of *'ḤRM* king of *GBL* made"
(Ph. Byblos: KAI/I p. 1, ins. #1, line 1)

b) *B'RN ZN 'NK BTN'M 'M MLK 'ZB'L*
"in this sarcophagus I, *BTN'M* mother of king *'ZB'L*"
(Ph. Byblos: KAI/I p. 2, ins. #11, line 1)

c) *HN 'NK ŠKB B'RN ZN*
"behold, I lie in this sarcophagus"
(Ph. Byblos: MUSJ 45 [1969] p. 262, line 1)

d) *ḤRŠ 'RNT*
"maker of sarcophagi"
(Pu. Carthage: CIS I, ins. #3333, line 1)

e) *'Š TPQ 'YT H'RN Z*
"who shall remove this sarcophagus"
(Ph. Sidon: KAI/I p. 2, ins. #13, line 3)

2 a) *'RN Z[N] MGN 'MTB'L BT PṬ'S*
"this chest *'MTB'L* daughter of *PṬ'S* offered"
(Ph. Carchemish: KAI/I p. 7, ins. #29, line 1)

Bibl. Harris 81; DISO 25; KAI/II 2, 15-16, 47; MUSJ 45 (1969) 263; EI V 84-86.

'RṢ C.S. 1. "land" n.f. 2. names of specific places. 3. in religious contexts. 4. in titles. 5. name of a district in a city.

1 a) *ṢDN 'RṢ YM*
"*ṢDN*, land of the sea"
(Ph. Sidon: KAI/I p. 3, ins. #14, line 16)

b) *'RṢT DGN H'DRT*
"the glorious corn lands"
(Ph. Sidon: KAI/I p. 3, ins. #14, line 19)

c) *'Š B'RṢ*
"which are in the land"
(Ph. Ma'ṣub: KAI/I p. 4, ins. #19, line 10)

d) *KL HR' 'Š KN B'RṢ*
"all the evil which was in the land"
(Ph. Karatepe: KAI/I p. 5, ins. #26, line A I,9)

2 a) *'RṢ 'MQ 'DN*
"the land of the plain of *'DN*"
(Ph. Karatepe: KAI/I p. 5, ins. #26, line A I,4)

b) *ẆṪḤ 'Š 'L 'RṢT TŠK'T*
"*ẆṪḤ* who is over the land of *TŠK'T* (?)"
(N.Pu. Dschebel Massoudj: KAI/I p. 26, ins. #141, line 1)

3 a) *'L QN 'RṢ*
"*'L*, the creator of earth"
(Ph. Karatepe: KAI/I p. 5, ins. #26, line A III,18)

b) *'RṢ 'LM*
"ancient earth"
(Ph. Arslan Tash: BASOR 197 [1970] pp. 44-45, lines rev. 13-14)

4 a) *MYŠR 'RṢT RBT*
"the bringer of prosperity to the great lands"
(N.Pu. Cherchel: KAI/I p. 29, ins. #161, line 2)

b) *YTNB'L RB 'RṢ*
"*YTNB'L* the district chief (?)"
(Ph. Larneka: KAI/I p. 10, ins. #43, line 2)

5 a) *'RṢ RŠPM*
"the district (?) of *RŠPM*"
(Ph. Sidon: KAI/I p. 3, ins. #15, line 2)

Bibl. Harris 81; NE 227; ANET 653, 662; DISO 25-26; KAI/II 19, 27, 36, 43, 60, 139, 150; LS I 59-60.

'RR Akk. *'aRRu* "bird used as a decoy"; J.Aram. *'aRa'* "fowler". 1. "calling birds" n.m.

a) *SYPRM 'RRM [B]HMQM*
"calling birds (?) [in] the temple"
(N.Pu. Tripolitania: Or 33 [1964] p. 4, line 7)

Bibl. Or 33 (1964) 13; ZA 41 (1933) 227.

'RŠ B.Heb. *'aReŠeT* "desire"; Ug. *'RŠ* "to request"; Akk. *eRēŠu', eRiŠTu* "desire". 1. "to request" vb.

a) *K 'ŠTRT 'RŠ BDY*
"because *'ŠTRT* requested (it) from me" (or "on my behalf")
(Ph. Pyrgi: Amadasi p. 161, ins. #2, line 6)

Bibl. Benz 276; Amadasi 165-66.

'Š I Heb. *'eŠ* "fire"; Q.Aram. *'ŠH*; Ug. *'ŠT*; Akk. *iŠāTu*; Anc.Aram. *'Š*; Geez *'eSaT*; J.Aram. *'eŠTa'*; Syriac *'eŠTa'*; Mandaic *'Ša'Ta'*; N.Syr. *ŠaTa'*; Amh. *əSaT*. 1. "fire" n.f.

a) *KM 'Š 'KLT ZQN*
"as a fire consumes a beard"
(Ph. Zinjirli: KAI/I p. 4, ins. #24, lines 6-7)

b) *W[KM] 'Š 'KLT YD*
"and [as] a fire consumes a hand"
(Ph. Zinjirli: KAI/I p. 4, ins. #24, line 7)

Bibl. KAI/II 31; ANET 654; DISO 27; Harris 82.

'Š II Heb. *'iyŠ* "man"; Akk. *iŠŠu*; Moab. *'Š*; ESArab. *'YS*; Anc.Aram. *'Š*; Q.Heb. *YŠ*; Emp.Aram. *'YŠ*; Palm. *'YŠ*; N.Syr. *'iyŠ*; Arabic *NāSuN*; Ph., Pu. *'Š* (N.Pu. *'YŠ*). 1. "man" n.m. 2. in gentilic relationship. 3. "worshiper"

1 a) *'ŠM R'M*
"evil men"
(Ph. Karatepe: KAI/I p. 5, ins. #26, line A I,15)

b) *W'D[R] ḤMŠM H'Š*
"the might[iest] of the fifty men"
(Pu. Dougga: KAI/I p. 20, ins. #101, line 4)

c) *'YŠ L'*
"her husband"
(N.Pu. Henschir Guergonr: KAI/I p. 27, ins. #143, line 3)

2 a) *B'LḤN' 'Š ṢDN*
"*B'LḤN* the man of *ṢDN*"
(Pu. Carthage: Slouszch p. 263, ins. #335, lines 2-3)

b) *PNSMLT 'Š KTY*
"*PNSMLT* the man of *KTY*"
(Ph. Piraeus: KAI/I p. 13, ins. #57, line 1)

c) *'BD'ŠMN BN M'DR 'Š KN'N*
"*'BD'ŠMN* son of *M'DR*, the man of *KN'N*"
(Pu. Constantine: Berthier/ Charlier, p. 83, ins. #102, lines 2-3)

3 a) *LB'LYTN 'Š 'LM 'Š LMLQRT*
"for *B'LYTN* the worshiper (?) of (the god) *MLQRT*"
(Ph. Beirut: NSI p. 36, no. 5, lines 1-3)

b) *'Š B'MT 'Š 'ŠTRT*
"who is among the worshipers (?) of *'ŠTRT*"
(Pu. Carthage: Slouszch p. 235, ins. #258, lines 3-4)

Bibl. Slouszch 46-47; Harris 79; KAI/II 36, 71, 110, 140; ANET 653; PPG 115; DISO 26-27; NSI 361; Leš 30 (1965) 36-40.

'Š III B.Heb. *ša*; Heb. *še*; Amm. *'Š*; Ph., Pu. *'Š* (Pu. *'*, *'Š*). 1. rel. pr. 2. in combinations

1 a) *MṢBT 'Z 'Š YṬN' 'RŠ RB SRSRM*
"this monument (is that) which *'RŠ* the chief of the brokers erected"
(Ph. Kition: KAI/I p. 8, ins. #34, line 1)

b) *NDR 'Š NDR B'LPD'*
"the vow which *B'LPD'* vowed"
(Pu. Constantine: KAI/I p. 20, ins. #103, line 2)

c) *MQDŠM ŠNM 'Š P'L B'L TNSMT*
"the two sanctuaries which the citizens of *TNSMT* made"
(N.Pu. Bir Bou-Rekba: KAI/I p. 26, ins. #137, line 1)

d) *ND'R 'Š N'DR' B'L'MY*
"the vow which *B'L'MY* vowed"
(N.Pu. Henschir Meded: KAI/I p. 29, ins. #155, lines 1-2)

e) *' NDR TPṬ BN MGN*
"that which *TPṬ* son of *MGN* vowed"
(Pu. Carthage: CIS I, ins. #2683, line 3)

f) *KL 'DM 'Š YPTḤ*
"any man who shall open"
(Ph. Sidon: KAI/I p. 3, ins. #14, line 7)

g) *W'NḤN 'Š BNN*
"and it is we who built"
(Ph. Sidon: KAI/I p. 3, ins. #14, line 17)

h) *'Š NDR 'MT'ŠTRT*
"that which *'MT'ŠTRT* vowed"
(Pu. Carthage: Slouszch p. 323, ins. #515, lines 2-3)

2 a) *KM 'Š LMLKYT 'Š KN LPNY*
"as with the royalty which was before me"
(Ph. Byblos: KAI/I p. 2, ins. #11, line 2)

b) *KM 'Š QR'T 'T RBTY*
"when I invoked my lady"
(Ph. Byblos: KAI/I p. 2, ins. #10, line 7)

c) *KM 'Š BN KL 'ḤRY H[MQDŠ]M*
"when they built all the remainder of the [sanctuari]es"
(Ph. Ma'ṣub: KAI/I p. 4, ins. #19, lines 9-10)

d) *BMQMM B'Š KN 'ŠM R'M*
"in the places where there were evil men"
(Ph. Karatepe: KAI/I p. 5, ins. #26, lines A I,14-15)

Bibl. DISO 285-86; Harris 82; NE 227-28; Benz 277-78, 412; JNES 16 (1957) 124-27; ANET 653, 656, 662; KAI/II 12, 15-16, 19, 27, 36, 52, 114, 136, 147; PPG 54-55, 148; Branden 59-62; LS I 74.

'ŠR I   Heb. *'oŠeR* "happiness"; Akk. *iŠaRiŠ* "to prosper"; Arabic *YaSiRuN* "easy, possible".
1. "happiness" n.m.

a) *B'ŠR LB*
"with happiness of heart"
(N.Pu. Maktar: KAI/I p. 27, ins. #145, line 11)

Bibl. KAI/II 141; DISO 28; LS III 110.

'ŠR II — Ug. *'ṮR* "place"; Akk. *'aŠRu*; Anc.Aram. *'ŠR*; B.Aram. *'aTaR*; Emp.Aram. *'TR*; J.Aram. *'aTRa'*; Syriac *'aTRa'*; Mandaic *'aTRa'*; Nab. *'TR*; Palm. *'TR*; ESArab. *'ṮR* "a footstep, tract", *'SR* "basis"; Arabic *'aṮRuN* "impression"; Geez *'aŠaR* "track"; Eg. *'iSR* "tamarisk"; Heb. *'aŠeR* rel. pr. Soq. *'iHoR* "trace"; B.Heb. *'aŠeR* "place" (Jud. 17:9). 1. "place" n.m.

a) *[B]'ŠR HQDŠ*
"[in] the holy place"
(Pu. Carthage: Slouszch p. 351, ins. #584, line 6)

b) *'ŠR QDŠ 'Z*
"this holy place"
(Ph. Pyrgi: Amadasi p. 160, ins. #2, lines 1-2)

Bibl. Slouszch 352; Harris 83; DISO 27-28; Amadasi 162.

'ŠR III — B.Heb. *'aŠeRiM* "sacred trees or poles." 1. "sacred image" n.m.

a) *NŠ' 'BD'NT 'ŠRM M'Š LḤN BTY*
"*'BD'NT* set up the sacred image (?) for *ḤN* his daughter"
(Pu. Carthage: Slouszch p. 173, ins. #152, lines 1-2)

Bibl. Slouszch 173.

'ŠRT — Heb. *'aŠeRā* "sacred tree or pole"; Akk. *'aŠiRTu* "temple"; Eg. *'iSR* "tamarisk". 1. "sacred grove" n.f.

a) *L'ŠTRT B'ŠRT 'L ḤMN*
"for *'ŠTRT* (who is) in the sacred grove (?) of *'L ḤMN*"
(Ph. Ma'ṣub: KAI/I p. 4, ins. #19, line 4)

Bibl. Harris 83; Slouszch 45; KAI/II 27; DISO 28.

'ŠT I — B.Heb. *ŠeT* "pillar"; Akk. *iŠDu* "leg"; Ug. *'iŠD*; N.Heb. *ŠiT* "foundation"; B.Aram. *'eŠ'*; J.Aram. *'ūŠa'*; Syriac *'eŠTa'* "the bottom"; Arabic *'uSSuN* "foundation"; Q.Heb. *'WŠ*; Q.Aram. *'Š*. 1. "pillar" n.f.

a) *LḤRŠM 'Š P'L 'ŠTT*
"for the masons who made the pillars"
(Ph. Kition: KAI/I p. 8, ins. #37, line A 14)

b) *LNPŠ BT 'Š L'ŠTT MKL*
"for the personnel of the temple which (is by) the pillars of *MKL*"
(Ph. Kition: KAI/I p. 8, ins. #37, line B 5)

Bibl. Or 37 (1968) 316 note 3; DISO 28; Harris 83; RB 37 (1928) 359; Dahood I 69; Slouszch 79, 81-82; KAI/II 54.

'ŠT II Heb. *'iššā* "wife, woman"; Ug. *'aṮṮ*; Akk. *'aššaTu*; Emp.Aram. *'NTH*; ESArab. *'NṮṮ*; J.Aram. *'aTTa'*; Mandaic *'NTa'*; Syriac *'aNTa'*; Palm. *'TT'*; Nab. *'TTH*; Geez *'aNṮH*; Arabic *'uNṮa*; Amh. *'əṆeST*; Ph., Pu., N.Pu. *'ŠT* (Pu. *'S̄T*, N.Pu. *'ŠT*). 1. "wife" n.f. 2. "woman"

1 a) *WŠMNH 'ŠT B'L QDŠ*
"and the eight wives of *B'L*, the holy one"
(Ph. Arslan Tash: BASOR 197 [1970] p. 45, rev. lines 17-18)

b) *Y'Š 'ŠT [B'LT]YTN*
"*Y'Š* the wife of *[B'LT]YTN*"
(Ph. Kition: KAI/I p. 7, ins. #33, line 2)

c) *WL'ŠTY L'MT'ŠTRT BT T'M*
"and to my wife, to *'MT'ŠTRT* daughter of *T'M*"
(Ph. Kition: KAI/I p. 8, ins. #35, lines 2-3)

d) *'RŠṬB'L HKHNT 'ŠT MLQRTḤLṢ*
"*'RŠTB'L* the priestess, wife of *MLQRTḤLṢ*"
(Pu. Carthage: Slouszch p. 184, ins. #158, line 1)

e) *'ŠḌNT 'ŠT MGN*
"*'ŠDNT* wife of *MGN*"
(Pu. Carthage: Slouszch p. 184, ins. #302, line 4)

f) *T'NBR' 'ŠT[']*
"*T'NBR'* his wife"
(N.Pu. El-Amruni: KAI/I p. 22, ins. #117, lines 3-4)

g) *'ŠT M'GRS'N*
"wife of *M'GRS'N*"
(N.Pu. Maktar: KAI/I p. 28, ins. #149, line 3)

2 a) *'ŠT TK LḤDY DL PLKM*
"a woman walked by herself without supports"
(Ph. Karatepe: KAI/I p. 5, ins. #26, lines A II,5-6)

Bibl. Benz 280-81; DISO 26-27; Harris 79; ANET 653, 658; BASOR 197 (1970) 44-45; PPG 48, 106, 112, 115; KAI/II 36, 43, 51-52, 122, 145; Slouszch 252.

'T I C.S. 1. "you" pers.pr. f.

a) *WŠLM 'T 'P 'NK ŠLM*
"is it well with you, even (as) I am well"
(Ph. Saqqara: KAI/I p. 12, ins. #50, line 2)

Bibl. KAI/II 67; DISO 29; PPG 22, 45; Branden 46-47.

'T II C.S. 1. "you" pers.pr. m.

a) *MY 'T KL 'DM 'Š TPQ*
"whoever you are, any man who shall remove..."
(Ph. Sidon: KAI/I p. 2, ins. #13, line 3)

b) *QNMY 'T KL MMLKT WKL 'DM*
"whoever you are, any prince and any man"
(Ph. Sidon: KAI/I p. 3, ins. #14, line 4)

Bibl. DISO 29; ANET 662; KAI/II 17, 19; Harris 79; PPG 22, 45; Branden 46-47; Slouszch 16, 20.

'T III B.Heb. *'eT* "with"; Akk. *iTTi*. 1. "with, to" prep. 2. in combinations

1 a) *WYSGRNM H'LNM HQDŠM 'T MMLK<T> 'DR*
"may the holy gods deliver them up to a mighty ruler"
(Ph. Sidon: KAI/I p. 3, ins. #14, line 9)

b) *MŠKB 'T RP'M*
"a resting place with the shades"
(Ph. Sidon: KAI/I p. 3, ins. #14, line 8)

c) *'T KL MLK*
"with all kings"
(Ph. Karatepe: KAI/I p. 5, ins. #26, lines A I,11-12)

2 a) *'Š 'L' BBN M'T M'QR BN G'Y*
"who was adopted (?) as a son through *M'QR* son of *G'Y*"
(N.Pu. Leptis Magna: KAI/I p. 23, ins. #124, line 3)

b) *'Š P'L MŠRT 'T PN GW*
"who performed service before the community"
(Ph. Piraeus: KAI/I p. 13, ins. #60, lines 7-8)

Bibl. ANET 653, 662; NE 230; DISO 29; Harris 83, 84; Benz 281; KAI/II 19, 36, 73, 130; PPG 125; Branden 116.

'T' B.Heb. *'āTā* "to come"; Ug. *'TY*; Anc.Aram. *'TH*; Saftartic *'T*; Emp.Aram. *'TH*; ESArab. *'TW* "to return"; Geez *'TW*; J.Aram. *'aTa'*; Syriac *'eTa'*; Mandaic *'aTa'*; Arabic *'aTa'*; Palm. *'T'*; Nab. *'T'*; Soq. *'eTe* "to go".
1. "to come" vb.

a) *W'T' DN'Ṭ' B'T 'T' Š'M*
"and *DN'Ṭ'* came during the time in which he came there"
(N.Pu. Tripolitania: Or 33 [1964] p. 4, line 2)

Bibl. Or 33 (1964) 9.

'TNM B.Heb. *'eTaNiM* "name of a Hebrew month"; Ph. *'TNM* (N.Pu. *'TNYM*). 1. name of a month. pr. n.

a) *BYRḤ 'TNM*
"in the month of *'TNM*"
(Ph. Tamassos: KAI/I p. 9, ins. #41, line 4)

b) *ṬKLT YRḤ 'TNM*
"accounts of the month of *'TNM*"
(Ph. Kition: Or 37 [1968] p. 305, line A 1)

c) [ ]*MYK' 'TNYM*
"(?) of the (month) of *'TNYM*"
(N.Pu. Tripolitania: Or 33 [1964] p. 9, line 1)

Bibl. Or 33 (1964) 7; Harris 84; KAI/II 54, 58; PPG 42; Or 37 (1968) 307; Slouszch 76.

B

B C.W.S. 1. "in" prep. 2. "from" 3. "among" 4. with the force of comparison 5. as a temporal conj. 6. with a causal force

1 a) *BMŠKB ZN 'Š ŠKB BN*
"in this resting place, in which I rest"
(Ph. Byblos: KAI/I p. 2, ins. #9, line A 3)

b) *'Š BTKT 'BN*
"which is in the midst of a (semiprecious) stone"
(Ph. Byblos: KAI/I p. 2, ins. #10, line 5)

c) *B'RN ZN 'NK BTN'M*
"in this sarcophagus I, *BTN'M*..."
(Ph. Byblos: KAI/I p. 2, ins. #11, line 1)

d) *'Š BGW HQDŠ*
"who is in the midst of the sanctuary"
(Ph. Tyre: KAI/I p. 3, ins. #17, line 1)

e) *BNTY BŠT 180 L'DN MLKM*
"I built in the one hundred and eightieth year of the Lords of Kingdoms"
(Ph. Umm el-Awamid: KAI/I p. 3, ins. #18, lines 4-5)

f) *BPLG L'DK*
"in the district of *L DK*"
(Ph. Umm el-Awamid: KAI/I p. 3, ins. #18, line 3)

g) *'ṬRT ḤRṢ BDRKNM 20 LMḤT*
"a gold crown, twenty drachmas sterling in value (?)"
(Ph. Piraeus: KAI/I p. 13, ins. #60, line 3)

h) *BŠT ŠPṬM ḤMLK WḤMLK BN 'NKN*
"in the year of the magistrates *ḤMLK* and *ḤMLK* son of *'NKN*"
(N.Pu. Bir Bou-Rekba: KAI/I p. 26, ins. #137, lines 1-2)

2 a) *W'L Y'MSN BMŠKB Z*
"and may he not carry me from this resting place"
(Ph. Sidon: KAI/I p. 3, ins. #14, lines 5-6)

b) *WYQDŠT ḤYT ŠĠYT BGBL ŠD NRNK*
"and consecrated many animals from the territory of the fields of *NRNK*"
(Ph. Larnaka: KAI/I p. 10, ins. #43, line 9)

c) *BḤDR ḤSK 'BR*
"from the underworld (?) pass"
(Ph. Arslan Tash: KAI/I p. 6, ins. #27, lines 19-20)

d) *[MŠ Z Y]Ḃ' 'BB'L MLK [GBL BYḤMLK MLK] GBL BMṢRM*
"[the statue which] *'BB'L* king of [*GBL* son of *YḤMLK* king of] *GBL* [br]ought from *MṢRM*"
(Ph. Byblos: KAI/I p. 1, ins. #5, lines 1-2)

3 a) *ZR' BḤYM*
"offspring among the living"
(Ph. Sidon: KAI/I p. 2, ins. #13, line 7)

b) *WMY BBNY 'Š YŠB TḤTN*
"and whoever among my sons who shall sit in my place"
(Ph. Zinjirli: KAI/I p. 4, ins. #24, lines 13-14)

c) *'Š B'M 'YTNM*
"who is among the people of the Island of Jackels"
(Pu. Sousse: KAI/I p. 19, ins. #99, line 5)

4 a) *W'P B'BT P'LN KL MLK*
"and moreover, all kings made me as (an) intercessor"
(Ph. Karatepe: KAI/I p. 5, ins. #26, line A I,12)

5 a) *MṢBT LMBḤYY YṬN'T*
"a monument during my lifetime, I erected"
(Ph. Kition: KAI/I p. 8, ins. #35, lines 1-2)

b) *'Š BN...'YT BT Z*
"while...this temple"
(Ph. Sidon: KAI/I p. 3, ins. #15, line 2)

6 a) *BṢDQY WBḤKMTY WBN'M LBY*
"because of righteousness and my wisdom and with the goodness of my heart"
(Ph. Karatepe: KAI/I p. 5, ins. #26, lines A I,12-13)

b) *BY PY 'NK*
"without my word"
(Pu. Carthage: KAI/I p. 17, ins. #79, line 8)

Bibl. DISO 30-31; Harris 84; ANET 653-54, 656-58, 662; Branden 114-15; PPG 126-28; KAI/II 7, 10, 12, 15, 17, 25-26, 30, 36, 43, 52, 60, 97, 107, 136; BASOR 197 (1970) 46, esp. note 23; JNES 10 (1951) 228-30.

B' Heb. *Bō'* "to come", *HeBī'* "to bring"; Ug. *BW'*; Akk. *Bāu*; Arabic *Bāa'* "to return, come back"; Geez *Bo'a* "to enter"; ESArab. *BH'*. 1. "to enter" vb. 2. "to bring" 3. "to fall"

1 a) *BT 'B' BL TB'N*
"the house which I enter you shall not enter"
(Ph. Arslan Tash: KAI/I p. 6, ins. #27, obv. lines 5-6)

b) *B' H'LNM 'L 'LT HMQDŠM 'L*
"these gods came into these sanctuaries"
(N.Pu. Bir Bou-Rekba: KAI/I p. 26, ins. #137, lines 4-5)

2 a) *[MŠ Z Y]Ḃ' 'BB'L MLK GBL*
"[the statue which] *'BB'L* king of *GBL* [br]ought"
(Ph. Byblos: KAI/I p. 1, ins. #5, line 1)

3 a) *'Š YB' 'LT HḤRZ*
"that which falls (?) upon the fence (?)"
(Pu. Carthage: KAI/I p. 17, ins. #81, line 4)

Bibl. KAI/II 7, 43, 98, 136; Harris 84; DISO 32; ANET 658; Slouszch 158; BASOR 197 (1970) 44-45; PPG 78.

**B'R* C.S. N.Pu. *B''R, BHR*. 1. "well" n.f.

a) *HB''R HDBR Š'MMQM*
"the well of the innermost room of the sanctuary"
(N.Pu. Bitia: Amadasi p. 134, ins. #8, line 5)

b) *HQṢ'H ŠHBHRM*
"the edge of the wells"
(N.Pu. Sardinia: Amadasi 134, ins. #8, line 3)

Bibl. KAI/II 157; DISO 32; Amadasi 135.

BD I — B.Heb. *BaD* "empty idle talk"; Syriac *BeDya'* "vain talk". 1. "vanity" n.m.

a) *'L TŠM' BDNM*
"do not listen to their vanity (?)"
(Ph. Sidon: KAI/I p. 3, ins. #14, line 6)

Bibl. ANET 662; Harris 86.

BD II — 1. "on behalf of" prep. (only in combinations)

a) *TM BD ṢDNYM*
"it was decided on behalf of the *ṢDNYM*"
(Ph. Piraeus: KAI/I p. 13, ins. #60, line 1)

b) *BD MNḤM B[N] B'L[Š]M'*
"on behalf of *MNḤM* s[on] of *B'L[Š]M'*"
(Ph. Kition: Slouszch p. 82, ins. #67, lines 3-4)

c) *'Š NDR B'LHN' 'Š ṢDN BD 'DNY BD 'ŠMNYTN'*
"that which *B'LHN'* the man of *ṢDN* vowed on behalf of his lord, on behalf of *'ŠMNYTN*"
(Pu. Carthage: Slouszch p. 263, ins. #335, lines 2-4)

d) *K 'ŠTRT 'RŠ BDY*
"because *'ŠTRT* requested (it) from me" (or "on my behalf")
(Ph. Pyrgi: KAI/I p. 53, ins. #277, line 6)

Bibl. DISO 104; Harris 85; KAI/II 73; Slouszch 82-83, 117; Benz 283-86; Amadasi 166; PPG 23, 31, 127.

BDD — B.Heb. *BāDaD* "to be separate"; N.Heb. *BāDāD* "loneliness"; Arabic *BaDDa* "to be separate". 1. "to be separate"

a) *BDD BR'Š MGMR BNT*
"separate at once (?) O destroyer of intelligence (?)"
(Ph. Arslan Tash: BASOR 209 [1973] p. 19, rev. lines 3-4)

Bibl. BASOR 209 (1973) 25; Syria 48 (1971) 404.

BDLḤ Heb. *BeDoLaḤ* "Bdellium gum"; Akk. *BuDuLḪu*; J.Aram. *BeDuLḤa'*; Syriac *BeDuLḤa'*; Lat. *Bdellium*; Gk. *Bdellion*. 1. "bdellium gum" n.m.

a) *'SP BMR WBDL[Ḥ]*
"gathered in myrrh and bdell[ium]"
(Ph. Byblos: MUSJ 45 [1969] p. 262, line 1)

Bibl. MUSJ 45 (1969) 264.

BWṢ Heb. *BūṢ* "byssus"; Akk. *BūṢu*; J.Aram. *BūṢa'*; Syriac *BūṢa'*; Arabic *BaZZuN*; Ph. *BṢ* (Pu. *BWṢ*). 1. "byssus" n.m.

a) *WBYMY KSY BṢ*
"and in my days byssus covered him"
(Ph. Zinjirli: KAI/I p. 4, ins. #24, lines 12-13)

b) *BWṢ WMKS'*
"byssus and a covering"
(Pu. Carthage: KAI/I p. 17, ins. #76, line A 6)

Bibl. NE 235; KAI/II 30-31, 93; ANET 654; DISO 41.

**BṬN* Heb. *BeṬeN* "belly, body, womb"; Q.Heb. *BṬN* "sheath"; Amar.Akk. *BaṬNu* "belly"; Emp.Aram. *BṬN*; J.Aram. *BaṬNa'*; Syriac *BaṬNa'*; Amm. *BṬN* "bowl"; Mandaic *BuṬNa'* "pregnancy". 1. "embossment" n.m.

a) *DL HKT'RT 'L B'ṬN'*
"the possessor of a capital (?) with its embossment (?)"
(N.Pu. Leptis Magna: KAI/I p. 22, ins. #119, line 2)

Bibl. KAI/II 124; DISO 34; BASOR 193 (1969) 19, esp. note 15.

BL I Heb. *BūL* "name of the eighth month." 1. name of a month. n.m.

a) *BYRḤ BL*
"in the month of *BL*"
(Ph. Sidon: KAI/I p. 3, ins. #14, line 1)

b) *BYMM 6 LYRḤ BL*
"on the sixth day of the month of *BL*"
(Ph. Kition: KAI/I p. 7, ins. #32, line 1)

Bibl. Harris 87; Slouszch 59; KAI/II 19, 50.

BL II

B.Heb. *BaL* "not"; Ug. *BL*; Akk. *BaLu* "without"; Arabic *BaL* particle of digression. 1. "not" adv.

a) *NGZLT BL 'TY*
"I have been snatched away before my time"
(Ph. Sidon: KAI/I p. 3, ins. #14, lines 2-3)

b) *KN BMH WBL P'L*
"there was *BMH* and he was ineffective"
(Ph. Zinjirli: KAI/I p. 4, ins. #24, line 3)

c) *'Š BL 'N KL HMLKM 'Š KN LPNY*
"which all the kings who were before me did not humble"
(Ph. Karatepe: KAI/I p. 5, ins. #26, line A I,19)

d) *WḤṢR 'DRK BL TDRKN*
"and the court which I tread, you shall not tread"
(Ph. Arslan Tash: KAI/I p. 6, ins. #27, rev. lines 7-8)

e) *BL YKN LKHN MNM*
"nothing shall go to the priest"
(Pu. Carthage: KAI/I p. 16, ins. #74, line 6)

f) *BL YKN LKHN*[*M MNM*]
"[nothing] shall go to the priests"
(Ph. Marseilles: KAI/I p. 15, ins. #69, line 15)

Bibl. ANET 653-54, 656-58, 662; Harris 87; PPG 125, 161; NE 236; Branden 114; KAI/II 19, 30-31, 36, 43, 83, 92; Amadasi 169; Slouszch 19; Gaster-Fs 135.

BLL

B.Heb. *BeLiL* "fodder"; N.Heb. *BeLiLā* "mixture"; Akk. *BaLLu* "fodder". 1. "fodder" n.m.

a) [']*L BLL W'L ḤLB W'L ḤLB*
"[f]or fodder for milk and for fat"
(Pu. Marseilles: KAI/I p. 15, ins. #69, line 14)

b) *'L BLL W'L ḤLB*
"for fodder and for milk"
(Pu. Carthage: KAI/I p. 16, ins. #75, line 1)

c) *ḂLL WQDMT*
"fodder and first fruits"
(Pu. Carthage: KAI/I p. 16, ins. #76, line A 7)

Bibl. Amadasi 169; Harris 87; DISO 37; KAI/II 83, 92, 93; ANET 656-57, esp. note 2; Slouszch 147; NE 236.

BLT B.Heb. *BiLTi* "not, except"; Ug. *BLT*.
1. "only" adv.

a) *BLT 'NK ŠKB B'RN Z*
"only I lie in this sarcophagus"
(Ph. Sidon; KAI/I p. 2, ins. #13, line 5)

Bibl. Slouszch 17; ANET 662; Harris 87; DISO 37; PPG 125; KAI/II 17; Branden 114.

BN I C.S. Ph., Pu., N.Pu. (Ph. *BL*, *BM*, *'BL*, *'BN*; N.Pu. *B'N*). 1. "son" n.m. 2. "nephew" 3. "grandson" 4. relationship of age 5. with legal meaning 6. in group association 7. referring to an ethnic group

1 a) *ŠLM BN 'BDSSM*
"*ŠLM* son of *'BDSSM*"
(Ph. Abydos: KAI/I p. 11, ins. #49, line 46)

b) *BNḤDŠ BN B'LYTN*
"*BNḤDŠ* son of *B'LYTN*"
(Ph. Piraeus: KAI/I p. 13, ins. #58, line 1)

c) *'BDṢPL BL 'BDMLKT*
"*'BDṢPL* son of *'BDMLKT*"
(Ph. Abydos: KAI/I p. 11, ins. #49, line 18)

d) *GRHKL BM ḤLM*
"*GRHKL* son of *ḤLM*"
(Ph. Abu Simbel: Slouszch p. 62, ins. #54, line 2)

e) *'B'L 'BL MTL*
"*'B'L* son of *MTL*"
(Ph. Abydos: KAI/I p. 11, ins. #49, line 30)

f) *B'LYTN BN ḤN'*
"*B'LYTN* son of *ḤN'*"
(N.Pu. Leptis Magna: KAI/I p. 23, ins. #122, line 2)

g) *WL'BNY WL'ŠTY*
"and for his son and for his wife"
(N.Pu. Tripolitania: LibAnt 1 [1964] p. 57, line 4)

2 a) *BN' ḤYM*
"his brother's sons"
(N.Pu. Guelma: JA Series 11 vol. 8 [1916] p. 494, ins. #10, line 6)

3 a) *BN BN 'RMLK MLK GBL*
"grandson of *'RMLK*, king of *GBL*"
(Ph. Byblos: KAI/I p. 2, ins. #10, line 1)

b) *BN BN MLK 'ŠMN'ZR*
"grandson of king *'ŠMN'ZR*"
(Ph. Sidon: KAI/I p. 3, ins. #15, line 1)

4 a) *BN ŠNT ŠNM*
"two years of age"
(N.Pu. Maktar: KAI/I p. 28, ins. #151, line 3)

b) *BN Š'NT ŠB'M*
"seventy years of age"
(N.Pu. Tunisia: KAI/I p. 25, ins. #133, line 3)

c) *BN ŠŠM ŠT WŠLŠ*
"sixty-three years of age"
(N.Pu. Maktar: KAI/I p. 28, ins. #152, line 3)

5 a) *WBN ṢDQ YTNMLK MLK ṢDNM*
"and the legitimate heir, *YTNMLK* king of the *ṢDNM*"
(Ph. Sidon: KAI/I p. 3, ins. #16, line 1)

6 a) *DR BN 'LM*
"assembly of the gods"
(Ph. Karatepe: KAI/I p. 5, ins. #26, line A III,19)

b) *WKL BN 'LM*
"and all the sons of *'L*"
(Ph. Arslan Tash: BASOR 197 [1970] p. 44, rev. line 15)

c) *'WGSTS BN 'LM*
"the divine Augustus"
(N.Pu. Leptis Magna: KAI/I p. 22, ins. #120, line 1)

d) *WBN 'DM*
"and man(kind)"
(Ph. Memphis: KAI/I p. 11, ins. #48, line 4)

7 a) *BN ṢR*
"son of *ṢR*" (i.e. Tyrian)
(Pu. Carthage: RES, ins. #891, line 4)

Bibl. JA Series 11 vol. 8 (1916) 494; Harris 87; Benz 287-88; Slouszch 64; DISO 37; BASOR 197 (1970) 44-45; KAI/II 12, 19, 43, 64, 65, 122, 126, 128, 135, 146; NE 237; PPG 21, 109, 116; ANET 653, 656, 658, 662; Branden 34; LibAnt 1 (1957) 58-59; AJSL 41 (1925) 84.

BN II — Heb. *BaiN* "in the interval of, between"; Ug. *BN*; Anc.Aram. *BN*; Emp.Aram. *BYN*; J.Aram. *BaiN*; Syriac *BaiNaT*; Nab. *BYN*; Palm. *BYN*; Mandaic *BiNaT*; Arabic *BaiNa*. 1. "either" conj.

a) *BN YD B'L WBN YD 'DM*
"either by the hand(s) of *B'L*, or by the hand(s) of man"
(Ph. Cyprus: KAI/I p. 7, ins. #30, line 4)

Bibl. KAI/II 48; DISO 34; PPG 130, 163.

BNY — Heb. *BāNā* "to build"; Ug. *BNY*; Akk. *BaNū* "to build, create, produce"; Moab. *BNH*; Anc.Aram. *BNY* (?); Emp.Aram. *BNH*; J.Aram. *BeNa'*; Syriac *BeNa'*; Palm. *BN'*; Nab. *BNH*; Mandaic *BN'*; ESArab. *BNY*; Arabic *BaNa*; Ph. *BNY*, *BN*; Pu. *BN'* (N.Pu. *B'N*, *B'N*, *BN'*, *B'N*). 1. "to build" vb. 2. "builder" 3. "construction" (infinitive) 4. "was built" (N)

1 a) *BT Z BNY YḤMLK MLK GBL*
"the temple which *YḤMLK* the king of *GBL* built"
(Ph. Byblos: KAI/I p. 1, ins. #4, line 1)

b) *QR Z BNY ŠPṬB'L MLK GBL*
"the wall which *ŠPṬB'L* king of *GBL* built"
(Ph. Byblos: KAI/I p. 1, ins. #7, lines 1-2)

c) *W'NḤN 'Š BNN BTM L'LN ṢDNM*
"and it is we who built temples for the gods of *ṢDNM*"
(Ph. Sidon: KAI/I p. 3, ins. #14, lines 17-18)

d) *HBT Z BN L'LY L'ŠMN*
"this temple, he built for his god, for *'ŠMN*"
(Ph. Sidon: KAI/I p. 3, ins. #16, line 2)

e) *'Š BN H'LM ML'K MLK'ŠTRT*
"which the chiefs, the envoys of *MLK'ŠTRT* built"
(Ph. Ma'ṣub: KAI/I p. 4, ins. #19, lines 2-3)

f) *WBN 'NK*
"and I built"
(Ph. Karatepe: KAI/I p. 5, ins. #26, line A II,9)

g) *T MQDŠ Z BN' B'L' TBGG*
"this sanctuary the citizens of *TBGG* built"
(Ph. Dougga: KAI/I p. 20, ins. #101, line 1)

2 a) *YTNB'L HBN'*
"*YTNB'L* the builder"
(N.Pu. Leptis Magna: KAI/I p. 23, ins. #123, lines 3-4)

3 a) *KN' 'L MLKT HBN'*
"were (appointed) over the labor of construction"
(N.Pu. Bir Bou-Rekba: KAI/I p. 26, ins. #137, line 2)

4 a) *NBN' [K]' HMQDŠ S*
"this sanctuary was built [here]"
(N.Pu. Maktar: KAI/I p. 28, ins. #146, line 1)

b) *NBN' HMNBṢBT Z*
"this (grave)stone was built"
(N.Pu. Maktar: KAI/I p. 28, ins. #149, line 1)

Bibl. DISO 38; Harris 87-88; Benz 288; NE 238; Branden 9, 103-4; PPG 23-24, 41, 81-82, 84-85; KAI/II 6, 9, 19, 25, 27, 36, 110, 130, 144, 145; ANET 656, 662.

BNT I Heb. *BiNā* "intelligence"; B.Aram. *BīNā*; J.Aram. *BīNāTa'*. 1. "intelligence" n.f.

a) *BDD BR'Š MGMR BNT*
"separate at once (?), O destroyer of intelligence (?)"
(Ph. Arslan Tash: BASOR 209 [1973] p. 19, rev. lines 3-4)

Bibl. BASOR 209 (1973) 25; Syria 48 (1971) 404-5.

BNT II for etymology see under *PNT*. 1. "before" prep.

a) ['*Š*] *Y'MS BNT 'LM*
"[that which] will be set before the gods"
(Pu. Carthage: KAI/I p. 16, ins. #74, line 8)

Bibl. KAI/II 92; DISO 230; Harris 138; NE 352; Slouszch 167; PPG 17, 125; Branden 6.

B'L C.S. 1. "citizen" n.m. 2. "husband" 3. n. of relation

1 a) *W'BDY B'L ḤMN*
"and her servants, the citizens of *ḤMN*"
(Ph. Ma'ṣub: KAI/I p. 4, ins. #19, line 3)

b) *B'L ṢDN*
"the citizens of *ṢDN*" (or "*B'L* of *ṢDN*")
(Ph. Piraeus: KAI/I p. 13, ins. #60, line 6)

c) *B'L' TBGG*
"the citizens of *TBGG*"
(Pu. Dougga: KAI/I p. 20, ins. #101, line 1)

d) *MTNB'L B'L YRM*
"*MTNB'L*, the citizen of *YRM*"
(Pu. Constantine: Berthier/Charlier p. 91, ins. #113, line 1)

2 a) *BD'ŠTRT* [*BN*] *MRŠ B'L 'RŠT*
"*BD'ŠTRT* [son] of *MRŠ*, husband of *'RŠT*"
(Pu. Carthage: Slouszch p. 261, ins. #329, lines 3-4)

3 a) *B'L 'DR*
"possessor of a flock"
(Ph. Zinjirli: KAI/I p. 4, ins. #24, line 11)

b) *B'L BQR*
"possessor of cattle"
(Ph. Zinjirli: KAI/I p. 4, ins. #24, lines 11-12)

c) *W'ḤRY HŠ'R LB'L HZBḤ*
"and the remainder of the flesh shall go to the owner of the sacrifice"
(Pu. Marseilles: KAI/I p. 15, ins. #69, line 8)

d) *B'L ḤRDT*
"master of terror (?)"
(N.Pu. Maktar: KAI/I p. 27, ins. #145, line 5)

e) *B'L ŠLM HRŠT/N*
"donor (?) of a *ŠLM* offering of first fruits"
(N.Pu. Leptis Magna: KAI/I p. 22, ins. #120, line 2)

f) *'ŠM R'M B'L 'GDDM*
"evil men, the leaders of troops"
(Ph. Karatepe: KAI/I p. 5, ins. #26, line A I,15)

g) *B'L ḤRŠ 'KBRM*
"the master craftsman, *'KBRM*"
(Pu. Carthage: KAI/I p. 17, ins. #81, line 9)

Bibl. Benz 288-90; Branden 16; PPG 42; Harris 88; DISO 40, 105; NE 239; KAI/II 27, 30, 36, 73, 83, 98, 118, 141; ANET 653-54, 656; Amadasi 169; VT 10 (1960) 141; JAOS 74 (1954) 231; Albright 108-12.

B'LT Heb. *Ba'aLā* "mistress of the house"; Akk. *BēLTu*; Ug. *B'LT*; ESArab. *B'LT*; J.Aram. *Ba'aLTa'*. 1. "mistress" n.f.

a) *LB'LT GBL 'DTW*
"for the Mistress of *GBL*, his lady"
(Ph. Byblos: KAI/I p. 1, ins. #7, lines 3-4)

b) *T'RK B'LT GBL YMT ŠPṬB'L WŠNTW*
"may the Mistress of *GBL* lengthen the days of *ŠPṬB'L* and his years"
(Ph. Byblos: KAI/I p. 1, ins. #7, lines 4-5)

c) *KM 'Š QR'T 'T RBTY B'LT GBL*
"when I invoked my lady, the Mistress of *GBL*"
(Ph. Byblos: KAI/I p. 1, ins. #10, lines 7-8)

Bibl. Benz 288-90; Harris 88-90; NE 239-40; DISO 40; KAI/II 9, 12; ANET 656; Slouszch 11.

B'T etymology unknown. 1. "tariff" n.f. (from context)

a) *B'[T HMŠ]'TT*
"tar[iff of pay]ments
(Pu. Marseilles: KAI/I p. 15, ins. #69, line 1)

b) *B'T HMŠ'TT*
"tariff of payments"
(Pu. Carthage: KAI/I p. 16, ins. #74, line 1)

c) *'T KL HB'T*
"with the entire tariff (?)"
(N.Pu. Leptis Magna: KAI/I p. 22, ins. #119, lines 7-8)

d) *BKL B'T LKNṢWL'T*
"with the entire tariff (?) of the consulate"
(N.Pu. Maktar: KAR 12 [1963-64] p. 52, col. II, line 3)

Bibl. KAI/II 83, 92, 124; DISO 39; Harris 88; NE 242; Slouszch 142; KAR 12 (1963-64) 52; ANET 656-57; LS I 79.

BṢL C.S. 1. "onion" n.m.

a) *WBṢL R'ŠY*
"and onion *R'ŠY*"
(Ph. Egypt: KAI/I p. 12, ins. #51, line obv. 4)

Bibl. KAI/II 69.

BṢ' I [B.Heb. *BeṢ'a* "profit, cut"]. 1. "contribution" n.m. (etymology doubtful)

a) *BṢ'M N'MM*
"kindly (?) contributions (?)"
(N.Pu. Leptis Magna: KAI/I p. 22, ins. #119, line 6)

Bibl. KAI/II 124; DISO 41.

BṢ' II [B.Heb. *BāṢa'* "to act, to make a large profit"; N.Heb. *BāṢa'* "to break bread"; J.Aram. *BeṢa'*; Arabic *BaṢa'a* "to cut pieces"; ESArab. *BṢ'* "to behead"]. 1. "to contribute" vb. (etymology doubtful)

a) *'T M'NŠ' WMBṢ' LMLKT HMQ[M]*
"with the donors (?) and the contributors (?) to the labor of the tem[ple]"
(N.Pu. Leptis Magna: KAI/I p. 22, ins. #119, line 6)

Bibl. KAI/II 124; DISO 41.

BQY N.Heb. *BāQi* "expert"; J.Aram. *BeQa'* "to search, investigate"; Syriac *BeQa'*; Mandaic *BQ'*; Arabic *BaQi* "to remain". 1. "to remain" vb.

a) *TBQY ''LK*
"remain O passerby"
(N.Pu. Guelaat Bou-Sba: KAI/I p. 30, ins. #165, line 1)

Bibl. KAI/II 154; OrAnt 4 (1965) 64.

BQR Heb. *BāQāR* "cattle"; J.Aram. *BaQRa'* "herd"; Syriac *BaQRa'*; ESArab. *BQR* "bovines"; Arabic *BaQRuN* "cattle". 1. "cattle" n.m.

a) *Š̌TY B'L BQR*
"I established him (as) the possessor of cattle"
(Ph. Zinjirli: KAI/I p. 4, ins. #24, lines 11-12)

Bibl. DISO 41; ANET 654; KAI/II 31.

BQŠ̌ Heb. *BiQQeŠ̌* "to seek"; Ug. *BQṮ*; N.Heb. *NiTBaQQeŠ̌* "to be sought". 1. "to seek" vb.

a) *W'L YBQŠ̌ BN MNM*
"and may he not seek anything within it"
(Ph. Sidon: KAI/I p. 3, ins. #14, lines 4-5)

b) *H'G YTBQŠ̌N H'DR*
"the '*G* shall seek me, the Mighty one"
(Ph. Byblos: MUSJ 45 [1969] p. 262, line 2)

Bibl. ANET 662; Harris 91; Slouszch 21; Benz 290; MUSJ 45 (1969) 264; KAI/II 19.

BR B.Heb. *BR* (Prov. 31:2) "son"; Anc.Aram. *BR*; Emp.Aram. *BR*; J.Aram. *BeRa'*; Syriac *BeRa'*; Mandaic *BRa'*; Nab. *BR*; Palm. *BR*; Soq. *BaR* "child". 1. "son" n.m.

a) *'NK KLMW BR ḤY[']*
"I am *KLMW* son of *ḤY[']*"
(Ph. Zinjirli: KAI/I p. 4, ins. #24, line 1)

b) *KLMW BR ḤY*
"*KLMW* son of *ḤY*"
(Ph. Zinjirli: KAI/I p. 5, ins. #25, lines 2-3)

Bibl. Harris 91; KAI/II 31, 35; ANET 654; DISO 41-42.

BR' Heb. *BāRā* "to create"; Q.Aram. *BRY*; ESArab. *BR'* "to build"; J.Aram. *BeRa'* "to create"; Syriac *BeRa'*; Mandaic *BR'*; Arabic *BaRa* "to form, fashion by cutting"; Akk. *BaRū* "to look upon, to observe omens". 1. "diviner" n.m.

a) *'Š NDR MTN HBR'*
"that which *MTN* the diviner (?) vowed"
(Pu. Carthage: Slouszch p. 303, ins. #452, lines 3-4)

Bibl. Slouszch 303; DISO 43; Harris 91; NE 244; Leš. 6 (1930) 352-54.

BRZL Heb. *BaRZeL* "iron"; Ug. *BRḎL*; Akk. *PaRZiLLu*; Emp.Aram. *PRZL*; J.Aram. *BaR̄ZeLa'*; Syriac *PaRZeLa'*; Mandaic *PaRZLa'*; Arabic *FarZiLuN* "iron horse fetters". 1. "iron" n.m.

a) *NSK BRZL*
"the iron caster"
(Ph. Kition: Slouszch p. 94, ins. #83, lines 2-5)

b) *HNSKM Š BRZL*
"the casters of iron"
(Ph. Dougga: KAI/I p. 19, ins. #100, line 7)

c) *'KBRM NSK HBRZL*
"*'KBRM*, the iron caster"
(Pu. Carthage: Slouszch p. 195, ins. #186, lines 1-2)

Bibl. Harris 91; NE 244; KAI/II 107; DISO 43; Slouszch 95, 195, 212; JNES 28 (1969) 263, also n. 3; Leš 4 (1932) 115-18.

BRḤ Heb. *BāRaḤ* "to flee"; Ug. *BRḤ* (?); N.Heb. *HiBRiaḤ* "to drive out, exclude"; J.Aram. *'aBRaḤ* "to withhold"; Arabic *BaRaḤa* "to withdraw, flee". 1. "to depart" vb. 2. "to waste"

1 a) *WNḤT TBRḤ 'L GBL*
"may calm depart from *GBL*"
(Ph. Byblos: KAI/I p. 1, ins. #1, line 2)

2 a) *BKSP* <*'Š*> *'BRḤT*
"with the silver which I wasted (?)"
(Ph. Carthage: KAI/I p. 18, ins. #89, line 4)

Bibl. KAI/II 2, 102; DISO 43; Harris 91; MUSJ 45 (1965) 315-16; PPG 67.

BRK C.S. 1. "to bless" vb. 2. "blessed" p.p.

1 a) *K Š M' QL YBRK*
"because he heard (his) voice, may he bless him"
(Ph. Idalion: KAI/I p. 8, ins. #38, line 2)

b) *K ŠM' QL YBRK*
"because he heard (his) voice, mey he bless him"
(Ph. Tamassos: KAI/I p. 9, ins. #41, line 6)

c) *K ŠM' QL' YBRK'*
"because he heard his voice, may he bless him"
(Pu. Sicily: KAI/I p. 14, ins. #63, line 3)

d) *YBRKY WYŠM' QL 'D 'LM*
"bless him and hear (his) voice for eternity"
(Pu. Carthage: KAI/I p. 17, ins. #78, line 1)

e) *TŠM' QL' TBRK'*
"hear his voice (and) bless him"
(Pu. Carthage: KAI/I p. 18, ins. #84, line 1)

f) *K ŠM' QL' BRKY'*
"for he heard his voice (and) blessed him"
(Pu. Constantine: KAI/I p. 20, ins. #105, line 4)

g) *K ŠM' QL' YBRK''*
"because he heard his voice, may he bless him"
(Pu. Carthage: Slouszch p. 313, ins. #485, lines 2-4)

h) *B'L YBRK WYḤWW*
"may *B'L* bless and preserve him"
(Pu. Byblos: KAI/I p. 2, ins. #12, line 4)

i) *TBRKY BYMY*
"may she bless her in her lifetime"
(Ph. Ur: KAI/I p. 7, ins. #29, line 2)

2 a) *'NK 'ZTWD HBRK B'L*
"I am *'ZTWD*, the blessed of *B'L*" (or "steward of *B'L*")
(Ph. Karatepe: KAI/I p. 5, ins. #26, line A I,1)

Bibl. Harris 91; NE 244-45; Benz 291-92; PPG 49, 89; DISO 44; Slouszch 176, 313; ANET 653; KAI/II 16, 36, 47, 56, 58, 96, 100, 114; Leš 32 (1967-68) 59-62.

BRKT Heb. *BeRāKā* "blessing"; J.Aram. *BiRKeTa'*; Syriac *BūRKeTa'*; Mandaic *BRaKa'*; Arabic *BaRaKaTuN*. 1. "blessing" n.f.

a) *L'B BRKT ML[KYM]*
"to the father, the blessing(s) of ki[ngs] (?)"
(N.Pu. Maktar: KAI/I p. 28, ins. #147, line 3)

Bibl. KAI/II 144.

BRŠ N.Heb. *NiBReŠeT* "candlestick"; J.Aram. *NaBRaŠTa'*; Syriac *NaBReŠTa'*; Arabic *NiBRāŠuN*. 1. "candlestick maker" n.m.

a) *'Š NDR 'BDMLQRT BN ḤMLKT HBRŠ*
"that which *'BDMLQRT* son of *ḤMLKT* the candlestick maker (?) vowed"
(Pu. Carthage: Slouszch p. 311, ins. #480, lines 2-3)

Bibl. NE 246; DISO 45; Harris 92; Slouszch 312.

BŠM Heb. *BoŚeM* "spice", "balsam"; J.Aram. *BuSMa'*; Syriac *BeSMa'*; Arabic *BaŠāMuN*. 1. "spice" n.m.

a) *Š'G' ŠBŠM*
"for bread cake (?), for spice (?)"
(N.Pu. Bir-Tlesa: KAI/I p. 26, ins. #138, line 4)

Bibl. KAI/II 137; DISO 45; LS I 99.

BŠR Heb. *BāŚāR* "flesh"; Ug. *BŠR*; Emp.Aram. *BŠR*; J.Aram. *BiSRa'*; Syriac *BeSRa'*; B.Aram. *BiŚRa'*; Mandaic *BiSRa'*; Arabic *BaŠaRaTuN* "epidermis"; Geez *BaSoR* "flesh"; Pu. *BŠR*, *BŠ'R*, *BŠ'R*; N.Pu. *BŠR*, *BŠ'R*. 1. type of sacrifice. n.m.

a) *MLK 'DM BŠ'RM BTM*
"a *MLK 'DM* sacrifice whose flesh (is) intact"
(Pu. Constantine: KAI/I p. 20, ins. #105, line 3)

b) *BŠR'M BTM*
"(whose) flesh (is) intact"
(Pu. Constantine: KAI/I p. 21, ins. #108, lines 3-4)

c) *'Š NDR 'BD'ŠMN BN 'RŠ BŠ'R*
"that which *'BD'ŠMN* son of *'RŠ* vowed, a flesh offering"
(Pu. Carthage: Slouszch p. 309, ins. #471, lines 3-6)

d) *MLK 'DM BŠRM BN' TM*
"a *MLK 'DM* sacrifice, its flesh, of his son (is) intact"
(Pu. Constantine: KAI/I p. 21, ins. #107, line 4)

e) *MLK 'DM BŠ'RM BTM*
"*MLK 'DM* sacrifice, whose flesh (is) intact"
(Pu. Constantine: Slouszch p. 223, ins. #229, line 2)

f) *BŠRM BTM*
"whose flesh (is) intact"
(N.Pu. Constantine: Slouszch p. 222, ins. #228, line 2)

Bibl. Albright 205-6; ANET 658; Harris 118; PPG 48, 110; KAI/II 114-15; DISO 45.

BT I

C.S. Ph., Pu. *BT* (N.Pu. *BYT*). 1. "house, dwelling place, temple, place" 2. "room (of a palace, house, tomb)" 3. n. of relationship referring to family, royal name and dynasty 4. unknown

1 a) *W'NḤN 'Š BNN BT L'ŠMN*
"and it is we who built a temple for *'ŠMN*"
(Ph. Sidon: KAI/I p. 3, ins. #14, lines 16-17)

b) *W'NḤN 'Š BNN BTM L'LN ṢDNM*
"and it is we who built temples for the gods of *ṢDNM*"
(Ph. Sidon: KAI/I p. 3, ins. #14, lines 17-18)

c) *HBT Z BN L'LY L'ŠMN*
"this temple he built for his god, for *'ŠMN*"
(Ph. Sidon: KAI/I p. 3, ins. #15, line 2)

d) *BT 'LM*
"temple"
(Ph. Piraeus: KAI/I p. 13, ins. #60, line 2)

e) *WYṬN' 'NK BT 'DNY*
"and I erected my lordly house(s)"
(Ph. Karatepe: KAI/I p. 5, ins. #26, lines A I,9-10)

f) *BT LB'L ṢDN WBT L'ŠTRT ŠM B'L*
"a temple for *B'L* of *ṢDN* and a temple for *'ŠTRT ŠM B'L*"
(Ph. Sidon: KAI/I p. 3, ins. #14, line 18)

g) *'RPT BT 'LM*
"the portico of the temple"
(Ph. Piraeus: KAI/I p. 13, ins. #60, line 5)

h) ['']*BD BT ŠMŠ*
"[ser]vant of the temple of *ŠMŠ*"
(Pu. Carthage: Slouszch p. 306, ins. #462, line 4)

i) *'BD BT MLK'ŠTRT*
"servant of the temple of *MLK'ŠTRT*"
(Pu. Carthage: Slouszch p. 280, ins. #385, line 5)

j) *BT B'L 'DR*
"the temple of *B'L 'DR*"
(Pu. Constantine: Berthier/Charlier p. 28, ins. #27, line 2)

k) *BT 'B' BL TB'N*
"the house I enter you shall not enter"
(Ph. Arslan Tash: BASOR 197 [1970] p. 44, obv. lines 5-6)

2 a) *ḤDR BT 'LM*
"the chamber of the tomb"
(Ph. Malta: Slouszch p. 126, ins. #109, line 1)

3 a) *BT MPŠ*
"the house of *MPŠ*"
(Ph. Karatepe: KAI/I p. 5, ins. #26, line A I,16)

b) *KN BT 'BY BMTKT MLKM 'DRM*
"my father's house was in the midst of mighty kings"
(Ph. Zinjirli: KAI/I p. 4, ins. #24, lines 5-6)

c) *RKB'L B'L BT*
"*RKB'L* master of the dynasty"
(Ph. Zinjirli: KAI/I p. 4, ins. #24, line 16)

d) *L'DN LBL ḤMN K BL BT*
"to the lord, to *B'L ḤMN*, for (he is) the master of the dynasty"
(Pu. Constantine: Berthier/Charlier p. 27, ins. #25, lines 1-2)

4 a) *BYT Š'T*
"container of (?)"
(N.Pu. Henscher Medina: KAI/I p. 29, ins. #160, line 2)

Bibl. ANET 662; DISO 35-36; Harris 86; PPG 116; Slouszch 126, 280; Amadasi 18; KAI/II 19, 23, 30, 36, 73, 149; Berthier/Charlier 27-28; NE 235-36; Benz 294.

BT II C.S. Ph., Pu., N.Pu. *BT* (N.Pu. *B'T*).
1. "daughter" n.f. 2. relationship of age

1 a) *'MTB'L BT PṬ'S*
"*'MTB'L* daughter of *PṬ'S*"
(Ph. Ur: KAI/I p. 7, ins. #29, line 1)

b) *'ṬHD BT 'BD'ŠMN*
"*'ṬHD* daughter of *'BD'ŠMN*"
(Ph. Kition: KAI/I p. 8, ins. #36, lines 1-2)

c) *ṢPNB'L HKHNT BT 'ZRB'L*
"*ṢPNB'L* the priestess, daughter of *'ZRB'L*"
(Pu. Carthage: KAI/I p. 19, ins. #93, line 1)

d) *'ṘŠṬ BT YTNB'L*
"*'RŠT* daughter of *YTNB'L*"
(N.Pu. Leptis Magna: KAI/I p. 23, ins. #123, line 3)

e) *B'L'NG B'T ŠPṬ*
"*B'L'NG* daughter of *ŠPṬ*"
(N.Pu. Carthage: JA Series 11 vol. 10 [1917] p. 32, lines 2-3)

2 a) *MT' BT Š'NT ŠB'M WŠB'*
"she died at seventy-seven years of age"
(N.Pu. Tunisia: KAI/I p. 25, ins. #136, lines 2-3)

b) *BT HSRM WŠB'*
"(who died) at twenty-seven"
(N.Pu. Maktar: KAI/I p. 28, ins. #148, lines 2-3)

Bibl. DISO 37; Benz 293; Harris 87; PPG 43, 116, 119; KAI/II 47, 53, 104, 130, 135, 145.

G

GBL Heb. *GeBūL* "territory, boundary"; Anc.Aram. *GBL* "territory"; ESArab. *GBLT* "region(s)"; Palm. *GBL* "totality"; Arabic *JaBaLuN* "mountain". 1. "boundary" n.m. 2. "territory"

1 a) *BKL QSYT L'GBLM*
"at all the edges, upon their boundary"
(Ph. Karatepe: KAI/I p. 5, ins. #26, line A I,14)

b) *BQṢT GBLY*
"at the edge(s) of my border"
(Ph. Karatepe: KAI/I p. 5, ins. #26, line A I,21)

2 a) *BKL GBL 'MQ 'DN*
"in the entire territory of the plain of *'DN*"
(Ph. Karatepe: KAI/II p. 5, ins. #26, lines A II,1-2)

b) *BGBL ŠD NRNK*
"from the territory of the field of *NRNK*"
(Ph. Larnaka: KAI/I p. 10, ins. #43, line 9)

Bibl. DISO 47; Harris 93; NE 248; KAI/II 36, 60; ANET 653; Fitzmyer 119.

GBR Heb. *GeBeR* "young, vigorous man"; Anc.Aram. *GBR*; B.Aram. *GeBaR*; Emp.Aram. *GBR*; J.Aram. *GaBRa'*; Syriac *GaBRa'*; Mandaic *GaBRa'*; Nab. *GBR*; Palm. *GBR*. 1. "man" n.m.

a) *'LMT YTN BŠ WĠBR BSWT*
"(who) gave a maid for a sheep and a man for a garment"
(Ph. Zinjirli: KAI/I p. 4, ins. #24, line 8)

b) *HGBR Z'*
"this man"
(Ph. Cyprus: KAI/I p. 7, ins. #30, line 2)

Bibl. DISO 47; KAI/II 30, 31, 48; ANET 654.

GRBT Heb. *GeBūRā* "strength, might"; B.Aram. *GeBūRTa'*; J.Aram. *GeBūRTa'*; Syriac *GaBRūTa'* "vigour, force"; Mandaic *GaBaRuaTa'* "great might"; Arabic *JaBRūTuN* "magnification, pride". 1. "mighty deed" n.f.

a) *'L GBRTM K'TBTY*
"I wrote about their mighty deeds"
(N.Pu. Maktar: KAI/I p. 27, ins. #145, line 6)

Bibl. DISO 50; Leš. 16 (1947-48) 9; KAI/II 141; PPG 48.

GG I — Heb. *GaG* "roof"; Ug. *GG*; Amar.Akk. *GaGGi* (?); N.Heb. *GiGiT* "roofing, tub, tank"; J.Aram. *GiGiTa'*. 1. "roofer" n.m.

a) *NDR ḤN' HGG'*
"the vow of *ḤN'* the roofer"
(Pu. Constantine: Berthier/Charlier p. 41, ins. #42, line 2)

b) *'DR' HGG*
"*'DR'* the roofer"
(Pu. Antas: RPA p. 70, ins. #4, line 6)

Bibl. Berthier/Charlier 41; RPA 72-73.

GG II — for etymology, see *GG* I. 1. "roof" n.m.

a) *HGG 'L 'MDM*
"the roof upon the columns"
(Pu. Sardinia: Amadasi p. 109, ins. #32, line 2)

b) *WHGG*
"and the roof"
(Pu. Sardinia: Amadasi p. 109, ins. #32, line 3)

Bibl. Amadasi 111.

GGP — N.Heb. *GaPPā* "stone fence with a gate"; J.Aram. *GaPPa'* "city gate". 1. "fence" n.f.

a) *'BD'ŠTRT P'L HGGPM* (possible dittography of the Gimel or reflection of Dageš following the definite article)
"*'BD'ŠTRT*, the maker of fences"
(Pu. Carthage: CIS I, ins. #339, lines 3-4)

Bibl. Harris 93; Slouszch 279; NE 248; DISO 47.

GDD — Heb. *GeDūD* "band, raid"; Akk. *GuDūDāNu* "military detachment" (only pl.); J.Aram. *GuNDa'*; Mandaic *GuNDa'*; Arabic *JuNDuN*. 1. "troop" n.m.

a) *B'L 'GDDM*
"leaders of troops"
(Ph. Karatepe: KAI/I p. 5, ins. #26, line A I,15)

Bibl. ANET 653-54; KAI/II 36; DISO 3.

**GDY* C.S. 1. "kid" n.m.

a) *B'MR 'M BGD'*
"for a lamb or for a kid"
(Pu. Marseilles: KAI/I p. 15, ins. #69, line 9)

Bibl. KAI/II 83; Harris 93; Slouszch 145; DISO 47; Amadasi 179.

GW I J.Aram. *GaWWa'*; Anc.Aram. *GW* "interior"; B.Aram. *Gō'*; Emp.Aram. *GW*; Syriac *GaWa'*; Mandaic *GaWa'*; Arabic *JaWuN* "the air between the sky and the earth; the interior of a house, or tent". 1. "midst" n.m.

a) *'Š BGW HQDŠ*
"who is in the midst of the sanctuary"
(Ph. Tyre: KAI/I p. 3, ins. #17, line 1)

Bibl. KAI/II 25; DISO 48; PPG 126; Harris 94.

GW II Heb. *Gōy* "nation"; B.Heb. *GeW* "folk"; Akk. *Gā'u* "group, gang of workmen"; Syriac *GaWa'* "a body of people, congregation, community"; ESArab. *GW* "community". 1. "community" n.m.

a) *'Š NŠ' HGW*
"the chief of the community"
(Ph. Piraeus: KAI/I p. 13, ins. #60, line 2)

b) *K YD' HGW*
"that the community knows"
(Ph. Piraeus: KAI/I p. 13, ins. #60, line 7)

c) *NDR 'Š NDR 'KBRT BT ḤṬML[ ] LHGW*
"a vow which *'KBRT* daughter of *ḤṬML*[ ] vowed on behalf of the community"
(N.Pu. Constantine: Berthier/ Charlier p. 26, ins. #24, lines 2-3)

Bibl. Slouszch 117; Harris 94; DISO 48; NE 249; Tur-Sinai 422; JAOS 82 (1962) 143, note 3; KAI/II 73, 153; Berthier/ Charlier 25; JBL 79 (1960) 157-63; Bib 48 (1967) 573.

**GZ* Heb. *GāZaZ* "shear"; Akk. *GaZāZu*; J.Aram. *GaZaZ*; Syriac *GaZ*; Arabic *JaZZa*; Mandaic *GZZ*; Soq. *GeZZ*. 1. "shearer" n.m.

a) *MTHQŠ' HG'Z*
"*ṀṬHQŠ̬'* the shearer"
(N.Pu. Tripolitania: Libya 3 [1927] p. 110, line 1)

Bibl. DISO 49.

GZL

Heb. *GāZaL* "to tear away, rob"; Syriac *GeLaZ* "to cheat, seize"; Mandaic *GZL* "to steal, separate"; J.Aram. *GeZaL* "to acquire something illegitimately"; Arabic *JaZaLa* "to cut". 1. "to be snatched" vb. (N) 2. "gamble" n.m.

1 a) *NGZLTY BL ʿTY*
"I have been snatched away before my time"
(Ph. Sidon: KAI/I p. 3, ins. #14, lines 2-3)

2 a) *'DNBʿL BN Ḥ̣N' HGZL*
"*'DNBʿL* son of *Ḥ̣N'* the gambler"
(See Talmud Babli Tractate Sanhedrin, page 25, side 2)
(Pu. Carthage: Slouszch p. 233, ins. #251, line 2)

Bibl. Albright-Fs 259-60; Harris 94; Slouszch 9, 233; ANET 662; DISO 49; PPG 65; KAI/II 19.

GZT

Heb. *GaZiT* "hewn stone"; [ESArab. *GZYT* "an edict"]. 1. "stone wall" n.f.

a) *'YT HGZT ST*
"this hewn stone wall (?)"
(Pu. Ibiza: Amadasi p. 143, ins. #10, line B 1)

Bibl. DISO 49; ClassFol 22 (1968) 170-71; KAI/II 88; Amadasi 144.

GLB

Heb. *GaLLāB* "barber"; Akk. *GaLLāBu*; J.Aram. *GaLLāBa'*; [Syriac *GeLaB* "to answer, to disperse"]; Nab. *GLB'*; Eg. *D̲D̲B* "to stab, prick". 1. "barber" n.m.

a) *LGLBM P'LM 'L ML'KT QP' 2*
"for the barbers carrying out the cultic service, two *QP'*"
(Ph. Kition: Or 37 [1968] p. 305, line A 13)

b) *B'LŠLK GLB 'LM*
"*B'LŠLK* the cultic barber"
(Pu. Carthage: Slouszch p. 264, ins. #338, line 4)

c) *'RŠM GLB 'LM*
"*'RŠM* the cultic barber"
(Pu. Carthage: Slouszch p. 239, ins. #268, lines 4-5)

d) *'BDMLQRT GLB 'LM*
"*'BDMLQRT* the cultic barber"
(Pu. Carthage: Slouszch p. 279, ins. #382, lines 4-5)

Bibl. Slouszch 239; DISO 50; Harris 94; Benz 296; KAI/II 54; EncMiq vol. 2 col. 485-86 (sub. *GaLLāB*).

**GLY*

Heb. *GāLā* "to reveal, uncover"; Akk. *GaLū* "to go into exile"; Ug. *GLY* "to leave"; Syriac *GeLa'* "to uncover, reveal"; J.Aram. *GeLa'*; Arabic *JaLa* "to become clear, unobscured"; Emp.Aram. *GLY*; Mandaic *GL'*; Te. *GeLa* "to take away". 1. "to uncover" vb.

a) *WYGL 'RN ZN*
"who shall have uncovered this sarcophagus"
(Ph. Byblos: KAI/I p. 1, ins. #1, line 2)

Bibl. DISO 50; KAI/II 2; Harris 94; PPG 24; Branden 9.

GLM

B.Heb. *GeLōM* "garment", *GoLeM* "embryo"; N.Heb. *GāLaM* "to roll up, to unshape", *GoLeM* "lump, shapeless or lifeless substance"; J.Aram. *GoLMa'*, *GeLīMa'* "wrapper, cloak, hill, height"; Syriac *GeLiMa'*; Mandaic *GLM* "to roll up, encompass", *GLuM* "spirit invoked in exorcisms"; [Soq. *GLM* "to pick, to gather"; Arabic *JaLaMa* "to cut, intercept"]. 1. "type of spirit" n.m.

a) *BD'ŠṬRT 'LM HGLM*
"*BD'ŠTRT* the exorciser (?) of the *GLM* spirit (?)"
(Pu. Carthage: CIS I, ins. #3427, line 3)

Bibl. DISO 50.

GLGL

N.Heb. *GiLGeL* "to roll upon, to burden, tax"; J.Aram. *GaLGeL*. 1. "wrapper" n.m.

a) *'Š NḌR ḤMLKT HGLGL HMŠ*
"that which *ḤMLKT*, the wrapper (?) of (?) vowed"
(Pu. Constantine: Berthier/Charlier p. 45, ins. #48, lines 1-2)

Bibl. Berthier/Charlier 45; DISO 50.

GL'N

precise meaning unknown. 1. "open eyed" adj. m.

a) *WGL'N BŠDH 'Y 'LŠYY*
"and an open eyed one from the field of (that) island, a *'LŠYY* (?)"
(Ph. Arslan Tash: BASOR 209 [1973] p. 18, obv. lines 4-6)

Bibl. BASOR 209 (1973) 21-22, esp. note 13; Syria 48 (1971) 399-401.

GM meaning and etymology unknown.
1. "majesty" n.m. (from context)

a) *'L GM 'DR*
"for glorious majesty (?)"
(N.Pu. Cherchel: KAI/I p. 29, ins. #161, line 5)

Bibl. KAI/II; DISO 51.

GMR I B.Heb. *GāMaR* "to do good, spare" (Ps. 57:3). 1. "to spare" vb.

a) *'Š GMR 'ŠTRT*
"whom *'ŠTRT* spared"
(Pu. Carthage: Slouszch p. 203, ins. #198, line 2)

Bibl. Slouszch 204; DISO 51.

GMR II Heb. *GāMaR* "to end, come to an end, complete"; Akk. *GaMāRu*; J.Aram. *GeMaR*; Syriac *GeMaR*; Mandaic *GMR*; Arabic *JaMaRa* "to assemble, collect"; B.Aram. *GaMaR*.
1. "to destroy" vb. 2. "to complete"

1 a) *MGMR BNT*
"O destroyer of intelligence (?)"
(Ph. Arslan Tash: BASOR 209 [1973] p. 19, rev. lines 3-4)

2 a) *GMR' B*[ ]
"they finished (?) with the [ ]"
(Pu. Carthage: CIS I, ins. #3919, line 2)

Bibl. BASOR 209 (1973) 25-26; Syria 48 (1971) 404; DISO 51; Dahood I 45.

GNB Heb. *GāNaB* "to steal"; Anc.Aram. *GNB*; J.Aram. *GeNaB*; Mandaic *GNB*; Emp.Aram. *GNB*; Palm. *GNB*; Arabic *JaNaBa* "to put aside". 1. "to steal" vb.

a) *WKL 'DM 'Š GNB*
"and all men who would steal"
(Pu. Carthage: Slouszch p. 346, ins. #573, line 5)

b) *KL 'Š LGNB*
"all who (would come) to steal"
(Pu. Carthage: Slouszch p. 347, ins. #574, lines 1-2)

Bibl. Slouszch 347-48; Harris 94; DISO 51; PPG 59; JNES 32 (1973) 477, also note 13.

GR Heb. *GūR* "young animal, whelp"; Akk. *GuRRu* "young of animals"; J.Aram. *GūRYa'*; Syriac *GūRYa'*. 1. "lion whelp" n.m.

a) *LKLBM WLGRM QR 3*
"for the dogs and for the lions 3 *QR*"
(Ph. Kition: Or 37 [1968] p. 305, line B 10)

Bibl. Or 37 (1968) 317, esp. note 4; KAI/II 54; DISO 53; Harris 92; Slouszch 80-81.

**GNN* Heb. *HāGeN* "to protect"; Akk. *GaNNu* "cover"; Emp.Aram. *GNN* "to protect"; J.Aram. *GeNaN*; Syriac *GeNa'* "shelter, shadow"; Chr.Pal.Aram. *'GN* "to protect"; Palm. *'GN*; Arabic *JaNNa* "to cover, to wrap". 1. "to cover"

a) *T 'MDM WT HM'Q'M YGN*
"...covered the pillars and the temple"
(N.Pu. Leptis Magna: KAI/I p. 23, ins. #124, lines 1-2)

Bibl. DISO 52; KAI/II 130.

GRGNT J.Aram. *GūRGaNTa'* "type of large drum" (reading uncertain; see Aruch vol. 2, p. 350, col. 2). 1. type of instrument used in a religious ceremony. n.f.

a) *WYLK RBM 'DNB'L BN GRSKN... 'YT 'GRGNT*
"and their chiefs *'DNB'L* son of *GRSKN* and...offered the *GRGNT* instrument"
(Pu. Carthage: CIS I, ins. #5510, lines 9-10)

GRR Heb. *GāRaR* "to drag away"; Akk. *GaRāRu* "to flow, run"; J.Aram. *GeRaR*; Arabic *JaRRa* "to drag along"; Mandaic *GRR* "to scrape, drive off"; Syriac *GeRaR*. 1. "hauler" n.m.

a) *BD'ŠMN HGRR Š'ZRT B'LYSP*
"*BD'ŠMN*, the hauler, of the family (?) of *B'LYSP*"
(Pu. Carthage: CIS I, ins. #4873, line 3)

Bibl. DISO 54.

GRŠ Heb. *GeRaŠ* "to drive out"; Ug. *GRS*; Moab. *GRS*. 1. "to drive out" vb.

a) *BTRŠŠ WGRŠ H'*
"from *TRŠŠ* he was driven"
(Ph. Sardinia: Or 41 [1972] p. 459, lines 1-2)

Bibl. Or 41 (1972) 460-63.

GT Heb. *GaT* "wine vat"; Ug. *GT*; P.S. *GNT*. 1. "wine vat" n.f.

a) *GT KR*[*ML*]
"the vat of *KR*[*ML*]"
(Ph. Shiqmona: IEJ 18 [1968] p. 227, line 2)

Bibl. IEJ 18 (1968) 233.

D

D Heb. *Dai* "enough". 1. "sufficiency" subst.

a) *YM MD YM*
"day by day"
(Ph. Larnaka: KAI/I p. 10, ins. #43, line 11)

b) *YRḤ MD YRḤ*
"month by month"
(Ph. Larnaka: KAI/I p. 10, ins. #43, line 12)

Bibl. DISO 56; Harris 95; Slouszch 111-12; KAI/II 43.

DBR I Heb. *DāBāR* "matter, thing"; Ug. *DBR*; B.Aram. *DiBRā* "cause"; Emp.Aram. *DBR* "word"; J.Aram. *DiBūRa'*. 1. "thing" n.m.

a) *K T'BT 'ŠTRT HDBR H'*
"because that thing is an abomination to *'ŠTRT*"
(Ph. Sidon: KAI/I p. 2, ins. #13, line 6)

Bibl. ANET 662; KAI/II 17; DISO 55; Slouszch 17.

DBR II Heb. *DiBBeR* "to speak". 1. "to speak" vb.

a) *DBR MLK 'ŠMN'ZR MLK ṢDNM L'MR*
"thus spake king *'ŠMN'ZR*, king of the *ṢDNM* saying"
(Ph. Sidon: KAI/I p. 3, ins. #14, line 2)

b) *'P 'M 'DMM YDBRNK*
"yea, even if men speak with you" (or "impel you")
(Ph. Sidon: KAI/I p. 3, ins. #14, line 6)

Bibl. ANET 662; KAI/II 19; Slouszch 21; DISO 55.

DBR III B.Heb. *HiDBīR* "to lead"; N.Heb. *HiDBīR* "to persuade"; Akk. *DuBBuRu* "to expel"; Emp.Aram. *DBR* "to tread"; J.Aram. *DeBaR* "to lead, guide"; Syriac *DeBaR*; Mandaic *DBR*; Arabic *DaBaRa* "to follow". 1. "to impel" vb.

a) *'P 'M 'DMM YDBRNK*
"yea, even if men impel you"
(or "speak with you")
(Ph. Sidon: KAI/I p. 3, ins. #14, line 6)

Bibl. ANET 662; KAI/II 19; Slouszch 21; DISO 55.

DBR IV — See under *DBR* I for etymology. 1. "word" (of supplication) n.m. 2. "affair"

1 a) *K ŠM' QL DBRY*
"because he heard the sound of his words"
(Pu. Malta: Amadasi p. 20, lines 5-6)

b) *K ŠM' QL DBRY*
"because he heard the sound of his words"
(Ph. Tortozah: Slouszch p. 48, ins. #32, line 5)

c) *K ŠM' QL DBRW*
"because he heard the sound of his words"
(Pu. Carthage: Slouszch p. 347, ins. #576, line 7)

2 a) *BKTBT DBR' HBT ŠG'Y BN ḤN'*
"by the document of the affairs of the house of *G'Y* son of *ḤN'*"
(N.Pu. Leptis Magna: KAI/I p. 23, ins. #124, lines 3-4)

Bibl. Harris 95; DISO 55; NE 254; KAI/II 76, 130; Slouszch 348.

DBR V — Heb. *DeBīR* "innermost chamber of the temple"; Syriac *DeBRa'* "outlying country, wilderness"; J.Aram. *DaBRa'*; Mandaic *DiBRa'*; Arabic *DaBRuN* "part behind". 1. "innermost room" n.m.

a) *HB''R HDBR Š'MMQM*
"the wall of the innermost room of the sanctuary"
(N.Pu. Bitia: Amadasi p. 134, ins. #8, line 5)

Bibl. Leš. 32 (1967-68) 10-11; Amadasi 135; DISO 55; KAI/II 158.

DGN — Heb. *DāGāN* "corn"; Ug. *DGN*; Emp.Aram. *DGN*; J.Aram. *DeGāNa'*. 1. "corn" n.m.

a) *'RṢT DGN H'DRT*
"the glorious corn lands"
(Ph. Sidon: KAI/I p. 3, ins. #14, line 19)

Bibl. Harris 95; DISO 55; ANET 662; NE 254; Slouszch 27; KAI/II 19; Albright 108.

DḤY Heb. *DāḤā* "to push, thrust"; J.Aram. *DeḤa'*; Syriac *DeḤa'*; Mandaic *DH'*; Arabic *DaḤa* "to drive along". 1. "to break" vb.

a) *YDḤ 'YT HPS Z*
"break this tablet"
(Pu. Carthage: KAI/I p. 16, ins. #75, line 6)

Bibl. KAI/II 93; PPG 82, 85; DISO 56; Harris 95.

DKY Heb. *DiKKe* "to crush, humble"; Akk. *DaKū* "to kill". 1. "depressed" adj. (from context)

a) *'NK P'L'BST BN ṢDYTN BN GRṢD YŠB DKY** (?) *B'N BMṢRM*
"I, *P'L'BST* son of *ṢDYTN*, son of *GRṢD* dwell depressed (?) in *'N*, in *MṢRM*"
(Ph. Abydos: KAI/I p. 11, ins. #49, line 34)

*The reading of Dalet is not certain.

Bibl. Slouszch 56; KAI/II 65; DISO 57; Harris 95.

**DL* I B.Heb. *DaL* "door" (Ps. 141:3); Heb. *DeLeT*; Ug. *DLT*; J.Aram. *DaLTa'*; Akk. *DaLTu*. 1. "door" n.f.

a) *HŠ'R Z WHDLHT*
"this gate and the doors"
(Ph. Umm el-Awamid: KAI/I p. 3, ins #18, line 3)

b) *DLHT ŠNḤŠT*
"doors of bronze"
(N.Pu. Leptis Magna: KAI/I p. 23, ins. #122, line 2)

Bibl. KAI/II 26, 128; DISO 58; Harris 95; NE 256; Branden 32; PPG 116.

DL II [Akk. *DaLāLu* "to proclaim, glorify"; Mandaic *DLL* "to point out, designate"; Arabic *Dalla* "to direct, guide"]. 1. "to glorify" vb.

a) *K RḤ DL QDŠM*
"because (my) spirit glorified (?) the holy ones"
(Pu. Carthage: Slouszch p. 180, ins. #155, line 4)

Bibl. Slouszch 181.

DL III rel.pr. plus possessive (see under *Z* I). 1. particle indicating possession. prep.

a) *WDL MLKT ḤHRṢ WDL KL MNM*
"and with all the word of gold and with all vessels (?)" (or "every thing")
(Pu. Carthage: KAI/I p. 17, ins. #81, line 2)

b) *WDL KL MNM BM'ZNM*
"and with all vessels (?) in the scales (?)"
(Pu. Carthage: KAI/I p. 17, ins. #81, line 3)

c) *DL 'ṬRT WDL ŠM T'ṢMT*
"the possessor of glory (?) and the possessor of honor (?)"
(N.Pu. Guelaat Bou-Sba: KAI/I p. 30, ins. #165, lines 6-7)

d) *DL HKT'RT 'L B'ṬN'*
"the possessor of a capital (?) with its embossment (?)"
(N.Pu. Leptis Magna: KAI/I p. 22, ins. #119, line 2)

e) *W'ḤDR DL 'QBR'*
"and the chamber with its grave"
(N.Pu. Cherchel: KAI/I p. 29, ins. #161, line 3)

Bibl. JNSL 1 (1971) 54-56; KAI/II 98, 124, 150, 154; Harris 96.

DL IV Heb. *DaL* "poor, thin"; Akk. *DaLāLu* "to be humble, miserable, pitiful"; Syriac *'iTDeLaL* "to be diminished"; J.Aram. *DeLaL* "to be poor"; Soq. *DeLeL* "humiliate". 1. "deficient" adj. m. 2. "without" prep.

1 a) *DL MQN' 'M DL ṢPR*
"deficient with regard to cattle or deficient with regard to birds"
(Pu. Marseilles: KAI/I p. 15, ins. #69, line 15)

b) *HMṬBḤ Z DL P'MM*
"this slaughtering place deficient with regard to feet"
(Pu. Carthage: KAI/I p. 17, ins. #80, line 1)

c) *[BKL ZBḤ 'Š YZB]Ḥ DL MQN'*
"[for every sacrifice which shall be offered by persons] deficient with regard to cattle"
(Pu. Carthage: KAI/I p. 16, ins. #74, line 6)

2 a) *WBYMTY 'NK 'ŠT TK LḤDY DL PLKM*
"but in my days, a woman walked by herself without supports"
(Ph. Karatepe: KAI/I p. 5, ins. #26, lines A II,5-6)

Bibl. PPG 126; Harris 95-96; Slouszch 148, 162; KAI/II 36, 83, 92, 98; ANET 653, 656; DISO 58; LS I 77-78; JNSL 1 (1971) 53-54; NE 256; JQR 16 (1904) 283.

DLḤT etymology unknown; perhaps related to *DLHT*. 1. "tablet" n.f.

a) *ŠPṬ SPR HDLḤT*
"*ŠPṬ*, the tablet scribe (?)"
(Pu. Carthage: Slouszch p. 333, ins. #544, line 3)

Bibl. DISO 58.

DLT I Heb. *DeLeT* "tablet, door"; Ug. *DLT*. 1. "plaque" n.f.

a) *KM HDLT HNḤŠT* (reading of Mem uncertain)
"as the bronze plaque"
(Ph. Larnaka: KAI/I p. 10, ins. #43, line 12)

Bibl. KAI/II 60; DISO 58.

DLT II B.Heb. *DLT* "tablet of wood" (see Lachish ostracon #3, line 3); Ug. *DLT*; Syriac *'āDLāTa'* "double doors". 1. "tablet" n.f.

a) *BDLT 'Š ḤTM LBTM*
"by the tablet, which...sealed in his house"
(Pu. Carthage: CIS I, ins. #5522, line 5)

Bibl. Gibson 42; LS I 416.

DN'R Gk. *Denarius*; Lat. *Denarius*; N.Heb. *DiNāR*; J.Aram. *DiNāRa'*; Syriac *DiNaRa'*; Arabic *DiNāRuN*. 1. "type of coin". n.m.

a) *DN'RY' M'T WŠLŠM WŠLŠ*
"one hundred and thirty-three *DN'RY'*"
(N.Pu. Leptis Magna: KAI/I p. 25, ins. #130, lines 1-2)

Bibl. KAI/II 133.

D'T Heb. *Da'aT* "knowledge"; Akk. *Di'aTu*; ESArab. *D'W* "known"; J.Aram. *Da'aTa'* "knowledge"; Soq. *Do'oH*. 1. "knowledge" n.f.

a) *MḤB D'T HTMT*
"(he who is the) lover of the knowledge of harmony (?)"
(N.Pu. Leptis Magna: KAI/I p. 23, ins. #121, line 1)

Bibl. KAI/II 128; DISO 59; ZDMG 69 (1961) 513f.

DṢ etymology unknown. 1. "contrary" adv. (from context)

a) *BDṢ L'Š*
"contrary to that which"
(Pu. Marseilles: KAI/I p. 15, ins. #69, line 20)

Bibl. KAI/II 69; DISO 59; Harris 95; Amadasi 182; Slouszch 150.

DQ Heb. *DaQ* "thin, fine"; Akk. *DaQQu* "small"; Ug. *DQ*; Syriac *DaQDeQa'* "minute, light, small"; J.Aram. *DaQQa'*; Mandaic *DQaTa'* "small pieces"; Arabic *DaQQaTuN* "smallness, littleness". 1. "fine" adj. f.

a) *LBNT DQT*
"fine frankincense"
(Pu. Carthage: KAI/I p. 16, ins. #76, line B 6)

Bibl. Harris 96; DISO 60; KAI/II 93; NE 257; Slouszch 168.

DR I Heb. *DōR* "generation, contemporaries, assembly" (Ps. 14:5); Ug. *DR*; Akk. *DāRu* "generation"; [Mandaic *DuRa'* "circumstances]; ESArab. *DR* "one time"; Geez *DaR* "age"; Arabic *DaWRuN* "circle". 1. "assembly" n.m.

a) *DR BN 'LM*
"assembly of the gods"
(Ph. Karatepe: KAI/I p. 5, ins. #26, line A III,19)

b) *WRB DR KL QDŠṀ* (or *QDŠṄ*)
"and the great of the assembly of all the holy ones"
(Ph. Arslan Tash: BASOR 197 [1970] p. 44, rev. line 12)

Bibl. ANET 653, 658; DISO 60; JNES 9 (1950) 215-17; KAI/II 36, 43; BASOR 197 (1970) 44-45, esp. note 10; Dahood I 82; ZDMG 69 (1961) 501, note 3.

DR II   for possible etymology, see *DR* I.
1. "family" n.m.

a) *[SK]R DR' L'WLM*
"[a memor]ial of his family, for eternity"
(N.Pu. Leptis Magna: KAI/I p. 25, ins. #128, line 2)

b) *SK'R DR' L'LM*
"a memorial of his family, for eternity"
(N.Pu. Guelaat Bou-Sba: KAI/I p. 30, ins. #165, lines 7-8)

c) *DR' KN' ŠLM*
"they have named their family"
(N.Pu. Maktar: KAR 12 [1963-64] p. 54, col. IV, line 1)

Bibl. DISO 60; PPG 48, 234; KAI/II 132, 154; KAR 12 (1963-64) 54.

DR III   for possible etymology, see *DR* I.
1. "perpetuity" n.f.

a) *HMZRḤ 'Š LDRT*
"the council which (was established) in perpetuity (?)"
(N.Pu. Maktar: KAI/I p. 27, ins. #145, line 1)

Bibl. DISO 60; KAI/II 141.

DRK I   B.Heb. *DeReK* "power" (Prov. 31:3); Ug. *DRKT* "rule, dominion". 1. "commander" n.m.

a) *'Š NDR W'Š Ṭ[N'] DRK 'DNB'L*
"which *'DNB'L* the commander vowed and er[ected]"
(N.Pu. Kef Bezioun: KAI/I p. 31, ins. #170, lines 1-2)

Bibl. KAI/II 156; Leš. 33 (1968-69) 76, 90-92.

DRK II   Heb. *DāRaK* "to tread"; Emp.Aram. *DRK*; J.Aram. *DeRaK*; Mandaic *DRK*; Syriac *DeReK*; ESArab. *HDRK* "to reach"; Arabic *'aDRaKa* "to attain or overtake". 1. "to tread" vb.

a) *WḤṢR 'DRK BL TDRKN*
"and the court which I tread, you shall not tread"
(Ph. Arslan Tash: BASOR 197 [1970] p. 44, obv. lines 7-8)

Bibl. ANET 658; KAI/II 43; BASOR 197 (1970) 44-45; PPG 61.

DRK III Heb. *DeReK* "way, road"; J.Aram. *DaRKa'*; Syriac *DeRāKa'* "a step"; Akk. *DaRaGGu* "path". 1. "road" n.f.

a) *'Š YŠT' 'DM LLKT DRK*
"where a man was afraid to walk on the road"
(Ph. Karatepe: KAI/I p. 5, ins. #26, lines A II,4-5)

Bibl. ANET 653; KAI/II 36.

DRKMN Gk. *Drachmae* "silver drachmas"; B.Heb. *'aDaRKōN, DaRKōN, DaRKeMōN*; Syriac *DeRiKoNa'*. 1. "silver drachmae" n.m.

a) *'ṬRT ḤRṢ BDRKNM 20 LMḤT*
"a crown of gold, twenty drachmas sterling in value (?)"
(Ph. Piraeus: KAI/I p. 13, ins. #60, line 3)

b) *YŠ'N BKSP 'LM B'L ṢDN DRKMNM 20 LMḤT*
"let the citizens of *ṢDN* bring twenty drachmas in value (?) of the finest silver"
(Ph. Piraeus: KAI/I p. 13, ins. #60, line 6)

Bibl. DISO 60; Harris 96; KAI/II 73; NE 257; PPG 99; Slouszch 118.

DRŠ Heb. *DāRaŠ* "to search into, inquire"; Syriac *DeRaŠ* "to beat a path, discuss"; Mandaic *DRŠ*; J.Aram. *DeRaŠ*; Arabic *DaRaSa* ["to efface, to disappear"] "to study a book". 1. "to inquire into". vb. (from context)

a) *TDRŠ' T.N'M*
"may you inquire into him, may you do good (?)"
(Pu. Morocco: BAC [1955] p. 31, line 1)

Bibl. BAC (1955) 31.

H

H Heb. *Ha* the definite article; Moab. *H*; Saftaitic *H*; Thamudic *H*; Ph., Pu. *H* (N.Pu., Pu. ', '). 1. the definite article joined with nouns 2. with the gentilic 3. with participles 4. with relative force 5. to mark the vocative

1 a) [ ]*D'* *BN GBR HMLK*
"[ ]*D'* son of *GBR* the king"
(Ph. Abydos: Slouszch p. 61, ins. #51, line 1)

b) *LSM*['] *BT* *'Z*[*R*]*B'L HMḤQ*
"for *ŠM*['] the daughter of *'Z*[*R*]*B'L* the scraper"
(Ph. Kition: Slouszch p. 90, ins. #74, lines 1-2)

c) *WHSLMT 'Š LMPQD*
"and the stairs of the tower"
(Ph. Idalion: Slouszch p. 98, ins. #88, line 4)

d) *QBR MTR HYṢR*
"the grave of *MTR* the potter"
(Pu. Motya: Slouszch p. 132, ins. #116, lines 1-2)

e) *P'LT LY HMŠKB ZN*
"I made for myself this resting place"
(Ph. Byblos: KAI/I p. 2, ins. #9, line A 1)

f) *HŠ'R Z WHDLHT*
"the gate and the doors"
(Ph. Umm el-Awamid: KAI/I p. 3, ins. #18, line 3)

g) *B'T HMŠ'TT*
"tariff of payments"
(Pu. Carthage: KAI/I p. 16, ins. #74, line 1)

h) *'ZMLK 'ŠPṬ*
"*'ZMLK* the magistrate"
(Pu. Carthage: Slouszch p. 287, ins. #406, line 6)

2 a) *GRṢD HṢRY*
"*GRṢD* the *ṢRY*"
(Ph. Abydos: KAI/I p. 11, ins. #49, line 34)

b) *'BD'ŠMN BN ŠLM HKTY*
"*'BD'ŠMN* son of *ŠLM* the *KTY*"
(Ph. Abydos: KAI/I p. 11, ins. #49, line 13)

c) *'BDŠMŠ HṢDNY*
"*'BDŠMŠ* the *ṢDNY*"
(Ph. Athens: KAI/I p. 13, ins. #53, line 2)

3 a) *'NK 'ZTWD HBRK B'L*
"I am *'ZTWD* the blessed of *B'L*" (or "steward of *B'L*")
(Ph. Karatepe: KAI/I p. 5, ins. #26, line A I,1)

4 a) *LPN HMLKM HLPNYM*
"before those kings who were before me"
(Ph. Zinjirli: KAI/I p. 4, ins. #24, lines 9-10)

b) *BL P'L HLPNYHM*
"those who were before me were ineffective"
(Ph. Zinjirli: KAI/I p. 4, ins. #24, line 5)

c) *''W' Š'NT 'RBM WḤD*
"who lived forty-one years"
(N.Pu. Henschir Guergour: KAI/I p. 27, ins. #143, lines 3-4)

Bibl. Albright-Fs 326-30; Harris 96; NE 257; JBL 56 (1937) 141; DISO 61; PPG 52-53, 150; EHO 16-17; Slouszch 288; Branden 4, 5, 63-64; KAI/II 30, 140; Les 14 (1945-46) 19-38.

H' I — Heb. *Hu'* "he"; Ug. *HW*; Moab. *H'*; Anc.Aram. *H'*; ESArab. *HWT*; Meh. *He*; Geez *Ue'eTū*; Arabic *HuWa*. 1. m. pr. of the third person sing.

a) *WH' YMḤ SPRH LPP ŠBL*
"and as for him, let a (?) efface his inscription"
(Ph. Byblos: KAI/I p. 1, ins. #1, line 2)

b) *K̇ MLK ṢDQ H'*
"for he is a righteous king"
(Ph. Byblos: KAI/I p. 2, ins. #10, line 9)

c) *BTRŠŠ WGRŠ H'*
"from *TRŠŠ* he was driven"
(Ph. Sardinia: Or 41 [1972] p. 459, lines 1-2)

d) *B'L ḤRŠ H'*
"and he (himself) was the master craftsman"
(Pu. Ibiza: KAI/I p. 16, ins. #72, line B 4)

Bibl. DISO 61-62; KAR 12 (1963-64) 52; KAI/II 6, 19, 57, 63, 88, 97, 124; Harris 96; ANET 656; NE 257; Amadasi 84, 86, 143; Or 41 (1972) 460-63; BASOR 208 (1972) 15-16; PPG 45, 51; Branden 46-47, 57-59.

H' II Heb. *Hi'* "she"; Ug. *HY*; ESArab. *H'T*; Palm. *HY*; Meh. *HY*; Geez *Ye'eTī*; Arabic *HiYa*; Ph. *H'* (N.Pu. *HY*). 1. f. pr. of the third person sing. 2. with demonstrative force

1 a) *'Š H' ŠT 57 L'Š KTY*
"which is the fifty-seventh year of the men of *KTY*"
(Ph. Idalion: Slouszch p. 102, ins. #93, line 2)

2 a) *HY 'L H[M]'QM*
"that (one) is over the [san]ctuary"
(N.Pu. Maktar: KAR 12 [1963-64] p. 52, col. II, line 3)

b) *'L ML'KT H'*
"upon that labor"
(Ph. Byblos: KAI/I p. 2, ins. #10, line 13)

c) *HMMLKT H'*
"that ruler"
(Ph. Sidon: KAI/I p. 3, ins. #14, line 22)

d) *'Š KN' BHŠT HY*
"who were in that year"
(N.Pu. Leptis Magna: KAI/I p. 25, ins. #130, line 3)

Bibl. Slouszch 102-3; KAR 12 (1963-64) 52; KAI/II 12, 19, 133.

H' III Heb. *Hu'* "he"; Ug. *HW*, *HWT*; Moab. *H'*; Anc.Aram. *H'*; J.Aram. *Hā'*; Mandaic *Hu*; ESArab. *H'*; Meh. *He*; Arabic *HuWa*.
1. m. dem. pr. of the third person sing.

a) *HR H'*
"that (sacred) hill"
(Pu. Carthage: KAI/I p. 17, ins. #81, line 4)

b) *YKN HLḤM H'*
"that bread shall be"
(Pu. Carthage: KAI/I p. 16, ins. #76, line B 4)

c) *L'DM H' L'DRB'L*
"for that man, for *'DRB'L*"
(N.Pu. Leptis Magna: KAI/I p. 22. ins. #119, line 5)

Bibl. see under *H'* I.

H' IV — Heb. *Hā'* "lo, behold"; J.Aram. *Hā'*; Syriac *Ha'*; Mandaic *Ha'*; Arabic *Hā'*.
1. "behold" interjection

a) *WH' 'Y ṀPT WR'Š̌*
"and behold, there is no dignitary (?) or leader"
(Ph. Cyprus: KAI/I p. 7, ins. #30, line 1)

Bibl. KAI/II 48; PPG 131.

H'T — for etymology, see under *H'* III.
1. m. pr. of the third person sing.

a) *Ḣ'T ḤWY KL MPLT HBTM 'L*
"he restored all the ruins of these temples"
(Ph. Byblos: KAI/I p. 1, ins. #4, lines 2-3)

Bibl. see under *H'* I.

HBRK — Akk. *'aBaRRaKu* "steward"; Sum. L.W. *'aBaRaG*; B.Heb. *'aBReK* (Gen. 41:43).
1. "steward" n.m.

a) *'NK 'ZTWD HBRK B'L*
"I am *'ZTWD*, the steward of *B'L* (or "the blessed of *B'L*")
(Ph. Karatepe: KAI/I p. 5, ins. #26, line A I,1)

Bibl. ANET 653.

HWN — Heb. *HōN* "power, wealth"; J.Aram. *HaWNa'*; [Syriac *HaWNa'* "the mind, reason"].
1. "wealth" n.m.

a) *HWN YM*
"the wealth (?) of the sea (?)"
(Ph. Byblos: MUSJ 45 [1969] p. 262, line 5)

Bibl. MUSJ 45 (1969) 271; Bib 47 (1966) 266.

HLK — Heb. *HāLaK* "to go, walk"; Ug. *HLK*; Akk. *'aLāKu*; Syriac *HaLeK*; Moab. *HLK*; Anc.Aram. *HLK*; Emp.Aram. *HLK*; Nab. *HLK*; Palm. *HLK*; J.Aram. *HLK*; Mandaic *HLK*; Arabic *HaLaKa* "to perish". 1. "to walk" vb. 2. "to travel" 3. "to establish, offer" 4. "to produce" 5. "passerby" n.m. Ph., Pu. *HLK* (N.Pu. *'LK*)

1 a) *'ŠT TK LḤDY DL PLKM*
"a woman walked by herself without supports"
(Ph. Karatepe: KAI/I p. 5, ins. #26, lines A II,5-6)

b) *'Š YŠT' 'DM LLKT DRK*
"where a man was afraid to walk on the road"
(Ph. Karatepe: KAI/I p. 5, ins. #26, lines A II,4-5)

2 a) *'Š NDR '[RŠ] BN [ ]RB[ ] 'N[Y] HLK[ ] QR[ ]*
"that which '[RŠ] son of [ ] the captain (?) of the fleet (?) traveling (?) to *QR* (?) vowed"
(Pu. Carthage: Slouszch p. 244, ins. #280, lines 2-3)

3 a) *WYLK ZBḤ LKL HMSKT*
"and I established (?) a sacrificial order (?) for all the molten images"
(Ph. Karatepe: KAI/I p. 5, ins. #26, lines A II,19)

b) *WYLK RBM 'DNB'L*
"and their chiefs *'DNB'L*... offered"
(Pu. Carthage: CIS I, ins. #5510, line 9)

4 a) *YLK HTM 'T PRY*
"the total (?) will produce (?) fruit"
(N.Pu. Tripolitania: Or 33 [1964] p. 4, line 6)

5 a) *TBQY ''LK*
"remain O passerby"
(N.Pu. Guelaat Bou-Sba: KAI/I p. 30, ins. #165, line 1)

Bibl. DISO 65; Slouszch 244; ANET 654; KAI/II 36, 154; Or 33 (1964) 13; LS I 77, 79; OrAnt 4 (1965) 64.

HLM B.Heb. *HāLaM* "to strike"; Ug. *HLM*; Te. *HaLaMa* "slap in the face". 1. "to strike" vb.

a) *BR'Š ḤLM KY HLMT 'N BTM*
"from the head of the dreamer, when you smote his eye completely"
(Ph. Arslan Tash: BASOR 209 [1973] p. 19, rev. lines 4-5)

Bibl. BASOR 209 (1973) 25; Syria 48 (1971) 405.

HMT I — Heb. *HeM*; B.Heb. *HeM*, *HeMā* "they"; Ug. *HM*, *HMT*; B.Aram. *HiNō*; Arabic *HuMMa*; ESArab. *HMW*. 1. m. dem. pr. of the third person pl.

a) *'M 'DMM HMT*
"or those men"
(Ph. Sidon: KAI/I p. 3, ins. #14, line 11)

b) *H'DMM HMT*
"those men"
(Pu. Marseilles: KAI/I p. 15, ins. #69, line 17)

Bibl. DISO 61-62; Harris 97; Amadasi 169; KAI/II 19, 30, 31, 60, 83; ANET 656, 662; NE 257; PPG 45, 51; Branden 96-97, 57-59; Slouszch 23, 149.

HMT II — for etymology, see under *HMT* I. 1. m. pr. of the third person pl.

a) *'Š HMT L'M LPṬ ŠNT 33*
"which is the thirty-third year of the people of *LPṬ*"
(Ph. Larnaka: KAI/I p. 10, ins. #43, line 5)

b) *WHMT ŠT NBŠ*
"and as for them (each) placed himself"
(Ph. Zinjirli: KAI/I p. 4, ins. #24, line 13)

Bibl. see under *HMT* I.

HN — Heb. *HiNNE*, *HeN* "behold, here is"; Ug. *HN*; Anc.Aram. *HN*; Akk. *'aNNuMa* "now"; Arabic *'iNNa* "surely"; J.Aram. *HN*; Palm. *HN*; Nab. *HN*; Ph. *HN* (N.Pu. *'N'*).
1. "here" adv. 2. "behold" interjection

1 a) *'N' ŠM'TM*
"and here are their names"
(N.Pu. Maktar: KAR 12 [1963-64] p. 54, col. IV, line 2)

2 a) *WKN HN 'NK ŠKB B'RN ZN*
"and thus, behold, I lie in this sarcophagus"
(Ph. Byblos: MUSJ 45 [1969] p. 262, line 1)

b) *LD'T HN YPD LK THT ZN*
"attention! behold, you shall come to ruin below this"
(Ph. Byblos: KAI/I p. 1, ins. #2, lines 1-3)

Bibl. DISO 66; MUSJ 45 (1969) 263; Harris 97; PPG 131; Branden 123-24; KAI/II 4; KAR 12 (1963-64) 50-51.

HNK Arabic *HuNNāKa* "there"; Akk. *'aNNaKaM* "here". 1. "here" dem. part.

a) *N'PŠ 'DYT HNKT 'BNT*
"the gravestone of *'DYT*. Here she lies buried (?)"
(N.Pu. Tunisia: KAI/I p. 25, ins. #136, lines 1-2)

b) *HNKT 'BNT TḤT 'BN ZT QBRT*
"here she lies buried under this stone, laid to rest"
(N.Pu. Tunisia: NSI p. 142, ins. #54, line 4)

c) *HNKT 'BNT T'T HBNT ZT QBRT*
"here she lies buried under this stone, laid to rest"
(N.Pu. Tunisia: NE p. 436, ins. #9, lines 4-5)

Bibl. NSI 142-43; Muséon 84 (1971) 534-35; DISO 179; Harris 97; KAI/II 135; NE 260.

HPK Heb. *HāPaK* "to overthrow, demolish"; Ug. *HPK*; Akk. *'aBāKu* "to send away", "to upset"; Syriac *HePaK* "to turn, change"; Anc.Aram. *HPK*; Palm. *HPK*; J.Aram. *HePaK*; Mandaic *'PK* "to reject, convert, turn back"; Arabic *'aFaKa* "to change a manner of being"; Nab. *HPWK* "return". 1. "to overturn" vb.

a) *THTPK KS' MLKH*
"may the throne of his kingdom be overturned"
(Ph. Byblos: KAI/I p. 1, ins. #1, line 2)

Bibl. DISO 68; Harris 97; Albright-Fs 254-57; KAI/II 2; Slouszch 4; Branden 81; PPG 69.

HR Heb. *HaR* "mountain"; Amar.Akk. *ḪaRRi*. 1. "hill" n.m. 2. "mountain"

1 a) *KM ŠḤGR HŠMRT LHR H'*
"as also the protective wall for that (sacred) hill (?)"
(Pu. Carthage: KAI/I p. 12, ins. #81, line 4)

2 a) *'N YDLL BHR*
"the spring of *YDLL*, in the mountain"
(Ph. Sidon: KAI/I p. 3, ins. #14, line 17)

Bibl. DISO 68; Harris 97; Albright-Fs 254-57; KAI/II 2; Slouszch 4; Branden 81; PPG 69.

W

W C.S. 1. "and" conj., connecting both words and sentences 2. with infinitive absolute used as a finite vb. 3. connecting verbs 4. the Waw consecutive 5. with the infinitive construct 6. the conditional sentence

1 a) *WMPḤRT 'L GBL QDŠM*
"and the assembly of the gods of *GBL*, the holy ones"
(Ph. Byblos: KAI/I p. 1, ins. #4, lines 4-5)

b) *WMR'Š 'LY WMḤSM ḤRṢ LPY*
"and a *MR'Š* headdress (?) upon me and a muzzle of gold upon my mouth"
(Ph. Byblos: KAI/I p. 2, ins. #11, line 2)

c) *WKL 'DM 'Š YPTḤ*
"and any man who opens"
(Ph. Sidon: KAI/I p. 3, ins. #14, line 4)

d) *BŠNT 'SR W'RB'*
"in the fourteenth year"
(Ph. Sidon: KAI/I p. 3, ins. #14, line 1)

e) *HŠ'R Z WHDLHT*
"this gate and the doors"
(Ph. Umm el-Awamid: KAI/I p. 3, ins. #18, line 3)

f) *KTY W'DYL*
"*KTY* and *'DYL*"
(Ph. Idalion: KAI/I p. 8, ins. #38, line 1)

g) ['*L BLL W*]'*L ḤLB*
["for fodder and] for milk"
(Ph. Carthage: KAI/I p. 16, ins. #74, line 10)

h) *L'DN LŠDRP' WLMLK'ŠTRT*
"for the lord, for *ŠDRP'* and for *MLK'ŠTRT*"
(N.Pu. Leptis Magna: KAI/I p. 22, ins. #119, line 1)

2 a) *WŠKR 'NK 'LY MLK 'ŠR*
"and I hired against him the king of *'ŠR*"
(Ph. Zinjirli: KAI/I p. 4, ins. #24, lines 7-8)

b) *WBN 'NK HQRT Z*
"and I built this city"
(Ph. Karatepe: KAI/I p. 26,
ins. #21, line A II,9)

c) *WQR' 'NK 'T RBTY*
"and I invoked my lady"
(Ph. Byblos: KAI/I p. 2,
ins. #10, lines 2-3)

3 a) *'Š YTN WYṬN'*
"that which...offered and erected"
(Ph. Tamassos: KAI/I p. 9,
ins. #41, lines 1-2)

b) *BḤY 'BY YTT WYQDŠT*
"in the lifetime of my father
I offered and consecrated"
(Ph. Larnaka: KAI/I p. 10,
ins. #43, lines 8-9)

c) *P'L WḤDŠ 'M GWL*
"the people of *GWL* made and
repaired"
(Ph. Malta: KAI/I p. 14,
ins. #62, line 1)

d) *ḤYDŠ W'YQDŠ*
"(he) repaired and consecrated"
(N.Pu. Bir Tlesa: KAI/I p. 26,
ins. #138, line 6)

e) *BN W'YQDŠ*
"he built and consecrated"
(N.Pu. Leptis Magna: KAI/I p.
25, ins. #129, lines 1-2)

4 a) *WKN H'RT*
"and the skin shall belong to..."
(Pu. Marseilles: KAI/I p. 15,
ins. #69, line 10)

b) *WKN-H'RT H'ZM LKHNM*
"and the skin of the goats shall
belong to the priests"
(Pu. Carthage: KAI/I p. 10,
ins. #74, line 4)

5 a) *W'M PTḤ TPTḤ*
"and if you shall open"
(Ph. Sidon: KAI/I p. 2,
ins. #13, lines 6-7)

b) *WRGZ TRGZN*
"and if you shall disturb me"
(Ph. Sidon: KAI/I p. 2,
ins. #13, line 7)

6 a) *W'L MLK BMLKM*
"and if any king"
(Ph. Byblos: KAI/I p. 1,
ins. #1, line 2)

Bibl. DISO 69; Harris 97; PPG 129, 162;
Branden 108-9, 119-20; KAI/I 69, 92;
Amadasi 169; ANET 653-54, 656, 662.

Z

Z I B.Heb. *Zu, Zeh* "which"; Ug. *D, DT*; Emp.Aram. *ZY*; B.Aram. *Di*; J.Aram. *D*; Syriac *D*; Arabic *Du*. 1. rel. pr.

a) *ṀŠ Z P'L 'LB'L*
"the statue which *'LB'L*...made"
(Ph. Byblos: KAI/I p. 1, ins. #6, line 1)

b) *QR Z BNY ŠPṬB'L*
"the wall which *ŠPṬB'L*...built"
(Ph. Byblos: KAI/I p. 1, ins. #7, line 1)

c) *BT Z BNY YḤMLK MLK GBL*
"the temple which *YḤMLK* king of *GBL* built"
(Ph. Byblos: KAI/I p. 1, ins. #4, line 1)

d) *'RN Z P'L [']TB'L BN 'ḤRM MLK GBL*
"the sarcophagus which [']*TB'L* son of *'ḤRM* king of *GBL* made"
(Ph. Byblos: KAI/I p. 1, ins. #1, line 1)

Bibl. ANET 653; KAI/II 2, 6-9; DISO 70-71; Harris 98; EHO 13; PPG 55, 149; Branden 60; Slouszch 2, 4, 5.

Z II Heb. *Zeh, Z'ōT, Zū, Zō* "this"; Moab. *Z'T*; Emp.Aram. *Z*; B.Aram. *Dā*; J.Aram. *Dā, Deh*; Syriac *HāDe', HāD*; Mandaic *HaZa*; ESArab. *DN, DT*; Arabic *Da, Diy*; Ph., Pu., N.Pu. *Z* (Ph. *'Z, Z'*; N.Pu. *S, Z, H'Z, Š', ZT, HYZ, ST, 'Š*). 1. dem. pr.

a) *HŠ'R Z WHDLHT*
"this gate and the doors"
(Ph. Umm el-Awamid: KAI/I p. 3, ins. #18, line 3)

b) *B'RN Z*
"in this sarcophagus"
(Ph. Sidon: KAI/I p. 2, ins. #13, lines 2-3)

c) *'L Y'MSN BMŠKB Z*
"may he not carry me from this resting place"
(Ph. Sidon: KAI/I p. 3, ins. #14, lines 5-6)

d) *W'LT 'RPT Z'*
"and upon this portico"
(Ph. Byblos: KAI/I p. 2, ins. #10, line 12)

e) *H'RPT Z' W'MDH*
"this portico and its pillars"
(Ph. Byblos: KAI/I p. 2, ins. #10, line 6)

f) *SML 'Z 'Š YTN MLK MLKYTN*
"this statue (is that) which king *MLKYTN* gave"
(Ph. Idalion: Slouszch p. 100, ins. #91, line 1)

g) *MṢBT 'Z*
"this monument"
(Ph. Kition: KAI/I p. 8, ins. #34, line 1)

h) ['Š] *'YBL ŠT BPS Z*
"(which) is not set down on this tablet"
(Ph. Carthage: KAI/I p. 16, ins. #74, line 11)

i) *HMQDŠ S*
"this sanctuary"
(N.Pu. Maktar: KAI/I p. 28, ins. #146, line 1)

j) *M'Š Z ṬYN'*
"this statue...erected"
(N.Pu. Leptis Magna: KAI/I p. 24, ins. #127, line 1)

k) *HM'Š ST*
"this statue"
(N.Pu. Cherchel: KAI/I p. 29, ins. #161, line 3)

l) *HBN 'ST*
"this (grave) stone"
(N.Pu. Maktar: KAI/I p. 28, ins. #151, line 1)

m) *L'DN LŠDRP MZBḤ ZṬ*
"to the lord, to *ŠDRP*, this altar"
(N.Pu. Carthage: Slouszch p. 164, ins. #141, line 1)

n) *'T NDR Š*
"this vow"
(Pu. Constantine: Berthier/Charlier p. 42, ins. #93, line 5)

o) *ND'R Š 'Š NDR LB'L'DR*
"this offering (is that) which was vowed to *B'L'DR*"
(N.Pu. Masculula: JA Series 11 vol. 7 [1916] p. 460, ins. #9, line 1)

p) *NP'L' HMNṢBT Š'*
"this pillar was made"
(N.Pu. Tripolitania: LibAnt 1 [1964] p. 62, line 1)

Bibl. Berthier/Charlier 42; JA Series 11 vol. 7 (1916) 460; KAI/II 12, 17, 19, 26, 52, 92, 132, 146, 150; Slouszch 100, 165; ANET 662; DISO 70-71; Harris 97-98; Branden 56-57; PPG 8, 50-52, 147-48; NE 264; VT 5 (1955) 309-12.

ZBḤ I C.S. 1. "to slaughter" vb. 2. "sacrificial priest" n.m.

1 a) *WKL 'DMM 'Š YZBḤ*
"and all men who would slaughter"
(Pu. Marseilles: KAI/I p. 15, ins. #69, line 16)

2 a) *LZBḤM 2 QR*
"for the sacrificial priests, two *QR*"
(Ph. Kition: KAI/I p. 8, ins. #37, line A 9)

b) *ZBḤ B'LŠLK BN ḤN'*
"the sacrificial priest, *B'LŠLK* son of *ḤN'*"
(Pu. Malta: KAI/I p. 16, ins. #62, line 6)

c) *BYRḤ KRR ŠT BLL HZBḤ BN*
"in the month of *KRR* the sacrificial priest son of (?) placed fodder"
(N.Pu. Henschir Medina: KAI/I p. 29, ins. #159, line 5)

d) *KNT 'ZBḤ*
"*KNT* the sacrificial priest"
(N.Pu. Constantine: Slouszch p. 219, ins. #223, line 3)

Bibl. Slouszch 219; DISO 71; Amadasi 169; Harris 98; NE 265; KAI/II 54, 78, 83, 148; Or 37 (1964) 313; Levine 115f.

ZBḤ II C.S. 1. "sacrifice" Ph., Pu., N.Pu. *ZBḤ* (N.Pu. *Z'B'*, *ZB'*, *Š'B'*, *Š'B'Ḥ*, *ZB*). 2. in combinations

1 a) *L'LMT WL'LMT 22 BZBḤ*
"for the prostitutes (?) and the twenty-two musicians (?) at the sacrifice"
(Ph. Kition: Or 32 [1964] p. 305, line B 9)

b) *W'L KL ZBḤ*
"and for all sacrifices"
(Pu. Marseilles: KAI/I p. 15, ins. #69, line 14)

c) *ŠBḤ MGNM BN ʿBDK[Š]R*
"the sacrifice of *MGNM* son of *ʿBDK[Š]R*"
(N.Pu. Guelma: JA Series 11 vol. 8 [1916] p. 508, ins. #31, line 1)

d) *ŻBʾ ṬYṬʾ PLʿẆY*
"the sacrifice of *ṬYṬʾ PLʿWY*"
(N.Pu. Guelma: JA Series 11 vol. 8 [1916] p. 509, ins. #32, line 1)

e) *ŻʿBʾ MYLKYTN BN BʿLYTN*
"the sacrifice of *MYLKYTN* son of *BʿLYTN*"
(N.Pu. Guelma: JA Series 11 vol. 8 [1916] p. 500, ins. #19, lines 1-2)

f) *ʾŠ NDR ʿRŠ HMYŠṬR BN BNTʾ ZBḤ*
"that which *ʿRŠ* son of *BNTʾ* the officer vowed, a sacrifice"
(N.Pu. Guelma: JA Series 11 vol. 8 [1916] p. 513, lines 2-3)

g) *ŠʿBʿḤ BLBṬʿR*
"the sacrifice of *BLBṬʿR*"
(N.Pu. Guelma: JA Series 11 vol. 8 [1916] p. 510, ins. #35, line 1)

h) *ZB MTNBʿL BN YG*
"the sacrifice of *MTNBʿL* son of *YG*"
(N.Pu. Guelma: JA Series 11 vol. 8 [1916] p. 510, ins. #34, lines 1-2)

2 a) *ZBḤ YMM ʾLP*
"(as an) annual slain sacrifice, oxen"
(Ph. Karatepe: KAI/I p. 5, ins. #26, line A III,1)

b) *ʾM ZBḤ ṢD ʾM ZBḤ ŠMN*
"or (as a) sacrifice of game or (as a) sacrifice of oil"
(Pu. Marseilles: KAI/I p. 15, ins. #69, line 12)

c) *ʿL ZBḤ BMNḤT*
"for a sacrifice as an offering"
(Pu. Carthage: KAI/I p. 16, ins. #74, line 10)

Bibl. JA Series 11 vol. 8 (1916) 511-13; DISO 71; Harris 98; ANET 653, 656; KAI/II 36, 54, 83, 92; LS I 79; EncMiq vol. 2, cols. 901-4; Slouszch 147; VT 19 (1969) 11-22; Levine 115-16, 132-35.

ZBḤ ŠMŠ 1. name of month n.

a) *BYRḤ ZBḤ ŠMŠ*
"in the month of *ZBḤ ŠMŠ*"
(Ph. Pyrgi: Amadasi p. 161, ins. #2, lines 4-5)

Bibl. Amadasi 164.

ZBḤ ŠŠM 1. name of month n.

a) *BḤDŠ ZBḤ ŠŠM*
"on the new moon of *ZBḤ ŠŠM*"
(Ph. Larnaka: KAI/I p. 10, ins. #43, line 4)

b) *BYMM 20 LYRḤ ZBḤ ŠŠM*
"on the twentieth day of the month *ZBḤ ŠŠM*"
(Ph. Kition: Slouszch p. 72, ins. #61, line 1)

Bibl. KAI/II 60; NE 265; Harris 98; Slouszch 72.

ZBR N.Heb. *ZiBBūRiT* "a receptacle for drippings fastened to the bottom of a vessel"; Syriac *ZaBūRa'* "a pitcher with a long spout"; Q.Heb. *ZRB* "basin". 1. "pitcher" n.m.

a) *WZBRM ŠNM*
"and two pitchers"
(N.Pu. Leptis Magna: KAI/I p. 26, ins. #137, line 6)

Bibl. DISO 72; KAI/II 136; Leš 33 (1968-69) 106.

ZYB B.Heb. *ZiW* "name of the second month"; J.Aram. *ZiW* "month of bright flowers". 1. name of a month n.

a) *B'SR W'ḤD LZYB*
"on the eleventh day of the (month) *ZYB*"
(N.Pu. Constantine: Slouszch p. 222, ins. #228, line 4)

Bibl. Harris 98; Slouszch 223; NSI 78.

ZYT Heb. *ZaiiT* "olive (tree)"; Ug. *ZT*; Emp.Aram. *ZYT*; J.Aram. *ZaiTa'*; Syriac *ZaiTa'*; Mandaic *ZaiTa'*; Arabic *ZaiTuN*. 1. "olive" n.m. Ph. *ZYT* (Ph. *ZT*)

a) *WZYT ṀŠQN 25*
"and twenty-five olive (?)"
(Ph. Egypt: KAI/I p. 12, ins. #51, obv. line 6)

b) *B'LY ZT*
"the possessors of olive trees"
(Ph. Cyprus: RES, ins. #1526, line 1)

Bibl. Harris 99; DISO 80; KAI/II 69.

ZK' B.Heb. *ZaK* "clear, pure"; Akk. *ZaKū* "to become clean, clear or light"; J.Aram. *DeKa'*; Syriac *DeKa'*; Mandaic *DaKia'* "clean, pure"; ESArab. *ḎKW* "to eradicate, purge out"; Arabic *ḎaKā* "to clean or purify". 1. "pure" adj. m.

a) *PTR' MKR HQN' ZK'*
"*PTR'*, the seller of pure reed"
(Ph. Carthage: Slouszch p. 337, ins. #557, lines 1-2)

Bibl. DISO 76; Harris 99; PPG 107; Slouszch 337.

ZKR Heb. *ZeKeR* "mention, memorial"; Akk. *ZiKRu* "discourse, mention, oath, etc." Anc.Aram. *ZKR* "memorial"; J.Aram. *DKR*, *DūKRaN*; Arabic *ḎuKRuN* "remembrance". 1. "memory" n.m.

a) *LZKR H'LM*
"in memory of the youth
(Pu. Carthage: Slouszch p. 208, ins. #209, line 1)

Bibl. DISO 77; Slouszch 208; Benz 305-6; Harris 99.

ZKRN Heb. *ZiKKāRōN* "record" (Neh. 2:20), "memorial"; Emp.Aram. *ZKRN*; B.Aram. *DiKRoN*; J.Aram. *DūKRaN*; Syriac *DuKRaN*; Mandaic *DuKRaN*; Nab. *DKRWN*. 1. "commemoration offering" n.m.

a) *L'DNY LMLK'ŠTRT 'ḤMN 'Š NDR 'BDK 'BD'SR BN 'RŠ ZKRN*
"to his lord, to *MLK'ŠTRT* (who is) *'ḤMN* that which your servant *'BD'SR* son of *'RŠ* vowed, a commemorative offering"
(Ph. Umm el-Awamid: Leš 30 [1966] p. 234, ins. #11, lines 1-2)

Bibl. DISO 78; Leš 30 (1966) 233-34; Leš 29 (1965) 53-54.

ZN B.Heb. *ZN* "this (?)" (Ps. 144:13); Anc.Aram. *ZNH*; B.Aram. *DeNā*; Emp.Aram. *ZNH*, *DNH*; J.Aram. *DeNa'*, *DaiN*; Nab. *ZNH*, *DNH*; ESArab. *ḎN*. 1. dem. pr. "this"

a) *P'LT LY HMŠKB ZN*
"I made for myself this resting place"
(Ph. Byblos: KAI/I p. 2, ins. #9, line A 1)

b) *BMŠKB ZN*
"in this resting place"
(Ph. Byblos: KAI/I p. 2, ins. #9, line A 3)

c) *LD'T HN YPD LK TḤT ZN*
"attention! behold, you shall come to ruin below this"
(Ph. Byblos: KAI/I p. 1, ins. #2, lines 1-3)

d) *HMZBḤ NḤŠT ZN*
"this bronze altar"
(Ph. Byblos: KAI/I p. 2, ins. #10, line 4)

e) *'Š 'L PTḤ ḤRṢ ZN*
"which is upon this gold engraving"
(Ph. Byblos: KAI/I p. 2, ins. #10, line 5)

f) *'RN [Z]N*
"th[is] chest"
(Ph. Carchemish: KAI/I p. 7, ins. #29, line 1)

Bibl. DISO 78-79; Harris 98; PPG 51, 52, 147; Branden 56-57; KAI/II 4, 10, 12, 97; ANET 656.

ZQN Heb. *ZāQāN* "beard"; Ug. *DQN*; Akk. *ZiQNu*; J.Aram. *DiQNa'*; Mandaic *DiQNa'*; Arabic *D̲iQNuN*. 1. "beard" n.m.

a) *'Š 'KLT ZQN*
"a fire consumes a beard"
(Ph. Zinjirli: KAI/I p. 4, ins. #24, lines 6-7)

Bibl. ANET 654; KAI/II 31; DISO 79.

ZR I Heb. *ZāR* "stranger, oppressor, enemy"; Akk. *ZēRu* "to dislike, hate"; Soq. *ZRY* "to hate". 1. "enemy" n.m.

a) *[MM]LKT L'BYTY ZR*
"a [ru]ler (who was) an enemy (?) to my fathers"
(Ph. Byblos: MUSJ 95 [1969] p. 262, line 6)

b) *SML ZR*
"hated (?) image"
(Ph. Karatepe: KAI/I p. 5, ins. #26, line C IV,18)

c) *Š'R ZR*
"a hated (?) gate"
(Ph. Karatepe: KAI/I p. 5, ins. #26, line A III,16)

Bibl. MUSJ 45 (1969) 272; JNES 32 (1973) 480.

ZR II — etymology unknown. 1. unit/type of money n.m.

a) *ZR 2 B'ḤD*
"two *ZR* for each"
(Pu. Marseilles: KAI/I p. 15, ins. #69, line 7)

b) *KSP RB' ŠLŠT ZR 2 B'ḤD*
"three-quarters of a silver (shekel), two *ZR* for each"
(Pu. Marseilles: KAI/I p. 15, ins. #69, line 11)

c) *KSP ZR 2 'L 'ḤD*
"two silver *ZR* for each"
(Pu. Carthage: KAI/I p. 16, ins. #74, line 7)

Bibl. NE 268; Slouszch 145; Harris 99; DISO 80; Amadasi 169; KAI/II 83, 92; ANET 656-57.

ZR' — Heb. *ZeRa'* "seed, offspring"; Ug. *DR'* "to sow"; Akk. *ZaRū*; Anc.Aram. *ZR'*; J.Aram. *ZaR'a'*; Syriac *ZaR'a'*; Arabic *ZaR'uN*; Mandaic *ZR'* "to sow". 1. "offspring" n.m.

a) *H'DM H' WZR'W*
"that man and his offspring"
(Ph. Byblos: KAI/I p. 2, ins. #10, line 15)

b) *BN WZR'*
"son and offspring"
(Ph. Sidon: KAI/I p. 3, ins. #14, line 8)

c) *H'DMM HMT WZR'M L'LM*
"those men and their offspring for eternity"
(Ph. Sidon: KAI/I p. 3, ins. #14, line 22)

d) *'L ḤYY W'L ḤY ZR'Y*
"for my life and for the life of my offspring"
(Ph. Larnaka: KAI/I p. 10, ins. #43, line 11)

Bibl. DISO 80; Harris 99; Slouszch 17; NE 269; KAI/II 12, 17, 19, 60; ANET 656, 662.

Ḥ

ḤBL B.Heb. *ḤōBeL* "sailor". 1. "sailor" n.m.

a) *'Š NDR MLKYTN '[Ḥ]BL*
"that which *MLKYTN* the [sa]ilor vowed"
(Pu. Carthage: Slouszch p. 297, ins. #437, lines 2-3)

Bibl. Slouszch 298; Harris 99.

ḤBR I B.Heb. *ḤāBeR* "fellow being"; N.Heb. *ḤeBeR* "company, association"; Akk. *eBRu* "friend"; Geez *ḤaBaRa* "to be united"; Ug. *ḤBR* "companion"; Syriac *ḤaBRa'* "comrade"; J.Aram. *ḤaBRa'*; Mandaic *ḤaBRa'*; Nab. *ḤBR*; Palm. *ḤBR*; B.Aram. *ḤaBaR*; Amh. *MaHBaR* "association". 1. "associate" n.m.

a) *ḤLSB'L BN BD'ŠMN WḤBRNM*
"*ḤLSB'L* son of *BD'ŠMN* and their associates"
(Pu. Marseilles: KAI/I p. 15, ins. #69, line 19)

b) *WḤBRNM HMZRḤ*
"the associates of the citizen's council"
(N.Pu. Henschir Medina: KAI/I p. 29, ins. #159, line 4)

c) *BN ḤN' WḤBRNM*
"son of *ḤN'* and their associates"
(Pu. Carthage: CRAI [1968] p. 117, line 3)

Bibl. DISO 82; Amadasi 174; ANET 656; KAI/II 83, 148; Harris 100.

ḤBR II B.Heb. *ḤōBeR* "conjurer" (Dt. 18:11); N.Heb. *ḤaBBāR*; J.Aram. *ḤaBBāRa'*; Syriac *ḤaBBaRa'*. 1. "conjurer" n.m.

a) *ḤBRY TNT* (or *'ŠTRTḤR RBTN*
"the conjurers of *TNT*" (or "*'ŠTRTḤR* our lady")
(Pu. Spain: Amadasi p. 150, ins. #16, line 4)

Bibl. Amadasi 151; JBL 75 (1956) 328-31; HTR 64 (1971) 191.

ḤGR N.Heb. *ḤaGiRā* "wall"; Arabic *ḤāJiRuN*; Nab. *ḤGR'*; Soq. *ḤeGHeR*. 1. "wall" n.m.

a) *KM Š ḤGR HŠMRT*
"as also the protective wall"
(Pu. Carthage: KAI/I p. 17, ins. #81, line 4)

Bibl. KAI/II 98; Harris 100; Slouszch 158; DISO 82; Bib 48 (1967) 564.

ḤDR Heb. *ḤeDeR* "room, interior of the body, mystery, burial chamber"; ESArab. *ḤDR* "chamber, hall"; Ug. *ḤDR* "room"; [Ṡyriac *ḤeDāRa'* "suburbs, surroundings"; Mandaic *ḤDaR'* "circuit"; N.Syr. *ḤeDaRaT'* "course"]; Geez *MaḪDaR* "habitation". 1. "burial chamber" n.m. 2. "underworld" (?)
Pu., N.Pu. *ḤDR* (N.Pu. *'DR*)

1 a) *ḤDR BT 'LM*
"the chamber of the tomb"
(Pu. Malta: Amadasi p. 18, ins. #2, line 1)

b) *W'ḤDR DL 'QBR'*
"and the chamber with its grave"
(N.Pu. Cherchel: KAI/I p. 25, ins. #161, line 3)

c) *'DR TKLT*
"a communal (?) burial chamber"
(N.Pu. Bitia: OrAnt 4 [1965] p. 69, line 1)

2 a) *L'PT' BḤDR ḤŠK 'BR*
"O fliers, from the underworld (?) pass"
(Ph. Arslan Tash: BASOR 197 [1970] p. 46, col. B, line 1)

Bibl. DISO 82; Amadasi 18; NE 271; Slouszch 126; Harris 100; KAI/II 43, 150; PPG 15; BASOR 197 (1970) 46; OrAnt 4 (1965) 70; Leš 33 (1968-69) 302-3.

ḤDRT for etymology, see under *ḤDR*. 1. "chamber" n.f. 2. "mystery" n.f.

1 a) *BḤDRT WLḤM QṬ[RT]*
"in the chamber, bread, inc[ense]"
(Pu. Carthage: KAI/I p. 16, ins. #76, line B 3)

b) *LŠT 'LT HḤDRT NPT*
"to set upon the chamber honey (?)"
(Pu. Carthage: KAI/I p. 16, ins. #76, line B 8)

2 a) *LRBT L'M' LB'LT HḤDRT*
"to the lady, to *'M'*, to the mistress of the mysteries (?)"
(Pu. Carthage: KAI/I p. 18, ins. #83, line 1)

Bibl. DISO 83; Harris 100; Slouszch 168, 171; NE 271; KAI/II 93, 100.

ḤDŠ I

Heb. *ḤiDDeŠ* "to renew, repair"; Akk. *uDDuŠu* "to renew"; Ug. *ḤDT*; J.Aram. *ḤaDDeT*; Syriac *ḤaDeT*; Mandaic *ḤḊT*; Nab. *ḤDT*; Palm. *ḤDT*; Ȧrabic *ḤaDuṮa* "to be new, young". 1. "to repair" vb. (Q)

a) *P'L WḤDŠ 'M GWL*
"the people of *GWL* made and repaired"
(Pu. Malta: KAI/I p. 14, ins. #62, line 1)

b) *P'L WNDR WḤDŠ 'YT HGZṪ ST*
"*PN* made, dedicated and repaired this hewn stone wall (?)"
(Pu. Ibiza: KAI/I p. 16, ins. #72, line B 1)

c) *ḤYDŠ W'YQDŠ*
"he repaired and consecrated"
(N.Pu. Bir Tlesa: KAI/I p. 26, ins. #138, line 6)

Bibl. DISO 83; PPG 42, 66; KAI/II 78, 88, 137; Harris 100; Slouszch 128, 162; ClassFol 22 (1968) 170; Amadasi 23, 143; LS I 100.

ḤDŠ II

Heb. *ḤoDeŠ* "new moon"; Ug. *ḤDṮ*. 1. "new moon" n.m.

a) *BḤDŠ YRḤ 'TNM*
"on the new moon of the month of *'TNM*"
(Ph. Kition: KAI/I p. 8, ins. #37, line A 2)

b) *BḤDŠ YRḤ P'LT*
"on the new moon of the month of *P'LT*"
(Ph. Kition: KAI/I p. 8, ins. #37, line B 2)

c) *BḤDŠ ZBḤ ŠŠM*
"on the new moon of the month of *ZBḤ ŠŠM*"
(Ph. Larnaka: KAI/I p. 10, ins. #43, line 4)

Bibl. DISO 83; KAI/II 54, 60; Harris 100; Slouszch 76; Benz 308.

ḤDŠ III Heb. *ḤāDāŠ* "new"; Akk. *eŠŠu*; Syriac *ḤaDTa'*; J.Aram. *ḤaDaTa'*; Arabic *ḤaDiṮuN*; Mandaic *ḤaDTa'*. 1. "new" adj. m.

a) *MQDŠM ḤDŠM*
"new sanctuaries"
(Pu. Carthage: CIS I, ins. #3914, line 1)

b) *Š'R HḤDŠ*
"the new gate"
(Pu. Carthage: CRAI [1968] p. 117, line 1)

Bibl. CRAI (1968) 122; DISO 83; KAI/II 98; Harris 100.

ḤWY C.S. (except for Akk.) 1. "to preserve" (keep alive) vb. 2. "to restore" 3. "to live" Ph. *ḤWY* (N.Pu. *ḤW'*, *'W'*, *'WH*, *'W'*, *ḤW'*, *'WḤ*, *'WḤ'*)

1 a) *TBRK B'LT GBL 'YT YḤWMLK MLK GBL WTḤWW*
"may the mistress of *GBL* bless *YḤWMLK* king of *GBL* and preserve him"
(Ph. Byblos: KAI/I p. 2, ins. #10, lines 8-9)

2 a) *Ḣ'T ḤWY KL MPLT HBTM 'L*
"(it was) he who restored all these temple ruins"
(Ph. Byblos: KAI/I p. 1, ins. #4, line 2)

b) *YḤW 'NK 'YT DNNYM*
"I have restored the *DNNYM*"
(Ph. Karatepe: KAI/I p. 5, ins. #26, lines A I,3-4)

3 a) *'WH Š'N'[T] Š['Š]M WŠ'Š*
"he lived s[ixty]-six years"
(N.Pu. Henschir Brigitta: KAI/I p. 26, ins. #142, line 2)

b) *ḤW' ŠNT ŠB'M*
"she lived seventy years"
(N.Pu. Algeria: KAI/I p. 31, ins. #171, lines 3-4)

c) *'W' Š'NT 'RBM WḤD*
"she lived forty-one years"
(N.Pu. Tunisia: KAI/I p. 27, ins. #143, line 4)

d) *'WḤ ŠNT ŠLŠ*
"he lived three years"
(N.Pu. Tunisia: KAI/I p. 25, ins. #134, line 2)

Bibl. DISO 87; Harris 100; PPG 23, 24, 82, 84-85; JAOS 74 (1954) 232; NE 273; Benz 308-9; KAI/II 6, 12, 36, 135, 139, 156; ANET 653, 656; JSS 17 (1972) 79-81.

**ḤZY*

Heb. *ḤāZā* "to see"; Emp.Aram. *ḤZH*; J.Aram. *ḤaZa'*; Syriac *ḤeZa'*; Palm. *ḤZY*; Mandaic *HZ'*; Arabic *ḤaZa* "to perceive with inner vision". 1. "to see" vb.

a) *WMY BL ḤZ PN Š*
"and whoever had never seen the face of a sheep"
(Ph. Zinjirli: KAI/I p. 4, ins. #24, line 11)

b) *WMY BL ḤZ PN 'LP*
"and whoever had never seen the face of an ox"
(Ph. Zinjirli: KAI/I p. 4, ins. #24, line 11)

c) *ḤZT 'T KL MḤ[PṢ] HBT*
"I have seen to all the ve[ssels] of the temple"
(Ph. Abydos: Slouszch p. 59, ins. #45, line 1)

Bibl. KAI/II 30; PPG 23, 81, 84; DISO 84; Branden 9; Harris 101.

**ḤZN*

Akk. *ḤaZiāNu* (ARM XIII letter #143) "chief magistrate of a town or of a quarter of a large city"; J.Aram. *ḤaZZāNa'* "overseer especially in synagogue matters, a town guard"; N.Heb. *ḤaZZāN*. 1. "inspector" n.m.

a) *MLKYTN BN 'ZR RB ḤZ'NM*
"*MLKYTN* son of *'ZR* the chief inspector (?)"
(Ph. Kition: KAI/I p. 8, ins. #34, lines 4-5)

Bibl. KAI/II 52; Harris 101; DISO 85; LS I 442.

ḤZT

B.Heb. *ḤāZā* "to see, behold"; J.Aram. *ḤaZa'*; Syriac *ḤeZa'*; Arabic *ḤaZa* "perceive with inner vision"; Te. *ḤaZa* "to look". 1. "omen sacrifice" (?) n.f.

a) *'M ŠṢP 'M ḤZT*
"or a *ŠṢP* sacrifice or an omen sacrifice (?)"
(Pu. Marseilles: KAI/I p. 15, ins. #69, line 11)

Bibl. DISO 84; ANET 656; KAI/II 83; Slouszch 146; Amadasi 180.

ḤṬR Heb. *ḤoṬeR* "rod"; Akk. *ḤuṬaRu*; Anc.Aram. *ḤṬR*; Emp.Aram. *ḤṬR*; Syriac *ḤuṬRa'*; J.Aram. *ḤuṬRa'*; Mandaic *ḤuṬRa'*; Arabic *H̱iṬRuN* "twig". 1. "scepter" n.m.

a) *TḤTSP ḤṬR MŠPṬH*
"may the scepter of his rule be removed"
(Ph. Byblos: KAI/I p. 1, ins. #1, line 2)

Bibl. KAI/II 2; Harris 101; Slouszch 4; DISO 86; PPG 153; Branden 31.

ḤYM I Heb. *ḤaYYīM* "life, lifetime"; Saftaitic *ḤYWT*; Ug. *ḤYM*; Syriac *ḤaYTa'*; J.Aram. *ḤaYYiN*; Arabic *ḤaYāTuN*; Amar.Akk. *H̱aYa* "alive"; Ph., Pu. *ḤYM* (Ph. *ḤYYM*, N.Pu. *'YM*). 1. "life" n.m. 2. "lifetime"

1 a) *[WY]TN LM ḤN WḤYM*
"[may he gr]ant them favor and life"
(Ph. Memphis: KAI/I p. 11, ins. #48, line 4)

b) *L'NT 'Z ḤYM*
"to *'NT*, (who is) the strength of life" (or "strength of mortals")
(Ph. Larnaka: KAI/I p. 10, ins. #42, line 1)

c) *ḤRPKRṬ YTN ḤYYM L'MS BN 'ŠMNYTN*
"*ḤRPKRṬ* granted life to *'MS* son of *'ŠMNYTN*"
(Ph. Egypt: BMQ 27 [Winter 1963-64] p. 82)

d) *ḤRPKRṬ YTN ḤYM L'BDY*
"*ḤRPKRṬ* granted life to his servant"
(Ph. Egypt: Slouszch p. 65, ins. #55, lines 1-2)

e) *YTN LH RKB'L 'RK ḤY*
"may *RKB'L* grant him long life"
(Ph. Zinjirli: KAI/I p. 5, ins. #25, lines 5-7)

f) *TM B'YM*
"upright in life"
(N.Pu. Tunisia: KAI/I p. 25, ins. #134, line 3)

2 a) *'BḤY 'BY*
"in the lifetime of my father"
(Ph. Larnaka: KAI/I p. 10, ins. #43, line 7)

b) *MṢBT LMBḤYY*
"a monument during my lifetime"
(Ph. Kition: KAI/I p. 8, ins. #35, lines 1-2)

Bibl. KAI/II 35, 59-60, 64, 135; Slouszch 65; Harris 100; DISO 86; Branden 5, 8-9, 32; PPG 12, 23, 24, 43, 153; AJSL 41 (1925) 82.

ḤYM II — for etymology see *ḤYM* I. 1. "living" n.m.

a) *MṢBT BḤYM 'Š YTN' 'BD'SR L'BY*
"a monument among the living which *'BD'SR* erected for his father"
(Ph. Kition: Slouszch p. 92, ins. #78, lines 1-2)

b) *MṢBT BḤYM L'BD'ŠMN*
"a monument among the living for *'BD'ŠMN*"
(Ph. Kition: Slouszch p. 94, ins. #81, lines 1-2)

c) *WT'R BḤYM TḤT HŠMŠ*
"and fame (?) among the living under the sun"
(Ph. Sidon: KAI/I p. 3, ins. #14, line 12)

d) *ZR' BḤYM*
"offspring among the living"
(Ph. Sidon: KAI/I p. 2, ins. #13, line 7)

Bibl. Slouszch 17, 23, 93; KAI/II 17, 19; ANET 662; Albright-Fs 265.

ḤWT — for etymology see under *ḤYM*. 1. "lifetime" n.f.

a) *BKL ḤWT BN'*
"during the entire lifetime (?) of his son"
(N.Pu. Cherchel: KAI/I p. 29, ins. #161, line 9)

Bibl. KAI/II 150; DISO 84.

ḤYR — etymology unknown. 1. "name of a month" n.

a) *BYMM 7 LYRḤ ḤYR*
"on the seventh day of the month of *ḤYR*"
(Ph. Idalion: KAI/I p. 9, ins. #40, line 1)

b) *BYRḤ ḤYR*
"in the month of *ḤYR*"
(N.Pu. Leptis Magna: KAI/I p. 22, ins. #119, line 3)

Bibl. Slouszch 58; KAI/II 57, 124; Harris 101; JNSL 2 (1972) 43.

ḤYT I — Heb. *ḤaYYā* "living thing, animal, usually wild"; B.Aram. *ḤeWa'*; J.Aram. *ḤaYiTa'*; Syriac *ḤaYiTā'*; Mandaic *HiWa'*; Arabic *ḤaYaWāNuN*. 1. "animal" n.f.

a) *YQDŠT ḤYT ŠGYT*
"and I consecrated many animals"
(Ph. Larnaka: KAI/I p. 10, ins. #43, line 9)

Bibl. KAI/II 60; PPG 24, 107; Harris 100; Slouszch 110; DISO 86.

ḤYT II — C.S. root (except Akk.). 1. "life" n.f.

a) *BḤYTNM WBḤYT BN'M 'RŠM W'Y'ṢDN*
"during their life and the life of his children *'RŠM* and *'Y'ṢDN*"
(N.Pu. Tripolitania: LibAnt 1 [1964] p. 57, line 6)

Bibl. LibAnt 1 (1964) 59-60.

ḤKMT — Heb. *ḤoKMā* "wisdom"; Anc.Aram. *ḤKMT*; Emp.Aram. *ḤKMT*; Syriac *ḤeKMeTa'*; J.Aram. *ḤuKMeTa'*; Mandaic *HuKuMTa'*; Soq. *ḤiKMeT*; Akk. *ḪaKāMu* "to know, understand". 1. "wisdom" n.f.

a) *BṢDQY WBḤKMTY*
"because of my righteousness and my wisdom"
(Ph. Karatepe: KAI/I p. 5, ins. #26, lines A I,12-13)

Bibl. ANET 653; KAI/II 36; DISO 88.

ḤLB I — Heb. *ḤeLeB* "fat"; Syriac *ḤeLBa'* "fat, diaphram" [Arabic *ḪiLBuN* "midriff"]. 1. "fat" n.m.

a) *'L ḤLB W'L ḤLB*
"for milk and for fat"
(Pu. Marseilles: KAI/I p. 15, ins. #69, line 14)

Bibl. ANET 655; KAI/II 83; Harris 101; Amadasi 181; Slouszch 147-48; DISO 88.

ḤLB II — C.S. 1. "milk" n.m.

a) *'L ḤLB W'L ḤLB*
"for milk and for fat"
(Pu. Marseilles: KAI/I p. 15, ins. #69, line 14)

b) [*'L BLL W*]*'L ḤLB*
"[for fodder and] for milk"
(Pu. Carthage: KAI/I p. 16, ins. #74, line 10)

c) *ḤLB*
"milk"
(Pu. Carthage: RES, ins. #1924, line 1)

Bibl. ANET 657; KAI/II 83, 92; DISO 88; Slouszch 147-48; Amadasi 181; Harris 101.

ḤLL B.Heb. *ḤāLaL* "to play the pipe"; Akk. *ḪaLāLu* "to play the pipe"; J.Aram. *ḤaLiLa'* "flute"; N.Heb. *ḤāLiL* "pipe, flute". 1. "to play the flute" vb.

a) *'BD'ŠMN BN MLKYTN [H]M[Ḥ]LL*
"*'BD'ŠMN* son of *MLKYTN* the [flau]tist"
(Ph. Kition: Slouszch p. 94, ins. #81, line 2)

Bibl. Slouszch 94.

ḤLM C.S. 1. "to dream" vb.

a) *BR'Š ḤLM KY HLMT 'N BTM*
"from the head of the dreamer, when you smote his eye completely"
(Ph. Arslan Tash: BASOR 209 [1973] p. 19, rev. lines 4-5)

Bibl. BASOR 209 (1973) 25; Syria 48 (1971) 405.

ḤLPT B.Heb. *ḤeLeP* "exchange" (Num. 18:21); J.Aram. *ḤaLaP* "in place of"; Syriac *ḤeLāP*. 1. "change" n.f.

a) *K YD' HGW LŠLM ḤLPT 'YT H'DMM*
"that the community knows how to requite the men"
(Ph. Piraeus: KAI/I p. 13, ins. #60, line 7)

Bibl. DISO 89; KAI/II 73; Harris 101; Slouszch 118.

ḤLṢ I Heb. *ḤiLLeS* "to deliver, strengthen"; [Akk. *ḪaLāṢu* "to press, squeeze out"]; Syriac *ḤeLaṢ* "to gird oneself, to set out briskly to work"; [J.Aram. *ḤaLaṢ* "to take off, undress";] Mandaic *HLṢ* "to be brave"; Arabic *ḪaLaṢa* "to save". 1. "deliver" vb.

a) *YD'MLK BN PDYHLS 'Š ḤLṢ PGMLYN*
"*YD'MLK* son of *PDYḤLṢ* whom *PGMLYN* did deliver"
(Pu. Carthage: Slouszch p. 199, ins. #194, lines 3-6)

Bibl. Harris 101; Slouszch 201; Benz 311; DISO 89.

ḤLṢ II — B.Heb. *ḤāLūṢ* "man girded for war"; Akk. *ḪaNṢāTu* "one whose loins are girded"; [ESArab. *ḪLS* "sincerity, loyalty"]; Heb. *ḤaLāṢaYYiM* "loins". 1. "chief warrior" n.m.

a) *'DNB'L ḤLṢ HRB*
"*'DNB'L*, the chief warrior"
(Pu. Carthage: CIS I, ins. #4823, lines 1-2)

Bibl. A History of the Jews in Babylonia, Leiden, 345-46.

ḤLT I — Heb. *ḤaLLā* "bread used for offerings"; J.Aram. *ḤaLTa'*. 1. "bread used in sacrificial ceremony" n.f. (reading uncertain)

a) *L'PM 2 'Š 'P 'YT ṬN' ḤLT LMLKT*
"for the two bakers who baked. A basket of bread (?) for the queen"
(Ph. Kition: Or 37 [1968] p. 305, lines 10-11)

Bibl. Or 37 (1968) 315, esp. note 1.

ḤLT II — Akk. *ḪaLLaTu* "a kind of basket"; ESArab *ḪLT* "case, covering, casket"; J.Aram. *ḤaLTa'* "sarcophagus"; Syriac *ḤeLTa'* "sheath, scabbard"; Arabic *ḪiLLaTuN*. 1. "sarcophagus"

a) *WŠKB 'NK BḤLT Z*
"and I lie in this sarcophagus"
(Ph. Sidon: KAI/I p. 3, ins. #14, line 3)

b) *W'L YŠ' 'YT ḤLT MŠKBY*
"and may he not carry away the sarcophagus of my resting place"
(Ph. Sidon: KAI/I p. 3, ins. #14, line 5)

c) *'M 'Š YŠ' 'YT ḤLT MŠKBY*
"or shall carry away the sarcophagus of my resting place"
(Ph. Sidon: KAI/I p. 3, ins. #14, line 7)

Bibl. KAI/II 19; ANET 662; DISO 88; Harris 101; Slouszch 20.

ḤMD — Heb. *ḤāMaD* "to desire, covet"; Ug. *ḤMD* "to covet"; J.Aram. *ḤaMaD*; Amar.Akk. *ḪaMūDu* "desirable"; ESArab. *ḤMD* "to praise"; Mandaic *HMD*; Arabic *ḤaMiDa*. 1. "to desire" vb.

a) *'M 'P YḤMD 'YT HQRT Z*
"even if he should desire (good for) this city"
(Ph. Karatepe: KAI/I p. 5, ins. #26, lines A III,14-15)

Bibl. ANET 653; KAI/II 36; DISO 90.

ḤMDT for etymology see under *ḤMD* (vb).
1. "good intention" n.f.

a) *'M BḤMDT YS'*
"whether with good intention (?) he removes (it)"
(Ph. Karatepe: KAI/II p. 5, ins. #26, line A III,17).

Bibl. ANET 653; KAI/II 36; DISO 90.

ḤMR Heb. *ḤeMeR* "wine"; Ug. *ḤMR*; J.Aram. *ḤaMRa'*; Mandaic *HaMRa'*; Syriac *ḤaMRa'*; Arabic *ḪaMRuN*; Meh. *ḪaMeR*. 1. "wine" n.m.

a) *[Ḥ]MR GT KRML*
"[wi]ne of the vat of *KRML*"
(Ph. Shiqmona: IEJ 18 [1968] p. 227)

b) *ḤMR GT KR[ML]*
"wine of the vat of *KR[ML]*"
(Ph. Shiqmona: IEJ 18 [1968] p. 227)

ḤMŠ C.S. num. 1. "five" Pu., N.Pu. *ḤMŠ* (N.Pu. *'MŠ*) 2. in combinations 3. in weights.

1 a) *BḤMŠ LYRḤ P'LT*
"on the fifth (day) of the month of *P'LT*"
(Pu. Constantine: Berthier/Charlier p. 52, ins. #57, line 3)

b) *TŠMḤ QL' BRK' BḤMŠ LMLKY*
"hear his vows and bless him in the fifth (year) of his king" (or "my king")
(Pu. Constantine: Slouszch p. 226, ins. #236, lines 2-3)

2 a) *B'SR W'MŠ LYRḤ P'LT*
"on the fifteenth (day) of the month of *P'LT*"
(Pu. Constantine: Berthier/Charlier p. 59, ins. #63, lines 3-4)

b) *'W' Š'NT 'SRM W'MŠ*
"she lived twenty-five years"
(N.Pu. Tunisia: KAI/I p. 25, ins. #135, lines 3-4)

3 a) *KSP ḤMŠT*
"five silver (shekels)"
(Pu. Marseilles: KAI/I p. 15, ins. #69, line 5)

Bibl. DISO 91; Harris 102; Slouszch 226; PPG 15, 120; Amadasi 169.

ḤMŠY C.S. 1. "fifth" num.

a) *YM HḤMŠY*
"the fifth day"
(Pu. Carthage: KAI/I p. 16, ins. #76, line B 7)

Bibl. DISO 91; KAI/II 93; PPG 40, 123; Harris 102.

ḤMŠM C.S. num. 1. "fifty" 2. in combinations 3. in weights. Pu., N.Pu. *ḤMŠM* (N.Pu. *'MŠM*)

a) *WḤW' Š'NT 'MŠM*
"and he lived fifty years"
(N.Pu. Dschebel Mansur: KAI/I p. 26, ins. #140, line 7)

b) *'W' Š'NT 'MŠM*
"he lived fifty years"
(N.Pu. Guelaut Bou-Sba: KAI/I p. 30, ins. #165, line 7)

2 a) *BŠŠT ḤMŠM ŠT LMLKNM*
"in the fifty-sixth year of their reign"
(Pu. Constantine: Berthier/Charlier p. 59, ins. #63, lines 4-5)

3 a) *Š'R MŠQL M'T WḤMŠM*
"flesh, weighing one hundred and fifty (shekels)"
(Pu. Marseilles: KAI/I p. 15, ins. #69, line 6)

b) *DN'RY' ḤMŠM WŠNM*
"fifty-two *DN'RY'*"
(N.Pu. Leptis Magna: KAI/I p. 25, ins. #130, line 3)

Bibl. Harris 102; DISO 91; KAI/II 83, 133, 138, 154; ANET 656; Amadasi 69; Branden 16.

ḤMT Heb. *ḤōMā* "wall"; Moab. *ḤMT*; Amar.Akk. *ḪuMiTu*; Ug. *ḤMT*; Syriac *ḤōMa'*.
1. "fortress" n.f.

a) *WBN 'NK ḤMYT 'ZT*
"and I built mighty fortresses"
(Ph. Karatepe: KAI/I p. 5, ins. #26, lines A I,13-14)

Bibl. ANET 653; KAI/II 36; PPG 98; DISO 90.

ḤN Heb. *ḤeN* "favor"; Ug. *ḤNT*; Anc.Aram. *ḤN*; Emp.Aram. *ḤN*. 1. "favor" n.m. 2. in combinations

1 a) *ḤN L'N 'LNM*
"favor in the sight of the gods"
(Ph. Byblos: KAI/I p. 2, ins. #10, line 10)

b) *WḤN ʿM ʾRṢ Z*
"and the favor of this people"
(Ph. Byblos: KAI/I p. 2, ins. #10, lines 10-11)

c) *[WY]ṬN LM ḤN WḤYM*
"[may he g]rant them favor and life"
(Ph. Memphis: KAI/I p. 11, ins. #48, line 4)

2 a) *MNḤT ḤNY*
"my free will offering"
(Ph. Larnaka: KAI/I p. 10, ins. #43, line 13)

Bibl. KAI/II 12, 60, 64; DISO 91-92; Harris 102; Slouszch 112-13; ANET 656.

ḤNWṬ etymology unknown. 1. "statue" n.m. (from context)

a) *HḤNWṬM ʾL PʿLT ʾNK ʿBDʾŠMN*
"these statues (?) I, *ʿBDʾŠMN* ...made"
(Ph. Sidon: KAI/I p. 2, ins. #12, lines 1-2)

b) *WḤNWṬM ŠNM*
"and two statues (?)"
(Pu. Sardinia: KAI/I p. 14, ins. #64, line 1)

Bibl. DISO 92; KAI/II 16, 79; Harris 102; Amadasi 102; Slouszch 133-34.

ḤNN Heb. *ḤāNaN* "to show favor, be gracious"; Akk. *eNēNu* "to grant a privilege"; Amar.Akk. *ḤaNāNu*; Ug. *ḤNN* "to be kind"; Syriac *ḤaN* "to be gracious"; J.Aram. *ḤaNaN* "to show mercy"; Mandaic *HNN*; Arabic *ḤaNNa* "to yearn towards, be merciful"; B.Aram. *ḤaNaN*.
1. "to show favor" vb.

a) *K ʾNK NḤN**
"for I am to be pitied (?)"
(Ph. Sidon: KAI/I p. 3, ins. #14, line 12)

*See Jeremiah 22:23 for Niqṭal of vb. *ḤNN*.

b) *ʾS NDR ʾRŠ BN ʿBDʾ[ŠMN] ʾŠ ṢWʾṬ ŠT BN [BN ʾ]DNBʿL WTḤNʾ* (reading of line uncertain)
"that which *ʾRŠ* son of *ʿBDʾ[ŠMN]* the (?) *ŠT* grand[son] (?) of [ʾ]*DNBʿL* vowed, may she show him favor (?)"
(Pu. Carthage: Slouszch p. 242, ins. #277, lines 3-5)

Bibl. Slouszch 243; DISO 92; Harris 102;
KAI/II 19; JSS 2 (1957) 128-48; ANET
662; Branden 93; JBL 73 (1954) 36-41;
VT 4 (1954) 277.

ḤNM Heb. *ḤiNNāM* "gratuitously". 1. "gratuitously" adv.

a) *ḤNM BY KSP*
"gratuitously, without silver"
(Pu. Carthage: CIS I, ins.
#5522, line 4)

Bibl. DISO 92.

ḤNQ Heb. *ḤāNaQ* "to strangle"; Ug. *H̱NQ* (?); Geez *H̱aNaQa*; Akk. *H̱aNāQu*; J.Aram. *ḤeNaQ*; Mandaic *HNQ*; Arabic *H̱aNaQa*; Amh. *'aNNaQa*; Shauri *H̱NQ*. 1. "to strangle" vb.

a) *LḤNQT 'MR*
"O stranglers of lamb(s)"
(Ph. Arslan Tash: BASOR 197
[1970] p. 44, lines 4-5)

Bibl. BASOR 197 (1970) 44-45; KAI/II 43;
ANET 656; LS I 58; PPG 64; DISO 92.

ḤNT B.Heb. *ḤāNūT* "cell"; N.Heb. *ḤāNūT* "tent, tavern, meat market"; J.Aram. *ḤāNūTa'*; Syriac *ḤaNūTa'* "vaulted room"; Palm. *ḤNWT'* "shop"; Nab. *ḤNWT*; Mandaic *HaNuTa'* "tavern"; Eg. *H̱N* "tent". 1. "arch" n.f.

a) *MQDŠ ḤṢRT PḤNT QDŠM*
"(the) sanctuary, courts also (?)
the arches (?) of the temples"
(N.Pu. Maktar: KAI/I p. 27,
ins. #145, lines 1-2)

Bibl. DISO 92; KAI/II 141; JAOS 47 (1927)
226.

ḤSP Heb. *ḤāSaP* "to strip, lay bare"; Akk. *H̱aSāPu* "to pluck out, remove". 1. "to remove" vb.

a) *TḤTSP ḤṬR MŠPṬH*
"may the scepter of his rule be
removed"
(Ph. Byblos: KAI/I p. 1,
ins. #1, line 2)

Bibl. KAI/II 2; Harris 103; Slouszch 3-4.

ḤṢ I — Heb. *ḤaYYiṢ* "type of wall". 1. "wall" n.m. (reading uncertain)

a) *[L'DN L'ŠMN BN MQDŠ Z WHḤṢRT W]ḤṢ' KM KL 'Š*
"[for the lord for *'ŠMN* this temple and courtyards and] its wall (?), as all which..."
(Pu. Carthage: Slouszch p. 160, ins. #138, line 1)

Bibl. Slouszch 161.

ḤṢ II — Heb. *ḤūṢ* "street, outside, market". 1. "street" n.m.

a) *PTḤ W P'L 'YT HḤṢ Z*
"this street was opened and made"
(Pu. Carthage: CRAI [1968] p. 117, line 2)

Bibl. RSO 43 (1968) 11-12; CRAI (1968) 122-23.

ḤṢ III — Heb. *ḤeṢ* "arrow"; Akk. *uṢṢu*; Ug. *ḤẒ*; Emp.Aram. *ḤṬ'*; Arabic *ḤuẒWaTuN*. 1. "arrowhead" n.m. 2. in names of gods.

1 a) *ḤṢ 'D' BN 'KY*
"the arrowhead of *'D'* son of *'KY*"
(Ph. Rueisseh: KAI/I p. 4, ins. #20, line 1)

b) *ḤṢ 'BDLB<'>T*
"the arrowhead of *BDLB<'>T*"
(Ph. El-Hadr: KAI/I p. 4, ins. #21, line 1)

c) *ḤṢ ZKR {B} BN BN'N*
"the arrowhead of *ZKR* son of *BN'N*"
(Ph. Lebanon: KAI/I p. 4, ins. #22, line 1)

2 a) *RŠP ḤṢ*
"*RŠP* of fortune (?)" (or "*RŠP* of the arrow")
(Ph. Kition: KAI/I p. 7, ins. #32, line 4)

Bibl. Harris 104; DISO 94; KAI/II 29-30, 50; JAOS 81 (1961) 27-32.

ḤṢB — Heb. *ḤāṢaB* "to hew, cleave"; J.Aram. *ḤeṢaB*; Syriac *ḤeṢBa'* "large wine jar". 1. "urn" n.m.

a) *ḤṢB BRK*
"the urn (?) of *BRK*"
(Ph. Egypt: ESE III p. 125, lines 1-2)

Bibl. ESE III 126; DISO 94.

ḤṢY Heb. *ḤaṢiy* "half"; Moab. *ḤṢY*; Nab. *ḤṢ*.
1. "half" n.m.

a) *P'L ḤṢY HSP Z*
"he made half of this basin"
(Ph. Tyre: NSI p. 43, ins. #8, line 5)

b) *ḤṢY LKL 'DM*
"half to all men"
(Pu. Carthage: CIS I, ins. #169)

c) *YTN 'YT HḤSY HSP Z*
"he gave half of this basin"
(Ph. Tyre: NSI p. 43, ins. #8, line 6)

Bibl. NSI 44; Harris 104; Slouszch 35; DISO 95.

ḤṢR B.Heb. *ḤāṢeR* "enclosure, permanent settlement"; N.Heb. *ḤāṢeR* "a gated arch close to a building especially for the placement of utensils"; Ug. *ḤẒR* "courtyard"; Akk. *ḪaṢāRu* "enclosure for sheep"; Amh. *'aṬṬaRa* "to make a fence"; J.Aram. *ḤuṬRa'*; Arabic *ḤaẒīRaTuN*; Syriac *ḤeRTa'* "depot"; Ph., N.Pu. *ḤṢR* (N.Pu. *HṢR*). 1. "court" n.m.

a) *WḤṢR 'DRK BL TDRKN*
"and the court which I tread, you shall not tread"
(Ph. Arslan Tash: KAI/I p. 6, ins. #27, rev. lines 7-8)

b) *ḤṢR BT 'LM*
"temple court"
(Ph. Piraeus: KAI/I p. 13, ins. #60, line 2)

c) *MQDŠ ḤṢRT*
"a sanctuary, courts"
(N.Pu. Maktar: KAI/I p. 13, ins. #145, line 1)

d) *B'N' ḤṢRT Š MḤQM*
"the builder of the court(s) of the temple"
(N.Pu. Maktar: KAR 12 [1963-64] p. 46, line 1)

Bibl. DISO 95; KAR 12 (1963-64) 46; KAI/II 43, 73, 141; Harris 104; Slouszch 117; BASOR 197 (1970) 44; ANET 658; LS I 58.

*ḤRB — Ug. *ḪRB* "become dry"; B.Heb. *ḤāReB*; J.Aram. *ḤuRBa̅'* "drought". 1. "drying shed" n.m.

a) *PTḤ' Š'M' ḤR'B K'*
"the drying sheds (?) were set open (?) here"
(N.Pu. Tripolitania: Or 33 [1964] p. 4, line 1)

Bibl. Or 33 (1964) 7.

ḤRDT — B.Heb. *ḤaRāDā* "trembling, fear, terror"; Arabic *ḪaRiDa* "to keep silent"; Syriac *'eTḤeReD̲* "to tremble". 1. "terror" n.f.

a) *B'L ḤRDT*
"master of terror (?)"
(N.Pu. Maktar: KAI/I p. 27, ins. #145, line 5)

Bibl. KAI/II 141; DISO 96.

ḤRZ — Heb. *ḤāRūZ* "beads"; Q.Aram. *ḤRZ* "to string"; N.Heb. *MaḤaZōRaT* "row, string of fish"; J.Aram. *ḤiRZa'* "a thorny bush used for hedges"; Syriac *ḤaRaZa'* "row, series"; Arabic *ḪaRZuN* "necklace". 1. "fence" n.m. (etymology doubtful)

a) *'Š YB' 'LT HḤRZ ŠMQDŠM 'L*
"that which falls (?) upon the fence (?) of these sanctuaries"
(Pu. Carthage: KAI/I p. 17, ins. #81, line 4)

Bibl. KAI/II 98; Harris 104; Slouszch 158; DISO 96.

*ḤRṬ — B.Heb. *ḤeReṬ* "mould (?)" (Ex. 32:4); N.Heb. *ḤāRaṬ* "to scrape, chisel"; Syriac *ḤeRaṬ*. 1. "sculpture" n.m.

a) *WHḤRṬYT 'Š BMQDŠM 'L*
"and the sculptures (?) which are in these sanctuaries"
(Pu. Carthage: KAI/I p. 17, ins. #81, line 2)

Bibl. KAI/II 98; PPG 108; Harris 104; Slouszch 157; LS I 414-16.

ḤRM — N.Heb. *ḤāRRāM* "fisherman". 1. "fisherman" n.m.

a) *[B]ḌB'L RB ḤRM LYM*
"*[B]DB'L* chief fisherman of the sea"
(Ph. Egypt: KAI/I p. 12, ins. #51, rev. line 2)

b) *B'LḤN' HḤRM*
"*B'LḤN'* the fisherman"
(Pu. Carthage: CIS I, ins. #324, line 3)

Bibl. DISO 96; Harris 104; KAI/II 69.

ḤRṢ B.Heb. *ḤāRūṢ* "gold"; Ug. *ḪRṢ*; Akk. *ḪuRāṢu*; Gk. *Khrusos*; J.Aram. *ḤaRiʿaʾ* "safflower"; Syriac *ḤaRaʿaʾ* "yellow, yellowish"; Arabic *ḪuRṢuN* "gold or silver earring"; [ESArab. *ḪRṢ* "wages in kind"]. 1. "gold" n.m.

a) *MḤSM ḤRṢ LPY*
"a muzzle of gold upon my mouth"
(Ph. Byblos: KAI/I p. 2, ins. #11, line 1)

b) *ʿL PTḤ ḤRṢ ZN*
"upon this gold engraving"
(Ph. Byblos: KAI/I p. 2, ins. #10, line 5)

c) *BʿL ḤRṢ*
"possessor of gold"
(Ph. Zinjirli: KAI/I p. 4, ins. #24, line 12)

d) *MSP NSK HḤRṢ*
"*MSP* the goldsmith"
(Pu. Carthage: Slouszch p. 260, ins. #328, lines 4-5)

e) *ʿLT MṢBT ḤRṢ*
"upon the gold monument"
(Ph. Piraeus: Slouszch p. 116, ins. #99, line 5)

f) *ʿṬRT ḤRṢ*
"a crown of gold"
(Ph. Piraeus: Slouszch p. 118, ins. #99, line 3)

Bibl. Slouszch 117-18, 261; DISO 96; PPG 12; Harris 104; KAI/II 12, 15-16, 30, 73; ANET 656.

ḤRŠ I Heb. *ḤāRāŠ* "artist, artisan"; Akk. *eRŠu* "wise"; Ug. *ḤRṮ*; J.Aram. *ḤaRaT* "to engrave"; Arabic *ḤaRaTa* "to dip"; Syriac *ḤaRaT* "to dip out, hollow"; Mandaic *HRT*. 1. "craftsman" n.m. 2. "mason" 3. in compounds 4. "wood craftsman"

1 a) *ŠPṬ ʾḤRŠ*
"*ŠPṬ* the craftsman"
(Pu. Carthage: Slouszch p. 330, ins. #535, line 2)

b) *ḤMLKT BN ʾRŠ ʾḤRŠ*
"*ḤMLKT* son of *ʾRŠ* the craftsman"
(Pu. Carthage: CIS I, ins. #325, line 5)

2 a) *LḤRSM 'Š P'L 'ŠTT 'DN* (reading uncertain)
"for the masons who made the pillars of the lord (?)"
(Ph. Kition: Or 37 [1968] p. 305, line A 14)

3 a) *B'L ḤRṢ 'KBRM*
"the master craftsman *'KBRM*"
(Pu. Carthage: NSI p. 127, ins. #45, line 9)

b) *WB'L ḤRŠ H' BTM*
"and he (himself) was the master craftsman at his own expense"
(Pu. Ibiza: KAI/I p. 16, ins. #72, line B 4)

4 a) *HḤRŠM ŠYR*
"the wood craftsman"
(Pu. Dougga: KAI/I p. 19, ins. #100, line 6)

Bibl. DISO 97; Slouszch 331; Harris 104; KAI/II 88, 107; NSI 129; Or 37 (1968) 316; Amadasi 145; ClassFol 22 (1968) 170-71.

ḤRŠ II Heb. *ḤāRīš* "ploughing"; Ug. *ḤRṮ* "to plow"; Amar.Akk. *ḪaRāšu*; Akk. *eRēšu*; Syriac *ḤeRaṬ*; Arabic *ḤaRṮuN* "tillage"; Amh. *'aRša* "field", *'aRaš* "farmer". 1. "ploughing" n.m.

a) *B'T ḤRŠ*
"at the time of ploughing"
(Ph. Karatepe: KAI/I p. 6, ins. #26, lines C IV,4-5)

Bibl. ANET 653; DISO 97; KAI/II 36.

ḤRT Heb. *ḤāRaT* "to engrave"; Ug. *ḤRṮ*; J.Aram. *ḤaRaṬ*. 1. "engraver" n.m.

a) *ḤRT BMḤSP*
"(the) engraver (?) upon (?) pottery (?)"
(Pu. Carthage: CIS I, ins. #6002, line 2)

Bibl. Slouszch 208.

ḤŠ Heb. *Ḥūš*, *ḤuS* "to be sorry for"; N.Heb. *Ḥūš* "to feel pain, be affected"; Akk. *Ḫāšu* "to grieve"; J.Aram. *Ḥūš*; Syriac *ḤuS*, *ḤaS*; Mandaic *HuS* "to feel, be troubled about"; Arabic *ḤaSSa*. 1. "woe" interjection.

a) *ḤŠ L'RBTNM*
"woe for the four of them"
(N.Pu. Tripolitania: LibAnt 1 [1964] p. 57, line 5)

Bibl. LibAnt 1 (1964) 59.

ḤŠB I B.Heb. *ḤiŠŠeB* "to be mindful, devise"; Eg. *ḤŠB*; N.Heb. *ḤiŠŠeB* "to account, figure"; J.Aram. *ḤaŠŠeB*, *ḤaŠŠāBBa'* "accountant"; Syriac *ḤaŠeB*; Mandaic *HŠB*; Nab. *ḤSB*; Arabic *ḤaSiBa*; Soq. *ḤoSeB* "to compute"; [Akk. *ePēŠu* "to do, make"]. 1. "accountant" n.m.

a) *[B'L] Ḥ[N]' HḤŠB*
"[*B'L*] *Ḥ*[*N*]' the accountant"
(Ph. Kition: Slouszch p. 74, ins. #64, lines 3-4)

Bibl. Slouszch 75; Harris 104; DISO 97; AJSL 34 (1918) 237.

ḤŠB II for etymology see *ḤŠB* I. 1. "to plan" vb.

a) *ḤŠB N'M*
"the planner of good"
(N.Pu. Cherchel: KAI/I p. 29, ins. #161, line 2)

Bibl. DISO 97; Harris 104.

ḤŠK Heb. *ḤoŠeK* "darkness"; J.Aram. *ḤaŠōKa'*; Syriac *ḤaŠuKTa'*; Mandaic *HŠuKa'*. 1. "underworld" n.m.

a) *L'PT' BḤDR ḤŠK 'BR*
"O fliers, from the underworld (?) pass"
(Ph. Arslan Tash: BASOR 197 [1970] p. 46, col. B 1)

Bibl. DISO 98; KAI/II 43; ANET 658; LS I 62; BASOR 197 (1970) 46 (for parallel in Akkadian, see CT 15 45:4).

ḤTM I Heb. *ḤāTaM* "to seal"; Emp.Aram. *ḤWTM*; J.Aram. *ḤeTaM*; Syriac *ḤeTaM*; Chr.Pal.Aram. *ḤTM*; Mandaic *HTM*; Arabic *ḪaTaMa*. 1. "to complete" vb. 2. "to seal"

1 a) *K'S LP'L WḤTM*
"he commissioned (?) the work (?) to be completed (?)"
(N.Pu. Leptis Magna: KAI/I p. 23, ins. #124, line 4)

2 a) *BDLT 'Š ḤTM LBTM*
"by the tablet, which...sealed in his house"
(Ph. Carthage: CIS I, ins. #5522, line 5)

Bibl. KAI/II 130; DISO 125 (see under *K'S*).

ḤTM II — N.Heb. *ḤōTāM* "seal, stamp"; Syriac *ḤaTMa'* "seal, signet ring"; Arabic *H̱āTiMuN* "seal, stamp"; J.Aram. *ḤaTMūTa'* "signature"; Chr.Pal.Aram. *ḤTM'*; Mandaic *HaTMa'*.
1. "seal" n.m.

a) *ḤTMM BṬB'T*
"and seals on the signet ring(s)"
(Ph. Egypt: KAI/I p. 12, ins. #51, lines obv. 9-10)

b) *ḤTM Š ṢRY*
"the seal of a *ṢRY*"
(Ph. Cilicia: JKF 1 [1950-51] p. 44, line 1)

Bibl. KAI/II 69; JKF 1 (1950-51) 93-94; DISO 98.

ḤTM III — B.Heb. *ḤāTaM* "to seal"; N.Heb. *ḤāTaM* "to complete a prayer or a cycle of readings"; J.Aram. *ḤaTaM* "to seal, to close up"; Eg. *H̱TM* "seal"; Syriac *ḤeTaM*; Arabic *H̱aTaMa*.
1. "keeper of the seal" n.m.

a) *B'LYTN HŠPṬ BN 'BD'ŠMN HḤTM*
"*B'LYTN* the magistrate, son of *'BD'ŠMN* the keeper of the seal (?)"
(Ph. Athens: Slouszch p. 120, ins. #103, line 1)

Bibl. Slouszch 120; Harris 105; DISO 98.

Ṭ

ṬBḤ B.Heb. *ṬaBBāḤ* "officer (?)"; Heb. *ṬaBBāḤ* "cook"; B.Aram. *ṬaBBāḤa* "officer"; Akk. *ṬaBāH̱u* "to slaughter"; Syriac *ṬaBāḤa'* "cook"; J.Aram. *ṬaBBāḤa'*; Mandaic *ṬaBaḤa'*; ESArab. *ṬBH̱* "cooked meat"; Arabic *ṬaBBāH̱uN* "cook". 1. "cultic slaughterer" n.m.

a) *'Š NDR BDMLQRT HṬBḤ*
"that which *BDMLQRT* the cultic slaughterer vowed"
(Pu. Carthage: Slouszch p. 257, ins. #319, line 2)

b) *[B]'LYTN HṬBḤ*
"*[B]'LYTN* the cultic slaughterer"
(Pu. Carthage: Slouszch p. 266, ins. #344, line 3)

c) *BDḤDŠṬ HṬBḤ*
"*BDḤDŠṬ* the cultic slaughterer"
(Pu. Carthage: Slouszch p. 319, ins. #504, line 5)

Bibl. DISO 99; NE 282; Harris 105; PPG 15; Slouszch 258.

ṬB' Heb. *ṬāBa'* "to sink, sink down"; J.Aram. *ṬeBa'*, *MaṬBe'a* "coin, medal"; Syriac *ṬeBa'*; Arabic *ṬaBa'a* "to seal, stamp"; N.Heb. *MaṬBe'a* "coin, medal". 1. "coinage" n.m.

a) *ṬB' ṢR*
"coinage of *ṢR*"
(Ph. Tyre: NSI p. 43, ins. #8, line 2)

Bibl. NSI 44; DISO 100.

ṬB'T Heb. *ṬaBa'aT* "a signet ring"; Akk. *ṬiMBu'u*, *ṬiBuTTu*; Eg. *D̲B'T*. 1. "signet ring" n.f.

a) *WḤTMM BṬB'T*
"and seals upon the signet ring(s)"
(Ph. Egypt: KAI/I p. 12, ins. #51, lines obv. 9-10)

Bibl. KAI/II 69; Bib 30 (1949) 314-38.

ṬHRT Heb. *ṬāHeR* "to be ritually clean"; Ug. *ṬHR*; ESArab *ṬHR*; J.Aram. *ṬeHaR*; Arabic *ṬaHaRa*; Soq. *ṬaHiR*. 1. "purification" n.f.

a) *LŠRT ŠNT ḤMŠM B'YḤŠBR LṬHRT*
"to serve (?) fifty years in the Island of *ḤŠBR* (?) for (the purpose) of purification (?)"
(N.Pu. Cherchel: NSI p. 147, ins. #58, line 4)

Bibl. DISO 100; NSI 148.

ṬḤ for etymology, see under *MṬḤ*. 1. "plastered" p.p. of *ṬeYYeḤ*.

a) *WHGG...MṬḤT*
"and the roof...plastered (?)"
(Pu. Sardinia: Amadasi p. 109, ins. #32, line 3)

Bibl. Amadasi 111.

ṬM' meaning and etymology unknown. 1. "section" n.m.

a) [ ]*MYK' 'TNYM ṬM' LKN ŠLM*
"reports (of the month) of *'TNYM*. Section (?) of that which is to be settled in full"
(N.Pu. Tripolitania: Or 33 [1964] p. 4, line 1)

Bibl. Or 33 (1964) 7.

ṬN' I Heb. *ṬeNe'* "basket"; Eg. *DN'* "basket for fruit". 1. "to set up, erect" vb. 2. "to donate, namely to have fashioned" 3. "to appoint"

1 a) *WYṬN' 'NK BT 'DNY*
"and I erected my lordly houses"
(Ph. Karatepe: KAI/I p. 5, ins. #26, lines A I,9-10)

b) *HMṢBT 'Z 'Š YṬN'T 'NK* [*M*]*NḤM BN* [*BD*]*'ŠMN*
"this gravestone (is that) which I [*M*]*NḤM*, son of [*BD*]*'ŠMN* set up"
(Ph. Kition: CIS I, ins. #57, lines 1-2)

c) *WYṬN'Y B'RPT*
"and I set it up in the portico"
(Ph. Piraeus: KAI/I p. 13, ins. #60, line 5)

d) *'BN 'Š T'N' LMTNB'L BT PRYM'*
"a (grave) stone which was erected for *MTNB'L* daughter of *PRYM'*"
(N.Pu. Henschir Guergour: KAI/I p. 27, ins. #143, lines 1-2)

e) *'BN Z T'N' LŠBLT BT M'LL*
"this (grave) stone was erected for *ŠBLT* daughter of *M'LL*"
(N.Pu. Guelma: KAI/I p. 30, ins. #169, lines 1-2)

f) *M'Š Z ṬYN' L'DN ŠDRP'*
"this statue was set up for the lord *ŠDRP'*"
(N.Pu. Leptis Magna: KAI/I p. 24, ins. #127, line 1)

2 a) *MNḤT 2 'L '[Š YTN W]YTN'*
'BD'L[M BN] 'BDMLQRT BN ['BDR]ŠP
"these two offerings (are those) which *'BD'L[M* son of] *'BDMLQRT* son of [*'BDR]ŠP* donated"
(Ph. Kition: CIS I, ins. #14, line 5-7)

b) *MTNT 'Š ṬN' LB'L*
"a present which he donated to *B'L*"
(Pu. Constantine: Berthier/Charlier p. 153, ins. #250, lines 2-4)

c) *MTNT 'Š ṬN' B'LYTN*
"a present which *B'LYTN* donated"
(Pu. Constantine: Berthier/Charlier p. 59, ins. #63, lines 1-2)

d) *MTNT 'Š ṬN' YḤW'LN BN 'BD'ŠMN*
"a present which *YḤW'LN* son of *'BD'ŠMN* donated"
(Pu. Constantine: KAI/I p. 20, ins. #102, lines 2-3)

3 a) *ṬN'M 'L H[MLKT Z]*
"appointed over [this work]"
(Pu. Sardinia: Amadasi p. 117, ins. #36, lines 4-5)

b) *ṬN'M 'L MLKT Z*
"appointed over this work"
(Pu. Dougga: KAI/I p. 20, ins. #101, line 5)

c) [*M*]*ṬN'M 'L MLKT Z*
"[app]ointed over this work"
(Pu. Carthage: Slouszch p. 160, ins. #138, line 5)

Bibl. DISO 101; Harris 105; KAI/II 36, 73, 110, 113, 132, 140; Berthier/Charlier 59, 153; Amadasi 119; PPG 80-81, 88-89; Branden 4, 101-2; NE 283-84; ANET 653.

ṬN' II — B.Heb. *ṬeNe'* "basket"; N.Heb. *ṬeNi* "basket, traveling box". 1. "type of cultic basket" n.m. (reading uncertain)

a) *ṬṄ' ḤLT LMLKT*
"the basket of bread (?) for the queen"
(Ph. Kition: Or 33 [1963] p. 305, line 10)

Bibl. Or 33 (1968) 314, esp. note 4.

Y

Y' B.Heb. **Yā'ā* "to befit"; N.Heb. *Yā'ūT* "right"; Syriac *Yā'e'* "to be fair," "suitable," J.Aram. *Yāe(y)*; Mandaic *Y''*; Soq. *DiYe* "good". 1. "fine" adj. m. 2. "fair"

1 a) *ŠḤ PR Y'*
"plants of fine fruit"
(Pu. Carthage: KAI/I p. 16, ins. #76, line B 2)

2 a) *WTYN Y' LBN*
"and figs, fair (and) white"
(Pu. Carthage: KAI/I p. 16, ins. #76, line B 5)

b) *'Š KN Y' WMḤ*
"which is fair and rich"
(Pu. Carthage: KAI/I p. 16, ins. #76, line A 5)

Bibl. DISO 103; Harris 105; NE 284; Slouszch 168; KAI/II 93; LexSoq 126.

YBL Heb. *YōBeL* "ram"; Akk. *YaBiLu*; J.Aram. *YuBLa'*; Arabic *WāBiLuN* "young sheep". 1. "ram" n.m.

a) *BYBL 'M B'Z*
"for a ram or for a goat"
(Pu. Marseilles: KAI/I p. 15, ins. #69, line 7)

Bibl. KAI/II 83; NE 285; DISO 103; Harris 106; Amadasi 178; Slouszch 144-45; ANET 656.

YD I C.S. 1. "hand" n.f.

a) *WKL ŠLḤ YD*
"and everybody sent forth his hand"
(Ph. Zinjirli: KAI/I p. 4, ins. #24, line 6)

b) *WKT BYD MLKM*
"and I was in the hands of kings"
(Ph. Zinjirli: KAI/I p. 4, ins. #24, line 6)

c) *W'NK TMKT MŠKBM LYD*
"and I supported the *MŠKBM* by the hand"
(Ph. Zinjirli: KAI/I p. 4, ins. #24, line 13)

d) *BN YD B'L WBN YD 'DM*
"either by the hand(s) of *B'L* or by the hand(s) of man"
(Ph. Cyprus: KAI/I p. 7, ins. #30, line 4)

Bibl. KAI/II 31, 48; ANET 654; DISO 103-4; Harris 106; EHO 17; Branden 19; PPG 109, 116.

YD II — 1. "side" n.f.

a) *'Š LYD' 'LNM*
"which are on the sides of the divine (statues)"
(N.Pu. Maktar: KAR 12 [1963-64] p. 53, col. III, line 1)

YD' — Heb. *YāD'* "to know"; Ug. *YD'*; Akk. *eDū*; ESArab. *HYD'* "to give some information"; Anc.Aram. *YD'*; Emp.Aram. *YD'*; J.Aram. *YeDa'*; Mandaic *YD'*; Syriac *YeDa'*; Soq. *'eDaḤ*. 1. "to know" vb.

a) *LD'T HN YPD LK TḤT ZN*
"attention! behold, you shall come to ruin below this"
(Ph. Byblos: KAI/I p. 1, ins. #2, lines 1-3)

b) *LKN YD' HṢDNYM K YD' HGW*
"therefore the *ṢDNYM* shall know that the community knows"
(Ph. Piraeus: KAI/I p. 13, ins. #60, line 7)

Bibl. DISO 104; Harris 106; Benz 321-22; Slouszch 118; KAI/II 4, 73.

YLD I — C.S. 1. "to multiply; namely to beget children" vb.

a) *WBRBM YLḊ*
"and may they greatly multiply"
(Ph. Karatepe: KAI/I p. 5, ins. #26, lines C IV,10)

Bibl. DISO 107; ANET 653; KAI/II 36.

YLD II — C.S. 1. "youth" n.m. (interpretation and reading very uncertain)

a) *'ZRB'L HYLḊ ŠḤRB'L B'N ŠQLN*
"*'ZRB'L* the youth (?) (and) *ŠḤRB'L*, son of *ŠQLN*"
(N.Pu. Cherchel: NSI p. 147, ins. #56, line 3)

YLL B.Heb. *HāLaL* "to be boastful, to praise"; Ug. *HLL* "shouting"; Akk. *'aLāLu* "to sing pleasurably"; Syriac *HaLeL* "to praise"; Mandaic *HLL* "to utter cries of joy"; Arabic *HaLLa* "to shout"; J.Aram. *HaLeL* "praise".
1. "to be exalted" vb.

a) *HMYLL MYŠR 'RṢT RBT*
"the exalted (?), the bringer of prosperity to the great lands"
(N.Pu. Cherchel: KAI/I p. 29, ins. #161, line 2)

Bibl. KAI/II 150; DISO 107.

YM I C.S. 1. "day" n.m.

a) *YMT YḤMLK*
"the days of *YḤMLK*"
(Ph. Byblos: KAI/I p. 1, ins. #4, line 5)

b) *YMT ŠPṬB'L*
"the days of *ŠPṬB'L*"
(Ph. Byblos: KAI/I p. 1, ins. #7, line 5)

c) *YMW WŠNTW 'L GBL*
"his days and his years over *GBL*"
(Ph. Byblos: KAI/I p. 2, ins. #10, line 9)

d) *L'ZTWD 'RK YMM*
"to *'ZTWD* length of days"
(Ph. Karatepe: KAI/I p. 5, ins. #26, line A III,5)

e) *YM MD YM*
"day by day"
(Ph. Larnaka: KAI/I p. 10, ins. #43, line 11)

f) *YM HḤMŠY*
"the fifth day"
(Pu. Carthage: KAI/I p. 16, ins. #76, line B 7)

g) *YM N'M*
"good day"
(N.Pu. Constantine: Berthier/Charlier p. 81, ins. #98, line 4)

Bibl. Harris 106; NE 287; PPG 11, 117, 153; Branden 32, 65; DISO 107-8; Berthier/Charlier 81; ANET 656; KAI/II 7, 9, 12, 36, 60, 94.

YM II

Heb. *YaM* "sea"; Ug. *YM*; Akk. *YaMu*; Emp.Aram. *YM* ; Palm. *YM'*; J.Aram. *YaMa'*; Syriac *YaMa'*; Mandaic *YaMa'*; Arabic *YaMMuN*. 1. "sea" n.m. 2. in place names.

1 a) *RB ḤRM LYM*
"chief fisherman of the sea (?)"
(Ph. Egypt: KAI/I p. 12, ins. #51, rev. line 2)

b) *HWN YM*
"the wealth (?) of the sea (?)"
(Ph. Byblos: MUSJ 45 [1969] p. 262, line 5)

2 a) *BṢDN YM*
"in *ṢDN* of the sea"
(Ph. Sidon: KAI/I p. 3, ins. #15, line 1)

b) *BṢDN 'RṢ YM*
"in *ṢDN*, the land of the sea"
(Ph. Sidon: KAI/I p. 3, ins. #14, line 18)

Bibl. DISO 107; Harris 106; EncMiq vol. III cols. 691-92; MUSJ 45 (1969) 271; KAI/II 19, 22, 69; ANET 662; Slouszch 24.

YSP

Heb. *YāSaP* "to add"; Moab. *YSP*; Anc.Aram. *HWSP*; Emp.Aram. *HWSP*; B.Aram. *HuSaP* (only Hoqtal); J.Aram. *YeSaP*; Syriac *'aWSeP*; Nab. *'WSP*; Soq. *SeF* "augment". 1. "to add" vb. 2. "unknown".

1 a) *WYSPNNM 'LT GBL 'RṢ*
"and we added them to the borders of the land"
(Ph. Sidon: KAI/I p. 3, ins. #14, lines 19-20)

b) *WKL 'DM 'Š YSP*
"and all men who (continue) to add"
(Ph. Byblos: KAI/I p. 2, ins. #10, line 11)

2 a) *'BDMSKR RB 'BR LSPT*
"*'BDMSKR* chief of *'BR LSPT* (?)"
(Ph. Tyre: Slouszch p. 42, ins. #26, line 1)

Bibl. Harris 107; Benz 323-24; NE 289; PPG 50, 74, 90, 92; KAI/II 12, 19; Slouszch 13, 27, 42-43; ANET 662.

*Y'Ṣ B.Heb. *Yā'aṢ* "to advise"; B.Aram. *Ye'aṬ*; Emp.Aram. *Y'Ṭ*; J.Aram. *Ye'aṬ*; Arabic *Wa'aẒa* "to exhort". 1. "advisor" n.m.

a) *'BDMLQRT Y'Ṣ*
"*'BDMLQRT* (the) advisor"
(Pu. Sousse: RES ins. #906, line 1)

Bibl. DISO 110.

*Y'R Heb. *Ya'aR* "thicket, wood"; Ug. *Y'R*; J.Aram. *Y'aRa'*; Moab. *Y'R*; Syriac *Y'aRa'*; [Arabic *W'aRuN* "to be hard uneven" (soil)]. 1. "wood" n.m.

a) *HḤRŠM ŠYR*
"the artisans of wood"
(Ph. Dougga: KAI/I p. 19, ins. #100, line 6)

Bibl. DISO 110; KAI/II 108; PPG 13.

YP' Heb. *YāPā* "to be beautiful"; Amar.Akk. *YaPu* "beautiful"; [ESArab *WPY* "to be whole, safe"]; Syriac *Piy* "to be becoming"; [Arabic *WaFi* "to be whole, safe"]. 1. "suitable" adj. m.

a) *KM YP' 'YBL 'M 'T 'BTM*
"as it is suitable (?), (but) only with his forefathers"
(N.Pu. Leptis Magna: KAI/I p. 22, ins. #119, line 7)

Bibl. KAI/II 124; DISO 110.

YṢ' Heb. *YāṢa'* "to go out, come forth"; Ug. *YṢ'*; Akk. *'aṢū*; J.Aram. *Ye'a'* "to sprout, bud"; Syriac *Ye'a'*; Mandaic *Y''*; Arabic *WaḌaa'* "to shine (sun)"; ESArab *WḌ'* "to go out"; Amh. *WaṬṬa*. 1. "to rise" vb. 2. "to attack".

1 a) *YṢ' ŠMŠ LSSM*
"the sun rises, O *SSM*"
(Ph. Arslan Tash: BASOR 197 [1970] p. 47 D, lines 5-6)

b) *WRB'N 'TY 'LŠYY YṢ'*
"and a large eyed *'LŠYY* has attacked with him"
(Ph. Arslan Tash: BASOR 109 [1973] p. 18, obv. lines 2-3)

2 a) *NṢḤT 'T [ ]Y HYṢ'M W'ZRNM*
"I conquered the [ ] of the attackers and their helpers"
(Ph. Idalion: Slouszch p. 100, ins. #91, line 2)

Bibl. DISO 110; BASOR 197 (1970) 47; Harris 107; NE 290; LS I 63-64; ANET 658; PPG 73; KAI/II 43; Slouszch 101.

YṢLT Heb. *'āṢīL* "corner, side", *'aṢṢīL* "joint, joining"; Syriac *YaṢiLa'* "elbow"; Mandaic *YaṢiLa'*; Arabic *'aṢLuN* "root". 1. "joint" n.f.

a) *QṢRT WYṢLT*
"ribs and joints"
(Pu. Marseilles: KAI/I p. 15, ins. #69, line 4)

Bibl. Slouszch 143-44; NE 290; Harris 107; DISO 110; KAI/II 83; Amadasi 177; ANET 656.

YṢQ Heb. *YāṢaQ* "to pour, cast"; B.Heb. *YeṢūQā* "casting of metal"; Ug. *YṢQ*. 1. "statue" n.m.

a) *YṢQ Z 'ŠMN*
"this statue (?) of *'SMN*"
(Ph. Sidon: ESE II, p. 161, lines 1-2)

Bibl. DISO 110.

YṢR Heb. *YōṢeR* "potter, creation"; Ug. *YṢR*; Akk. *eṢēRu* "to make a statue," *YaṢiRuMa*. 1. "potter" n.m.

a) *QBR MTR HYṢR*
"the grave of *MTR* the potter"
(Pu. Motya: Amadasi p. 56, ins. #3, lines 1-2)

Bibl. DISO 110; Harris 107; NE 290; Amadasi 56; Slouszch 132.

YRD Heb. *YāRaD* "to go down"; Ug. *YRD*; Akk. *'aRāDu*; Moab. *YRD*; ESArab *WRD*; Geez *WaRaDa*; Arabic *WaRaDa* "to descend". 1. "to come down" vb. 2. "to bring down"

1 a) *W'[L] ẎRD LMZZT*
"and let him [n]ot come down to (my) doorposts"
(Ph. Arslan Tash: BASOR 197 [1970] p. 46 D, lines 3-5)

b) *WYRD B'RṢH MLK 'Š[R]*
"and the king of *'Š[R]* came down into his land"
(Ph. Hasan Beyli: KAI/I p. 4, ins. #23, Winckler line 3)

2 a) *YRDM 'NK*
"I brought them down"
(Ph. Karatepe: KAI/I p. 5, ins. #26, line A I,20)

b) *YRD B'MQ HLḤ W'ḤRST*
"he brought (?) down the tablet and the (?) into the valley (?)"
(N.Pu. Maktar: KAI/I p. 27, ins. #145, line 8)

Bibl. DISO 111; ANET 653, 658; Leš 16 (1947) 10; BASOR 197 (1970) 46-47; PPG 50, 74, 90, 92; Branden 8; KAI/II 30, 36, 43, 141.

YRḤ I — Heb. *YaReaḤ* "moon," *YeRaḤ* "month"; Ug. *YRḤ* "month"; Eg. *ỉ'Ḥ* "moon"; Akk. *'aRḪu*; ESArab *WRḤ*; Emp.Aram. *YRḤ*; Syriac *YaRḤa'*; J.Aram. *YaRḤa'*; Mandaic *YaHRa'*; Arabic *TāRiḪuN* "date, era," "history"; Meh. *WaRḤ* "month"; Shauri *'oRaḤ*. 1. "month" n.m.

a) *[BY]RḤ KRR*
"[in the mo]nth of *KRR*"
(Ph. Idalion: Slouszch p. 102, ins. #92, line 2)

b) *BYRḤ BL*
"in the month of *BL*"
(Ph. Sidon: KAI/I p. 3, ins. #14, line 1)

c) *ṬKLT YRḤ 'TNM*
"accounts (?) of the month of *'TNM*"
(Ph. Kition: Or 37 [1968] p. 305, line A I)

Bibl. See under *YRḤ* II.

YRḤ II — Heb. *YaReaḤ* "moon"; Eg. *ỉ'Ḥ*; Akk. *'aRḪu*. 1. "moon" n.m.

a) *KM ŠM ŠMŠ WYRḤ*
"as the name of the sun and the moon"
(Ph. Karatepe: KAI/I p. 5, ins. #26, lines A IV,2-3)

Bibl. DISO 111; Harris 107; Benz 326; NE 290; ANET 653; JNSL 1 (1971) 39-45; JNSL 2 (1972) 53-59; EncMiq vol. III, cols. 837-39; KAI/II 19, 36, 54; LS I 146; Gibson 3.

YŠB I — Heb. *YāŠaB* "to sit, remain, dwell"; Ug. *YṮB*; Akk. *'aŠāBu*; Anc.Aram. *YŠB*; Emp.Aram. *YṮB*; J.Aram. *YeTiB*; Syriac *YeTeB*; Mandaic *YTB*; Palm. *YTB*; Arabic *WaṮaBa* (only in the Himyaric dialect). 1. "sit upon a throne" vb. 2. "to dwell". 3. "to cause to dwell, to establish" (Y).

1 a) *YŠBT 'L KS' 'BY*
"I sat upon the throne of my father"
(Ph. Zinjirli: KAI/I p. 4, ins. #24, line 9)

b) *WMY BBNY 'Š YŠB TḤTN*
"and whoever among my sons who shall sit in my place"
(Ph. Zinjirli: KAI/I p. 9, ins. #24, lines 13-14)

c) *WYŠB 'NK 'L KS' 'BY*
"and I sat upon the throne of my father"
(Ph. Karatepe: KAI/I p. 5, ins. #26, line A I,11)

2 a) *W'Ṁ Z '[Š] YŠB BN*
"and this people wh[ich] dwells among us"
(Ph. Karatepe: KAI/I p. 5, ins. #26, lines C IV,7-8)

3 a) *YŠBM 'NK BQṢT GBLY*
"and I caused them to dwell at the edge(s) of my border"
(Ph. Karatepe: KAI/I p. 5, ins. #26, lines A I,20-21)

b) *WDNNYM YŠBT ŠM*
"and I established the *DNNYM* there"
(Ph. Karatepe: KAI/I p. 5, ins. #26, lines A I,21-II,1)

c) *WYŠBNY ŠMN 'DRM*
"and we established him (in) the high heavens"
(Ph. Sidon: KAI/I p. 3, ins. #14, line 17)

Bibl. ANET 653-54, 662; DISO 111-12; Harris 107; EHO 17; NE 291; PPG 8, 49, 75, 90; Branden 88-89; Slouszch 25.

YŠB II — B.Heb. *ŠeBeT* "seat"; Arabic *WiṮāBuN* "seat, throne". 1. "seat" n.m.

a) *NP'L' ŠŠ HYSBM 'L'*
"there were made these six seats"
(N.Pu. Leptis Magna: KAI/I p. 25, ins. #130, line 1)

Bibl. KAI/II 133; DISO 112.

YŠ' Heb. *HōŠi'a* "to deliver, support, save," *YeŠūa'* "salvation, welfare"; ESArab *YṮ'*; Moab. *HŠ'*; [Arabic *WaSi'a* "to make wide, spacious"]. 1. "preservation" n.m.

a) *LYŠ' R'Y*
"for the preservation of his eyesight"
(Ph. exact site unknown: JAOS [1907] p. 353, line 3)

Bibl. Benz 327; VT 6 (1956) 196.

YŠR I Heb. *YāŠaR* "to be smooth, right"; Ug. *YŠR* "uprightness"; Akk. *ŠuTēŠuRu* "to make thrive or prosper"; J.Aram. *YeŠaR* "to be firm, sound". 1. "to provide" vb. (Y).

a) *MYŠR 'RṢT RBT*
"the bringer of prosperity to the great lands"
(N.Pu. Cherchel: KAI/I p. 29, ins. #161, line 2)

Bibl. KAI/II 150; DISO 112-13.

YŠR II Heb. *YāŠāR* "upright, straight"; Ug. *YŠR* "uprightness"; Akk. *eŠēRu* "to make straight"; Emp.Aram. *HWŠR*; J.Aram. *YaŠRa'* "upright man"; Arabic *YaSaRa* "to be gentle, easy". 1. "upright" adj. m.

a) *MLK YŠR*
"upright king"
(Ph. Byblos: KAI/I p. 1, ins. #4, lines 6-7)

Bibl. DISO 113; KAI/II 6; Harris 108.

YT see entry under *'YT*.

a) *'Š NDR BDMLQRT BN ḤMLK' ŠM'T YT [QL']*
"that which *BDMLQRT*, son of *ḤMLK'* vowed, you heard [his voice]"
(Pu. Constantine: Berthier/Charlier p. 126, ins. #181, lines 2-4)

Bibl. DISO 28-29; Berthier/Charlier 126.

YTM Heb. *YāTōM* "be bereaved of parents"; Ug. *YTM*; J.Aram. *YāTōMa'*; Syriac *YaTMa'*; Mandaic *YaTiMa'*; Arabic *YaTiMuN*. 1. "orphan" n.m.

a) *KM NBŠ YTM B'M*
"as the desire of an orphan (is) for his mother"
(Ph. Zinjirli: KAI/I p. 4, ins. #24, line 13)

b) *YTM BN 'LMT*
"an orphan, son of a widow"
(Ph. Sidon: KAI/I p. 3, ins. #14, line 3)

Bibl. ANET 654, 662; DISO 113; Harris 108; NE 291; Slouszch 20; KAI/II 19, 31.

YTN Heb. *NāTaN* "to give"; Ug. *YTN*; Akk. *NaDāNu*; Anc.Aram. *NTN*; J.Aram. **NeTaN*; B.Aram. *NeTaN*; Syriac *NeTaL* (?); Mandaic *NTN*; Ph., Pu., N.Pu. *YTN* (N.Pu. *Y'TN*). 1. "to give, grant (offerings, life, rule)" vb. 2. "to be given" (N).

1 a) *WTTN [LW HRBT B]'LT GBL HN*
"may the [lady, the M]istress of *GBL* grant him favor"
(Ph. Byblos: KAI/I p. 2, ins. #10, lines 9-10)

b) *HSML 'Z 'Š YTN*
"this (is) the image which...gave"
(Ph. Cyprus: Slouszch p. 96, ins. #88, line 2)

c) *HMNḤT Z 'Š YTN 'BDMSKR*
"this (is) the offering which *'BDMSKR* gave"
(Ph. Tyre: Slouszch p. 42, ins. #26, line 1)

d) *YTT WYQDŠT*
"I gave and I consecrated"
(Ph. Larnaka: KAI/I p. 10, ins. #43, line 9)

e) *ḤRPKRT YTN ḤYM L'BDY*
"*ḤRPKRT* granted life to his servant"
(Ph. Egypt: KAI/I p. 12, ins. #52, lines 1-2)

f) *W'LKY HMZR' 'Š Y'TN' T ŠB'T*
"and because the association (?) which has given the oath"
(N.Pu. Maktar: KAR 12 [1963-64] p. 53, col. III, line 2)

2 a) *WNTN LPY HKTBT*
"and be given according to the document"
(Pu. Marseilles: KAI/I p. 15, ins. #69, line 18)

b) *WNNTN 'T HKHNM*
"and they were given to the priests"
(N.Pu. Bir Bou-Rekba: KAI/I p. 26, ins. #137, lines 6-7)

Bibl. DISO 113, 188-89; Harris 108; NE 292; PPG 22, 71-73; Branden 88-89; ANET 656; Benz 328-29, 364; KAI/II 12, 60, 64, 70, 83, 136; KAR 12 (1963-64) 53; Amadasi 169; JBL 72 (1953) 32, note 91; Bib 46 (1965) 324-25.

**YTR* Heb. *NōTāR* "to be left over"; Akk. *'aTāRu* "to exceed in number or size"; J.Aram. *'iyTaR* "to be left over"; Syriac *'iyTaR* "to be left over, to have over and above"; Mandaic *YTR* "to be supreme, surpass".

1. "remaining" adj. m.

a) *NLQḤ' BTṢ'T MQM N'TR* "(these) were bought at the expense of the remaining temple" (N.Pu. Leptis Magna: KAI/I p. 23, ins. #122, line 2)

Bibl. PPG 74-75; KAI/II 128.

K

K I Heb. *Ki* "that, for, when"; Akk. *Kī* "when, how"; Ug. *K*; Anc.Aram. *Ky*; Moab. *Ky*; Emp.Aram. *Ky*; Ph., Pu., N.Pu. *K* (N.Pu. *K'*, *KḤ*, *KY*, *KḤN*). 1. "for, because" conj. 2. "when" 3. "because" 4. "that"

1 a) *K ŠM' QL YBRK*
"because he heard his voice, may he bless him"
(Ph. Idalion: KAI/I p. 8, ins. #38, line 2)

b) *K ŠM' QL' YBRK'*
"because he heard his voice, may he bless him"
(Pu. Sicily: KAI/I p. 14, ins. #63, line 3)

c) *K ŠM QL' BRK'*
"for he heard his voice and blessed him"
(N.Pu. Constantine: Slouszch p. 222, ins. #228, lines 5-8)

d) *K' ŠM' QL'*
"for he heard his voice"
(N.Pu. Maktar: JA Series 11 vol. 7 [1916] p. 97, lines 1-2)

e) *KḤ Š[M]' [Q]L[']*
"for he h[ear]d [his v]oic[e]"
(N.Pu. Toisson d'ob: JA Series 11 vol. 9 [1917] p. 147, ins. #3, line 5)

f) *K ŠM' QL' BRK'*
"for he heard his voice and blessed him"
(N.Pu. Leptis Magna: KAI/I p. 25, ins. #129, line 4)

g) *KḤN ŠM' ML' BDK'* (should read *BRK'*)
"for he heard his word(s) and blessed him"
(N.Pu. Toisson d'ob: JA Series 11 vol. 9 [1917] p. 149, ins. #6, lines 3-4)

2 a) *K ŠTḤ B'LM*
"when he placed him in the tomb"
(Ph. Byblos: KAI/I p. 1, ins. #1, line 1)

3 a) *K T'BT 'ŠTRT HDBR H'*
"because that thing is an abomination to *'ŠTRT*"
(Ph. Sidon: KAI/I p. 2, ins. #13, line 6)

b) *K 'NK 'ŠMN'ZR MLK ṢDNM*
"because I *'ŠMN'ZR*, king of the *ṢDNM*"
(Ph. Sidon: KAI/I p. 3, ins. #14, line 13)

c) *W'L KY HMZR' 'Š*
"and because the citizens council which"
(N.Pu. Maktar: KAR 12 [1963-64] p. 53, col. III, line 2)

4 a) *K YD' HGW*
"that the community knows"
(Ph. Piraeus: KAI/I p. 13, ins. #60, line 7)

Bibl. DISO 117-18; NE 295; Harris 109; PPG 44, 130, 163; Branden 121, 131-32; KAI/II 2, 17, 19, 56, 79; ZDMG 74 (1910) 441, note 1.

K II — Heb. *K* "like, as"; Ug. *K*; Anc.Aram. *K*; Arabic *Ka*. 1. "as" comparative 2. used quantiatively

1 a) *'D 'LM KQDM*
"for ever, as of old"
(Ph. Larnaka: KAI/I p. 10, ins. #43, line 12)

2 a) *KMDT ŠT BKTB[T]*
"in proportion to as is set down in the documen[t]"
(Pu. Marseilles: KAI/I p. 15, ins. #69, line 17)

Bibl. Amadasi 169; KAI/II 60, 83; DISO 113-14; PPG 126; Harris 109; Branden 115; Slouszch 112, 178.

K' — B.Heb. *Kō* "thus, here"; N.Heb. *KāN*; Syriac *LeKa'* "hither," *'ayKa'* "where"; J.Aram. *Ka'*; Mandaic *Ka'*. 1. "here" adv.

a) *PTḤ' Š'M' ḤR'B K'*
"the drying sheds (?) were set open (?) here"
(N.Pu. Tripolitania: Or 37 [1968] p. 4, line 1)

Bibl. PPG 124; Or 37 (1968) 7-8.

KBD I — Heb. *KiBBeD* "to honor"; Akk. *KaBāTu* "become important, honored"; Ug. *KBD* "to honor"; ESArab *KBWDT* "honor". 1. "to honor" vb.

a) *MŠKBM 'L YKBD LB'RRM*
"may the *MŠKBM* not honor the *B'RRM*"
(Ph. Zinjirli: KAI/I p. 4, ins. #24, line 14)

b) *KBD H'DMM HMT RBTN*
"those men honored our lady"
(Pu. Carthage: CIS I, ins. #5510, line 1)

Bibl. ANET 654; DISO 114; Harris 110; EHO 18-19; KAI/II 30; BAC (1941-42) 389.

KBD II — Heb. *KāBōD* "honor, distinction"; Akk. *KuBāTu* "honors," *KaBTuTu* "majesty"; ESArab *KBWDT* "honor". 1. "honor" n.m.

a) *SKR KBD 'L P'LT M'ŠRT*
"a monument of honor for honest deed(s)"
(N.Pu. Leptis Magna: KAI/I p. 23, ins. #123, lines 4-5)

b) *SKR KBD 'L GM 'DR*
"a monument of honor for glorious majesty (?)"
(N.Pu. Cherchel: KAI/II p. 29, ins. #161, line 5)

Bibl. KAI/II 130, 150; DISO 114; Benz 330; ZA 43 (1935) 111.

KBDT — for etymology, see under *KBD* II. 1. "honor" n.m.

a) *BKBDT 'ṢMTY*
"in honor (?) of his bones (?)"
(Pu. Carthage: Slouszch p. 182, ins. #155, line 7)

Bibl. Slouszch 183; DISO 332; Harris 110; ESE I 168.

KBL — etymology and meaning unknown. 1. "to offer" vb. (from context)

a) *KBL L' BṢMḤ Š'RM*
"he offered (?) for him from (?) the offspring (?) of his flesh (?)"
(N.Pu. Constantine: KAI/I p. 30, ins. #163, line 3)

Bibl. KAI/II 153; AIPHOS 13 (1953) 166-71; DISO 114.

KBS — B.Heb. *KāBaS* "to press, tread"; N.Heb. *KiBBeS* "to wash (clothes)"; Akk. *KaBāSu* "to trample, defeat"; Ug. *KBS* "launderer"; Mandaic *KBaSTa'* "oppression" (?); Arabic *KaBaSa* "to knock, stamp". 1. "to launder" vb.

a) [ ] *ḤY HKBS*
"[ ]*ḤY* the launderer"
(Pu. Carthage: Slouszch p. 192, ins. #177, line 2)

Bibl. Slouszch 192.

KBRT

B.Heb. *KeBāRā* "a good distance"; Akk. *KiBRāTu* "referring to the four regions of the inhabited world," *KiBRu* "ledge, border". 1. "direction" n.m.

a) *'RPT KBRT MṢ' ŠMŠ*
"the portico in the direction (?) of sunrise"
(Ph. Ma'ṣub: KAI/I p. 4, ins. #19, line 1)

Bibl. DISO 45; Slouszch 44; Harris 110; NE 293; KAI/II 28.

KDŠ

C.S. for etymolgoy see under *QDŠ*. 1. "sanctuary" n.m.

a) *BKDŠ B'L ḤMN*
"in the sanctuary of *B'L ḤMN*"
(Ph. Carthage: KAI/I p. 17, ins. #78, line 5)

Bibl. KAI/II 96; PPG 17; Branden 7; Harris 110, 143; DISO 253.

KHN

Heb. *KōHeN* "priest"; Ug. *KHN*; Emp.Aram. *KHN*; Mandaic *KaHNa'* "Jewish priest"; J.Aram. *KaHaNa'*; Syriac *KaHaNa'*; Nab. *KHN'*; Arabic *KāHiNuN* "seer"; Ph., Pu., N.Pu. *KHN* (Pu. *KḤN*, *K'N*). 1. "priest" n.m. (of specific deities) 2. "cultic priest" 3. "royal priest" 4. "priest"

1 a) *PLṬB'L KHN B'LT*
"*PLṬB'L*, priest of the Mistress"
(Ph. Byblos: KAI/I p. 2, ins. #11, line 1)

b) *BD' KHN RŠP ḤṢ*
"*BD'* priest of *RŠP* of fortune (?)" (or "of the arrow")
(Ph. Kition: KAI/I p. 7, ins. #32, line 3)

c) *BD'ŠṬRT KHN MLQRT*
"*BD'ŠTRT* priest of *MLQRT*"
(Ph. Constantine: Berthier/Charlier p. 69, ins. #68, lines 2-3)

d) *ḤMLKT KHN B'L ŠMM*
"*ḤMLKT*, priest of *B'L ŠMM*"
(Pu. Carthage: Slouszch p. 191, ins. #176, line 1)

e) *['ŠM]NḤLṢ KHN 'LT*
"['ŠM]NḤLṢ, priest of *'LT*" (or "priest of the goddess")
(Pu. Carthage: Slouszch p. 254, ins. #308, line 4)

f) *LHN LB'L ḤMN*
"priest of *B'L ḤMN*"
(N.Pu. Henschir Medina: KAI/I p. 29, ins. #159, line 7)

2 a) *KL KHN 'Š YQḤ*
"all priests who would take"
(Pu. Carthage: KAI/I p. 16, ins. #75, line 3)

b) *LKHNM KSP 'ŠRT B'ḤD*
"the priests shall have ten silver (shekels) for each"
(Pu. Marseilles: KAI/I p. 15, ins. #69, line 3)

c) *LKHNM KSP RB' ŠLŠT*
"the priests shall have three quarters of a silver (shekel)"
(Ph. Marseilles: KAI/I p. 15, ins. #69, line 9)

3 a) *KHN L'DN MLKM*
"priest to the Lord of Kingdoms"
(Ph. Larnaka: KAI/I p. 10, ins. #43, line 5)

4 a) *'ZRB'L 'KHN*
"*'ZRB'L* the priest"
(Pu. Carthage: Slouszch p. 318, ins. #498, lines 3-4)

b) *ṬPN RB ḤK'N*
"*ṬPN* the high priest"
(Pu. Constantine: Berthier/Charlier p. 62, ins. #65, lines 2-3)

Bibl. NE 294; Harris 110; Amadasi 169; DISO 116; KAI/II 15-16, 50, 60, 83, 93, 148; EncMiq vol. IV Sub. *KōHeN*, cols. 14-15; EH 63-64; ANET 656; JSS 18 (1973) 282-85.

KHNT for etymology, see under *KHN*. N.Heb. *KōHeNeT* "priest's daughter"; J.Aram. *KaHaNTa'*; Pu., N.Pu. *KHNT* (N.Pu. *KNT*, *K'NT*). 1. "priestess" n.f.

a) *QBR 'RŠTB'L HKHNṬ*
"the grave of *'RŠTB'L*, the priestess"
(Pu. Carthage: Slouszch p. 184, ins. #158, line 1)

b) *QBR GRTMLKṬ HKHNT*
"the grave of *GRMLQRT* the priestess"
(Pu. Carthage: Slouszch p. 188, ins. #170, line 1)

c) *R'G'Ṭ' BN HKHNT*
"*R'G'Ṭ'* son of the priestess"
(N.Pu. Maktar: KAI/I p. 27, ins. #145, line 45)

d) *ŠBTB'L BT 'WL' HKNT*
"*ŠBTB'L*, daughter of *'WL'* the priestess"
(N.Pu. Uzappa: JA Series 11 vol. 11 [1918] p. 252, ins. #2, lines 1-2)

e) *ḤMLKT BN ḤMLKY HK'NT*
"*ḤMLKT*, son of *ḤMLKY* the priestess"
(N.Pu. Constantine: Berthier/Charlier p. 66, ins. #72, line 2)

f) *QBR Ḥ[L]D RB KHNT*
"the grave of *Ḥ[L]D* the chief priestess"
(Pu. Carthage: Slouszch p. 189, ins. #172, line 1)

Bibl. DISO 116; NE 294; Harris 110; JA Series 11 vol. 11 (1918) 252; Slouszch 189; KAI/II 141; Berthier/Charlier 66.

KWLB Heb. *KeLūB* "basket, cage"; Akk. *KiLuBu* "bird trap"; Te. *KeLaB* "pen for animals"; Gk. *Kelubos* "basket, cage". 1. "capital" (of a column) n.m.

a) *NP'L BKWLBM NS'M*
"the (?) was made with high capitals (?)"
(N.Pu. Maktar: KAR 12 [1963-64] col. II, line 1)

Bibl. KAR 12 (1963) 51-52.

**KWN* Heb. *KōNeN* "to establish," *NaKōN* "be firm, taut"; Ug. *KN* "exist"; Akk. *KāNu* "be firm, right"; ESArab *KWN* "to be"; Syriac *KaWeN* "to make straight"; Mandaic *KUN*; Arabic *KāNa* "to be"; N.Heb. *KeWWeN* "to make straight"; J.Aram. *KaWWeN*. 1. "to exist" vb. 2. "to establish" 3. "to prepare" (Y)

1 a) *'L YKN LM MŠKB*
"may they have no resting place"
(Ph. Sidon: KAI/I p. 3, ins. #14, line 8)

b) *'L YKN LM ŠRŠ LMṬ WPRY LM'L*
"may they have no stock downwards or branches upwards"
(Ph. Sidon: KAI/I p. 3, ins. #14, lines 11-12

c) *LKNY LY LSKR*
"that it may be for me as a memorial"
(Ph. Umm el-Awamid: KAI/I p. 3, ins. #18, line 6)

d) *KN BMH*
"there was *BMH*"
(Ph. Zinjirli: KAI/I p. 4,
ins. #24, line 3)

e) *WKT BYD MLḲM*
"and I was in the hands of kings"
(Ph. Zinjirli: KAI/I p. 4,
ins. #24, line 6)

f) *'PS Š̌M 'ZTWD YKN L'LM*
"only the name of *'ZTWD* shall
exist forever"
(Ph. Karatepe: KAI/I p. 5,
ins. #26, lines A IV,1-2)

g) *HNDR 'Š̌ KN NDR 'BNM MRḤY*
"the vow which their father
MRḤY has vowed"
(Ph. Idalion: KAI/I p. 9,
ins. #40, line 20)

2 a) *LKNNM LṢDNM L'L[M]*
"to establish them for the *ṢDNM*
for ev[er]"
(Ph. Sidon: KAI/I p. 3,
ins. #14, line 20)

3 a) *L'LM Z YKN GR'Š̌TRT*
"for this god (or "for these
gods") *GR'Š̌TRT* prepared"
(Pu. Carthage: Slouszch p. 178,
ins. #145, line 1)

Bibl. DISO 117; NE 294; Harris 109-10;
ANET 662; EHO 17; KAI/II 19, 26,
30-31, 36, 57; Benz 332; Slouszch
22, 28; Branden 95-97.

KKB Heb. *KōKāB*; Ug. *KBKB*; Akk. *KaKKaBu*; Arabic
KaWKaBuN; Syriac *KaWKeBa'*; Shauri *KiBKiB*;
Geez *KoKaB*; J.Aram. *KōKeBa'*; ESArab *KWKB*;
Soq. *KiBŠ̌iB*. 1. "star" n.m.

a) *KM HKKBM 'L*
"like the stars of *'L* (?)"
(Ph. Pyrgi: KAI/I p. 53,
ins. #277, lines 10-11)

Bibl. Or 34 (1965) 170-72; Amadasi 168;
JAOS 86 (1966) 295-96.

KKR Heb. *KiKāR* "talent"; Akk. *KiRKaR*; J.Aram.
KaKRa'; Syriac *KaKRa'*. 1. "talent" n.m.

a) *KKRM M'T*
"one hundred talents"
(Pu. Carthage: Slouszch p. 169,
ins. #144, line 4)

b) *'SR KKR' ṢMQ*
"ten talents of raisins"
(N.Pu. Tripolitania: Or 33 [1964] p. 4, line 2)

Bibl. Or 33 (1964) 8; Slouszch 169; PPG 105; JNES 31 (1972) 353, also note 20.

KL C.S. 1. "with a following genitive, usually rendered as the whole, all, any and every" prep. 2. "all" n.m.

a) *Ḥ'T ḤWY KL MPLT HBTM*
"(it was) he who restored all these temple ruins"
(Ph. Byblos: KAI/I p. 1, ins. #4, lines 2-3)

b) *KL 'DM 'Š TPQ 'YT H'RN Z*
"any man who shall remove this sarcophagus"
(Ph. Sidon: KAI/I p. 2, ins. #13, line 3)

c) *KL HR' 'Š KN B'RṢ*
"the evil which was in the land"
(Ph. Karatepe: KAI/I p. 5, ins. #26, line A I,9)

d) *WKL BN 'LM*
"and all the sons of *'L*"
(Ph. Arslan Tash: KAI/I p. 6, ins. #27, rev. line 11)

e) *WLKL 'L TḤPNṢ*
"and may all the gods of *TḤPNṢ*"
(Ph. Saqqara: KAI/I p. 12, ins. #50, line 3)

f) *WKL 'Š LSR T 'BN Z*
"and all who will remove this (grave) stone"
(Pu. Carthage: KAI/I p. 17, ins. #79, lines 7-8)

2 a) *'BD'ŠTRT BN ŠPṬ P'L KL*
"*'BD'ŠTRT* son of *ŠPṬ* the general contractor (?)"
(Pu. Carthage: Slouszch p. 315, ins. #489, lines 2-3)

Bibl. Harris 111; DISO 118-20; ANET 653, 656, 662; PPG 149; Branden 62-63; NE 296; Slouszch 315; KAI/II 6, 17, 36, 43, 67, 97; BASOR 197 (1970) 44-45.

KLB C.S. 1. "dog" n.m.

a) *YTLNN MŠKBM KM KLBM*
"the *MŠKBM* growled like dogs"
(Ph. Zinjirli: KAI/I p. 5, ins. #24, line 10)

b) *LKLBM WLGRM QR 3*
"for the dogs and for the lions three *QR*"
(Ph. Kition: KAI/I p. 8, ins. #37, line B 10)

Bibl. Benz 331; Or 37 (1968) 317; KAI/II 30, 54; DISO 120-21; NE 296; Slouszch 80; Harris 111.

**KLY* Heb. *KāLā* "to complete, accomplish"; Akk. *KaLū*; Ug. *KLY* "to be spent (of foods and drink)"; J.Aram. *KeLa'* "to finish, end"; Mandaic *KL'*. 1. "to complete" vb.

a) *N*[ ] *NQY BKLTY*
"clean upon its completion"
(Pu. Malta: Amadasi p. 18, ins. #2, lines 1-2)

b) *'BDMLKT KL T Š'T'*
"*'BDMLKT* completed (?) his offering (?)"
(Pu. Carthage: Slouszch p. 205, ins. #203, lines 1-2)

Bibl. DISO 121; Harris 111; Amadasi 19; NE 296; Slouszch 127, 206.

KLL Heb. *KāLiL* "whole offering" 1. "whole offering" n.m. 2. in combinations

1 a) *B'LP KLL 'M ṢW'T*
"for an ox, whole offering or *ṢW'T* offering"
(Pu. Marseilles: KAI/I p. 15, ins. #69, line 3)

b) [*B*]*ṢRB 'YL KLLM 'M ṢW'T*
"[for] the young of a hart (?) whole offerings or *ṢW'T* offering"
(Pu. Carthage: KAI/I p. 16, ins. #74, line 5)

2 a) *'M ŠLM KLL*
"or the *ŠLM* of the *KLL* offering"
(Pu. Marseilles: KAI/I p. 15, ins. #69, line 3)

Bibl. DISO 121; Slouszch 143, 166; NE 296; Harris 111; KAI/II 83, 92; PEQ 80 (1948) 67-71; Amadasi 175-76; Levine 118-22.

KM Heb. *KeMō* "like, as"; Ug. *KM*; Akk. *KīMa*; J.Aram. *KeMa'*; Syriac *'aKMa'* "as, as long as"; Mandaic *KM'*; Arabic *KaMa*. 1. "as" conj. 2. "when"

1 a) *KM NBŠ YTM B'M*
"as the desire of an orphan (is) for his mother"
(Ph. Zinjirli: KAI/I p. 4, ins. #24, line 13)

b) *KM ŠM ŠMŠ WYRḤ*
"as the name of the Sun and the Moon"
(Ph. Karatepe: KAI/I p. 5, ins. #26, lines A IV,2-3)

c) *KM 'Š BN 'YT KL 'ḤRY [HMQDŠ]Ṁ*
"as they built all the remainder of the [sanctuari]es"
(Ph. Ma'ṣub: KAI/I p. 4, ins. #19, line 9)

d) *KM 'Š LMLKYT 'Š KN LPNY*
"as with the royalty which was before me"
(Ph. Byblos: KAI/I p. 2, ins. #11, line 2)

e) *KM Š ḤGR HŠMRT*
"as also the protective wall"
(Pu. Carthage: KAI/I p. 17, ins. #81, line 4)

2 a) *KM 'Š QR'T*
"when I invoked"
(Ph. Byblos: KAI/I p. 2, ins. #10, line 7)

Bibl. KAI/II 12, 15, 27, 30, 36, 98; Harris 109; DISO 121-22, PPG 55, 130, 164; Branden 122-23; ANET 653-54, 656; Slouszch 12.

KMN C.S. 1. "cumin" n.m.

a) *ŠQḊM WKMN*
"almonds and cumin"
(Ph. Egypt: KAI/I p. 12, ins. #51, obv. lines 6-7)

Bibl. KAI/II 69.

KMR Heb. *KoMeR* "idolatrous priest"; Akk. *KuMRu* "priest"; Anc.Aram. *KMR*; Gk. *Komarios*; J.Aram. *KūMRa'*; Syriac *KuMRa'*; Mandaic *KuMRa'*. 1. "priest" n.m.

a) *KMR NY'ṬMN*
"*NY'ṬMN* the priest"
(N.Pu. Henschir Medina: KAI/I p. 29, ins. #159, line 7)

b) *Š'B'L KMR B'LŠMM*
"*Š'B'L*, the priest of *B'LŠMM*"
(Ph. Batsalos: RES ins. #1519B, line 1)

Bibl. DISO 122; Harris 111; NE 297; KAI/II 149; ZA 38 (1930) 244.

KN I Heb. *KeN* "thus, therefore"; J.Aram. *KeN*; Syriac *KeN* "and so, and then"; Arabic *LaKiN* "but". 1. "therefore" adv. 2. "thus"

1 a) *'L KN P'L[T]*
"therefore I made"
(Ph. Byblos: KAI/I p. 2, ins. #9, line A 2)

b) *LKN YD' HṢDNYM*
"therefore, the *ṢDNYM* shall know"
(Ph. Piraeus: KAI/I p. 13, ins. #60, line 7)

2 a) *WKN HN 'NK ŠKB B'RN ZN*
"and thus, behold, I lie in this sarcophagus"
(Ph. Byblos: MUSJ 45 [1969] p. 262)

Bibl. PPG 124; DISO 122; MUSJ 45 (1969) 263; KAI/II 10, 73; Slouszch 118; Harris 111.

**KN* II B.Heb. *KeN* "base"; Akk. *KaNNu*; J.Aram. *KeNNa'*; Syriac *KaNa'*; Mandaic *KaNa'*. 1. "base" n.m.

a) *WT 'KHNYM*
"and the bases"
(N.Pu. Cherchel: KAI/I p. 29, ins. #161, line 6)

Bibl. KAI/II 150.

**KNDR* etymology unknown. 1. "type of money" n.m. (from context)

a) *WKT / NDRM TŠ'*
"and nine *KT/NDRM*"
(N.Pu. Leptis Magna: KAI/I p. 25, ins. #139, line 2)

Bibl. DISO 123; KAI/II 133.

**KNY* Heb. *KiNNā* "to give a name, to circumscribe"; J.Aram. *KaNNi*; Syriac *KeNa'*; Mandaic *KN'*; Arabic *KaNa*. 1. "to designate" vb. 2. "to name"

1 a) *LKNT GW 'RB*
"that the community be designated as surety (for it)"
(Ph. Piraeus: KAI/I p. 13, ins. #60, lines 5-6)

2 a) *DR' KN' ŠLM*
"they have named their family"
(N.Pu. Maktar: KAR 12 [1963-64] p. 54, col. IV, line 1)

Bibl. Slouszch 118; NE 297; KAI/II 73; DISO 123; PPG 83, 85; Harris 111; KAR 12 (1963-64) 54.

KNṢWL'T Lat. *Consul.* 1. "consulate" n.f.

a) *HST BN YHB'T 'Š 'L KNṢWL'T*
"*HST* son of *YHB'T* who is over the consulate"
(N.Pu. Maktar: KAR 12 [1963-64] p. 50, col. I, line 1)

Bibl. KAR 12 (1963-64) 50.

KS' I C.S. "throne" n.m.

a) *THTPK KS' MLKH*
"may the throne of his kingdom be overturned"
(Ph. Byblos: KAI/I p. 1, ins. #1, line 2)

b) *YŠBT 'L KS' 'BY*
"I sat upon the throne of my father"
(Ph. Zinjirli: KAI/I p. 4, ins. #24, line 9)

c) *WYŠB 'NK 'L KS' 'BY*
"and I sat upon the throne of my father"
(Ph. Karatepe: KAI/I p. 5, ins. #26, line A I,11)

Bibl. DISO 124; Harris 112; ANET 653-54, 661; Slouszch 4; Fitzmyer 115.

KS' II B.Heb. *KeSe* "covered (?) or full (?) moon"; Ug. *KS'*; Syriac *KeSa'* "covered (?) or full (?) moon"; Arabic *KiSāuN* "latter part of the month". 1. "time of the covered or full moon" n.m.

a) *[BḤD]ŠṀ ẆḂK̇Ṡ'Ṁ*
"at the [time] of the [new mo]ons and at the [time] of the covered (?) moons"
(Ph. Larnaka: KAI/I p. 10, ins. #43, line 12)

Bibl. Slouszch 112; NE 298; Harris 112; DISO 124; KAI/II 60; EI V 81, notes 12, 13; Bib 46 (1965) 330.

KSY Heb. *KāSā* "to cover"; Ug. *MKS* "covering"; Emp.Aram. *KSH* "to cover"; J.Aram. *KeSa'*; Syriac *KeSa'*; Mandaic *KS'*; Arabic *KaSa*. 1. "to cover" vb.

a) *WBYMY KSY BṢ*
"and in my days byssus covered him"
(Ph. Zinjirli: KAI/I p. 4, ins. #24, lines 12-13)

Bibl. EHO 18; Harris 42, note 17, 117; DISO 124; KAI/II 30-31; ANET 654; PPG 83, 85, 88; Branden 107.

KS'T C.S. 1. "throne" n.f.

a) *WKS'T ŠHNSKT L'LM 'WGSṬS*
"and the throne of the statue of the divine Augustus"
(N.Pu. Leptis Magna: KAI/I p. 23, ins. #122, line 1)

Bibl. DISO 124; KAI/II 128; PPG 153.

KSP Heb. *KeSeP* "silver"; Akk. *KaSPu*; Ug. *KSP*; Anc.Aram. *KSP*; Emp.Aram. *KSP*; J.Aram. *KaSPa'*; Syriac *KeSPa'*; Mandaic *KaSPa'*; Nab. *KSP*; Palm. *KSP'*. 1. "silver" n.m. 2. with a following qualification.

1 a) *K 'Y 'DLN KSP*
"for there is not in it (?) silver"
(Ph. Sidon: KAI/I p. 2, ins. #13, line 8)

b) *B'L KSP*
"possessor of silver"
(Ph. Zinjirli: KAI/I p. 4, ins. #24, line 12)

c) *'ṖQN HKSP 'Š ŠLḤT LY*
"the silver which you sent me has reached me"
(Ph. Saqqara: KAI/I p. 12, ins. #50, line 3)

d) *KSP 'ŠRT B'ḤD*
"ten silver (shekels) for each"
(Ph. Marseilles: KAI/I p. 15, ins. #69, line 3)

e) *KSP RB' ŠLŠT*
"three quarters of a silver (shekel)"
(Pu. Marseilles: KAI/I p. 15, ins. #69, line 9)

2 a) *BKSP 'LM*
"of the finest silver" (or "of the silver of the god")
(Ph. Piraeus: KAI/I p. 13, ins. #60, line 6)

Bibl. Harris 112; DISO 124; NE 298; ANET 654-55, 662; KAI/II 17, 30, 64, 73, 83; Amadasi 169; Slouszch 143.

KST Heb. *KeSūT* "covering"; Ug. *KST* "garment"; ESArab *KSW*; Akk. *KuSiTu* "an elaborate garment"; J.Aram. *KeSūTa'* "cover, clothing"; Mandaic *KiSYa'*; Syriac *KeSuYa'*; Arabic *KiSWaTuN*. 1. "covering" n.f.

a) *KST W'TPT*
"coverings (?) and wrappings (?)"
(Pu. Carthage: Slouszch p. 162, ins. #140, line 1)

Bibl. Slouszch 162; DISO 124; Harris 112.

K'S etymology and meaning unknown. 1. "to commission" vb. (from context)

a) *K'S LP'L WḤTM*
"he commissioned (?) the work (?) to be completed (?)"
(N.Pu. Leptis Magna: KAI/I p. 23, ins. #124, line 4)

Bibl. KAI/I 130; DISO 125.

**KPP* [Heb. *KāPaP* "to bend, bend down"; Akk. *KaPāPu*; J.Aram. *KePaP*; Syriac *KaPa*; Arabic *KaFFa*]. 1. "to present" vb.

a) *LKP 'YT 'MTNT Z*
"to present this gift"
(Pu. Carthage: CIS I, ins. #5510, line 3)

Bibl. DISO 125.

KPT [Akk. *KuPPuTu* "to bring together"; N.Heb. *KāPaT* "to twist, tie"; B.Aram. *KePaT*; J.Aram. *KePaT*; Syriac *KaPeT* "to thicken, form into a knot"; Mandaic *KPT* "to tie, bind"; Arabic *KaFaTa* "to gather"]. 1. "to limit" vb.

a) *WKPT RBTN TNT PN B'L W'DN B['L] ḤMN*
"may our lady *TNT PN B'L* and the lord *B'L ḤMN* limit (?)"
(Pu. Carthage: CIS I, ins. #5510, p. 433, lines 4-5)

Bibl. DISO 126.

KR I etymology unknown. Akk. *KaR* measure of capacity; Emp. Aram. *KR*. 1. "type of measure of capacity" n.m.

a) *MŠQL KR 100*
"(by) weight one hundred *KR*"
(Ph. Larnaka: KAI/I p. 10, ins. #43, line 14)

Bibl. DISO 126; Slouszch 113; KAI/II 60; Harris 112.

KR II — B.Heb. *KaR* "pasture"; Akk. *KaRu* "garden, grove". 1. "pasturage" n.m.

a) *B'L KR*
"master of the pasturage"
(Ph. Sidon: Eretz Israel IX, p. 10)

Bibl. EI IX 10.

KR' — Heb. *KāRā* "to dig"; J.Aram. *KeRa'*; ESArab *KRW*; Mandaic *KR'*; Arabic *KaRa*. 1. "to dig" vb.

a) *MṬHQŠ' HG'Z WKR' T Š'KM*
"*MṬHQŠ'* the shearer and digger of pits (?)"
(N.Pu. Tripolitania: Libya 3 [1927] p. 110, lines 1-2)

Bibl. DISO 127.

**KRY* — Heb. *KāRā* "to get by trade"; N.Heb. *KāRā* "to purchase"; Arabic *KaRa* "to let for hire". 1. "to purchase" vb.

a) *W'TKD YKRY 'T HŠD*
"and he decided (?) to purchase the field"
(N.Pu. Tripolitania: Or 33 [1964] p. 4, line 3)

Bibl. Or 33 (1964) 11; PPG 82.

**KRM* — N.Heb. *KāRaM* "to pile up"; Akk. *KaRāMu* "to pile up, store, keep". 1. "to devote" vb.

a) *ŠM'T HMZRḤ 'Š 'YKRM T HMNḤT*
"the names of the citizens council (?) members who devoted (?) the offering(s)"
(N.Pu. Maktar: KAI/I p. 27, ins. #145, lines 12-13)

Bibl. DISO 127; KAI/II 141.

KRT — Heb. *KāRaT* "to cut off, make a covenant"; Akk. *KaRāTu* "to strike, break off"; Moab. *KRT* "to cut". 1. "to make an oath" vb. 2. "woodcutter" 3. "to hew" (Y)

1 a) *K{R}RT LN 'LT 'LM*
"the Eternal one has made a covenant with us"
(Ph. Arslan Tash: BASOR 197 [1970] p. 44, rev. lines 8-10)

b) *'ŠR KRT LN*
"*'ŠR* made a [covenant] with us"
(Ph. Arslan Tash: BASOR 197 [1970] p. 44, lines 10-11)

2 a) *NDR 'Š NDR 'ZMLK HḲRT*
"the vow which *'ZMLK* the woodcutter (?) made"
(Pu. Constantine: Berthier/ Charlier p. 79, ins. #94, line 2)

3 a) [*'LT*] *TYL' HYKRT R'QYM*
"[upon] its ruin he hewed (?) the foundations"
(N.Pu. Maktar: KAI 12 [1963-64] p. 50, col. I, line 2)

Bibl. BASOR 197 (1970) 44-45; DISO 127; KAI/II 43; LS I 58; KAR 12 (1963-64) 50; PPG 59; Berthier/Charlier 80; ANET 658.

KTB C.S. (except for Akk.). 1. "to write" vb. 2. "to be written" (N)

1 a) *'YT R'T Z LKTB H'DMM*
"with this (our) intention to write (the names) of the men"
(Ph. Piraeus: KAI/I p. 13, ins. #60, line 4)

b) *SPRY KTB BPS*
"my inscription (?) write on a tablet"
(Pu. Carthage: Slouszch p. 182, ins. #155, line 8)

c) *ŠM' 'T QL' KTB N'MT*
"hear his voice, write good (about him) (?)"
(N.Pu. Constantine: Slouszch p. 224, ins. #233, lines 3-4)

d) *'L GBRTM K'TBTY*
"I wrote about their mighty deeds"
(N.Pu. Maktar: KAI/I p. 27, ins. #145, line 6)

2 a) *NKTBT WNŠMR'*
"it was written (?) and guarded"
(N.Pu. Cherchel: NSI p. 147, ins. #56, lines 4-5)

Bibl. DISO 128-29; Harris 113; PPG 43, 57, 58, 60; Slouszch 184, 225; KAI/II 73, 141; NSI 148.

KTBT B.Heb. *KeTōBeT* "a writing"; N.Heb. *KeTōBeT* "inscription, writing". 1. "document" n.f.

a) *KMDT ŠT BKTB*[*T*]
"in proportion to as is set down in the docume[nt]"
(Pu. Marseilles: KAI/I p. 15, ins. #69, line 17)

b) *BKTBT DBR' HBT ŠG'Y BN ḤN'*
"by the document of the affairs of the house of *G'Y* son of *ḤN'*"
(N.Pu. Leptis Magna: KAI/I p. 23, ins. #124, lines 3-4)

Bibl. Slouszch 149; Harris 113; KAI/II 83, 130; ANET 656; Amadasi 169.

KTN B.Heb. *KeToNeT* "tunic"; N.Heb. *KiTaN* "linen"; Ug. *KTN* a type of robe"; Akk. *KiTū* "flax"; Emp.Aram. *KTN'*; J.Aram. *KiTNa'*; Syriac *KiTNa'*; Mandaic *KiTaNa'*.
1. "linen" n.m.

a) *WMY BL ḤZ KTN LMN'RY*
"and whoever had never seen linen since his youth"
(Ph. Zinjirli: KAI/I p. 5, ins. #24, line 12)

Bibl. Harris 113; DISO 129; ANET 654; KAI/II 30.

KTRT Heb. *KōTeReT* "crown, capital".
1. "capital" n.f.

a) *KT'RT 'L B'ṬN'*
"a capital (?) with its embossment (?)"
(N.Pu. Leptis Magna: KAI/I p. 22, ins. #119, line 2)

Bibl. DISO 130; KAI/II 124.

L

L I C.S. (except ESArab). 1. prep. expressing direction, very often denoting such ideas as "for" and "to" 2. of time, expressing a specific period 3. with an infinitive (denotes intention) 4. expressing a vocative 5. in combinations 6. expressing locality 7. expressing native relationship

1 a) *L B'LT GBL 'DTW*
"for the Mistress of *GBL*, his lady"
(Ph. Byblos: KAI/I p. 1, ins. #7, lines 3-4)

b) *L'LY L'ŠMN*
"for his god, for *'ŠMN*"
(Ph. Sidon: KAI/I p. 3, ins. #16, line 2)

c) *L'ḤRM 'BH*
"for *'ḤRM* his father"
(Ph. Byblos: KAI/I p. 1, ins. #1, line 1)

d) *LMTNB'L BT PRYM'*
"for *MTNB'L* daughter of *PRYM'*"
(N.Pu. Henschir Guergour: KAI/I p. 27, ins. #143, lines 1-2)

e) *LŠB' BT Y'SKT'N*
"for *ŠB'* daughter of *Y'SKT'N*"
(N.Pu. Maktar: KAI/I p. 28, ins. #149, line 2)

2 a) *BYMM 24 LYRḤ MRP'*
"on the twenty-fourth day of the month of *MRP'*"
(Ph. Kition: KAI/I p. 7, ins. #33, line 1)

b) *BYMM 6 LYRḤ BL*
"on the sixth day of the month of *BL*"
(Ph. Kition: KAI/I p. 7, ins. #32, line 1)

c) *BŠT 'SRM W'ḤT LMLKM*
"in the twenty-first year of his rule"
(N.Pu. Dschebel Massoudj: KAI/I p. 26, ins. #141, lines 3-4)

3 a) *LKNY LY LSKR*
"that it may be for me as a memorial"
(Ph. Umm el-Awamid: KAI/I p. 3, ins. #18, line 6)

b) *DBR MLK 'ŠMN'ZR MLK ṢDNM L'MR*
"thus spake *'ŠMN'ZR* king of the *SDNM*, saying"
(Ph. Sidon: KAI/I p. 3, ins. #14, line 2)

c) *LMḤT ŠM 'ZTWD*
"to efface the name of *'ZTWD*"
(Ph. Karatepe: KAI/I p. 5, ins. #26, line C IV,15)

d) *L'ṬR 'YT ŠM'B'L BN MGN*
"to crown *ŠM'B'L* son of *MGN*"
(Ph. Piraeus: KAI/I p. 13, ins. #60, lines 1-2)

4 a) *LḤŠT L'PT' 'LT*
"incantations, O fliers goddesses"
(Ph. Arslan Tash: BASOR 197 [1970] p. 44, obv. line 1)

5 a) *'L YKN LM ŠRŠ LMT WPRY LM L*
"may they have no stock downwards or branches upwards"
(Ph. Sidon: KAI/I p. 3, ins. #14, lines 11-12)

b) *LMB'BN 'Š 'L HSYW'T*
"from the (grave)stone which is on the tomb (?)"
(N.Pu. Maktar: KAI/I p. 20, ins. #141, line 4)

6 a) *BKL ''N 'Š LYD' 'LNM*
"in all the (?) which (are) on the sides of the divine (statues)"
(N.Pu. Maktar: KAR 12 [1963-64] p. 53, col. III, line 1)

7 a) *P'LT LY HMŠKB ZN*
"I make for myself this resting place"
(Ph. Byblos: KAI/I p. 2, ins. #9, line A 3)

b) *'Š YṬN' LY*
"that which...erected for me"
(Ph. Piraeus: KAI/I p. 13, ins. #59, line 1)

c) *L' ṬN' T HM'Š ST*
"he set up this statue for himself"
(N.Pu. Cherchel: KAI/I p. 29, ins. #161, line 3)

Bibl. KAR 12 (1963-64) 53; BASOR 197 (1970) 44-45; DISO 130-32; PPG 126-28, 140-42, 155; Branden 114-15; KAI/II 2, 9-10, 19, 25, 36, 43, 50-52, 72-73, 139-40, 145, 150; Harris 113-14.

L II Heb. *Lū*, *LeWay* "O that"; J.Aram. *LeWay*; Syriac *LeWay*; Akk. *Lū*; Arabic *LaW*. 1. "O that" conj.

a) *LYŠM' QLM BRK'*
"O that he hear his voice, bless him"
(Pu. Constantine: Berthier/Charlier p. 33, ins. #32, line 3)

b) *LŠM' QL' BRK'*
"O that he hear his voice, bless him"
(Pu. Constantine: Berthier/Charlier p. 139, ins. #216, line 3)

Bibl. Berthier/Charlier 34, 139; PPG 130; DISO 132-33.

L III B.Heb. *Le* assertative particle (Gen. 9:10); Emp.Aram. *L'*; Ug. *L*; Arabic *La*; Anc.Aram. *L*; Nab. *L'*. 1. assertative/optative particle.

a) *WLKL 'L TḤPNṠ*
"and may all the gods of *TḤPNS*"
(Ph. Saqqara: KAI/I p. 12, ins. #50, line 3)

Bibl. KAI/II 67; VT 3 (1953) 372-80; DISO 136; Bib 48 (1967) 549.

LB C.S. 1. "heart" n.m.

a) *WBN'M LBY*
"and because of the goodness of my heart"
(Ph. Karatepe: KAI/I p. 5, ins. #26, line A I,13)

b) *WNḤT LB*
"and satisfaction (i.e. peace of mind)"
(Ph. Karatepe: KAI/I p. 5, ins. #26, line A II,8)

c) *B'ŠR LB*
"with happiness of heart"
(N.Pu. Maktar: KAI/I p. 27, ins. #145, line 11)

Bibl. ANET 653; KAI/II 36; DISO 134.

LBN Heb. *LāBāN* "white"; Ug. *LBN*; J.Aram. *LaBNa'*; Arabic *LaBaNuN* "white sour milk"; Soq. *LiBeHoN* "white"; Meh. *LeBoN*. 1. "white" adj. m.

a) *WTYN Y' LBN*
"and figs, fair (and) white"
(Ph. Carthage: KAI/I p. 16, ins. #76, line B 5)

Bibl. DISO 134; NE 301; Harris 114; Slouszch 168; KAI/II 93.

LBNT Heb. *LeBōNā* "frankincense"; Geez *LeBoN* "stryrax"; Akk. *LaBaNāTu*; Gk. *Libanōs*; J.Aram. *LeBūNTa'*; Syriac *LeBuNTa'*; Arabic *LuBaNuN*. 1. "frankincense" n.f.

a) *QṬRT LBNT DQT*
"incense, fine frankincense"
(Ph. Carthage: KAI/I p. 16, ins. #76, line B 6)

Bibl. DISO 135; NE 302; Slouszch 168; Harris 114; KAI/II 93.

LHB'T B.Heb. *LeHāBā* "flame"; Akk. *La'āBu* "to infect"; J.Aram. *LaHaBūTa'*; Syriac *ŠaLHeB* "to inflame, glow"; Arabic *LaHHaBa* "to blaze fiercely". 1. "flame" n.f.

a) *BLHB'T*
"with a flame"
(N.Pu. Cherchel: KAI/I p. 29, ins. #161, line 7)

Bibl. DISO 135; KAI/II 150; EI IX 152.

LḤ Heb. *LuaḤ* "tablet"; Akk. *Lēu*; Emp.Aram. *LWḤ* (?); Ug. *LḤ*; J.Aram. *LuḤa'*; Syriac *LuḤa'*; Arabic *LaWḤuN*. 1. "tablet" n.m.

a) *HLḤ W'ḤRST*
"the tablet and the (?)"
(N.Pu. Maktar: KAI/I p. 27, ins. #145, line 8)

Bibl. DISO 136; KAI/II 141; Leš 16 (1947-48) 10.

LḤD Akk. *ēDu* "alone"; Ug. *'aḤDY*; Emp.Aram. *LḤD* "each"; J.Aram. *LeḤoD* "singly, only, for"; Mandaic *LHuD*; Syriac *LeḤoD*; Arabic *WaḤDy* "alone". 1. "alone" adv.

a) *WBYMTY 'NK 'ŠT TK LḤDY*
"but in my days, a woman walked by herself"
(Ph. Karatepe: KAI/I p. 5, ins. #26, lines A II,5-6)

b) *'NK LḤDY*
"I alone"
(Ph. Byblos: MUSJ 45 [1969] p. 262, line 1)

Bibl. DISO 82; ANET 653; KAI/II 36; MUSJ 45 (1969) 262-63.

LḤM Heb. *LeḤeM* "bread," "food"; Ug. *LḤM*; Akk. *LēMu* "to eat bread"; Anc.Aram. *LḤM*; Emp.Aram. *LḤM*; J.Aram. *LaḤMa'*; Syriac *LaḤMa'*; Palm. *LḤM*; Arabic *LaḤMuN* "meat"; Soq. *LeḤeM* "fish". 1. "bread" n.m.

a) *WLḤM QṬ[RT]*
"and bread, ince[nse]"
(Pu. Carthage: KAI/I p. 16, ins. #76, line B 3)

b) *YKN HLḤM H'*
"that bread shall be"
(Pu. Carthage: KAI/I p. 16, ins. #76, line B 4)

Bibl. DISO 137; KAI/II 93; Slouszch 168; Harris 114.

LḤŠT B.Heb. *LāḤaŠ* "whispering, charming"; Ug. *LḤŠT* "whisper"; Akk. *LuḪḪuŠu*; Syriac *LūḤāŠa'*; J.Aram. *LeḤaŠa'* "witchcraft, sorcery"; Mandaic *NḤŠ*, *LḤŠ* "to divine by omen, mutter incantations, *NḤaŠa'* "divination"; Geez *'a-LḤoSaSa*. 1. "incantation" n.f. 2. "charm"

1 a) *LḤŠT L'PT' 'LT*
"incantations, O fliers, goddesses"
(Ph. Arslan Tash: BASOR 197 [1970] p. 44, obv. line 1)

2 a) *LḤŠT LMZH*
"charm against the demon who drains his victims"
(Ph. Arslan Tash: BASOR 209 [1973] p. 18, obv. line 1)

Bibl. BASOR 197 (1970) 44-45; DISO 137; KAI/II 43; LS I 54-55; ANET 658; BASOR 209 (1973) 18, esp. note 1, 20-21; Syria 48 (1971) 397-98.

LṬR Gk. *Litra*. 1. "pound" n.m.

a) *LṬRM M'T*
"one hundred pounds"
(Pu. Sardinia: Amadasi p. 91, ins. #9, line 1)

Bibl. DISO 137; KAI/II 81; Amadasi 92; Harris 114; Slouszch 135; NE 302; PPG 16, 99.

LYN etymology and meaning uncertain, perhaps related to Heb. *LūN* "to stay overnight"; Ug. *LN*. 1. "innkeeper" n.m.

a) *BD[']ŠTRT HLYN*
"*BD'ŠTRT* the innkeeper (?)"
(Pu. Carthage: CIS I, ins. #5090, line 3)

LKD B.Heb. *LāKaD* "to capture"; Akk. *LaKāDu* "to run"; J.Aram. *LeKaD*; Arabic *LaKaDa*, *'aLa* "to rush upon". 1. "to catch" vb.

a) *LR'M 'Š BD *ŠP LKD QR 2* "for the shepherds who caught by means of trap(s), two *QR*" (Ph. Kition: Or 37 [1968] p. 305, line B 8)

*reading uncertain

Bibl. DISO 138; Harris 115; NE 303; KAI/II 54; Or 37 (1968) 323.

LL C.S. 1. "night" n.m.

a) *WBL KN MTM LDNNYM LL BYMTY* "and there was never night for the *DNNYM* in my days" (Ph. Karatepe: KAI/I p. 5, ins. #26, lines A II,16-17)

Bibl. ANET 653; KAI/II 36; LS I 79; DISO 155.

**LLYT* Heb. *LiLiT* "type of demon"; Ug. *LL*; Sum. *LíL* "wind"; Akk. *LiLīTu* "storm demon"; Syriac *LeLiTa'* "a night spectre"; J.Aram. *LiLiTa'*; Mandaic *LiLiTa'*. 1. "night demon" n.f.

a) *L'PT' BḤDR HŠK 'BR P'M P'M LLYN* "O fliers from the underworld pass, pass (at once) (?) O night demons" (Ph. Arslan Tash: BASOR 197 [1970] col. B, lines 1-2)

Bibl. LS I 62-63; BASOR 197 (1970) 46, esp. note 24; KAI/II 43; ANET 658.

LM B.Heb. *LāMMā* "lest" (Ex. 32:12); Q.Heb. *LMH*. 1. "lest" conj.

a) *LM YSGRNM 'LNM HQDŠM* "lest the holy gods deliver them up" (Ph. Sidon: KAI/I p. 3, ins. #14, lines 21-22)

Bibl. Harris 116; DISO 138; ANET 662; Gaster-Fs 138-39.

**LN* B.Heb. *HeLīN* "to complain"; N.Heb. *HiTLōNeN* "to murmur". 1. "to growl" vb.

a) *YTLNN MŠKBM KM KLBM* "the *MŠKBM* growled like dogs" (Ph. Zinjirli: KAI/I p. 4, ins. #24, line 10)

Bibl. DISO 136; EHO 18; JPOS 6 (1926) 84-85; Harris 114; ANET 654; PPG 69, 78.

LPY for etymology, see under *PY*. 1. "according to" adv. 2. "in conformity with"

1 a) *LPY HKTBT*
"according to the document"
(Pu. Marseilles: KAI/I p. 15, ins. #69, line 18)

b) *LPY M'S' 'BTY*
"according to the deeds of his fathers"
(N.Pu. Leptis Magna: KAI/I p. 24, ins. #126, line 8)

2 a) *LPY KL 'RK' ML'Ṭ*
"in conformity with all his estimation of the (?)"
(N.Pu. Leptis Magna: KAI/I p. 20, ins. #119, line 5)

Bibl. KAI/II 83, 124, 138; Harris 136; Slouszch 149; NE 349; DISO 227; PPG 127; Branden 117; Amadasi 182.

LPN Heb. *LiPNey* "before"; Akk. *LaPaN*; Ug. *LPN*; Moab. *LPNY*. 1. "before" prep. 2. "formerly" adv. 3. "anterior" adj. Ph., Pu., N.Pu. *LPN* (N.Pu. *LP'N'*)

1 a) *LPN 'L GBL*
"before the gods of *GBL*"
(Ph. Byblos: KAI/I p. 1, ins. #4, line 7)

b) *'Š KN LPNY*
"who were before me"
(Ph. Byblos: KAI/I p. 2, ins. #11, line 2)

c) *BL P'L HLPNYHM*
"those who were before me were ineffective"
(Ph. Zinjirli: KAI/I p. 4, ins. #24, line 5)

d) *LPNY 'DR' 'LPQY*
"before the nobles of *'LPQY*"
(N.Pu. Leptis Magna: KAI/I p. 24, ins. #126, line 7)

e) *LP'N' HB'T*
"before the payment"
(N.Pu. Tripolitania: Or 33 [1964] p. 4, line 6)

2 a) *WBMQMM 'Š KN LPNM NŠT'M*
"and in the places which had formerly been feared"
(Ph. Karatepe: KAI/I p. 5, ins. #26, line A II,3-4)

3 a) *BYRḤ MP' LPNY*
"in the month of anterior *MP'*"
(Pu. Constantine: Berthier/Charlier p. 51, ins. #56, line 3)

b) *BḤMŠ LYRḤ MP' LPNY*
"on the fifth of the month of anterior *MP'*"
(Pu. Constantine: Berthier/Charlier p. 61, ins. #64, lines 2-3)

Bibl. DISO 139; EHO 16-17; Harris 138; NE 352; ANET 653-54; Berthier/Charlier 52; PPG 124, 126, 128; KAI/II 6, 31, 36, 131; Or 33 (1964) 12; Branden 117.

LQḤ Heb. *LāQaḤ* "to take, seize, buy"; Ug. *LQḤ*; Akk. *LeQū*; Amar.Akk. *LaQā̱Ḫu*; Emp.Aram. *LQḤ*; Anc.Aram. *LQḤ*; Moab. *LQḤ*; Geez *LaQḤa* "to loan, lend". 1. "to take" vb. 2. "to be bought" (N) 3. "to purchase"

1 a) *L'DM 'Š LQḤ MKN BM*
"for the man who took his place (?) with him (?)"
(Ph. Kition: Or 37 [1968] p. 305, line B 7)

b) *KL KHN 'Š YQḤ*
"all priests who would take"
(Pu. Marseilles: KAI/I p. 15, ins. #69, line 20)

c) *KL KHN 'Š YQḤ*
"all priests who would take"
(Pu. Carthage: KAI/I p. 16, ins. #75, line 3)

d) *WTYN Y' LBN LQḤT TŠQD*
"and figs, fair (and) white, be mindful to fetch"
(Pu. Carthage: KAI/I p. 16, ins. #76, line B 5)

2 a) *NLQḤ' BTS'T MQM N'TR*
"(these) were bought at the expense of the remaining temple"
(N.Pu. Leptis Magna: KAI/I p. 23, ins. #122, line 2)

3 a) *'RŠ BN 'RŠM HTŠ' LQḤ*
"*'RŠ* son of *'RŠM* the (?) purchaser"
(Pu. Constantine: Berthier/Charlier p. 84, ins. #103, lines 2-3)

Bibl. Berthier/Charlier 85; DISO 139-40; Harris 115; PPG 42, 70-71; Branden 84; Amadasi 169; Slouszch 168.

*LŠKT Heb. *LiŠKā* "cell, chamber"; J.Aram. *LiŠKeTa'*. 1. "chamber" n.f.

a) *LYŠKT H' 'T M'WN*
"that chamber, with the temple"
(N.Pu. Maktar: BAC [1950] p. 112, line 2)

Bibl. BAC (1950) 111-12.

M

M' N.Heb. *Mā* "which, what"; Nab. *MH* "who".
1. rel. pr.

a) *MNSBT M' P'L' BN L'BN'M*
"the (grave)stone which the sons made for their father" (N.Pu. Tripolitania: LibAnt 1 [1964] p. 60, lines 1-2)

Bibl. LibAnt 1 (1964) 61.

M'ZN B.Heb. *Mo'ZNaiM* "scales"; Ug. *MZNM*; J.Aram. *M'oDNa'*; Syriac *MoZNeYa'*; Mandaic *MuZaNia'*; Emp.Aram. *MWZN'*; B.Aram. *M'oZNaia'*.
1. "scale" n.m.

a) *WDL KL MNM BM'ZNM HMQDŠM 'L*
"and with all vessels (?) in the scales (?) of these sanctuaries" (Pu. Carthage: KAI/I p. 17, ins. #81, line 3)

Bibl. DISO 141; KAI/II 98; Harris 75.

M'NN etymology and meaning unknown

a) *NSK ḤRṢ WM'NNM*
"goldsmiths and (?)" (Pu. Carthage: CRAI [1968] p. 117, line 6)

Bibl. CRAI (1968) 129.

M'S' Heb. *Maa'Se* "deed, work", *'āŚā* "to do, create"; ESArab *'SY* "to do, make".
1. "deed" n.m.

a) *LPY M'S' 'BTY WM'S' BT/N*
"according to the deeds of his fathers and (?) deeds" (N.Pu. Leptis Magna: KAI/I p. 24, ins. #126, line 8)

Bibl. KAI/II 131; PPG 19.

M'SP for etymology, see under *'SP*. 1. "totality" n.f.

a) *WM'SP HNSKT Š'LM 'WGSṬS*
"and the totality (?) of the statue of the divine Augustus" (N.Pu. Leptis Magna: KAI/I p. 23, ins. #122, line 1)

Bibl. KAI/II 128; DISO 141; PPG 21, 97.

M'SPT for etymology, see under *'SP*.
1. "gathering (place)" n.f.

a) *M'SPT 'ṢMY*
"gathering (place) of my bones"
(Pu. Carthage: ESE I 169, line 4)

Bibl. Harris 80; ESE I 165-66; Slouszch 181; DISO 141.

M'T C.S. 1. "one hundred" n.f. 2. "two hundred"

1 a) *MZBḤ NḤŠT MŠQL LṬRM M'T*
"the bronze altar, in weight one hundred pounds"
(Pu. Sardinia: KAI/I p. 14, ins. #66, line 1)

b) *Š'R MŠQL M'T WḤMŠM*
"flesh, in weight one hundred and fifty (shekels)"
(Pu. Marseilles: KAI/I p. 15, ins. #69, line 6)

c) [*KS*]*P KKRM M'T*
"one hundred [silve]r *KKRM*"
(Pu. Carthage: Slouszch p. 169, ins. #144, line 4)

d) *TMNM DN'RY' M'T WŠLŠM WŠLŠ*
"their total cost one hundred and thirty-three *DN'RY'*"
(N.Pu. Leptis Magna: KAI/I p. 25, ins. #130, lines 1-2)

2 a) *M'TM*
"two hundred"
(Pu. Carthage: KAI/I p. 17, ins. #76, line B 9)

b) *M'TM W'RB'M*
"two hundred and forty"
(N.Pu. Dschebel Massoudj: KAI/I p. 26, ins. #141, line 5)

Bibl. KAI/II 93, 139; Harris 115; DISO 140; Amadasi 91, 169; ANET 656; PPG 108, 121; Branden 31, 41.

MB' B.Heb. *MāBō'* "entrance, a coming in".
1. "west" n.m.

a) *LMMṢ' ŠMŠ W'D MB'Y*
"from the rising of the sun (east) and until its setting (west)"
(Ph. Karatepe: KAI/I p. 17, ins. #26, lines A I,4-5)

b) *PNY MB' HŠMŠ*
"its front side, facing west"
(Pu. Carthage: KAI/I p. 17, ins. #78, lines 5-6)

Bibl. KAI/II 36, 96; ANET 653; Harris 84; DISO 141; PPG 109.

MBNT B.Heb. *MiBNeh* "structure". 1. "building" n.f.

a) *W'L MBNT ḤṢR BT 'LM*
"and over the building of the temple court"
(Ph. Piraeus: KAI/I p. 13, ins. #60, line 2)

Bibl. KAI/II 73; Harris 88; DISO 141; NE 238; Slouszch 117.

MGLT Heb. *MeGiLLā* "scroll"; Arabic *MaJaLaTuN* "magazine"; B.Aram. *MeGiLLā*. 1. "scroll" n.f.

a) *MNTY KMGLT*
"my/his spell is like the scrolls"
(Ph. Arslan Tash: BASOR 209 [1973] p. 19, rev. line 7)

Bibl. BASOR 209 (1973) 26; Syria 48 (1971) 406.

MGN I B.Heb. *MāGeN* "shield"; Ug. *MGN*; Syriac *MeGeNa'*; J.Aram. *MeGiNa'*; Arabic *MiJaNuN*. 1. "shield" n.m.

a) *WP'L 'NK SS 'L SS WMGN 'L MGN*
"and I acquired horse upon horse and shield upon shield"
(Ph. Karatepe: KAI/I p. 5, ins. #26, lines A I,6-7)

Bibl. ANET 653; KAI/II 36; DISO 142.

MGN II B.Heb. *MiGGeN* "to hand over"; Ug. *MGN* "to beseech"; Akk. *MaGaNNu* "for nothing"; J.Aram. *MaGaNa'* "for nothing"; Syriac *MaGaNa'* "gratis, freely"; Arabic *MaJaNaN* "gratis". 1. "to offer" vb.

a) *'RN* [*Z*]*N MGN 'MTB'L BT PṬ'S*
"[thi]s chest *'MTB'L* daughter of *PṬ'S* offered"
(Ṗh. Carchemish: KAI/I p. 7, ins. #29, line 1)

Bibl. DISO 142; KAI/II 47; Harris 116; PPG 18; VT 14 (1964) 494-97.

MGRD N.Heb. *MaGReDā* "strigil"; J.Aram. *MaGRaDeTa'* "grater"; Syriac *GeRaD* "to scrape, lay bare"; Mandaic *GRiDa'* "scraped"; Arabic *JaRaDa* "to strip (a branch of its leaves)"; Soq. *GRD* "to clean, make neat". 1. "file" n.m.

a) *BD'ŠTRT BN B'LŠMM P'L HMGRDM*
"*BD'ŠTRT* son of *B'LŠMM* the file maker"
(Pu. Carthage: CIS I, ins. #338, line 4)

Bibl. Slouszch 241; DISO 142; Harris 95.

MGŠT B.Heb. *HiGîŠ* "to consult for an oracle" (I Sam. 14:18, Jud. 6:19); Ug. *MGṮ* "offering"; Arabic *TaNJiSuN* "charm amulet". 1. "oracle" n.f.

a) *MGŠTK 'LK WMGŠT 'LY*
"your oracle (?) will be incumbent upon you and my oracle will be incumbent upon me"
(Ph. Byblos: JAOS 81 [1961] p. 32, lines 4-5)

Bibl. Leš 14 (1946) 162-63; JAOS 81 (1961) 33-34; DISO 163; EHO 13; PPG 112; KAI/II 5; EI VIII 9 (English Section), note 9; BASOR 212 (1973) 18.

MD B.Heb. *MaD* "garment"; J.Aram. *MaD* "the priest's cloak". 1. "raiment" n.m.

a) *L' ṬN' T HM'Š ST BMD*
"he set up this statue for himself in raiment (?)"
(N.Pu. Cherchel: KAI/I p. 29, ins. #161, line 3)

Bibl. DISO 142; KAI/II 150.

MDD Heb. *MāDaD* "to measure"; Akk. *MaDāDu* "to measure"; Ug. *MDD* "to measure"; ESArab *MDD* "to measure"; Arabic *MaDDa* "to extend"; Syriac *'eMaD* "to reach, arrive at"; Soq. *MeD* "to extend, to expand"; Amh. *MaDaMMaDa* "to level off"; Saftaitic *MD* "pass along". 1. "surveyor" n.m.

a) *MTNB'L BN ḤMLK BN ḤMLKT 'MDD*
"*MTNB'L*, son of *ḤMLK* son of *ḤMLKT* the surveyor (?)"
(Pu. Carthage: CIS I, ins. #349, line 5)

Bibl. Slouszch 305; Harris 116; NE 306; DISO 142; PPG 75.

MDT Heb. *MiDDā* "measure, measurement, scale". 1. measure, scale n.f.

a) *LMDT 'ṢMT 'Š P'LT*
"in accordance with the mighty deeds which I performed"
(Ph. Sidon: KAI/I p. 3, ins. #14, line 19)

b) *KMDT ŠT BKTB[T]*
"in proportion to as is set down in the docume[nt]"
(Pu. Marseilles: KAI/I p. 15, ins. #69, line 17)

Bibl. Amadasi 182; NE 306; Slouszch 27, 149; KAI/II 83; DISO 143; PPG 126-27; Branden 115, 117; ANET 656, 662.

MZBḤ Heb. *MiZBeaḤ* "altar"; Syriac *MaDBeḤa'* "altar," "sanctuary"; J.Aram. *MaDBeḤa'* "altar"; Mandaic *MaDBHa'*; ESArab *MḎBḤ* "altar"; Arabic *MaḎBaḤun* "the place of the slaughter". 1. "altar" n.m.

a) *HMZBḤ NḤŠT ZN*
"this bronze altar"
(Ph. Byblos: KAI/I p. 2, ins. #10, line 4)

b) *WMZBḤT L'DN 'Š LY LMLQRT*
"and altars for my lord, for *MLQRT*"
(Ph. Larnaka: KAI/I p. 10, ins. #43, line 10)

c) *MZBḤ NḤŠT MŠQL LṬRM M'T*
"the bronze altar in weight one hundred pounds"
(Pu. Sardinia: KAI/I p. 14, ins. #66, line 1)

d) *MZBḤ 'BN*
"a stone altar"
(Pu. Carthage: KAI/I p. 17, ins. #77, line 1)

e) *MZBḤ WP'DY*
"altar and podium"
(N.Pu. Leptis Magna: KAI/I p. 24, ins. #126, line 10)

f) *HMZBḤM 'S 'L P'NY*
"the altars which stand in front"
(N.Pu. Bitia: Amadasi p. 134, ins. #8, line 1)

Bibl. KAI/II 12, 60, 81, 96, 131, 157; DISO 146; Harris 98; PPG 97, 104, 153; Slouszch 11; Branden 32; ANET 656.

MZH B.Heb. *MāZe* "sucked out"; Akk. *MaZā'u* "to press out fluid"; Heb. *MāṢaṢ*, *MāṢa* "to drain out"; Syriac *MeṢa'*; Arabic *MaZZa*; Amh. *MaṬaMMaṬa* "suck up"; Soq. *MZZ*. 1. type of sucking demon n.m.

a) *LḤŠT LMZH*
"charm against the demon who drains his victims"
(Ph. Arslan Tash: BASOR 209 [1973] p. 18, obv. line 1)

Bibl. BASOR 209 (1973) 18, esp. note 1, 20-21; Syria 48 (1971) 397-98.

MZZT Heb. *MeZūZa* "doorpost"; Akk. *MaZZaZu*.
1. "doorpost" n.f.

a) *W'[L] ẎRD LṀZZT* (reading uncertain) "and let him [n]ot come down to (my) doorposts" (Ph. Arslan Tash: BASOR 197 [1970] p. 46, D. lines 3-5)

Bibl. KAI/II 43; JNES 20 (1961) 171.

MZL B.Heb. *MaZZāL* "constellation"; Akk. *MaNZaLTu* "post, station constellation"; N.Heb. *MaZZāL* "planet, destiny, angel of destiny"; J.Aram. *MeZZaLa'* "planet, luck"; Syriac *MaWZaLTa'* "a sphere, an orbit"; Mandaic *MaNZaLa'* "horoscope, star, stellar influence". 1. "luck" n.m.

a) *MŠL N'M* "good luck" (Ph. Larnaka: KAI/I p. 10, ins. #43, line 1)

b) *[L]MẒ̇L̇ N'M* "[for] good luck" (Ph. Larnaka: KAI/I p. 10, ins. #42, line 5)

Bibl. KAI/II 59-60; Harris 123; Slouszch 107-8; NE 307, 318; PPG 19; DISO 146, 171; JNES 20 (1961) 171.

MZRḤ Heb. *'ZRḤ* "a native citizen"; Pu., N.Pu. *MZRḤ* (N.Pu. *MZR'*). 1. "citizen" n.m. 2. type of citizens council 3. meaning unknown

1 a) *KL MZRḤ WKL ŠPḤ* "every citizen (?) and every clan" (Pu. Marseilles: CIS I, ins. #165, line 16)

2 a) *RB MZRḤ SHLKNY BN M'NZM'R* "chief of the citizens council, *SHLKNY* son of *M'NZM'R*" (N.Pu. Maktar: KAI/I p. 27, ins. #145, line 16)

b) *ŠMT HMZRḤ* "the names of the citizens council members" (N.Pu. Maktar: KAI/I p. 27, ins. #145, line 12)

c) *W'L KY HMZR'* "and because the citizens council" (N.Pu. Maktar: KAR 12 [1963-64] p. 53, col. III, line 2)

3 a) *HMZRḤ 'S*
"this *MZRḤ*"
(N.Pu. Maktar: KAI/I p. 28, ins. #147, line 1)

Bibl. KAI/II 83, 141, 144, 148; Amadasi 169; Harris 99; DISO 146; Lešs 19 (1947-48) 7; Slouszch 140; ANET 656; NE 268.

MḤ B.Heb. *MeaḤ* "fattling"; J.Aram. *MeḤa'* "paste, stirred flour in a dish".
1. "rich" adj. m.

a) *'Š KN Y' WMḤ*
"which is fair and rich"
(Pu. Carthage: CIS I, ins. #166A, line 5)

Bibl. Slouszch 168; Harris 116; NE 307; DISO 146.

MḤB Heb. *ḤāBaB* "to love"; J.Aram. *ḤaBBeB* "to love, honor"; Syriac *ḤaB* "to be kindled, set on fire"; Mandaic *HBB*, *HMBB*; Arabic *ḤaBBa* "to love"; Soq. *ḤBB* "to love".
1. "to love" vb. (Y)

a) *MḤB D'T HTMT*
"(he who is) the lover of the knowledge of harmony (?)"
(N.Pu. Leptis Magna: KAI/I p. 23, ins. #121, line 1)

Bibl. DISO 81; PPG 76; KAI/II 128; Bib 48 (1967) 573, note 1.

MḤZ Heb. *MāḤōZ* "harbor, bay"; Ug. *MaḪāZu/Du*; Akk. *MaḪāZu* "market, city"; J.Aram. *MāḤōZa'* "market place, point, site"; Syriac *MāḤōZa'* "a little fortified town"; Mandaic *MaHuZa'* "town, small walled city or village"; Arabic *MāḪūZuN* "harbor".
1. "forum" n.m. 2. "market master"

1 a) *WT HMḤZ RBD*
"and the forum, he paved"
(N.Pu. Leptis Magna: KAI/I p. 23, ins. #124, line 2)

2 a) *'L HMḤZM 'DNB'L BN ḤNB'L...WḤN' BN 'RŠM*
"for the market masters (?) *'DNB'L* son of *ḤNB'L*...and *ḤN'* son of *'RŠM*"
(N.Pu. Leptis Magna: KAI/I p. 25, ins. #130, lines 5-6)

Bibl. KAI/II 130, 133; DISO 147; Lešs 34 (1969) 5-18; Dahood III 88; ZA 41 (1933) 289, note 2.

MḤZT Heb. *MeḤeZā* "light, window"; J.Aram. *MaḤZiTa'* "mirror"; Syriac *MaḤZiTa'* "example, window"; Mandaic *MaHZiTa'* "sign, sight". 1. "window" n.f.

a) *MQDŠ ḤṢRT PḤNT QDŠM MḤZT*
"sanctuary, courts, also (?) arches (?) of the temples, windows"
(N.Pu. Maktar: KAI/I p. 27, ins. #145, lines 1-2)

Bibl. KAI/II 141; DISO 9; Leš 19 (1947-48) 8.

**MḤY* I B.Heb. *MāḤā* "to blot out, to exterminate"; J.Aram. *MeḤa'* "to efface"; Anc.Aram. *MḤ'*; Emp.Aram. *MḤ'*; Arabic *MaḤa'* "to erase". 1. "to efface" vb.

a) *WH' YMḤ SPRH LPP ŠBL*
"as for him, let a (?) efface his inscription"
(Ph. Byblos: KAI/I p. 1, ins. #1, line 2)

b) *'Š YMḤ ŠM 'ZTWD*
"who shall efface the name of *'ZTWD*"
(Ph. Karatepe: KAI/I p. 6, ins. #26, lines A III,13-14)

c) *'Š Y'M[R] LMḤT ŠM 'ZTWD*
"who shall thin[k] to efface the name of *'ZTWD*"
(Ph. Karatepe: KAI/I p. 6, ins. #26, lines C IV,14-15)

d) *WMḤ B'L ŠMM W'L QN 'RṢ*
"let *B'L ŠMM* and *'L* the Creator of earth efface"
(Ph. Karatepe: KAI/I p. 6, ins. #26, line A III,18)

Bibl. KAI/II 2, 36; DISO 147; PPG 82-83; ANET 653; Harris 116; Slouszch 5.

**MḤY* II [J.Aram. *iTMḤy* "to be approved"]. 1. "to be of full weight" vb. 2. "to repay" (from context)

1 a) *'ṬRT ḤRṢ BDRKNM 20 LMḤT*
"a crown of gold, twenty drachmas sterling in value (?)"
(Ph. Piraeus: KAI/I p. 13, ins. #60, line 3)

2 a) *WLMḤT KM YP'*
"and to repay (?) as it is suitable (?)"
(N.Pu. Leptis Magna: KAI/I p. 22, ins. #119, line 7)

Bibl. DISO 147; Harris 116; KAI/II 73, 124; Slouszch 118.

MḤNT Heb. *MaHaNeh* "camp, army camp"; Anc.Aram. *MḤNT*. 1. "army" n.f. 2. in combinations

1 a) *MḤNT ʿL MḤNT*
"army upon army"
(Ph. Karatepe: KAI/I p. 5, ins. #26, lines A I,7-8)

b) *ʿM HMḤNT*
"the community (?) of the army (camp)"
(Pu. Sardinia: Slouszch p. 131, ins. #113, line 1)

2 a) *TMʾ MḤNT*
"army commander"
(Ph. Byblos: KAI/I p. 1, ins. #1, line 2)

b) *RB MḤNT*
"commander in chief"
(N.Pu. Leptis Magna: KAI/I p. 22, ins. #120, line 1)

Bibl. ANET 653; Branden 101; Harris 102; KAI/II 2, 36, 126; JNES 26 (1967) 15-16; Slouszch 131, 218; DISO 147.

MḤSM B.Heb. *MaḤSōM* "muzzle"; N.Heb. *ḤaSōM*. 1. "muzzle" n.m.

a) *WMḤSM ḤRṢ LPY*
"and a muzzle of gold upon my mouth"
(Ph. Byblos: KAI/I p. 2, ins. #11, line 2)

Bibl. Harris 103; DISO 147; Slouszch 340; KAI/II 15; PPG 96.

MḤSP J.Aram. *ḤaSPaʾ* "potsherd"; Akk. *ḪaṢBu* "clay pot, potsherd"; Syriac *ḤaṢP̄aʾ*; Mandaic *HaSPaʾ*; Arabic *ḪaZaFuN* "pottery". 1. "pottery" n.m.

a) *ḤLṢBʿL BN BʿLḤNʾ ḤRT BMḤSP*
"*ḤLṢBʿL* son of *BʿLḤNʾ* (the) engraver upon (?) pottery (?)"
(Pu. Carthage: CIS I, ins. #6002, line 2)

Bibl. Harris 103; DISO 147; Slouszch 208; EI VIII 276.

MḤSR B.Heb. *MaḤSōR* "need, lack". 1. "want" n.m.

a) *BʿGL ʾŠ QRNY LMBMḤSR*
"for a calf whose horns are wanting"
(Pu. Marseilles: KAI/I p. 15, ins. #69, line 5)

MḤṢRT B.Heb. *ḤāṢiR* "green grass, herbage"; Akk. *ḪaṢa/eRTu* "green wool, mucous"; J.Aram. *ḤaṢiRa'* "moss"; Arabic *ḪuḌRaTuN* "herbage". 1. "herbage" n.f.

a) *[B']RṢT HMḤṢRT ŠL'*
"[in] his [l]ands of herbage"
(N.Pu. Cherchel: KAI/I p. 29, ins. #161, line 10)

Bibl. KAI/II 150; DISO 95.

MḤṢB Heb. *ḤāṢaB* "to hew out," *MaḤṢaB* "quarry"; J.Aram. *ḤaṢaB* "to hew out," *MaḤṢBa'* "quarry". 1. "quarry" n.m.

a) *BL' BN KLM BN Y'ZR ŠMR MḤṢB*
"*BL'* son of *KLM* son of *Y'ZR*, guardian of the quarry"
(Pu. Malta: KAI/I p. 14, ins. #62, line 7)

Bibl. Amadasi 24; Harris 104; KAI/II 78; DISO 148.

MḤQ N.Heb. *MāḤaQ* "to scrape, erase". 1. "scraper" n.m.

a) *'Z[R]B'L HMḤQ*
"*'Z[R]B'L* the scraper"
(Ph. Kition: Slouszch p. 90, ins. #74, line 2)

Bibl. DISO 95; NE 307; Harris 117.

MḤŠB B.Heb. *ḤiŠŠeB* "to reckon, account". 1. "accountant" n.m.

a) *W'NŠ HMḤŠBM 'Š LN*
"may our accountants impose a fine"
(Pu. Carthage: CRAI [1968] p. 117, line 7)

b) *[']BDMLQRT HNG[R] ŠMḤŠBM*
"*[']BDMLQRT*, the carpent[er] of the accountants"
(Pu. Carthage: CIS I, ins. #5547, lines 4-5)

Bibl. CRAI (1968) 131.

MḤTT Heb. *MaḤTā* "coal pan"; J.Aram. *MaḤTiTa'*. 1. "coal pan" n.f.

a) *ŠQL MḤTT*
"the weighers of the coal pans (?)"
(Pu. Carthage: CRAI [1968] p. 117, line 5)

Bibl. RSO 43 (1968) 13; CRAI (1968) 128.

MṬ Heb. *MaṬā* "downwards"; Ph. *MṬ* (N.Pu. *MT'*). 1. "downwards" adv.

a) *'L YKN LM ŠRŠ LMṬ WPRY LM'L* "may they have no stock downwards or branches upwards" (Ph. Sidon: KAI/I p. 3, ins. #14, lines 11-12)

b) *QR' LMM'L' MT'* "read from upwards downwards" (N.Pu. Maktar: KAI/I p. 27, ins. #145, line 14)

Bibl. Harris 124; Slouszch 23; PPG 17, 124; DISO 148; ANET 662; NE 308.

MṬBḤ Heb. *MiṬBaḤ* "slaughtering place"; Akk. *NaṬBaḤu* "slaughter house"; J.Aram. *MaṬBaḤaYY'* "slaughtering place"; Arabic *MaṬBaḤuN* "kitchen". 1. "slaughtering place" n.m.

a) *HMTBḤ Z DL P'MM* "this slaughtering place deficient with regard to feet" (Pu. Carthage: KAI/I p. 17, ins. #80, line 1)

Bibl. DISO 148; Harris 105; Slouszch 162; KAI/II 98.

MṬḤ I Heb. *ṬūaḤ* "to coat, to plaster"; Ug. *ṬḪ* "to plaster"; J.Aram. *ṬaḤ* "to overspread"; Mandaic *ṬH'* "to squeeze"; Arabic *ṬaḪa* "to oversmear". 1. "plastering" n.m.

a) *W'L MLKT HMṬḤ* "and over the labor of plastering" (N.Pu. Bir Bou-Rekba: KAI/I p. 26, ins. #137, line 3)

Bibl. DISO 148; KAI/II 136; Harris 105; Slouszch 209.

MṬḤ II (see previous entry for etymology). 1. "plasterer" n.m.

a) *['B]DKŠR HMṬḤ* "*['B]DKŠR* the plasterer" (Pu. Sardinia: Amadasi p. 109, ins. #32, lines 8-9)

Bibl. Amadasi 112.

MṬN' B.Heb. *ṬeNe'* "basket"; N.Heb. *ṬeNi* "large metal vessel". 1. "offering" n.m.

a) *HMṬN' [Z] YṬN['T] 'NK* "[this] offering I...offered" (Ph. Egypt: KAI/I p. 11, ins. #48, line 1)

b) *MṬN' 'Z P'L B'LYTN BN D'MLK*
"this offering *B'LYTN* son of *D'MLK* made"
(Ph. Spain: Amadasi p. 150, ins. #16, lines 1-2)

c) *MṬN'*
"offering"
(Ph. Egypt: ESE III, p. 125, line 1)

Bibl. Harris 105; OrAnt 8 (1968) 22; KAI/II 64; DISO 149; PPG 96; Slouszch 52-53.

MY Heb. *Mī* interrogative pr.; Ug. *MY*; Amar.Akk. *MiYa*. 1. indefinite pr. 2. in combinations.

1 a) *MY 'T KL 'DM*
"whoever you are, any man"
(Ph. Sidon: KAI/I p. 2, ins. #13, line 3)

b) *LMY KT 'B WLMY KT 'M WLMY KT 'H*
"to some I was a father, to some I was a mother, to some I was a brother"
(Ph. Zinjirli: KAI/I p. 5, ins. #24, lines 10-11)

c) *WMY BL ḤZ PN Š*
"and whoever had never seen the face of a sheep"
(Ph. Zinjirli: KAI/I p. 4, ins. #24, line 11)

d) *WMY BBNY*
"and whoever among my sons"
(Ph. Zinjirli: KAI/I p. 4, ins. #24, lines 13-14)

e) *WMY YŠḤT HSPR Z*
"he who ruins this inscription"
(Ph. Zinjirli: KAI/I p. 4, ins. #24, line 15)

2 a) *QNMY 'T KL MMLKT WKL 'DM*
"whoever you are, any prince and any men"
(Ph. Sidon: KAI/I p. 3, ins. #14, line 20)

Bibl. NE 308; EHO 18; ANET 654, 662; Harris 117, 144; DISO 149; Branden 62; KAI/II 17, 31; PPG 54-55; Slouszch 16, 20.

MYṬB Heb. *MeṬeB* "the choice of"; J.Aram. *MeṬBa'* "of the best". 1. "best (of)" n.m.

a) *HPRṬ 'L MYṬB 'RŠ' HṠLKY* (my letter division) "the provider (?) for the best wishes of the (senators) of *SLKY*" (N.Pu. Sardinia: KAI/I p. 31, ins. #172, line 2)

Bibl. Amadasi 130-31; KAI/II 156; Harris 106; DISO 149; PPG 42, 105.

MYNKD etymology unknown. 1. "imperial leader" n.m. (from context)

a) *MYNKD Q'YSR 'WGSṬS* "the emperor Caesar Augustus" (N.Pu. Leptis Magna: KAI/I p. 22, ins. #120, line 1)

b) *WMYNKD P'M'T 'SR W'RB'* "and the emperor for the fourteenth time" (N.Pu. Leptis Magna: KAI/I p. 22, ins. #120, line 1)

c) *LMYNKD Q'YSR 'DNB'L BN 'RŠ* "for the emperor *'DNB'L*, son of *'RŠ*" (N.Pu. Leptis Magna: KAI/I p. 22, ins. #120, line 2)

Bibl. KAI/II 126; DISO 149; PPG 100.

MY'MS etymology and meaning unknown. 1. "command" n.m. (from context)

a) *LMY'MS 'M QRT* "according to the command (?) of the people of the city (of Carthage)" (Pu. Carthage: CIS I, ins. #270, line 3)

b) *LMY'MS 'M QRTḤDŠT* "according to the command (?) of the people of *QRTḤDŠT*" (Pu. Carthage: CIS I, ins. #4903, line 4)

Bibl. DISO 149; Slouszch 251; Harris 115.

MYP'L B.Heb. *MiP'āL* "work". 1. "employ" n.m.

a) *BMYP'L 'DN 'ŠMNHLS* "in the employ (?) of lord *'ŠMNḤLṢ*" (Pu. Carthage: CIS I, ins. #5522, lines 2-3)

**MKBRT*

B.Heb. *MiKBāR* "grating or lattice work"; N.Heb. *MaKBeRā* "sieve"; Akk. *NaKMaRu* "type of cultic basket". 1. type of cultic strainer n.f.

a) *TZNM 'L M'KBRT*
"*TZNM* (who) is over the cultic strainers (?)"
(N.Pu. Cherchel: KAI/I p. 28, ins. #161, line 7)

Bibl. DISO 150; KAI/II 150.

MKN

B.Heb. *MāKōN* "fixed or established place, foundation"; Ug. *MKNT* "place"; ESArab. *MKNT*; Arabic *MaKāNuN*; Ph. *MKN* (N.Pu. *M'KN*). 1. "base" n.m. 2. "place"

1 a) *M'Š HNḤŠT 'L M'KN'*
"the bronze statue upon its base"
(N.Pu. Leptis Magna: KAI/I p. 22, ins. #119, line 4)

2 a) *L'DM 'Š LQḤ MKN BM QP'* [ ]
"for the man who took his place (?) with him [ ] *QP'*"
(Ph. Kition: Or 37 [1968] p. 305, line B 7)

Bibl. KAI/II 124; DISO 150; Or 37 (1968) 322.

MKS' I

B.Heb. *MiKSeh* "covering"; Ug. *MKS* "cover, garment"; N.Heb. *MiKSeh* "tent, covering". 1. "covering" n.m.

a) *BWṢ WMKS'*
"byssus and a covering"
(Pu. Carthage: CIS I, ins. #166A, line 6)

Bibl. DISO 150; NSI 126; KAI/II 93; PPG 97; Harris 112; Slouszch 168; NE 298.

MKS' II

C.S. (denominative Q part. from the C.S. noun *KS'*). 1. "chair maker" n.m.

a) *HMKS'M 'Š B'MQ QRT*
"the chair makers who are in the plain of the city"
(Pu. Carthage: CRAI [1968] p. 117, line 5)

Bibl. Dahood III XXXIII; CRAI (1968) 127; RSO 43 (1968) 13.

MKST Heb. *MeKes* "tax"; Akk. *MiKSu*; Emp.Aram. *MKS*; J.Aram. *MiKSa'*; Syriac *MiKSa'*; Arabic *MaKSuN*. 1. "tax" n.f.

a) *MKST*
"the taxes (?)"
(Ph. Byblos: MUSJ 45 [1969] p. 262, line 4)

Bibl. MUSJ 45 (1969) 270.

MKR Heb. *MāKaR* "to sell"; Ug. *MKR* "merchant"; Akk. *MaKKāRu*; Syriac *MeKaR* "to betrothe"; J.Aram. *MeKaR*; Mandaic *MKR*; ESArab. *MKR* "to sell". 1. "to sell" vb. 2. "merchant" (seller)

1 a) *KL 'DM 'Š YMKR*
"all men who sell"
(Pu. Carthage: KAI/I p. 16, ins. #75, line 5)

b) *WKMST ŠḤ[]T ŠYMKR'*
"and according to the ti[me] (?) in which they will sell"
(N.Pu. Tripolitania: Or 33 [1964] p. 4, lines 4-5)

2 a) *'ŠMNḤLṢ BN...MKR HŠ[ ]*
"*'ŠMNḤLṢ* son of (?) the seller of (?)"
(Pu. Carthage: Slouszch p. 252, ins. #303, line 3)

b) *BḊ[']ŠTRT BN ['BD']LM MKR 'QṬRT*
"*BD'ŠTRT* son of *'BD'LM*, seller of incense"
(Pu. Carthage: Slouszch p. 337, ins. #555, line 3)

c) *ZYBQ MKR HPL*
"*ZYBQ*, seller of beans (?)"
(Pu. Carthage: Slouszch p. 349, ins. #578, lines 2-3)

d) [ ]*RT BN PTR' MKR HQN' ZK'*
"[ ]*RT* son of *PTR'*, the seller of pure reed"
(Pu. Carthage: Slouszch p. 337, ins. #557, lines 1-2)

Bibl. Harris 117; KAI/II 93; Or 33 (1964) 12; DISO 150.

ML Heb. *Millā* "word, utterance"; J.Aram. *MiLTa'* "action, cause, word"; Syriac *MaLaLaYuTa'* "utterance"; Mandaic *MaLaLa'*.
1. "utterance" n.f. 2. "word"

1 a) *ŠM' ML' BDK'* (error for *BRK'*)
"he has heard his word(s) and blessed him"
(N.Pu. Tunisia: JA Series 11 vol. 8 [1917] p. 149, ins. #6, lines 3-4)

2 a) *'L MLY 'Š NDRT*
"for my word which I vowed"
(N.Pu. Constantine: ZDMG 12 [1863] p. 654, line 3)

Bibl. ZDMG 17 (1863) 656-57.

ML' C.S. 1. "to fill" vb.

a) *WML' 'NK 'QRT P'R*
"and I filled the storehouse (?) of *P'R*"
(Ph. Karatepe: KAI/I p. 5, ins. #26, line A I,6)

Bibl. KAI/II 36; ANET 653; PPG 80.

ML'K Heb. *MaL'āK* "messenger"; Ug. *ML'K;* J.Aram. *MaL'aKa';* Syriac *MaLa'Ka';* Arabic *MaLa'KuN;* Amh. *MaLaK.* 1. "envoy" n.m.

a) *'Š BN H'LM ML'K MLK'ŠTRT*
"which the chiefs, the envoys of *MLK'ŠTRT* built"
(Ph. Ma'ṣub: KAI/I p. 4, ins. #19, lines 2-3)

b) *WML'K MLK'ŠTRT*
"and the envoys of *MLK'ŠTRT*"
(Ph. Umm el-Awamid: Dunand/Duru p. 192, ins. #13, line 3)

Bibl. DISO 151; Harris 114; NE 309; KAI/II 27.

ML'KT Heb. *MeL'āKā* "occupation, work"; Ph. *ML'KT* (Ph., N.Pu. *MLKT*). 1. "cultic service" n.f. 2. "work"

1 a) *LGLBM P'LM 'L ML'KT*
"for the barbers carrying out the cultic service"
(Ph. Kition: KAI/I p. 8, ins. #37, line A 13)

2 a) *WKL 'DM 'Š YSP LP'L ML'KT 'LT MZBḤ ZN*
"and men who (continue) to add work upon this altar"
(Ph. Byblos: KAI/I p. 2, ins ins. #10, lines 11-12)

b) *MṬN'M 'L HMLKT*
"appointed over this work"
(Pu. Carthage: KAI/I p. 19, ins. #96, line 5)

c) *KN' 'L MLKT HBN'*
"there was (appointed) over the labor of construction"
(N.Pu. Bir Bou-Rekba: KAI/I p. 26, ins. #137, line 2)

d) *'L 'RB MLKT HMQM*
"in exchange for labor (furnished) for the temple"
(N.Pu. Leptis Magna: KAI/I p. 22, ins. #119, line 7)

e) *LMBMLKTM BTM*
"his work at his (own) expense"
(N.Pu. Leptis Magna: KAI/I p. 23, ins. #124, line 2)

f) *MZBḤ WP'DY P'L LMBMLKTM BTM*
"he made the altar and podium, his work at his (own) expense"
(N.Pu. Leptis Magna: KAI/I p. 24, ins. #126, lines 10-11)

Bibl. DISO 151; Harris 114; PPG 10, 13, 96-97; Branden 4; KAI/II 12, 54, 105, 124, 130, 136; ANET 656.

MLḤ I Heb. *MāLaḤ* "to salt, to brine"; [Ug. *MLḤ* "to be good"]; J.Aram. *MeLaḤ* "to salt, to brine"; Syriac *MeLaḤ* "to be salt, to season with salt"; Arabic *MaLaḤa* "to become salt (water), [to become good, pretty]". 1. "salt worker" n.m.

a) *BN 'ZRB'L BN [ ] 'MMLḤ*
"son of *'ZRB'L* son of (?) the salt worker"
(Pu. Carthage: CIS I, ins. #351, line 4)

Bibl. Slouszch 316; Harris 117; NE 309; DISO 155.

MLḤ II Heb. *MaLLāḤ* "sailor"; Akk. *MaLāḪu* "sailor" (Sum. L.W. *Má-LaḪu* "boat-maker"); J.Aram. *MaLLāḤa'* "sailor, mariner"; Syriac *MaLāḤa'* "sailor, salt"; Mandaic *MaLaHa'*; Arabic *MaLāḤuN* "sailor". 1. "sailor" n.m.

a) *BN ṢNR HMLḤM*
"son of *ṢNR*, the sailor(s)"
(Ph. Egypt: KAI/I p. 11, ins. #49, line 2)

b) *L'GD LM MLḤM*
"the sailors did gather together for themselves"
(Ph. Byblos: MUSJ 45 [1969] p. 262, line 2)

Bibl. KAI/II 65; Slouszch 341; DISO 152; Harris 117; LS I 349.

MLK I   C.S. 1. "king of a country" n.m. 2. "king over a city" 3. "king of an ethnic group"

1 a) *WŠKR 'NK 'LY MLK 'ŠR*
"and I hired against him the king of *'ŠR*"
(Ph. Zinjirli: KAI/I p. 5, ins. #24, lines 7-8)

b) *'ŠMN'ZR MLK ṢDNM*
"*'ŠMN'ZR*, king of the *ṢDNM*"
(Ph. Sidon: KAI/I p. 3, ins. #14, line 1)

c) *BN MLK TBNT MLK ṢDNM*
"son of king *TBNṬ*, king of the *ṢDNM*"
(Ph. Sidon: KAI/I p. 3, ins. #14, line 2)

d) *'N'L MLK GBL*
"*'N'L* king of *GBL*"
(Ph. Byblos: Slouszch p. 14, ins. #6A, line 1)

e) *YḤWMLK MLK GBL*
"*YḤWMLK* king of *GBL*"
(Ph. Byblos: KAI/I p. 2, ins. #10, line 1)

2 a) *TBRY' WLNŠ MLK 'L KYŠRY'*
"*TBRY' WLNŠ* king over *KYŠRY'*"
(Ph. Pyrgi: KAI/I p. 53, ins. #277, lines 3-4)

3 a) *'WRK MLK DNNYM*
"*'WRK* king of the *DNNYM*"
(Ph. Karatepe: KAI/I p. 5, ins. #26, line A I,2)

b) *MKWSN MLK [M]ŠLYYM*
"*MKWSN* king of the *[M]ŠLYYM*"
(N.Pu. Cherchel: KAI/I p. 29, ins. #161, line 1)

Bibl. Harris 118; Benz 344-45; NE 310-11; KAI/II 12, 17, 19, 31, 150; ANET 653-54, 662; Amadasi 164; DISO 153; Leš 31 (1967) 85-96.

MLK II   C.S. 1. "to rule" vb.

a) *MLK GBR 'L Y'DY*
"*GBR* ruled over *Y'DY*"
(Ph. Zinjirli: KAI/I p. 4, ins. #24, line 2)

b) *BŠNT 2 LMLKY 'L KTY W'DYL*
"in the second year of his rule over *KTY* and *'DYL*"
(Ph. Idalion: KAI/I p. 3, ins. #38, line 2)

c) *BŠNT 'SR W'RB LMLKY*
"in the fourteenth year of his rule"
(Ph. Sidon: KAI/I p. 3, ins. #14, line 1)

d) *B'ḤT 'RB'M ŠT LMLKY*
"in the forty-first year of his rule"
(Ph. Constantine: Berthier/Charlier p. 51, ins. #56, lines 3-4)

e) *BŠŠT ḤMŠM ŠT LMLKY MSNSN*
"in the fifty-sixth year of his rule, of *MSNSN*"
(Ph. Constantine: Berthier/Charlier p. 59, ins. #63, lines 4-5)

f) *BŠT 'SRM W'ḤT LMLKM*
"in the twenty-first year of his rule"
(N.Pu. Dschebel Massoudj: KAI/I p. 26, ins. #141, lines 3-4)

Bibl. Harris 117; PPG 63, 88; DISO 152-53; ANET 662; Berthier/Charlier 52, 59; KAI/II 19, 31, 56, 139.

MLK III "kingdom" n.m.

a) *BŠNT 31 L'DN MLKM PTLMYS*
"in the thirty-first year of the Lord of Kingdoms, *PTLMYS*"
(Ph. Idalion: KAI/I p. 9, ins. #40, line 1)

b) *'Š BŠNT 11 L'DN MLKM PTLMYŠ*
"which is the eleventh year of the Lord of Kingdoms, *PTLMYŠ*"
(Ph. Larnaka: KAI/I p. 10, ins. #43, line 4)

c) *THTPK KS' MLKH*
"may the throne of kingdom be overturned"
(Ph. Byblos: KAI/I p. 1, ins. #1, line 2)

d) *BŠT 180 L'DN MLKM*
"in the one hundred and eightieth year of the Lords of Kingdoms"
(Ph. Umm el-Awamid: KAI/I pp. 3-4, ins. #18, lines 4-5)

Bibl. AJSL 57 (1940) 71-74; KAI/II 2, 26, 57, 60; Harris 118; PPG 109.

MLK IV   Heb. *MoLeK* "type of offering".
1. type of offering n.m.

a) *L'DN LB'L MTNT MTNT' MLK B'L*
"for the lord, for *B'L*, a gift; his gift is a *MLK B'L* sacrifice"
(Ph. Sousse: KAI/I p. 19, ins. #99, lines 1-2)

b) *NṢB MLK 'MR 'Š Š[M 'R]Š LB'L [ḤMN]*
"a pillar (upon which) [*'R*]*Š* p[ut] a *MLK 'MR* sacrifice for *B'L* [*ḤMN*]"
(Pu. Malta: KAI/I p. 14, ins. #61, lines B 1-2)

c) *L'DN LB'L ḤMN MLK 'DM*
"for the lord for *B'L ḤMN*, a *MLK 'DM* sacrifice"
(N.Pu. Constantine: KAI/I p. 20, ins. #103, lines 1-2)

d) *L'DN LBḤL ḤMN MLK 'DM*
"for the lord for *B'L ḤMN*, a *MLK 'DM* sacrifice"
(N.Pu. Constantine: KAI/I p. 21, ins. #106, lines 1-2)

e) *ML'K 'MR 'Š NDR YŠD'*
"a *ML'K 'MR* sacrifice which *YŠD'* vowed"
(Pu. Constantine: Berthier/Charlier p. 49, ins. #54, lines 2-3)

Bibl. DISO 154; Albright 205-12; Harris 118; Berthier/Charlier 50-51; KAI/II 76, 107, 114-15; Benz 20-23; deVaux 73-90; Slouszch 222; LS I 85-122; ANET 658.

MLKYT   B.Heb. *MaLKūT* "royalty, royal power"; B.Aram. *MaLKū* "kingdom"; Anc.Aram. *MLKT* "royalty"; N.Heb. *MaLKūT* "kingdom, office, government"; J.Aram. *MaLKūTa'* "kingdom, rulership"; Mandaic *MaLKuTa'* "government, kingship"; Syriac *MaLKūTa'* "reign, majesty, kingdom".
1. "royalty" n.f.

a) *KM 'Š LMLKYT 'Š KN LPNY*
"as with the royalty which was before me"
(Ph. Byblos: KAI/I p. 2, ins. #11, line 2)

Bibl. Slouszch 340; DISO 154; PPG 98, 108; Harris 118; KAI/II 15-16.

MLKT   C.S. 1. "queen" n.f.

a) *HMLKT BT MLK 'ŠMN'ZR*
"the queen, daughter of king *'ŠMN'ZR*"
(Ph. Sidon: KAI/I p. 3, ins. #14, line 15)

b) *MLKT QDŠT*
"the holy queen"
(Ph. Kition: CIS I, ins. #86, line A 7).

Bibl. KAI/II 19, 54; Slouszch 24, 78; Harris 118; ANET 662; DISO 153.

MLṢ I — perhaps related etymologically to *MLṢ* II. 1. type of spokesman n.m.

a) *B'BR B'L W'LM WŠBRT MLṢM*
"by the grace of *B'L* and the gods and the report(s) (?) of the messengers (?)"
(Ph. Karatepe: KAI/I p. 5, ins. #26, line A I,8)

Bibl. LS I 75-76; Tur-Sinai 127-28, 270; ANET 653; KAI/II 36; DISO 138; PPG 78; VT 5 (1955) 169; AJSL 40 (1924) 137.

MLṢ II — Heb. *MeLīṢ* "interpreter, one who speaks in behalf of or in defense of someone else"; Q.Heb. *MLYṢ* "spokesman"; Ph., Pu. *MLṢ* (Pu. *MLS*). 1. "interpreter" n.m.

a) *RŠPYTN MLṢ HKRSYM*
"*RŠPYTN* interpreter of the *KRSYM*"
(Ph. Kition: CIS I, ins. #44, line 2)

b) *'BDŠMN HMLṢ*
"*'BDŠMN* the interpreter"
(Pu. Carthage: CIS I, ins. #350, lines 3-4)

c) *B'LYTN BN MGN 'MLS*
"*B'LYTN* son of *MGN* the interpreter"
(Pu. Constantine: Berthier/Charlier p. 117, ins. #163, line 3)

Bibl. DISO 127, 138; Harris 114; Slouszch 84-85, 319; Tur-Sinai 269-70; PPG 20, 78; Branden 98; VT 5 (1955) 169; AJSL 40 (1924) 137.

MLQḤ — B.Heb. *MeLQāḤaYYiM* "tongs"; Ug. *MQḤM*; ESArab *MLQḤ* "chain". 1. "tongs" n.m.

a) *B'LḤN' BN ḤML[KT P'L M]LQḤM*
"*B'LḤN'* son of *ḤML[KT*, maker of t]ongs"
(Pu. Carthage: Slouszch p. 265, ins. #339, line 3)

b) *'RŠ BN 'KBR 'RG 'MLQḤ*
"*'RŠ* son of *'KBR*, sharpener (?) of the tongs (?)"
(Pu. Carthage: Slouszch p. 243, ins. #279, lines 3-4)

Bibl. DISO 155; Harris 115; NE 304.

MMLKT Heb. *MaMLāKā* "kingdom, royalty" (?); Mandaic *MaMLaKa'*; Arabic *MaMLaKaTuN*; Ph., Pu. *MMLKT* (N.Pu. *MMLK'T*).
1. "ruler" n.f. 2. "prince"

1 a) *MMLKT 'L GBL*
"ruler over *GBL*"
(Ph. Byblos: KAI/I p. 2, ins. #10, line 2)

b) *'YT HMMLKT H'*
"that ruler"
(Ph. Karatepe: KAI/I p. 5, ins. #26, line A III,19)

2 a) *BŠB'T '[SRT] ŠT LMLKY [MSN]SN HMMLKT*
"in the sevent[eenth] year of his rule, of [*MSN*]*SN*, the prince"
(Ph. Constantine: Berthier/Charlier p. 57, ins. #61, lines 3-5)

b) *'PŠN HMMLKT RBT*
"*'PŠN* the great prince"
(Pu. Dougga: KAI/I p. 20, ins. #101, line 2)

c) *MYŠR 'RṢT RBT MMLK'T*
"the bringer of prosperity to the great lands, prince"
(N.Pu. Cherchel: KAI/I p. 29, ins. #161, line 2)

Bibl. DISO 155; KAI/II 12, 36, 150; Harris 118; Slouszch 11; ANET 653-54; Leš 36 (1972) 249-56; PPG 99, 154.

MN C.S. (except ESArab., Akk. and Ug.).
1. partitively (in the sense of coming out, removing or expelling) 2. of time, marking the terminus a quo, the anterior limit of a continuous period of time 3. from that, which 4. in a geographic or local sense 5. in compounds

1 a) *[S]MLT '[Z] 'Š YTN WYṬN' MNḤŠT*
"th[is] [im]age of bronze (is that) which...offered and set up)
(Ph. Kition: Slouszch p. 70, ins. #60, line 2)

b) *MB'L ṢYṢ*
"from the citizens of *ṢYṢ*"
(Ph. Sicily: Slouszch p. 130, ins. #112, line 1)

2 a) *WMY BL ḤZ KTN LMN'RY*
"and whoever had never seen linen since his youth"
(Ph. Zinjirli: KAI/I p. 5, ins. #24, line 12)

b) *MṢBT LMBḤYY YṬN'T*
"a monument, during my lifetime
I erected"
(Ph. Kition: KAI/I p. 8,
ins. #35, lines 1-2)

3 a) *M'Š P'LT*
"from that which I did"
(Ph. Zinjirli: KAI/I p. 5,
ins. #24, line 4)

4 a) *LMMṢ' ŠMŠ W'D MB'Y*
"from the rising of the sun (east)
until its setting (west)"
(Ph. Karatepe: KAI/I p. 5,
ins. #26, lines A I,4-5)

b) *'NK MGN BN BḌ' ŠḤPṢB'L MNP*
"I am *MGN* son of *BḌ'* (who)
belongs to *ḤPṢB'L* of *NP*"
(Ph. Egypt: KAI/I p. 12,
ins. #49, line 36)

c) *'Š NDR 'BD'ŠMN BṆ M'DR 'Š KN'N MQRML*
"that which *'BD'ŠMN* son of *M'DR*
the man of *KN'N* from *QRML* vowed"
(Pu. Constantine: KAI/I p. 21,
ins. #116, line 4)

5 a) *B'GL 'Š QRNY LMBMḤSR*
"for a calf whose horns are
wanting"
(Pu. Marseilles: KAI/I p. 15,
ins. #69, line 5)

b) *LMBYRḤ ḤYR*
"from the month of *ḤYR*"
(Pu. Carthage: KAI/I p. 17,
ins. #81, line 5)

c) *G'Y BN ḤN' LMBŠM G'Y BN BNM M'QR*
"*G'Y*, son of *ḤN'*, in the name of
G'Y grandson of *M'QR*"
(N.Pu. Leptis Magna: KAI/I p. 23,
ins. #124, line 1)

d) *TMNM DN'RY' ŠMNM WKT/DRM TŠ' LMB'NŠM*
"their total, eighty *DN'RY'* and
nine *KT/NDRM* as their tax"
(N.Pu. Leptis Magna: KAI/I p. 25,
ins. #130, line 2)

e) *LMBMLKTM BTM*
"at his own cost"
(N.Pu. Leptis Magna: KAI/I p. 23,
ins. #124, line 2)

f) *LMB'BN 'Š 'L HSYẆ'T*
"from the stone which is over
the tomb (?)"
(N.Pu. Dschebel Massoudj: KAI/I
p. 26, ins. #141, line 4)

g) *QR' LMM'L' MT'*
"read from upwards downwards"
(N.Pu. Maktar: KAI/I p. 27, ins. #145, line 14)

Bibl. DISO 155-57; Harris 120; KAI/II 12, 31, 36, 65, 83, 98, 119, 130, 139; Amadasi 169; PPG 127; Branden 117-18; ANET 656.

MNḤ Heb. *MeNūḤā* "rest," *MaNōaḤ*; Ug. *MNḤ* [Soq. *MeNaḤa* "war"]; Nab. *NYḤ'* "resting place"; Palm. *NYḤ* "tomb"; Akk. *MaNaḪTu* "resting place". 1. "rest" n.m.

a) *ŠLM WMNḤ*
"peace and rest"
(Pu. Carthage: CIS I, ins. #5511, line 4)

MNḤT Heb. *MiNḤā* "offering"; Ug. *MNḤ* "offering"; Emp.Aram. *MNḤT* "offering to a god"; J.Aram. *MiNḤaTa'* "offering, meal offering"; Arabic *MiNḤaTuN* "gift, loan of money". 1. "offering" n.f.

a) *HMNḤT Z 'Š YTN 'BDMSKR*
"this offering (is that) which *'BDMSKR* offered"
(Ph. Tyre: ESE I, p. 16, line 1)

b) *MNḤT 2 'L*
"these two offerings"
(Ph. Kition: CIS I, ins. #14, line 5)

c) *W'L KL ZBḤ 'Š 'DM LZBḤ BMNḤ[T]*
"for every sacrifice which a man would sacrifice as an offer[ing]"
(Ph. Marseilles: KAI/I p. 15, ins. #69, line 14)

d) *ṢM'T HMZRḤ 'Š 'YKRM' T HMNḤT*
"the names of the citizens council (?) who devoted (?) the offerings(s)"
(N.Pu. Maktar: KAI/I p. 27, ins. #145, lines 12-13)

Bibl. DISO 159; Harris 120; Amadasi 169; Slouszch 73, 148; ANET 655; KAI/II 83, 141; NE 313; Levine 116.

MNY Heb. *MāNā* "to count number"; Akk. *MaNū*; Ug. *MNY*; ESArab. *MNW*; Emp.Aram. *MNH*; J.Aram. *MeNa'*; Syriac *MeNa'*; Nab. *MN(Y)*; Mandaic *MN'*; Arabic *MaNa* "to assign". 1. "to count" vb.

a) *MN' ḤMŠ PRṢM*
"he counted five *PRṢM*"
(N.Pu. Tripolitania: Or 33 [1964] p. 4, line 5)

Bibl. Or 33 (1964) 12; PPG 82.

MNM B.Heb. *Me'ūMā* "anything, something"; Ug. *MNM* "whatever, whoever," "rhyton"; Akk. *MeNuMMe* "any, anything"; [J.Aram. *Mā'Na'* "vessel"; Syriac *Mā'Na'* "vessel, garment"; B.Aram. *Mā'Na'* "instrument, utensil"; Mandaic *MaNa'* "implement, garment"].
1. "anything, nothing" indefinite pr.
2. "vessel" n.m. (i.e., "thing")

1 a) *W'L YBQŠ BN MNM*
"and may he not seek anything within it"
(Ph. Sidon: KAI/I p. 3, ins. #14, lines 4-5)

b) *K 'Y ŠM BN MNM*
"because there is nothing placed in it"
(Ph. Sidon: KAI/I p. 3, ins. #14, line 5)

c) *BL YKN LKHN MNM*
"nothing shall go to the priest"
(Pu. Carthage: KAI/I p. 16, ins. #74, line 6)

2 a) *WDL KL MNM*
"and with all vessels (?)"
(or "everything")
(Pu. Carthage: KAI/I p. 17, ins. #81, line 3)

Bibl. KAI/II 17, 19, 92, 98; JBL 56 (1937) 140; DISO 159; Harris 120; PPG 55; Branden 62; ANET 132, note 14, 662; Or 8 (1938) 275, note 32.

MN'L Heb. *MaN'ūL* "bolt". 1. "bolt" n.m.

a) *N'LT MN'L*
"I have fastened the bolt"
(Ph. Arslan Tash: BASOR 209 [1973] p. 19, rev. line 1)

Bibl. Syria 48 (1971) 404.

MN'M B.Heb. *MaNa'M* "dainties" (Ps. 141:4).
1. "well being" n.m.

a) *BŠB' WBMN'M*
"with corn and well being"
(Ph. Karatepe: KAI/I p. 5, ins. #26, lines A II,12-13)

b) *WKN BKL YMTY ŠB' WMN'M*
"and in all my days there was corn and well being"
(Ph. Karatepe: KAI/I p. 5, ins. #26, line A II,7)

Bibl. DISO 159; ANET 653; LS I 78; KAI/II 36.

MNT Ug. *MNT* formula for conjuration; Akk. *MiNūTu*. 1. "spell" n.f.

a) *MNTY KMGLT*
"my/his spell is like the scrolls"
(Ph. Arslan Tash: BASOR 209 [1973] p. 19, rev. line 7)

Bibl. BASOR 209 (1973) 26; Syria 48 (1971) 406.

MSWYT B.Heb. *MaSWeh* "veil, mask". 1. "covering" n.f.

a) *WMSWY'T ŠHNSKT*
"and the coverings of the statues"
(N.Pu. Leptis Magna: KAI/I p. 23, ins. #122, line 2)

Bibl. KAI/II 128; DISO 160; PPG 108.

MSK I etymology and meaning unknown.
1. "few" adj. m. (from context)

a) *BN MSK YMM 'ZRM*
"son of limited cursed days (?)"
(Ph. Sidon: KAI/I p. 3, ins. #14, line 3)

Bibl. DISO 160; Harris 120; ANET 662; KAI/II 19; Albright-Fs 260.

MSK II (for etymology, see under *NSK*). N.Heb. *MāSeK* "to cast (metal)". 1. "coppersmith" n.m.

a) *BD'ŠTRT MSK HNḤŠT*
"*BD'ŠTRT* the coppersmith"
(Pu. Carthage: CIS I, ins. #330, lines 3-4)

b) *MSK HNḤŠT*
"coppersmith"
(Pu. Carthage: CIS I, ins. #331, lines 2-3)

Bibl. Slouszch 287; DISO 180; Leš 33 (1968-69) 72-73.

MSK III B.Heb. *NeSeK* "molten image" (Is. 41:29).
1. "molten image" n.m.

a) *MSK LMGN BN ḤNB'L*
"an image of *MGN* son of *ḤNB'L*"
(Ph. Tharros: CIS I, ins. #153, line 1)

Bibl. Slouszch 138; DISO 160.

MSKT Heb. *MaSeKā* "molten image". 1. "molten image" n.f.

a) *WYLK ZBḤ LKL HMSKT*
"and I established (?) a sacrificial order (?) for all the molten images"
(Ph. Karatepe: KAI/I p. 6, ins. #26, lines A II,19)

Bibl. KAI/II 36; ANET 653; DISO 160.

MSPN see under *MSPNT* for comparative data.
1. "ceiling" n.m.

a) *WDLHT ŠNḤŠT WMSPN MH'ṘṖ[T]*
"doors of bronze and the ceiling (?) from the porti[co]"
(N.Pu. Leptis Magna: KAI/I p. 23, ins. #122, line 2)

Bibl. KAI/II 128; DISO 161.

MSPNT B.Heb. *SiPūN* "ceiling"; J.Aram. *SoPNa'* "storeroom"; Amh. *SaFFaNa* "to cover".
1. "roof" n.m.

a) *WHḰ[T]ṘM 'Š 'LHM WMSPNTH*
"the capitals which are upon them, and its roof"
(Ph. Byblos: KAI/I p. 2, ins. #10, line 6)

Bibl. NE 330; Harris 127; DISO 161; KAI/II 12; PPG 48, 96, 113; Slouszch 12; ANET 656.

MSPR Heb. *MiSPāR* "number". 1. "number" n.m.

a) *W'W' Š'NT MSPR Š'T*
"and he lived for years, one in number"
(N.Pu. Toison d'ob: JA Series 11 vol. 10 [1917] p. 21, ins. #2, line 4)

Bibl. DISO 161; Harris 127; JA Series 11 vol. 10 (1917) 22.

MSRW' Heb. *ŚaRu'a* "to be abnormally long" (Lev. 21:18); Ug. *ŠR'* "to surge upwards"; J.Aram. *ŚeRi'a* "to extend abnormally"; Syriac *SeRi'a* "malformed, injured in any way, especially a slit ear"; Arabic *'aSRa'u* "long nosed". 1. "long" n.m. (meaning uncertain)

a) *'RŠM HMSRW' BN ḤN'*
"*'RŠM* the long (?) son of *ḤN'*"
(Pu. Carthage: Slouszch p. 246, ins. #288, lines 3-4)

Bibl. Slouszch 247; DISO 161; Harris 121; LS II 132-33.

MST B.Heb. *MiSSaT* measure of sufficiency; J.Aram. *MiSTa'* "plenty"; Syriac *MeST* "quantity, sufficiency". 1. "quantity" n.f.

a) *WKMST ŠḤ[']T ŠYMKR'*
"and according to the ti[me] (?) in which they will sell"
(N.Pu. Tripolitania: Or 33 [1964] p. 4, lines 4-5)

Bibl. Or 33 (1964) 11-12.

M'WN Heb. *Mā'ōN* "refuge, habitation"; ESArab *M'WN*; Amar.Akk. *Ma'uNNu*. 1. "temple" n.m.

a) *LYŠKT H' 'T M'WN*
"that chamber, with the temple"
(N.Pu. Maktar: BAC [1950] p. 112, line 2)

Bibl. BAC (1950) 111-12; LS I 389, note 1.

M'ZRT Heb. *'eZRā* "help, assistance"; Ug. *'D̲R* "to help, assist"; J.Aram. *'aDaR* "to help"; Syriac *'eDaR* "to help, assist". 1. "assistance" n.f.

a) *LMDT Ṫ M'ŻRT*
"in proportion to the assistance (given)"
(N.Pu. Maktar: KAI/I p. 27, ins. #145, line 15)

Bibl. KAI/II 141; DISO 161.

M'L Heb. *Ma'Lā* "upward, above". 1. "upwards" adv.

a) *'L YKN LM ŠRŠ LMṬ WPRY LM'L*
"may they have no stock downwards or branches upwards"
(Ph. Sidon: KAI/I p. 3, ins. #14, lines 11-12

b) *QR' LMM'L' MT'*
"read from upwards downwards"
(N.Pu. Maktar: KAI/I p. 27, ins. #145, line 14)

Bibl. DISO 162; Harris 133; PPG 127; ANET 662; KAI/II 19, 141.

M'ṢRT Heb. *'āṢaR* "to retain"; Syriac *'aṢaR*; J.Aram. *'aṢaR*. 1. "walled enclosure" n.f. (also see *MṢR*)

a) *KM P'LT M'ṢRT*
"as a work of walled enclosure (?)"
(or "as a fortified construction")
(N.Pu. Maktar: KAR 12 [1963-64] p. 51, col. III, line 2)

Bibl. KAR 12 (1963-64) 52-53.

M'ŠN Heb. *'āšāN* "smoke"; Arabic *'uṮāNuN*.
1. "type of funerary urn" n.m.

a) *M'ŠN 'ṢMM 'BDMLQRT*
"the funerary urn of the bones of *'BDMLQRT*"
(Pu. Sousse: RES, ins. #906, line 1)

Bibl. DISO 163.

M'ŠRT for possible etymology, see *YŠR*.
1. "honest" adj. f. N.Pu. *M'ŠRT* (*MHŠ'RT*)

a) *'L P'LT M'ŠRT*
"for honest deed(s)"
(N.Pu. Leptis Magna: KAI/I p. 23, ins. #123, line 4)

b) *TM' BḤYM MHŠ'RT*
"perfectly honest while alive"
(N.Pu. Toisson d'ob: JA Series 11 vol. 9 [1917] p. 159, ins. #23, line 3)

Bibl. KAI/II 130; PPG 74-75; DISO 112-13; JA Series 11 vol. 9 (1917) 159-60.

MPḪRT Ug. *PḪR* "assembly"; Akk. *PuḪRu*; Syriac *PuḤRa'* "banquet, company"; Mandaic *PuHRa'*; Soq. *FaḤeRe* "all, together"; Mehri *FaḤeRe*; ESArab. *FḪR* "to gather together"; [Arabic *FuḪRuN* "glory, excellence"]. 1. "assembly" n.f.

a) *WMPḪRT 'L GBL QDŠM*
"and the assembly of the gods of *GBL*, the holy ones"
(Ph. Byblos: KAI/I p. 1, ins. #4, lines 4-5)

Bibl. KAI/II 6; Harris 137; DISO 163; ANET 653; PPG 96; JNES 2 (1943) 166, note 44. (On the possibility of *PoḤaR* in B.Heb., see JBL 92 [1973] 517-22.)

MPLT B.Heb. *MaPeLeT* "ruin"; Q.Aram. *MPLH* "downfall". 1. "ruin" n.f.

a) *Ḥ'T ḤWY KL MPLT HBTM 'L*
"(it was) he who restored all these temple ruins"
(Ph. Byblos: KAI/I p. 1, ins. #4, lines 2-3)

Bibl. KAI/II 6; DISO 163; Harris 125; PPG 97, 108; JNES 20 (1960) 178.

MP' etymology unknown. 1. "name of a month" n.

a) *WBYRḤ MP'*
"and in the month of *MP'*"
(Ph. Larnaka: KAI/I p. 10, ins. #43, line 6)

b) *BYRḤ MP' LPNY*
"in the month of anterior *MP'*"
(Pu. Constantine: Berthier/Charlier p. 51, ins. #56, line 3)

Bibl. KAI/II 60, 116; Harris 56; Berthier/Charlier 52.

MPQD I — B.Heb. *MePaQeD* "deputy, overseer"; Heb. *PāQīD* "officer". 1. "overseer" n.m. 2. "administration" n.m.

1 a) *K[BDMLQRT] BN BḌ'ŠTRT MPQD*
"*K[BDMLQRT]* son of *BD'ŠTRT*, the overseer"
(N.Pu. Leptis Magna: KAI/I p. 22, ins. #119, line 3)

2 a) *MPQD LPQY*
"the administration of *LPQY*"
(N.Pu. Leptis Magna: Harris p. 139, sub. *PQD*)

Bibl. DISO 234; Harris 139.

MPQD II — B.Heb. *MiPQāD* "tower" (Neh. 3:31) (?)" 1. "tower" n.m.

a) *HMPQD Z WHSLMT 'Š LMPQD*
"this tower and the stairs of the tower"
(Ph. Idalion: CIS I, ins. #88, line 4)

b) *SMLM BSLMT HMPQD*
"images on the stairs of the tower"
(Ph. Idalion: CIS I, ins. #88, line 5)

Bibl. DISO 163; Harris 139; NSI 74-75; Slouszch 98-99; NE 353.

MPT — etymology unknown; perhaps related to N.Heb. *MōPeT* "important person". 1. "dignitary" n.m.

a) *ẆH' 'Y ṀPT WR'Š*
"and behold there is no dignitary (?) or leader"
(Ph. Cyprus: KAI/I p. 7, ins. #30, line 1)

Bibl. KAI/II 48; DISO 164; LS III 122-23.

MṢ' — B.Heb. *MōṢā'* "place or act of going forth"; Akk. *MūṢū* "going forth"; Ug. *Ṣ'AT*, *ŠPŠ* "sunrise"; N.Heb. *MōṢā'* "the night following the Sabbath or a holy day"; Anc.Aram. *MWQ'* "going forth, east". 1. "east" n.m. (rising of the sun)

a) *'RPT KBRT MṢ' ŠMŠ WṢPLY*
"the portico in the direction (?) of sunrise and the north (side) of it"
(Ph. Ma'ṣub: KAI/I p. 4, ins. #19, lines 1-2)

b) *LMMṢ' ŠMŠ W'D MB'Y*
"from the rising of the sun (east) and until its setting (west)"
(Ph. Karatepe: KAI/I p. 5, ins. #26, lines A I,4-5)

c) *BQṢT GBLY BMṢ' ŠMŠ*
"at the edge(s) of my border, in the east"
(Ph. Karatepe: KAI/I p. 5, ins. #26, line A I,21)

d) *PNY MB' HŠMŠ WṢD' MṢ' HŠMŠ*
"its front facing west and its side, facing east"
(Pu. Carthage: KAI/I p. 17, ins. #78, lines 5-6)

Bibl. KAI/II 36, 96; NE 290; Harris 107; DISO 164; ANET 653; Slouszch 44, 177.

MṢB for etymology, see under *NṢB*.
1. "pillar" n.m.

a) *Z MṢB YTN WSTY*
"this is the pillar which *WSTY* gave"
(N.Pu. Malta: ZDMG 117 [1967] p. 19)

Bibl. ZDMG 117 (1967) 19-20.

MṢBT Heb. *MaṢeBā* "pillar, stone set up for worshiper," "a memorial"; Ug. *NṢBT* "monument"; ESArab. *NṢB* "statue, monument"; Arabic *NaṢiBaTuN* "stones set up about a pole"; Ph., N.Pu. *MṢBT* (Pu., N.Pu. *MNṢBT*).
1. "monument" n.f. 2. "gravestone"
3. "pillar" 4. unknown

1 a) *MṢBT LMBḤYY*
"a monument during my lifetime"
(Ph. Kition: KAI/I p. 8, ins. #35, lines 1-2)

b) *MṢBT 'Z 'Š YṬN' 'RŠ*
"this monument (is that) which *'RŠ*...erected"
(Ph. Kition: KAI/I p. 8, ins. #34, line 1)

c) *MṢBT SKR BḤYM*
"a memorial monument among the living"
(Ph. Athens: KAI/I p. 13, ins. #53, line 1)

d) *'LT MṢBT ḤRṢ*
"upon the gold monument"
(Ph. Piraeus: KAI/I p. 13, ins. #60, line 5)

2 a) *MNṢBT KTM BN YŠB'L*
"the (grave)stone of *KTM* son of *YSB'L*"
(Pu. Tharros: Slouszch p. 140, ins. #127, lines 1-3)

b) *NBN' HMNṢBT Z LŠB' BT Y'SKT'N*
"this (grave)stone was built for *ŠB'* daughter of *Y'SKT'N*"
(N.Pu. Maktar: KAI/I p. 28, ins. #149, lines 1-2)

c) *W'W' Š'NT 'ŠRM W'ḤD MNṢBT L'*
"he lived twenty-one years (this is) his (grave)stone"
(N.Pu. Guelma: JA Series 11 vol. 8 [1916] p. 496, ins. #13, lines 1-3)

3 a) *HMṢBT 'L L'ŠMN 'DNY*
"this pillar is for *'ŠMN* his lord"
(Ph. Kition: Slouszch p. 82, ins. #68, line 1)

b) *MNṢBT PSLT YQDŠ TMQ' BN 'RKT*
"hewn pillars (which) *TMQ'* son of *'RKT* dedicated"
(Pu. Carthage: CIS I, ins. #3778, lines 4-5)

4 a) *MṢBT L'ZR*
"a pillar (?) to *'ZR*"
(Pu. Carthage: ESE I, p. 169, line 3)

Bibl. Slouszch 82, 140, 176, 180-81; Harris 125; DISO 164; ESE I 165; PPG 22, 97; Branden 10; JA Series 11 vol. 8 (1916) 496.

***MṢR** B.Heb. *MāṢōR* "fortified place".
1. "fortified construction" n.f. (also see under *M'ṢRT*)

a) *KM P'LT M'ṢRT*
"as a fortified construction" (or "as a work of walled enclosure")
(N.Pu. Maktar: KAR 12 [1963-64] p. 51, col. III, line 2)

MQDŠ Heb. *MiQDāŠ* "sanctuary, sacred place"; J.Aram. *MaQDeŠa'*; Syriac *MaQDeŠa'*; Ph., Pu. *MQDŠ* (N.Pu. *MQD'Š, MYQDŠ*).
1. "sanctuary" n.m.

a) *'Š YṮN'T LY 'BMQDŠ MLQRT*
"that which I set up for myself in the sanctuary of *MLQRT*"
(Ph. Larnaka: KAI/I p. 10, ins. #43, line 3)

b) *MQDŠ BT ṢDMB'L*
"the sanctuary, the temple of *ṢDMB'L*"
(Pu. Malta: KAI/I p. 14, ins. #62, line 2)

c) *'BMQDŠ BT 'ŠTRT*
"in the sanctuary, the temple of *'ŠTRT*"
(Pu. Malta: KAI/I p. 10, ins. #43, line 3)

d) *'ŠRT H'ŠM 'Š 'L HMQDŠM*
"the ten men who are (appointed) over the sanctuaries"
(Pu. Carthage: CIS I, ins. #175, line 1)

e) *MQDŠM ḤDŠM*
"new sanctuaries"
(Pu. Carthage: CIS I, ins. #3914, line 1)

f) **HYKRM MQD'Š' NP'L* (*should read *HYKRT*)
"he built (for the god) his fallen temple"
(N.Pu. Maktar: KAR 12 [1963-64] p. 52, line 2)

g) *MYQDŠ QN'M*
"(my) sanctuary, whoever (you) are (?)"
(N.Pu. Cherchel: KAI/I p. 29, ins. #161, line 1)

Bibl. DISO 165; Harris 143; PPG 42, 96; KAI/II 60, 78, 150; Amadasi 24.

MQM I Heb. *MāQōM* "place, site"; Ug. *MQM*; ESArab *MQM*; Arabic *MaQāMuN*; Ph., Pu., N.Pu. *MQM* (N.Pu. *[M]'QM*, *MḤQM*, *M'Q'M*). 1. "place" n.m. 2. "sacred place"

1 a) *WBMQM [ZN]*
"and in [this] place"
(Ph. Byblos: KAI/I p. 2, ins. #9, line A 3)

b) *BMQM 'Š BNT*
"in the place which I built"
(Ph. Sidon: KAI/I p. 3, ins. #14, line 4)

c) *'L GBLM BMQMM B'Š KN 'ŠM R'M*
"at the borders, in places where there were evil men"
(Ph. Karatepe: KAI/I p. 5, ins. #26, lines A I,14-15)

d) *WBMQM 'Š KN LPNM NŠT'M*
"in places which had formerly been feared"
(Ph. Karatepe: KAI/I p. 5, ins. #26, line A II,3-4)

e) *WBN 'NK ḤMYT BMQMM HMT*
"and I built fortresses in those places"
(Ph. Karatepe: KAI/I p. 5, ins. #26, line A I,17)

f) *MQM S'R HḤDŠ*
"the place of the new gate"
(Pu. Carthage: CRAI [1968] p. 117, line 1)

2 a) *'LT MQM Z*
"upon this sacred place"
(Ph. Byblos: KAI/I p. 2, ins. #10, line 14)

b) *MTNB'L BN B'LYTN -ḤSGN Š HMQM*
"*MTNB'L* son of *B'LYTN*, overseer (?) of the sacred place"
(N.Pu. Maktar: KAI/I p. 28, ins. #146, line 4)

c) *HY 'L H[M]'QM*
"that one is over the sanctuary"
(N.Pu. Maktar: KAR 12 [1963-64] p. 52, col. III, line 2)

d) *HB''R HDBR Š HMMQM*
"the well of the innermost room of the sanctuary"
(N.Pu. Sardinia: KAI/I p. 31, ins. #173, line 5)

e) *B'N' HṢRT Š MḤQM*
"the builder of the court(s) of the temple"
(N.Pu. Maktar: KAR 12 [1963-64] p. 46, col. I, line 1)

f) *W'T HM'Q'M*
"and the temple"
(N.Pu. Leptis Magna: KAI/I p. 23, ins. #124, lines 1-2)

Bibl. KAI/II 10, 12, 36, 124, 130, 144, 150; DISO 165; ANET 656; Harris 142; CB 9 (1960-61) 33-36; PPG 96; Branden 31; CRAI (1968) 122; Bib 43 (1962) 360.

MQM II Heb. *MeQiM* "to cause to rise, to raise"; Ph., Pu. *MQM* (N.Pu. *MYQM*). 1. "cultic functionary" n.m.

a) *B'LMLK BN MLKYTN MQM 'LM*
"*B'LMLK* son of *MLKYTN* the awakener of the god(s) (?)"
(Ph. Larnaka: KAI/I p. 10, ins. #44, line 2)

b) *BDMLQRT MQM 'LM*
"*BDMLQRT* the awakener of the god(s) (?)"
(Pu. Carthage: KAI/I p. 18, ins. #90, line 3)

c) *'ZRB'L HRB MQM 'LM*
"*'ZRB'L* the chief, the awakener of the god(s) (?)"
(Pu. Carthage: CIS I, ins. #377, lines 5-6)

d) *MSNSN MYQM 'LM*
"*MSNSN* the awakener of the god(s) (?)"
(N.Pu. Cherchel: KAI/I p. 29, ins. #161, line 4)

Bibl. Leš 30 (1966) 163-74; BMB 5 (1941) 7-20; DISO 256; Harris 142; KAI/II 62, 103, 150.

MQN' Heb. *MiQNeh* "property, purchase, especially cattle"; Anc.Aram. *MQNH* "property, estate". 1. "cattle" n.m.

a) *BKL ZBḤ 'Š YZBḤ DL MQN'*
"for every sacrifice which shall be offered by persons deficient with regard to cattle"
(Pu. Marseilles: KAI/I p. 15, ins. #69, line 15)

b) *T HMZBḤ ŠHMQNT*
"and the altar for cattle"
(N.Pu. Bir Tlesa: KAI/I p. 26, ins. #138, line 3)

Bibl. KAI/II 83, 138; DISO 165; Harris 143; NE 363; PPG 96-97; ANET 656-57; Slouszch 148; LS I 98-99.

MQN'T Heb. *MiQNā* "purchase," *MiQNeh* "property, especially cattle"; Anc.Aram. *MQNH* "estate". 1. "property" n.f.

a) *[Q]B'R MQN'T 'TM'*
"a grave, the complete property"
(N.Pu. Tripolitania: LibAnt 1 [1964] p. 57, line 1)

Bibl. LibAnt 1 (1964) 58.

MQR Heb. *MāQōR* "fountain"; Ug. *MQR* "well, fountain". 1. "fountain" n.m.

a) *WRZT 'Š 'L HMQRM*
"*WRZT* (who is) over the fountains"
(Pu. Constantine: Berthier/Charlier p. 87, ins. #89, line 2)

Bibl. Berthier/Charlier 87; DISO 166.

MR C.S. 1. "myrrh" n.m.

a) *'SP BMR WBDL[Ḥ]*
"gathered in myrrh and bdell[ium]"
(Ph. Byblos: MUSJ 45 [1969] p. 262, line 1)

MR'Š B.Heb. *MeRa'ŠōT* "head place"; N.Heb. *MeRa'ŠōT* "pillow, head board, head part of the bed". 1. type of headdress n.m.

a) *WMR'Š 'LY*
"and a *MR'Š* headdress (?) upon me"
(Ph. Byblos: KAI/I p. 2, ins. #11, line 2)

Bibl. Slouszch 340; KAI/II 15; Harris 145; DISO 167; PPG 96.

MRGL B.Heb. *MiRaGGeL* "spy," *RaGLi* "soldier"; J.Aram. *RiGLa'* "footman" (reading of resh uncertain, perhaps to be read as *MDGL*). 1. "footman" n.m.

a) *HMRGL Š 'DRB'L*
"the footman of *'DRB'L*"
(Pu. Carthage: CIS I, ins. #5933, lines 4-5)

MRZḤ B.Heb. *MaRZeaḤ* "mourning cry or feast, cry of revelry"; N.Heb. *MaRZeaḤ* "merrymaking, mourning feast"; Ug. *MRZḤ* "type of celebration or festivity"; Akk. *MaRZiḤu, MaRZa'u* a type of priesthood; J.Aram. *M̄aRZeḤa'* "the place of the mourner's meal, those who cheer the mourners"; Arabic *MiRZaḤuN* "the raising of the voice in a cry or in happiness"; Palm. *MRZḤ*; Soq. *RZḤ* "to encircle"; Shauri *RiZeḤ* "to stamp, trample". 1. name of a festival n.m. 2. priestly guild

1 a) *BYM 4 LMRZḤ*
"on the fourth day of the festival"
(Ph. Piraeus: KAI/I p. 13, ins. #60, line 1)

2 a) *KL MZRḤ WKL ŠPḤ WKL MRZḤ 'LM*
"every citizen (?) and every clan and every priestly guild (?)"
(Pu. Marseilles: KAI/I p. 15, ins. #69, line 16)

Bibl. KAI/II 73, 83, 141; DISO 167; Harris 146; CRST 37-48, 52-54; NSI 303; Slouszch 148-49; OrAnt 6 (1966) 165-76; Amadasi 182; ANET 655; Archives From Elephantine, Los Angeles, 179-86.

MRKBT Heb. *MeRKāBā* "chariot"; Ug. *MRKBT*; Akk. *NaRKaBTu*; J.Aram. *MeRKaBTa'*; Syriac *MeRKaBTa'*; Eg. *MRKBT*. 1. "chariot"

a) *B'L 'SR MRKBTY*
"*B'L* has harnessed his chariot"
(Ph. Arslan Tash: BASOR 209 [1973] p. 18, obv. lines 1-2)

MRM B.Heb. *MāRōM* "height"; Ug. *MRYM* "height"; J.Aram. *MāRōM'* "height, on high"; Syriac *MeRaWM'* "height". 1. "raised" adv.

a) *WT 'KHNYM 'Š 'L MRM*
"and the bases which are raised"
(N.Pu. Cherchel: KAI/I p. 29, ins. #161, line 6)

Bibl. KAI/II 150; DISO 168.

MRP' etymology unknown. 1. "name of a month" n.m.

a) *BYMM 24 LYRḤ MRP'*
"on the twenty-fourth day of the month *MRP'*"
(Ph. Kition: CIS I, ins. #11, line 2)

Bibl. KAI/II 51; Harris 147; Slouszch 70.

MRP'M etymology unknown. 1. "name of a month" n.m.

a) *BYRḤ MRP'M*
"in the month of *MRP'M*"
(Pu. Carthage: CIS I, ins. #179, line 5)

b) *B'SR WŠMN LYRḤ MRP'M*
"on the eighteenth of the month of *MRP'M*"
(Pu. Constantine: KAI/I p. 21, ins. #111, lines 2-3)

Bibl. Slouszch 127, 262; Harris 127; KAI/II 117.

MRṢ B.Heb. *MeRūṢā* "running". 1. measure of distance n.m.

a) *MRṢM M'TM W'RB'M*
"a distance of two hundred and forty *MRṢM*"
(N.Pu. Dschebel Massoudj: KAI/I p. 26, ins. #141, line 5)

Bibl. DISO 168; KAI/II 139.

MRQ' B.Heb. *RāQia'* "extended surface," *RiQū'a* "expansion"; N.Heb. *MaRQa'* "piece of cloth, patch"; Mandaic *RQiHa'* "sky". 1. "plate" n.m.

a) *MRQ' ḤRṢ*
"a gold plate"
(Ph. Idalion: KAI/I p. 8, ins. #38, line 1)

Bibl. NE 370; Slouszch 100-101; Harris 147; DISO 168; KAI/I 56; LS III 195-96.

MS Eg. *MŚW(T)* "likeness," *MŚ* "statue" (cited in Harris, p. 122); Ph., Pu. *MS*, *M'S* (N.Pu. *M'S*). 1. "statue" n.m.

a) *ṀŠ Z P'L 'LB'L MLK GBL*
"the statue which *'LB'L*, king of *GBL* made"
(Ph. Byblos: KAI/I p. 1, ins. #6, line 1)

b) *HSML Z MŠ 'NK YTNB'L RB 'RṢ*
"this image is a statue of me *YTNB'L* the district chief (?)"
(Ph. Larnaka: KAI/I p. 10, ins. #43, line 2)

c) *M'Š 'LM*
"statue of the god"
(Ph. Pyrgi: KAI/I p. 53, ins. #277, line 9)

d) *MŠ NḤŠT 'Š NDR ḤMLKT*
"a bronze statue which *ḤMLKT* vowed"
(Pu. Antas: RPA p. 51, ins. #1, line 1)

e) *MŠ 'BN 'Š NDR 'BDKY*
"a stone statue which your servant vowed"
(Pu. Carthage: CIS I, ins. #3777, line 1)

f) *'Š NDR ḤMLKT HGLGL HMŠ*
"that which *ḤMLKT* the wrapper (?) of (?) vowed"
(Pu. Constantine: Berthier/Charlier p. 45, ins. #98, line 2)

g) *M'Š ST*
"this statue"
(N.Pu. Cherchel: KAI/I p. 29, ins. #161, line 3)

Bibl. RPA 55-57; DISO 168-69; Harris 122; Amadasi 167; Slouszch 8; KAI/II 8, 60, 123; Berthier/Charlier 45-46.

MŠ'T B.Heb. *MaŜ'eT* "rising column of smoke, tribute, portion of food"; Akk. *MaŠŠīTu* "cargo, supply". 1. "payment" n.f.

a) *BT Ḃ'LṢṖṄ B'[T HMŠ]'TT*
"temple of *B'LṢPN* tar[iff of pay]ments"
(Pu. Marseilles: KAI/I p. 15, ins. #69, line 1)

b) *[K]L MŠ'T 'Š 'YBL ŠT BPS Z*
"[eve]ry payment which is not set down on this tablet"
(Pu. Marseilles: KAI/I p. 15, ins. #69, line 18)

c) *B'T HMŠ'TT*
"tariff of payments"
(Pu. Carthage: KAI/I p. 16, ins. #74, line 1)

Bibl. Harris 126; NE 326; Slouszch 142; DISO 169; Amadasi 173; ANET 657; PPG 19, 96-97; Branden 30; Gibson 43.

MŠB Heb. *MoŠāB* "seat, assembly, dwelling place"; Ug. *MṮB*; Akk. *MuŠāBu*; Anc.Aram. *MŠB*; J.Aram. *MoTBa'*; Syriac *MoTBa'*; Mandaic *MuTBa'*; Nab. *MWTB*. 1. "dwelling place" n.m.

a) *MŠB' [B]'LM*
"his dwelling place (?) (in) the tomb"
(N.Pu. Ksar Toual Zouameul: BAC [1947] p. 253, line 3)

MŠWT for possible etymology, see under *MŠ'T*. 1. "payment" n.f.

a) *MŠWTM BTKLT MQM*
"his payment (?) for the completion of the temple"
(N.Pu. Leptis Magna: KAI/I p. 22, ins #119, line 5)

Bibl. DISO 169; KAI/II 124.

MŠṬR B.Heb. *MiŠṬāR* "rule, authority"; Akk. *ŠaṬāRu* "to write"; N.Heb. *ŠōṬeR* "overseer"; ESArab *ŚṬR* "to write"; J.Aram. *'aSṬeR* "to flatter"; Pu. *MŠṬR* (*MYŠṬR*). 1. "officer" n.m.

a) *'RŠ HMYŠṬR*
"*'RŠ* the officer"
(Pu. Constantine: Slouszch p. 219, ins. #223, line 2)

b) *'RŠ HMŠṬR*
"*'RŠ* the officer"
(Pu. Constantine: Berthier/Charlier p. 6, ins. #78, line 2)

Bibl. DISO 170; Berthier/Charlier 70; LS II 83.

MŠKB B.Ḥeb. *MiŠKāB* "place of lying"; J.Aram. *MaŠKeBa'* "couch, bed, grave"; Syriac *MaŠKeBa'* "couch, bedroom"; Nab. *MŠKB'* "couch". 1. "resting place" n.m.

a) *P'LTY LY HMŠKB ZN*
"I made for myself this resting place"
(Ph. Byblos: KAI/I p. 2, ins. #9, line A 1)

b) *BMŠKB ZN 'Š ŠKB BN*
"in this resting place, in which I rest"
(Ph. Byblos: KAI/I p. 2, ins. #9, line A 3)

c) *MŠKB 'T RP'M*
"resting place with the shades"
(Ph. Sidon: KAI/I p. 3, ins. #13, line 8)

d) *'L Y'MSN BMŠKB Z*
"may he not carry me from this resting place"
(Ph. Sidon: KAI/I p. 3, ins. #14, lines 5-6)

e) *'L MŠKB NḤTNM L'LM*
"over their resting place, forever"
(Ph. Kition: KAI/I p. 8, ins. #34, line 5)

Bibl. DISO 170; Harris 149; NE 375; KAI/II 10, 17, 19, 52; ANET 662; Slouszch 17.

MŠL Heb. *MāŠaL* "to rule, to manage"; Anc.Aram. *MŠL*. 1. "to rule" vb. 2. "royal" adj. m.

1 a) *'Š MŠL BNM*
"who shall rule over them"
(Ph. Sidon: KAI/I p. 3, ins. #14, line 9)

2 a) *ṢDN MŠL*
"*ṢDN*, the royal residence"
(Pu. Sidon: KAI/I p. 3, ins. #15, line 2)

Bibl. ANET 662; KAI/II 19, 126; DISO 171; NE 318; Benz 355; Slouszch 23.

MŠLT — for etymology, see under *MŠL*.
1. "might" n.f.

a) *MŠLT 'SR MŠLM*
"the might of ten rulers"
(N.Pu. Leptis Magna: KAI/I p. 22, ins. #120, line 1)

Bibl. KAI/II 126; DISO 171.

MŠ'RT — Heb. *Šō'eReT* (2 Sam. 4:6) "portress"; Ug. *ṮGR* "gatekeeper"; N.Heb. *MeŠō'eR* "gatekeeper"; B.Aram. **Tāʀa'*.
1. "gatekeeper" n.f.

a) *WKN' Š'NT 'SR WŠMN R'Š 'MŠ'ṘT NṢB*
"and she was for eighteen years appointed as the chief gatekeeper (or chief singer)"
(N.Pu. Tunisia: KAI/I p. 25, ins. #136, lines 5-6)

Bibl. KAI/II 135; DISO 298; LS I 456.

MŠPṬ — Heb. *MiŠPāT* "judgment," "law, decision"; Ug. *MṮPṬ* "sovereignty". 1. "rule" n.m.

a) *TḤTSP ḤṬR MŠPṬH*
"may the scepter of his rule be removed"
(Ph. Byblos: KAI/I p. 1, ins. #1, line 2)

Bibl. KAI/II 2; DISO 171; Harris 153; PPG 96; Slouszch 4.

MŠPN — etymology unknown. 1. "bust" n.m. (from context)

a) *MŠPN 'BY BNḤŠT*
"a bust (?) of (the face) of my father in bronze"
(Ph. Larnaka: KAI/I p. 10, ins. #43, line 7)

Bibl. DISO 171; Slouszch 110; Harris 122; KAI/II 60.

MŠQL — Heb. *MiŠQāL* "a weight"; Syriac *MaTQeLa'* "a weight, scale balance"; J.Aram. *MaTQaLa'* "heaviness, weight"; Mandaic *MaTQala'* "a large gold sheqel"; Arabic *MiṮQaLuN*. 1. "weight" n.m.

a) *MŠQL KR 100 W 2*
"in weight one hundred and two *KR*"
(Ph. Larnaka: KAI/I p. 10, ins. #43, line 14)

b) *MZBḤ NḤŠT MŠQL LṬRM M'T*
"the bronze altar, in weight one hundred pounds"
(Pu. Sardinia: KAI/I p. 14, ins. #66, line 1)

c) *Š'R MŠQL M'T WḤMŠM*
"flesh, in weight one hundred and fifty (shekels)"
(Pu. Marseilles: KAI/I p. 15, ins. #69, line 6)

d) *MŠQLM 100* (reading of numerical sign uncertain)
"its weight one hundred (shekels)"
(Pu. Carthage: Slouszch p. 203, ins. #197, line 1)

Bibl. Amadasi 91, 169; KAI/II 60, 83; Slouszch 135, 203; Harris 154; ANET 656; DISO 171.

MŠRT B.Heb. *ŠāReT* "to serve, minister"; N.Heb. *ŠeRūT* "ministry". 1. "service" n.f.

a) *LŠLM ḤLPT 'YT 'DMM 'Š P'L MŠRT 'T PNṬ GW*
"to requite the men who have performed service before the community"
(Ph. Piraeus: KAI/I p. 13, ins. #60, lines 7-8)

b) *WP'L 'YT KL 'Š 'LTY MŠRT*
"and he performed all the service which was incumbent upon him"
(Ph. Piraeus: KAI/I p. 13, ins. #60, lines 3-4)

Bibl. KAI/II 73; Harris 154; Slouszch 118; NE 383; DISO 171; PPG 96.

M'ŠRT for possible etymology see *YŠR* I. 1. "honest" adv. f.

a) *'L P'LT M'ŠRT*
"for honest deeds"
(N.Pu. Leptis Magna: KAI/I p. 23, ins. #123, lines 4-5)

b) *TM' BḤYM MHŠ'RT*
"perfectly honest while alive"
(N.Pu. Toison d'ob: JA Series 11 vol. 9 [1917] p. 159, ins. #23, line 3)

Bibl. KAI/II 130; PPG 74-75; DISO 112-13; JA Series 11 vol. 9 (1917) 159-60.

MT C.S. 1. "to die, be dead" vb.

a) *MT' BT Š'NT ŠB'M WŠB'*
"she died at age seventy-seven"
(N.Pu. Tunisia: KAI/I p. 25, ins. #136, lines 2-3)

b) *PḤL' L'B'NHM MṪ QBR Š'ṬRY WGD'Y*
"*Š'ṬRY* and *GD'Y* made it, a grave for their father who is dead"
(N.Pu. Henschir Brigitta: KAI/I p. 26, ins. #142, line 4)

c) *NPŠ MT*
"a monument to the dead" (or "a gravestone")
(N.Pu. Leptis Magna: KAI/I p. 25, ins. #128, line 3)

Bibl. KAI/II 132, 135, 139; DISO 145; PPG 77.

MTḤ etymology unknown, perhaps related to *MṬḤ* II. 1. "plasterer" n.m.

a) *MGN HMTḤ*
"*MGN* the plasterer (?)"
(N.Pu. Sousse: RES, ins. #952, line 1)

Bibl. DISO 271.

MTKT Heb. *TōK* "midst"; Ug. *TK*; J.Aram. *TeKaK* "to squeeze, press". 1. "midst" n.f.

a) *BMTKT MLKM 'DRM*
"in the midst of mighty kings"
(Ph. Zinjirli: KAI/I p. 9, ins. #24, lines 5-6)

Bibl. DISO 172; KAI/II 30; Harris 155; ANET 654; PPG 96, 97.

MTM I B.Heb. *MeTōM* "soundness". 1. "pure" adj. m. (Is. 1:6)

a) *ḤRṢ MTM*
"pure gold"
(Ph. Umm el-Awamid: Dunand/Duru p. 192, ins. #13, line 1)

Bibl. Leš 21 (1959-60) 281; Leš 19 (1957-58) 234.

MTM II Akk. *MaTīMa* "some time or other," *MaTīMe* "whenever". 1. "ever" adv.

a) *WBL KN MTM LDNNYM LL BYMTY*
"and there was never night for the *DNNYM* in my days"
(Ph. Karatepe: KAI/I p. 5, ins. #26, lines A II,16-17)

Bibl. KAI/II 36; ANET 653; DISO 155; Gaster-Fs 135.

MTN I — etymology unknown. 1. "name of a month"

a) *BYRḤ MTN*
"in the month of *MTN*"
(Ph. Larnaka: Mus 51 [1938] p. 286, line 3)

Bibl. Mus 51 (1938) 292.

MTN II — Heb. *MaTāN* "gift, giving"; J.Aram. *MeTaNa'* "gift, grant, donation"; Amar.Akk. *MaTNia* (?). 1. "gift" n.m.

a) *BMTN 'BBT*
"as a gift to the temple"
(Ph. Pyrgi: Amadasi p. 161, ins. #2, line 5)

Bibl. Amadasi 166; Benz 356-57.

MTNT — Heb. *MaTāNā* "present"; Ug. *YTNT*, *MTNT* "gift"; Akk. *MaNDaTTu* "tribute"; J.Aram. *MaTaNTa'* "gift". 1. "present" n.f.

a) *L'DN LB'L MTNT*
"for the lord, for *B'L*, a present"
(Pu. Sousse: KAI/I p. 19, ins. #99, line 1)

b) *MTNT 'Š TN' YḤW'LN BN 'BD'SMN*
"a present which *YḤW'LN* son of *'BD'SMN* donated"
(Pu. Constantine: KAI/I p. 20, ins. #102, lines 2-3)

c) *MTNT 'Š NDR ḤN' BN MGN*
"a present which *ḤN'* the son of *MGN* vowed"
(Pu. Constantine: KAI/I p. 20, ins. #104, lines 1-2)

d) *MTNT NDR 'Š NDR MQN BN 'BD'*
"a vowed present which *MQR* son of *'BD'* vowed"
(Pu. Constantine: ESE I p. 41, ins. #100, lines 1-2)

e) *WKL 'DM 'Š GNB T MTNT Z*
"and all men who steal this present"
(Pu. Carthage: CIS I, ins. #3783, lines 5-6)

Bibl. DISO 172; Harris 108; KAI/II 107, 113-14; Slouszch 226.

MTR — for possible etymology, see under *YTR*. 1. "reserves" n.m. (reading uncertain)

a) *'DNB'L RB HMṫRṁ*
"*'DNB'L*, the chief of the reserves"
(N.Pu. Constantine: Berthier/Charlier p. 73, ins. #84, lines 2-3)

MTRḤ Ug. *MTRḪT* "woman acquired by the payment of the *TeRḪaTū*"; Akk. *TeRḪaTu* "espoused price". 1. "espoused" n.m.

a) *B'LMLK BN MLKYTN MQM 'LM MTRḤ 'ŠTRNY*
"*B'LMLK* son of *MLKYTN* awakener of the god(s) (?), espoused of *'ŠTRT* (?)"
(Ph. Rhodos: KAI/I p. 10, ins. #44, line 2)

b) *'BDMLQRT HŠPṬ RB KHNM MQM 'LM MTRḤ 'ŠTRNY*
"*'BDMLQRT* the magistrate, chief priest, awakener of the god(s) (?) espoused of *'ŠTRT* (?)"
(Pu. Carthage: KAI/I p. 19, ins. #93, lines 3-4)

c) *MTNB'L BN B'LYTN MQM 'LM MTRḤ 'ŠTRNY*
"*MTNB'L* son of *B'LYTN*, awakener of the god (?), espoused of *'ŠTRT* (?)"
(Pu. Carthage: CIS I, ins. #261, lines 4-5)

Bibl. DISO 172-73; Harris 122; JNES 12 (1953) 150 note 8; KAI/II 62, 104; Slouszch 197.

MTT B.Heb. *MaTaT* "a gift". 1. "gift" n.f.

a) *MTT L'ŠTRT 'DTY*
"(as) a gift to *'STRT* her lady"
(Ph. Carchemish: KAI/I p. 7, ins. #29, line 2)

Bibl. DISO 172; KAI/II 47; Harris 108.

N

N' Heb. *Nā* "particle of entreaty".
1. particle of entreaty

a) *ṢBṬ N' HQŠ[B]*
"hold now, pay atten[tion] (?)
(reading of entire line uncertain)
(N.Pu. Sicily: Kokalos 13 (1967)
p. 70, ins. #6, line 1)

Bibl. RSO 40 (1965) 205-6.

N'LK Heb. *MaHaLāK* "way, journey"; Akk. *MaLāKu*
"way, road". 1. "way" n.m.

a) [*'L '*]*DT ŠMR N'LKY*
"[becaus]e of the guarding of my
way"
(Ph. Memphis: KAI/I p. 11,
ins. #48, line 2)

Bibl. KAI/II 64.

N'SPT for etymology, see under *'SP*.
1. "assembly" n.f.

a) *TM BD ṢDNYM BN'SPT*
"it was decided by the *ṢDNYM* in
assembly"
(Ph. Piraeus: KAI/I p. 13,
ins. #60, line 1)

Bibl. DISO 173; KAI/II 73; Harris 80;
PPG 21, 97; Slouszch 117; Branden 8;
NE 223.

N'QYDŠ C.S. rt. 1. "holy" adj. m.

a) *L'DN LB'L ḤMN N'QYDŠ* (perhaps
dittography of *N*)
"for the lord, for *B'L ḤMN* the
holy"
(N.Pu. Carthage: JA Series 11
vol. 9 [1917] p. 151, ins.
#10, line 1)

Bibl. JA Series 11 vol. 9 (1917) 152.

NBL Heb. *NeBeL* "large jar or flagon"; Ug. *NBL*.
1. "goblet" n.m.

a) *NBL NSKT*
"molten metal goblets"
(N.Pu. Bir Bou-Rekba: KAI/I
p. 26, ins. #137, lines 5-6)

Bibl. KAI/II 93; Harris 123; DISO 173.

NGR C.S. 1. "carpenter" n.m. (Sum. L.W. *NaGaR* "carpenter").

a) *'RŠ' HNGR*
"*'RŠ'* the carpenter"
(Pu. Carthage: CIS I, ins. #354, line 2)

b) *B'LYTN HNGR*
"*B'LYTN* the carpenter"
(Pu. Constantine: Berthier/Charlier p. 80, ins. #95, lines 1-2)

c) *'BDMLQRT HNGR*
"*'BDMLQRT* the carpenter"
(Pu. Constantine: Berthier/Charlier p. 81, ins. #97, lines 1-2)

d) *B'LYTN 'NGR*
"*B'LYTN* the carpenter"
(N.Pu. Constantine: Berthier/Charlier p. 80, ins. #96, line 1)

Bibl. DISO 174; Harris 123; Slouszch 246; Berthier/Charlier 80-81.

NDB Heb. *NāDaB* "to offer freely"; B.Aram. *NeDaB* "to be willing"; J.Aram. *NeDaB*; Mandaic *NDB* "to urge, prompt"; Akk. *NaDāBu* "to call in". 1. "to offer freely" vb.

a) *NDB' BDMLQRT* (reading uncertain)
"*BDMLQRT* offered freely (?)"
(Pu. Sousse: RES ins. #907, line 1)

Bibl. DISO 174.

NDR I Heb. *NāDaR* "to vow"; Ug. *NDR*; J.Aram. *NeDaR*; Syriac *NeDaR*; Mandaic *NDR*; Arabic *NaDaRa*; ESArab *ND̲R* "to make a penitential vow"; Ph., Pu. *ND̄R* (Pu. *N'DR*, *NDDR*, *BDR*, *N'R*, *NR*, *DR*; N.Pu. *N'D'R*, *N'DR*). 1. "to vow" vb.

a) *'Š NDR 'BD'LM BN MTN*
"that which *'BD'LM* son of *MTN* vowed"
(Ph. Umm el-Awamid: Slouszch p. 38, ins. #22, lines 1-2)

b) *HNDR 'Š KN NDR 'BNM*
"the vow which their father had vowed"
(Ph. Idalion: CIS I, ins. #93, line 5)

c) *MTNT 'Š NDR 'DNB'L*
"a present which *'DNB'L* vowed"
(Pu. Carthage: Slouszch p. 170, ins. #147, line 1)

d) *'Š NDR 'BD'ŠMN*
"that which *'BD'ŠMN* vowed"
(Pu. Constantine: Berthier/Charlier p. 83, ins. #102, line 2)

e) *ND'R 'Š NDR' B'L'MY*
"the vow which *B'L'MY* vowed"
(N.Pu. Henschir Meded: KAI/I p. 29, ins. #155, lines 1-2)

Bibl. DISO 174-75; Harris 123; KAI/II 147; PPG 38, 42, 49, 57, 59, 60, 69, 110; Branden 82-84; NE 322-23.

NDR II — for etymology, see under *NDR* I. Ph., Pu. *NDR* (Pu. *ND'R*; N.Pu. *N'DR*). 1. "vow" n.m.

a) *HNDR 'Š KN NDR 'BNM*
"the vow which their father had vowed"
(Ph. Idalion: KAI/I p. 4, ins. #90, line 5)

b) *NDR 'Š NDR MTN LM BN ŠPṬ*
"the vow which *MTN LM* son of *ŠPṬ* vowed"
(Pu. Constantine: Berthier/Charlier p. 44, ins. #47, lines 2-3)

c) *ND'R 'Š NDR ṢṢLGM BN YSRG*
"the vow which *ṢṢLGM* son of *YSRG* vowed"
(Pu. Constantine: Berthier/Charlier p. 106, ins. #142, lines 2-3)

d) *ND'R 'Š N'DR 'MY'L*
"the vow which *'MY'L* vowed"
(N.Pu. Henschir Meded: KAI/I p. 29, ins. #156, line 1)

e) *ND'R 'Š N'DR' B'L'MY*
"the vow which *B'L'MY* vowed"
(N.Pu. Henschir Meded: KAI/I p. 29, ins. #155, line 1)

Bibl. KAI/II 57, 147; Berthier/Charlier 106-7; DISO 175; Harris 123; PPG 38; NE 322.

**NZQ* — N.Heb. *NāZaQ* "to damage"; Akk. *NaZāQu* "to annoy, bother"; Emp.Aram. *NZQ* "to irritate"; J.Aram. *NeZaQ* "to suffer injury"; B.Aram. *NeZaQ*. 1. "to damage" vb.

a) *WYZQ BSPR Z*
"and damage this inscription"
(Ph. Zinjirli: KAI/I p. 5, ins. #24, line 14)

Bibl. DISO 176; Harris 123; PPG 70; ANET 654; KAI/II 31; ZDMG 69 (1905) 512.

NḤ Heb. *NaḤ* "to rest"; Ug. *NḤ* "to rest"; Akk. *NaḪu* "to rest"; Syriac *NuḤ* "to be at ease"; Mandaic *NuḤ*; J.Aram. *NuaḤ* "to be at ease"; Arabic *'aNāḤa* "to make a camel lie down"; Geez *NoḤa* "to take a rest". 1. "to set down" vb.

a) *MZBḤ Z 'Š YNḤ BNḤDŠ BN B'LYTN HŠPṬ* "this altar (is that) which *BNḤDŠ* son of *B'LYTN* the magistrate set down" (Ph. Piraeus: CIS I, ins. #118, line 1)

Bibl. KAI/II 72; Harris 123; Slouszch 120; PPG 78; DISO 176.

NḤL B.Heb. *NāḤaL* "to receive, take as a possession, [cast lots]"; Ug. *NḤL* "to inherit"; ESArab. *NḤL* "to make a gift"; Arabic *NaḤaLa* "to bestow"; Akk. *NaḪāLu* "to assign". 1. "to cast lots" vb. (Josh. 19:49 [?])

a) *'M NḤL TNḤL* "if you would cast lots" (Ph. Byblos: JAOS 81 [1961] p. 32, lines 3-4)

Bibl. DISO 176; KAI/II 5; LS I 39-40; JAOS 81 (1961) 33; BASOR 212 (1973) 20-21.

NḤR Heb. *Na'aR* "youth"; Ug. *N'R* "boy". 1. "youth" n.m.

a) *BN 'DM KN NḤR* (reading of line uncertain) "a person who was a youth (?)" (N.Pu. Guelaat Bou-Sba: KAI/I p. 30, ins. #165, line 3)

Bibl. OrAnt 4 (1965) 66; KAI/II 154 (also see under *N'R*).

NḤŠT Heb. *NeḤōŠeT* "bronze, copper"; Amar.Akk. *NuḪuŠTu*; B.Aram. *NeḤaŠa'*; J.Aram. *NeḤaŠa'*; Syriac *NeḤaŠa'* "brass"; Arabic *NuḤāSuN*. 1. "bronze" n.f.

a) *HMZBḤ NḤŠT ZN* "this altar of bronze" (Ph. Byblos: KAI/I p. 2, ins. #10, line 4)

b) *BR'ŠT NḤŠT* "of the choicest bronze" (Ph. Limassol: KAI/I p. 7, ins. #31, line 1)

c) *MSK HNḤŠT*
"copper smith"
(Pu. Carthage: CIS I, ins. #330, lines 3-4)

d) *M'Š HNḤŠT 'L M'KN'*
"the bronze statue upon its pedestal"
(N.Pu. Leptis Magna: KAI/I p. 22, ins. #119, line 4)

e) *DLHT ŠNḤŠT*
"doors of bronze"
(N.Pu. Leptis Magna: KAI/I p. 23, ins. #122, line 2)

Bibl. Slouszch 11, 69; KAI/II 12, 49, 124, 128; DISO 177; Harris 123; NE 322; ANET 656.

NḤT Heb. *NaH̱aT* "rest, case, comfort"; Akk. *NuH̱Tu*; Ūg. *NH̱T* "resting place". 1. "repose" n.f. 2. "pleasure" n.f. 3. "resting place" n.f.

1 a) *WNḤT TBRH 'L GBL*
"may calm depart from *GBL*"
(Ph. Byblos: KAI/I p. 1, ins. #1, line 2)

2 a) *WNḤT LB LDNNYM*
"and satisfaction to the *DNNYM*"
(Ph. Karatepe: KAI/I p. 5, ins. #26, line A II,8)

b) *WBŠBT N'MT WBNḤT LB*
"and with a favorable situation and with satisfaction"
(Ph. Karatepe: KAI/I p. 5, ins. #26, lines A II,13-14)

3 a) *'L MŠKB NḤTY*
"over my resting place"
(Ph. Kition: KAI/I p. 8, ins. #35, line 2)

b) *'L MŠKB NḤTNM L'LM*
"over their resting place, forever"
(Ph. Kition: KAI/I p. 8, ins. #34, line 5)

Bibl. Harris 123; Slouszch 4, 87, 89; DISO 177; NE 322; Fitzmyer 87.

NK'T B.Heb. *NeKe'oT* "tragacanth gum"; Arabic *NaK'aTuN*; Akk. *NuKKaTu*. 1. "tragacanth gum" n.f.

a) *NK'T*
"tragacanth gum"
(N.Pu. Henschir Medina: KAI/I p. 29, ins. #160, line 3)

Bibl. KAI/II 150.

NKS — N.Heb. *NāKaS* "to cut, slaughter"; Akk. *NaKāSu*; Emp.Aram. *NKS*; J.Aram. *NeKaS*; Syriac *NeKaS* "to slay, kill for sacrifice or food"; Mandaic *NKS*; Arabic *NaKaŠa* "to destroy". 1. "to cut" vb.

a) *NKST TNT PN B'L*
"may (your throat) be cut by *TNT PN B'L*"
(Pu. Carthage: CIS I, ins. #3783, lines 6-7)

Bibl. Bib 49 (1968) 364-65; DISO 179; Slouszch 347.

******NS'* — for possible etymology, see under *NŠ'* IV. 1. "clan or tribal representatives" coll. n.

a) *SḤRT NST*
"merchants, clan representatives"
(Pu. Carthage: CRAI [1968] p. 117, line 5)

Bibl. RSO 43 (1968) 13-14; CRAI (1968) 126-27 (see CIS I, ins. #5510, line 7 for p.p. of 'Alif verb written defectively).

NSK — Heb. *NāSaK* "to pour out, cast metal"; Ug. *NSK* "to pour or cast metal"; [Akk. *NaSāKa* "to make flat or smooth";] Anc.Aram. *NSK* "to pour"; Syriac *NeSaK* "to smelt or cast metal"; J.Aram. *NeSaK* "to pour, to cast metal"; Q.Aram. *NSK*; Arabic *NaSaKa* "to be poured"; B.Aram. *NeSaK* (Dan 2:46). 1. "iron caster" n.m. 2. "goldsmith" n.m.

1 a) *'KBRM NSK HBRZL*
"*'KBRM*, the iron caster"
(Pu. Carthage: Slouszch p. 195, ins. #186, lines 1-2)

b) *'RŠ NSK HBRZL*
"*'RŠ* the iron caster"
(Pu. Carthage: CIS I, ins. #3014, line 3)

2 a) *YTNB'L BN MSP NSK 'ḤRṢ*
"*YTNB'L* son of *MSP* the goldsmith"
(Ph. Carthage: CIS I, ins. #328, lines 3-4)

b) *BD'ŠTRT BN MSP NSK HḤRṢ*
"*BD'ŠTRT* son of *MSP* the goldsmith"
(Pu. Carthage: CIS I, ins. #327, lines 4-5)

Bibl. DISO 180; Harris 124; Slouszch 195, 242; NE 323-24; ZDMG 41 (1887) 719.

NSKT Heb. *MaSeKā* "molten image," "metal jar". 1. "statue" n.f. 2. type of metal goblet

1 a) *NSK HNSKT*
"the caster of statues (?)"
(Pu. Carthage: CIS I, ins. #3275, line 3)

b) *HNSKT Š'LM 'WGSṬS*
"the statue of the divine Augustus"
(N.Pu. Leptis Magna: KAI/I p. 23, ins. #122, line 1)

2 a) *NBL NSKT*
"molten metal goblets"
(N.Pu. Bir Bou-Rekba: KAI/I p. 26, ins. #137, lines 5-6)

Bibl. DISO 180; Harris 124; KAI/II 128, 136.

NS' Heb. *NāSa'* "to pull up or out"; ESArab *NZ'* "to desert"; Akk. *NeSū* "to become distant"; J.Aram. *'aS'a* "to remove"; Ug. *NS'* "to travel, to remove"; Arabic *NaZa'a* "to pull out". 1. "to remove" vb. (Y)

a) *WYS' HŠ'R Z*
"and shall remove this gate"
(Ph. Karatepe: KAI/I p. 6, ins. #26, line a III,15)

b) *'M BŠN'T WBR' YS' HŠ'R Z*
"or with hatred and with evil (intention) he shall remove this gate"
(Ph. Karatepe: KAI/I p. 6, ins. #26, lines A III,17-18)

Bibl. KAI/II 36; PPG 70; DISO 180.

N'L Heb. *Nā'aL* "to tie, lock up". 1. "to lock" vb.

a) *N'LT MN'L*
"I have fastened the bolt"
(Ph. Arslan Tash: BASOR 209 [1973] p. 19, rev. line 1)

Bibl. Syria 48 (1971) 404.

N'M I Heb. *Nā'iM* "pleasing, lovely"; Ug. *N'M* "goodness," "loveliness"; Arabic *Na'iMuN* "enjoyment". 1. "good" adj. m. 2. "rejoicing" n.m. 3. "kind" adj. m.

1 a) *MŠL N'M*
"good luck"
(Ph. Larnaka: KAI/I p. 10, ins. #43, line 1)

b) *LKNY LY LSKR WŠM N'M*
"that it may be established for me as a memorial and a good name"
(Ph. Umm el-Awamid: KAI/I p. 4, ins. #18, line 6)

2 a) *YM N'M HYM Z LMGN*
"a day of rejoicing is this day for *MGN*"
(N.Pu. Cirta: RES ins. #303, line 1)

3 a) *L'LM N'MM*
"for the kind gods"
(N.Pu. Constantine: KAI/I p. 30, ins. #162, line 3)

Bibl. DISO 180-81; Benz 362; Slouszch 227; KAI/II 26, 60, 152; Harris 124.

N'M II — for etymology, see under *N'M* I.
1. "good" adj. m.

a) *'RŠMLK HN'M*
"*'RŠMLK* the good (?)"
(N.Pu. Carthage: Mission à Carthage, p. 120, line 1)

Bibl. Sainte-Marie 121.

N'M III — B.Heb. *No'aM* "kindness, grace"; ESArab *N'MT* "prosperity"; Ug. *N'M* "goodness, charm"; Arabic *Naa'MaTuN* "favor, good".
1. "goodness" n.m. 2. "kindness" n.m. 3. "happiness" n.m.

1 a) *BN'M LBY*
"and because of the goodness of my heart"
(Ph. Karatepe: KAI/I p. 5, ins. #26, line A I,13)

b) *WKN BYMTY KL N'M LDNNYM*
"and there was in my days every goodness for the *DNNYM*"
(Ph. Karatepe: KAI/I p. 5, ins. #26, lines A I,5-6)

2 a) *WP'L LY N'M*
"and done kindness to me"
(Ph. Byblos: KAI/I p. 2, ins. #10, line 8)

3 a) *YTN L' N'M*
"he gave him happiness"
(N.Pu. Constantine: JA Series 11 vol. 10 [1917] p. 65, ins. # Costa 92, line 4)

Bibl. ANET 653, 656; JA Series 11 vol. 10 (1917) 65; NE 324; Benz 362; Harris 124; DISO 181-82; Slouszch 13.

N'M IV — for etymology, see under *N'M* I.
1. "good" adj. m.

a) *BYM N'M WBRK*
"on a good and blessed day"
(N.Pu. Dougga: CRAI [1916] p. 128, line 1)

N'MT — for etymology, see under *N'M* III.
1. "favorable" adj. f. 2. "good" n.f.

1 a) *WRŠ'T N'MT*
"and favorable rule"
(Ph. Karatepe: KAI/I p. 6, ins. #26, line A III,6)

b) *ŠBT N'MT*
"favorable situation"
(Ph. Karatepe: KAI/I p. 5, ins. #5, line A II,7-8)

2 a) *ŠM' 'T QL' KTB N'MT*
"hear his voice, write good (about him)"
(N.Pu. Constantine: Slouszch p. 224, ins. #233, lines 3-4)

Bibl. KAI/II 36; ANET 653; Slouszch 225; DISO 181.

N'R I — Heb. *Ne'ūRîM* "time of youth". 1. "time of youth" n.m.

a) *WMY BL ḤZ KTN LMN'RY*
"and whoever had never seen linen since his youth"
(Ph. Zinjirli: KAI/I p. 4, ins. #24, line 12)

Bibl. Harris 124; DISO 181; KAI/II 31; ANET 654; Branden 32; EHO 18.

N'R II — Heb. *Na'aR* "young man, attendant"; Ug. *N'R* "boy servant, squire". 1. "servant" n.m.

a) *LN'RM 2 QP' 2*
"for the two servants, two *QP'*"
(Ph. Kition: KAI/I p. 8, ins. #37, line A 8)

b) *LN'RM 3 QP' 3*
"for the three servants, three *QP'*"
(Ph. Kition: KAI/I p. 8, ins. #37, line A 12)

Bibl. Harris 124; DISO 181; KAI/II 54; Or 37 (1968) 313; Slouszch 78 (also see under *NḤR*).

**NPL*

Heb. *NāPaL* "to fall"; Ug. *NPL*; Akk. *NaPāLu* "to break off"; Amar.Akk. *NuPuL* "drop"; Syriac *NePaL* "to fall"; Mandaic *NPL*; Emp.Aram. *NPL*; Palm. *NPL*; J.Aram. *NePaL*; Arabic *NaFaLa* "to divide the spoils". 1. "fallen" adj. m.

a) *HYKRM MQD'Š' NP'L*
"he built (for the god) his fallen temple"
(N.Pu. Maktar: KAR 12 [1963-64] p. 52, line 2)

**NPQ*

Heb. *PuQ* (Hiqṭal) "to bring out, produce"; N.Heb. *NāPaQ* "to go out"; Ug. *PQ* "to get a wife"; Anc.Aram. *NPQ* "to go forth, to bring out"; Emp.Aram. *NPQ*; J.Aram. *NePaQ*; Syriac *NePaQ*; Mandaic *NPQ*; Geez *NaFaQa* "to split, cleave"; Arabic *NaFaQa* "to come out of its hole (mole)"; Soq. *NeFoG* "to come out, appear (heavenly bodies)". 1. "to remove" vb. 2. "to obtain"

1 a) *'Š TPQ 'YT H'RN Z*
"who shall remove this sarcophagus"
(Ph. Sidon: KAI/I p. 2, ins. #13, line 3)

2 a) *'PQN HKSP 'Š ŠLḤT LY*
"the silver which you sent me has reached me"
(Ph. Saqqara: KAI/I p. 12, ins. #50, line 3)

Bibl. DISO 226; Harris 136; Or 40 (1971) 404-5; ANET 662; KAI/II 17, 67; PPG 70; JNES 30 (1971) 90.

NPŠ

C.S. Ph., N.Pu. *NPŠ* (Ph. *NBŠ*; N.Pu. *N'PŠ*). 1. "self" n.f. 2. "desire" 3. "person" 4. "gravestone"

1 a) *WHMT ŠT NBŠ*
"and as for them (each) placed himself"
(Ph. Zinjirli: KAI/I p. 4, ins. #24, line 13)

2 a) *KM NBŠ YTM B'M*
"as the desire of an orphan (is) for its mother"
(Ph. Zinjirli: KAI/I p. 5, ins. #24, line 13)

3 a) *LNPŠ BT*
"for the personnel of the temple"
(Ph. Kition: KAI/I p. 8, ins. #37, line B 5)

4 a) *NPŠ MT*
"a gravestone" (or "a monument to the dead")
(N.Pu. Leptis Magna: KAI/I p. 25, ins. #138, line 3)

b) *Ṅ'PŠ Š 'DYT*
"the gravestone of *'DYT*" (or "a monument of *'DYT*")
(N.Pu. Tunisia: KAI/I p. 25, ins. #136, line 1)

Bibl. Harris 125; DISO 183-84; PPG 17 note 1, 38 note 1, 43; NE 325; ANET 655; KAI/II 31, 54, 132, 135; Slouszch 81; Or 37 (1968) 321.

NPT Heb. *NoPeT* "honey"; Ug. *NBT*; Akk. *NuBTu* "bee". 1. "honey" n.f.

a) *LŠT 'LT HḤDRT NPT*
"to set upon the chamber honey (?)"
(Pu. Carthage: KAI/I p. 16, ins. #76, line B 8)

Bibl. Harris 125; DISO 184; Slouszch 168; KAI/II 93.

NṢ Heb. *NeṢ* "hawk"; J.Aram. *NaṢṢa'*; Syriac *NeṢṢa'*. 1. "hawk" n.m. (only in place names)

a) *LB'L ŠMM B'Y NṢM*
"for *B'L ŠMM* of the Island of Hawks"
(Pu. Sardinia: KAI/I p. 14, ins. #64, line 1)

Bibl. Harris 76; KAI/II 79; Slouszch 133-34.

NṢB I Heb. *NiṢaB* "to put up, place"; Amar.Akk. *NaṢaBa* "to put in place"; Ug. *NṢB* "to stand, erect (a monument)"; J.Aram. *NaṢaB* "to put up, plant"; Syriac *NeṢaB*; Mandaic *NṢB* "to set up, establish"; Palm. *NṢB*; Soq. *NṢB*; ESArab. *NṢB*; Arabic *NaṢaBa*. 1. "to be appointed" vb.

a) *WKN' Š'NT 'SR WŠMN R'Š 'MŠ'RT NṢḂ*
"and she was for eighteen years appointed (?) as the chief singer" (or "chief gatekeeper")
(N.Pu. Tunisia: KAI/I p. 25, ins. #136, lines 5-6)

Bibl. KAI/II 135; JNES 32 (1971) 481.

NṢB II B.Heb. *NeṢīB* "pillar"; Anc.Aram. *NṢB* "monument"; ESArab. *NṢB* "funerary monument"; Arabic *NaṢBuN* "an idol set up by the pagan Arabs for sacrificial purposes"; [J.Aram. *NiṢBa'* "plant, shoots"; Syriac *NeṢBa'*; Mandaic *NaṢBa'* "creator, transplanter"]; Nab. *NṢYB* "stela"; Akk. *NaṢaBāTi* "columns" (?). 1. "pillar" n.m.

a) *NṢB MLKB'L*
"the pillar of *MLKB'L*"
(Pu. Malta: Slouszch p. 12, ins. #108, lines 1-2)

b) *NṢB MLK B'L 'Š NDR MTN'LM*
"the pillar of *MLK B'L* which *MTN'LM* vowed"
(Pu. Carthage: CIS I, ins. #194, lines 1-2)

c) *NṢB MLK 'MR 'Š Š[M] '[RS]*
"a pillar (upon which) '[*RŠ* pu]t a *MLK 'MR* sacrifice"
(Pu. Malta: Amadasi p. 22, ins. #5, lines 1-2)

d) *NṢB MLK B'L 'Š ŠM NḤM*
"a pillar (upon which) *NḤM* put a *MLK B'L* sacrifice"
(Pu. Malta: Amadasi p. 20, ins. #4, lines 1-2)

e) *HNṢB Z*
"this pillar"
(Pu. Carthage: CIS I, ins. #5632, line 6)

Bibl. DISO 184; Harris 125; Amadasi 20-21; Slouszch 49, 125-26; NE 325.

NṢB III B.Heb. *NeṢīB* "prefect"; N.Heb. *NeṢiB* "officer". 1. "deputy" n.m.

a) *NṢB MLKT BMṢRM*
"deputy work supervisor in *MṢRM*"
(Pu. Carthage: CIS I, ins. #98, line 4)

Bibl. Harris 125; DISO 184; NE 325.

NṢḤ B.Heb. *NāṢaḤ* "to be enduring, act as an overseer"; N.Heb. *NaṢaḤ* "to conquer"; J.Aram. *NeṢaḤ* "to be victorious"; Syriac *NeṢaḤ* "to shine out, be brilliant"; Arabic *NaṢaḤa* "to be pure, reliable". 1. "to conquer" vb.

a) *NṢḤT 'T [ ]Y HYṢ'M W'ZRNM*
"I conquered the [ ] of the attackers and their helpers"
(Ph. Idalion: CIS I, ins. #91, line 2)

Bibl. Slouszch 100; DISO 184; PPG 69; NE 325; Harris 125.

NṢR Heb. *NāṢaR* "to watch, guard"; Akk. *NaṢāRu*; Anc.Aram. *NṢR*; Emp.Aram. *NṢR*; J.Aram. *NeṬaR*; Syriac *NeṬaR*; Safaitic *NṢR* "aid"; Mandaic *NṬR* "to wait"; Arabic *NaŻaRa* "to look in order to see"; [Soq. *NṢR* "to be split; Geez *NaẒaRa* "to break, shatter"]. 1. "to watch" vb.

a) *ŠMR WNṢR ḤLṢB'L BN 'ŠY*
"*ḤLṢB'L* son of *'ŠY* guarded and watched"
(Pu. Carthage: RES 20, lines 1-2)

b) *NṢR WŠMR ḤLṢB'L BN 'RŠTB'L*
"*ḤLṢB'L* son of *'RŠTB'L* guarded and watched"
(Pu. Carthage: RES 19, lines 1-2)

Bibl. Slouszch 205; DISO 185; PPG 8; Harris 125; ESE I 185; JAOS 93 (1973) 193-96.

NQY B.Heb. *NāQī* "clean"; Syriac *NeQa'* "to be adapted, ready"; Mandaic *NaQia'* "clean, pure"; J.Aram. *NeQa'* "to cleanse, clear"; Arabic *NaQiya* "to clear, purify"; Soq. *NeQe* "to be proper". 1. "clean" adj. m.

a) *NQY BKLTY*
"clean, upon its completion"
(Pu. Malta: CIS I, ins. #124, line 2)

Bibl. Slouszch 109; Amadasi 18; Harris 125; DISO 185; PPG 110.

NQŠM etymology unknown. 1. "portion" n.m. (from context)

a) *'YŠ LNQŠMY KYTB*
"each was noted down according to his portion (?)"
(N.Pu. Henschir Medina: KAI/I p. 29, ins. #160, line 2)

Bibl. KAI/II 149.

NŠ' I C.S. Ph., Pu. *NŠ'* (N.Pu. *N'Š'*, *N'Š'*). 1. "to carry" vb. 2. "to raise, lift"; hence, "to offer"

1 a) *W'L YŠ' 'YT ḤLT MŠKBY*
"and may he not carry away the sarcophagus of my resting place"
(Ph. Sidon: KAI/I p. 3, ins. #14, line 5)

b) *'M 'Š YŠ' 'YT ḤLT Z*
"or shall carry away this sarcophagus"
(Ph. Sidon: KAI/I p. 3, ins. #14, lines 10-11)

c) *'M 'Š YŠ' 'YT ḤLT MŠKBY*
"or shall carry away the sarcophagus of my resting place"
(Ph. Sidon: KAI/I p. 3, ins. #14, line 7)

2 a) *'Š NŠ' 'RSTB'L BT B'LŠLK*
"that which *'RSTB'L* daughter of *B'LŠLK* offered"
(Pu. Carthage: CIS I, ins. #414, lines 3-4)

b) *'Š NŠ' SKNYTN BN BD'*
"that which *SKNYTN* son of *BD'* offered"
(Pu. Hadramatum: NE p. 432, ins. #2, line 2)

c) *N'Š' ŠDBR L'DN LB'LMN*
"*ŠDBR* offered to the lord, to *B'L ḤMN*"
(N.Pu. Guelma: JA Series 11 vol. 8 [1916] p. 504, ins. #24, lines 1-2)

d) *N'Š' PNṬN' BN MGNM*
"*PNṬN'* son of *MGNM* offered"
(N.Pu. Guelma: JA Series 11 vol. 8 [1916] p. 503, ins. #22, lines 1-2)

Bibl. NE 326; KAI/II 19; Harris 125; DISO 186-87; PPG 79; ANET 662.

***NŠ' II** 1. "to donate" perhaps denominative vb. from *NŠ'*, "offering".

a) *'T M'NŠ' WMBṢ' LMLKT HMQ[M]*
"with the donors (?) and the contributors (?) to the labor of the tem[ple]"
(N.Pu. Leptis Magna: KAI/I p. 22, ins. #119, line 6)

Bibl. KAI/II 124.

NŠ' III B.Heb. *Maŝŝ'ā* "tribute, load"; Akk. *Maššu*; N.Heb. *Maŝŝ'ā* "carrying, burden".
1. "offering" n.m. Pu. *NŠ'* (N.Pu. *N'Š'*)

a) *MTNT 'Š NDR [ ] BN MHRB'L NŠ' L'LM*
"a present which [ ] the son of *MHRB'L* vowed, an offering to the god(s)"
(Pu. Constantine: Berthier/Charlier p. 75, ins. #87, line 2)

b) *N'Š' ŠDBR*
"the offering of *ŠDBR*"
(N.Pu. Guelma: JA Series 11 vol. 8 [1916] p. 504, ins. #24, line 1)

Bibl. Berthier/Charlier 76; Harris 125; DISO 187; LS I 112.

NŠ' IV

Heb. *Nāśi'* "chief, officer, prince".
1. "chief" n.m.

a) *ŠM'B'L BN MGN 'Š NŠ' HGW*
"*ŠM'B'L* son of *MGN* who is the chief of the community"
(Ph. Piraeus: KAI/I p. 13, ins. #60, line 2)

b) *H'DMN 'Š NŠ'M LN*
"the men who (were) our chiefs"
(Ph. Piraeus: KAI/I p. 13, ins. #60, line 4)

Bibl. KAI/II 73; Harris 126; Slouszch 117; NE 326; DISO 187; CBQ 25 (1963) 111-17; Or 26 (1957) 343 note 2; Syria 20 (1939) 174 note 3.

NŠR

B.Heb. *MaSSōR* "saw"; Akk. *MaSSaRu*; N.Heb. *NiSSeR* "to cut"; J.Aram. *NeSaR*; Syriac *NeSaR*; Mandaic *NSR* "to lacerate"; Geez *NaSaRa* "to saw (wood)"; Arabic *NaŠaRa*; Soq. *MiNŠaR* "saw"; Geez *MoŠaRT*; Amh. *MəSaR* "ax". 1. "cutter" n.m.

a) *MTN NYŠR*
"*MTN* the cutter (?) (of trees)"
(Pu. Carthage: BAC [1917] p. 158, ins. #34, line 2)

NTK

[J.Aram. *TeKaK* "to squeeze, annoy"; Syriac *TeKaK* "to press hard, weigh upon"].
1. "to bind with magic" vb.

a) *'TK 'NKY MṢLH 'YT 'M'[Š]TRT*
"I *MṢLH* bind *'M'[Š]TRT*"
(Pu. Carthage: KAI/I p. 18, ins. #89, line 2)

Bibl. PPG 70, 75-76; DISO 328; Harris 155; Branden 93; KAI/II 102.

NTN

for etymology, see under *YTN*. 1. "to give" vb.

a) *'BRGD NT<N> ŠY*
"*'BRGD* offered a gift (to the god)"
(Ph. site unknown: IEJ 16 [1966] p. 243, lines 1-3)

Bibl. IEJ 16 (1966) 245.

S

SG B.Heb. *SūG* "to backslide". 1. "strife" n.m. (reading uncertain)

a) *TŠ'M ŠLM SG NŠBT*
"if you seek peace, we shall cease strife"
(Ph. Byblos: JAOS 81 [1961] p. 32, lines 2-3)

Bibl. JAOS 81 (1961) 32-33; KAI/II 5; LS I 38-40; BASOR 212 (1973) 19.

SGN B.Heb. *SeGaN* "head official, noble, prefect"; N.Heb. *SeGaN* "chief, adjutant, high priest"; Akk. *ŠaKNu* "prefect"; Emp.Aram. *SGN* "governor, prefect, chief"; B.Aram. *SeGaN*; J.Aram. *SeGaNa'* "chief, adjutant, high priest". 1. "temple functionary" n.m.

a) *MTNB'L BN B'LYTN -ḤSGN Š HMQM*
"*MTNB'L* son of *B'LYTN* the overseer (?) of the sacred place"
(N.Pu. Malta: KAI/I p. 28, ins. #146, line 4)

SGR Heb. *SāGaR, SāKaR* "to close"; Ug. *SKR*; Akk. *SaKāRu*; Arabic *SaKaRa*; Syriac *SeGaR*; J.Aram. *SeGaR*; Q.Aram. *SKR*; Mandaic *SKR, SGR*; Amh. *SaGG^{W}aRa* "to bolt the door". (I am not convinced that the roots *SKR* and *SGR* are phonetic variations of the same Proto-Semitic lexeme; they may represent two distinct roots.) 1. "to deliver up" vb. (Y)

a) *WYSGRNM H'LNM HQDŠM*
"may the holy gods deliver them up"
(Ph. Sidon: KAI/I p. 3, ins. #14, line 9)

b) *LM YSGRNM 'LNM HQDŠM*
"lest the holy gods deliver them up"
(Ph. Sidon: KAI/I p. 3, ins. #14, lines 21-22)

Bibl. ANET 662; KAI/II 19; DISO 190; Slouszch 22, 29; PPG 50, 62 note 2; 68, 90, 93; LS I 90-91.

SDL N.Heb. *SaNDāL* "sandal"; J.Aram. *SaNDLa'*; Syriac *SeDLa'*; Gk. *Sandelion*; Mandaic **SaNDLa'*. 1. "sandal" n.m.

a) *P'L SDLM*
"makers of sandals"
(Pu. Carthage: CRAI [1968] p. 117, line 6)

Bibl. CRAI (1968) 130-31.

SWYT Heb. *MaSWeh* "cover, veil". 1. "veil" n.f.

a) *LSWYT 'LT*
"veil (?) upon (?)"
(Pu. Carthage: KAI/I p. 17, ins. #76, line A 4)

Bibl. DISO 191; KAI/II 93; PPG 99; Slouszch 168; Harris 126.

SWT Heb. *SūT* (Gen. 49:11) "garment". 1. "burial robe" n.f. 2. "garment" n.f.

1 a) *ŠKBT BSWT*
"lie in a burial robe"
(Ph. Byblos: KAI/I p. 2, ins. #11, line 1)

2 a) *'LMT YTN BŠ WĠBR BSWT*
"(who) gave a maid for a sheep and a man for a garment"
(Ph. Zinjirli: KAI/I p. 5, ins. #24, line 8)

Bibl. KAI/II 15-16, 31; ANET 654; Slouszch 340; Harris 126; DISO 191.

SḤB B.Heb. *SāḤaB* "to drag"; N.Heb. *SāḤaP* "to rub, sweep"; Moab. *SḤB* "to drag"; Arabic *SaḤaBa*; Geez *SaḤaBa*; Soq. *SḤoB*. 1. "sweeper" n.m.

a) *BN 'BDŠ[ ]' HSḤB*
"son of *'BDŠ*[ ]', the sweeper (?)"
(Pu. Carthage: CIS I, ins. #355, line 2)

Bibl. Slouszch 262-63; Harris 126; DISO 192.

SḤR Heb. *SāḤaR* "to go around"; Akk. *SaḪāRu*, *SaḪiRu*; J.Aram. *SeḤaR*; Syriac *SeḤaR* "to go around begging"; Mandaic *SHR* "to move about". 1. "merchant" n.m.

a) *QBR B'L'ZR BN ḤNB'[L] ḤSḤR*
"the grave of *B'L'ZR*, son of *ḤNB'*[*L*] the merchant"
(Pu. Carthage: Slouszch p. 187, ins. #165, line 1)

b) *QBR ḤLṢB'L BN BD' SḤR 'WR*
"the grave of *ḤLṢB'L*, son of *BD'*, the blind (?) merchant"
(Pu. Carthage: Slouszch p. 190, ins. #174, line 4)

Bibl. DISO 192; Slouszch 186-87, 190; Harris 126; BASOR 164 (1961) 23-28; Albright 78 n. 92; ZA 43 (1935) 76.

SḤRT I — B.Heb. *SeḤoRā* coll. n. meaning "merchants" (Ez 27:15). 1. "the quality or profession of a merchant" coll. n.

a) *SḤRT NST*
"merchants, clan representatives"
(Pu. Carthage: CRAI [1968] p. 117, line 5)

Bibl. RSO 43 (1968) 14-15; CRAI (1968) 126-27.

SḤRT II — Heb. *SōḤeR* "traveller, vagabond, merchant"; Akk. *SaḪḪiRu* "vagabond". 1. "merchant" n.f.

a) *QBR ŠBLT SḤRT ḤQRT*
"the grave of *ŠBLT*, the merchant of the city"
(Pu. Carthage: CIS I, ins. #5948, line 1)

Bibl. Slouszch 198; Harris 126; PPG 99; DISO 192; KAI/II 104.

SYW'T — etymology unknown. 1. "tomb" n.m. (from context)

a) *LMB'BN 'Š 'L HSYWṬ*
"from the (grave)stone which is upon the tomb (?)"
(N.Pu. Dschebel Massoudj: KAI/I p. 26, ins. #141, line 4)

Bibl. KAI/II 139; DISO 192.

SYNṬR — Lat. *senator*. 1. "senator" n.m.

a) *'S NDR ḤMLK BN 'ŠMN'MS SYNṬR*
"that which *ḤMLK* son of *'ŠMN'MS* the senator vowed"
(Pu. Carthage: CIS I, ins. #3404, lines 2-3)

Bibl. Slouszch 349; PPG 43, 99; DISO 192; Harris 126.

SK' etymology unknown. 1. "to die" vb. (from context)

a) *SK' BN ŠNT ŠNM*
"he died (?) at two years of age"
(N.Pu. Maktar: KAI/I p. 28, ins. #151, line 3)

Bibl. KAI/II 146; DISO 192; PPG 79.

SKN B.Heb. *SōKeN* "steward"; N.Heb. *SeGaN* "assistant"; Amar.Akk. *ZuKiNi*; Akk. *ŠaKNu* "governor"; Ug. *SKN*; Anc.Aram. *SKN*; Q.Aram. *SGN* "ruler". 1. "governor" n.m. 2. "overlord" n.m.

1 a) *WSKN BS[K]NM*
"and a governor among governors" (or: "if any governor")
(Ph. Byblos: KAI/I p. 1, ins. #1, line 2)

b) *SKN QRTḤDŠT*
"governor of *QRTḤDŠT*"
(Ph. Limassol: KAI/I p. 7, ins. #31, line 2)

2 a) *L'SKN 'DR*
"to the mighty overlord (?)"
(Ph. Athens: Slouszch p. 120, ins. #103, line 2)

Bibl. DISO 193; KAI/II 2, 49; Slouszch 3, 66, 121; LS II 293-96; Harris 126; Benz 365-66; NE 329; JAOS 87 (1967) 517-24; JAOS 88 (1968) 461-82; Scripta Hierosolmitana VIII, Jerusalem, 395.

SKR I Heb. *ZāKaR* "to remember, call to mind"; Akk. *ZaKāRu* "to say, name"; Anc.Aram. *ZKR* "to remember, call to mind"; Emp.Aram. *ZKR*; J.Aram. *DeKaR*; Syriac *DeKaR*; Palm. *DKR*; Arabic *D̲aKaRa*; ESArab. *D̲KR* "to record". 1. "to remember" vb.

a) *WYSKRN MLQRT*
"may *MLQRT* remember me"
(Ph. Larnaka: KAI/I p. 10, ins. #43, line 15)

Bibl. Benz 305-6; Harris 99; DISO 76-77; PPG 61, 88, 91; KAI/II 60.

SKR II Heb. *ZeKeR* "memorial, remembrance"; Anc.Aram. *ZKR*; J.Aram. *DuKRāNa'*; Syriac *DuKRaNa'*; Mandaic *DuKRaNa'*; Arabic *D̲uKRuN*; ESArab *D̲KR* "thought". Ph., N.Ph. *SKR* (N.Pu. *SK'R*). 1. "memorial" n.m.

a) *LKNY LY LSKR*
"that it may be for me as a memorial"
(Ph. Umm el-Awamid: KAI/I p. 4, ins. #18, line 6)

b) *MṢBT SKR BḤYM*
"a memorial monument among the living"
(Ph. Athens: KAI/I p. 13, ins. #53, line 1)

c) *SKR KBD 'L P'LT M'ŠRT*
"a monument of honor for honest deed(s)"
(N.Pu. Leptis Magna: KAI/I p. 23, ins. #123, lines 4-5)

d) *SK'R DR' L'LM*
"the memorial of his family for eternity"
(N.Pu. Guelaat Bou-Sba: KAI/I p. 30, ins. #165, lines 7-8)

Bibl. DISO 77; PPG 19, 38; Harris 99; KAI/II 26, 70, 154; Branden 7; NE 267-68; Benz 305-6.

SKRN Heb. *ZiKKāRōN* "memorial, mention"; B.Aram. *DiKRōN*; J.Aram. *DuKRāNa'*; Nab. *DKRN*; Syriac *DuKRaNa'*; Mandaic *DuKRaNa'*.
1. "memorial" n.m.

a) *LSKRN BḤYM*
"as a memorial among the living"
(Ph. Larnaka: Mus 51 [1938] p. 286, line 3)

Bibl. DISO 78; Mus 51 (1938) 291.

SLM I Heb. *SuLLāM* "ladder, ascent"; Akk. *SiMMiLTu* "staircase, steps"; Syriac *SeBLeTa'* "staircase, ladder"; N.Syr. *SiMaLTa'*; J.Aram. *SuLMa'*; Mandaic *SuMBiLTa'*; Amh. *MaSaLaL*; Arabic *SuLLaMuN*. 1. "stairs" n.m.

a) *WHSLMT 'Š LMPQD*
"and the stairs of the tower"
(Ph. Idalion: CIS I, ins. #88, line 4)

b) *SMLM BSLMT HMPQD*
"images on the stairs of the tower"
(Ph. Idalion: CIS I, ins. #88, line 5)

Bibl. ZA 41 (1933) 230-31; Speiser 218; DISO 193; NSI 75; Harris 126; Slouszch 99; NE 329.

SLM II meaning and etymology unknown.

a) *'ZMLK SLM H'GLM*
(Pu. Carthage: CIS I, ins. #5601, lines 4-5)

SML Heb. *SeMeL* "image, statue". 1. "image" n.m.

a) *L'DNN WLSML B'L*
"for our lord and for the image of *B'L*"
(Ph. Sidon: KAI/I p. 2, ins. #12, lines 3-4)

b) *SML 'Z*
"this image"
(Ph. Tamassos: KAI/I p. 9, ins. #41, line 1)

c) *HSML Z MŠ 'NK YTNB'L*
"this image is a statue of me, *YTNB'L*"
(Ph. Larnaka: KAI/I p. 10, ins. #13, line 2)

d) *SML ZR*
"hated (?) image"
(Ph. Karatepe: KAI/I p. 6, ins. #26, line C IV,18)

e) *W'YT SML H'LM*
"and the image(s) of the god(s)"
(Ph. Karatepe: KAI/I p. 6, ins. #26, lines C IV,18-19)

f) *HSMLM H'L*
"these images"
(Ph. Idalion: KAI/I p. 9, ins. #40, line 3)

Bibl. ANET 653; KAI/II 16, 36, 58, 60; DISO 194-95; Benz 367; Harris 126; NE 329; LS II 286-87.

**SMLT* Heb. *SeMeL* "image, statue". 1. "image" n.f.

a) *[S]MLT '[Z]*
"t[his] [im]age"
(Ph. Kition: Slouszch p. 70, ins. #60, line 2)

Bibl. NSI 58; Harris 127; NE 329; DISO 194-95; Benz 367; LS II 286-87.

SMR I

N.Heb. *MaSMeR* "nail, spike"; J.Aram. *MaSMeRa'*; Arabic *MiSMaRuN*; [Akk. *'aSMaRu* "lance"], *SaMaRTuM* "nail".
1. "scepter" n.m.

a) *SMR Z QN KLMW BR ḤY*
"the scepter (?) which *KLMW* son of *ḤY* fashioned (?)"
(Ph. Zinjirli: KAI/I p. 5, ins. #25, lines 1-3)

Bibl. ANET 655; DISO 195; KAI/II 35.

SMR II

Heb. *MaSMeR* "nail"; J.Aram. *MaSMeRa'*; Amh. *MəSMaR*; Arabic *MiSMaRuN*; Akk. *SaMaRTuM*. 1. "to nail" vb.

a) *WSMRT BQR*
"and I nailed (?) to the wall"
(Ph. Larnaka: KAI/I p. 10, ins. #43, line 13)

Bibl. KAI/II 60; DISO 195.

SS

Heb. *SūS* "horse"; Akk. *SiSū*; Ug. *SSW*; Eg. *SSM.T*; Anc.Aram. *SSYH*; J.Aram. *SūSYa'*; Syriac *SūSYa'*; Mandaic *SuSYa'*; Nab. *SWSY'*; Palm. *SWSY*. 1. "horse" n.m.

a) *WP'L 'NK SS 'L SS*
"and I acquired horse upon horse"
(Ph. Karatepe: KAI/I p. 5, ins. #26, lines A I,6-7)

Bibl. DISO 195; KAI/II 36; Bib 44 (1963) 70; ANET 653; JAOS 64 (1944) 175, also note 41; JCS 20 (1966) 121-22.

SP

Heb. *SaP* "basin"; Akk. *Š/SaPPu*.
1. "basin, bowl" n.m.

a) *HSP Z*
"this basin"
(Ph. Tyre: NSI p. 43, ins. #8, line 1)

b) *ḤṢY HSP Z*
"half of this basin"
(Ph. Tyre: NSI p. 43, ins. #8, line 6)

c) *SPM ŠNM*
"two basins"
(N.Pu. Bir Bou-Rekba: KAI/I p. 26, ins. #137, line 6)

Bibl. NSI 43; DISO 196; Harris 127; KAI/II 136.

SPR I Heb. *SePeR* "missive, book, tablet"; Akk. *ŠiPRu*; Ug. *SPR*; Anc.Aram. *SPR*; Emp.Aram. *SPRH*; J.Aram. *SiPRa'*; Syriac *SePRa'*; Mandaic *SiPRa'*; Arabic *SiFRuN*; Saftaitic *SFR*. 1. "inscription" n.m. 2. "letter"

1 a) *WH' YMḤ SPRH LPP ŠBL*
"and as for him, let a (?) efface his inscription"
(Ph. Byblos: KAI/I p. 1, ins. #1, line 2)

b) *WMY YŠḤT HSPR Z*
"he who ruins this inscription"
(Ph. Zinjirli: KAI/I p. 4, ins. #24, line 15)

c) *WYZQ BSPR Z*
"and damage this inscription"
(Ph. Zinjirli: KAI/I p. 4, ins. #25, line 14)

2 a) *WŠLḤT LY 'T SPR HNQT*
"and you sent me the letter of (?)"
(Ph. Saqqara: KAI/I p. 12, ins. #50, lines 5-6)

Bibl. KAI/II 2, 31, 67; DISO 196-97; Harris 127; NE 330; Slouszch 5.

SPR II Heb. *SōPeR* "scribe"; Akk. *ŠāPiRu*; Anc.Aram. *SPR*; Emp.Aram. *SPR*; Ug. *SPR*; J.Aram. *SaPRa'*; Syriac *SaPRa'*; B.Aram. *SāPRa'*; Mandaic *SaPRa'*. 1. "scribe" n.m.

a) *MHRB'L HSPR*
"*MHRB'L* the scribe"
(Ph. Tharros: Slouszch p. 138, ins. #124, lines 3-4)

b) *ṢDN BT MṢRY HSPR*
"*ṢDN* daughter of *MṢRY* the scribe"
(Pu. Carthage: Slouszch p. 328, ins. #526, lines 3-4)

c) *'Š N[DR] ŠPṬ SPR HDLḤT*
"that which *ŠPṬ*, the tablet scribe (?) [vowe]d"
(Pu. Carthage: Slouszch p. 333, ins. #544, lines 2-3)

d) *B'LŠL[K] HSPR*
"*B'LŠL[K]* the scribe"
(Pu. Carthage: Slouszch p. 273, ins. #364, lines 3-4)

e) *'BD'ŠMN RB SPRM*
"*'BD'ŠMN*, the chief scribe"
(Ph. Kition: CIS I,
ins. #86, line A 15)

Bibl. DISO 196; Harris 127; NE 330;
Slouszch 138, 333; KAI/II 54.

SRSR N.Heb. *SaRSūR* "broker, middleman";
J.Aram. *SaRSūRa'*; [Arabic *SuRSuRuN*
"intelligent, skillful"]. 1. "broker"
n.m.

a) *'RŠ RB SRSRM*
"*'RŠ*, the chief of the brokers"
(Ph. Kition: NSI p. 70, ins.
#21, line 2)

b) *MNḤM RB SRSRM*
"*MNḤM*, the chief of the brokers"
(Ph. Kition: NSI p. 70, ins.
#21, line 2)

Bibl. NSI 70-71; Slouszch 84; Harris 127;
KAI/II 52; DISO 198.

SR Heb. *SūR* "to turn aside". 1. "to remove"
vb.

a) *W'M TSṘ M[L']ḲT Z'*
"and if you remove this w[or]k"
(Ph. Byblos: KAI/I p. 2,
ins. #10, lines 13-14)

b) *WKL 'Š LSR*
"and all who will remove"
(Pu. Carthage: KAI/I p. 17,
ins. #79, lines 6-7)

Bibl. DISO 191; PPG 79; KAI/II 97; ANET
656; Harris 126; Slouszch 175;
Branden 98.

ᶜ

ʿBD I

Heb. *ʿāBaD* "to work, serve"; Ug. *ʿBD*; Anc.Aram. *ʿBD* "to do, make"; Emp.Aram. *ʿBD*; Syriac *ʿaBaD*; Mandaic *ʿABD*; J.Aram. *ʿaBaD*; Nab. *ʿBD*; Palm. *ʿBD*; Arabic *ʿaBaDa* "to work, serve god". 1. "to serve" vb. 2. "to use"

1 a) *WBRBM YʿBD LʾZTWD*
"may they greatly serve *ʾZTWD*"
(Ph. Karatepe: KAI/I p. 5, ins. #26, line A III,10-11)

b) *ʾŠ BL ʾŠ ʿBD KN LBT MPŠ*
"none of whom served the house of *MPŠ*"
(Ph. Karatepe: KAI/I p. 5, ins. #26, lines A I,15-16)

2 a) *YTNʾ L ʿBD BṢPʿT KL Ḥʿ T*
"they allowed him to use (?) the tunic at all times"
(N.Pu. Leptis Magna: KAI/I p. 24, ins. #126, line 9)

Bibl. DISO 199-201; KAI/II 36, 131; ANET 653; Benz 369-72; Harris 128-30; JAOS 92 (1972) 77.

ʿBD II

C.S. 1. "servant of a god" 2. "slave of a person" 3. "temple slave"

1 a) *ʾNK ʾZTWD HBRK BʿL ʿBD BʿL*
"I am *ʾZTWD* the blessed of *BʿL*, the servant of *BʿL*"
(Ph. Karatepe: KAI/I p. 5, ins. #26, lines A I,1-2)

b) *ʾŠ NDR ʿBDK ʿBDʾSR*
"that which your servant *ʿBDʾSR* vowed"
(Ph. Malta: Slouszch p. 124, ins. #107, lines 1-2)

c) *ḤRPKRT YTN ḤYM LʿBDY*
"*ḤRPKRT* granted life to his servant"
(Ph. Egypt: Slouszch p. 65, ins. #55, lines 1-2)

2 a) *ʾŠ NDR KBRM ʿBD ʿBDMLQRT*
"that which *ʿKBRM*, the slave of *ʿDBMLQRT* vowed"
(Pu. Carthage: Slouszch p. 320, ins. #507, lines 3-4)

b) *'Š NDR KNMY 'BD 'ŠMN'MS*
"that which *KNMY*, the slave of *'ŠMN'MS* vowed"
(Pu. Carthage: Slouszch p. 174, ins. #153, lines 3-4)

c) *'BD ṢDMLQRT*
"the slave of *ṢDMLQRT*"
(Pu. Carthage: CIS I, ins. #256, lines 3-4)

3 a) *'BD BT 'RŠ[P]*
"the slave of the temple of *'RŠ[P]*"
(Pu. Carthage: Slouszch p. 277, ins. #376, line 2)

b) *'BD B[T] MLK'ŠTRT*
"the slave of the tem[ple] of *MLK'ŠTRT*"
(Pu. Carthage: Slouszch p. 263, ins. #334, lines 5-6)

Bibl. DISO 201-2; Slouszch 277; ANET 653; KAI/II 36; Harris 128; Benz 369-72; Amadasi 17.

'BN etymology unknown. 1. "to be buried" vb. (from context)

a) *N̈'PṢ 'DYT HNKT 'BNT*
"the gravestone of *'DYT*. Here she lies buried (?)"
(N.Pu. Tunisia: KAI/I p. 25, ins. #136, lines 1-2)

b) *HNKT 'BNT TḤT 'BN ZT QBRT*
"here she lies buried under this stone, laid to rest"
(N.Pu. Tunisia: NSI p. 142, ins. #54, line 4)

c) *HNKT 'BNT T'T HBNT ZT QBRT*
"here she lies buried under this stone, laid to rest"
(N.Pu. Tunisia: NE p. 436, ins. #9, lines 4-5)

Bibl. NSI 142-43; Mus 84 (1971) 534-35; DISO 3; Harris 97; KAI/II 135; NE 205.

'BR I Heb. *'aBūR* "for the sake of"; Geez *Ba'aBReT* "on account of". 1. "by the grace of" preposition

a) *B'BR B'L W'LM*
"by the grace of *B'L* and the gods"
(Ph. Karatepe: KAI/I p. 5, ins. #26, line A I,8)

b) *WBNY 'NK B'BR B'L WB'BR RŠP ṢPRM*
"and I built it by the grace of *B'L* and the grace of *RŠP ṢPRM*"
(Ph. Karatepe: KAI/I p. 5, ins. #26, line A II,11-12)

Bibl. ANET 653; KAI/II 36; PPG 126; Branden 117; DISO 202; LS I 75.

'BR II Heb. *'āBaR* "to pass on, cross"; Akk. *eBēRu*; Anc.Aram. *'BR*; Emp.Aram. *'BR*; J.Aram. *'aBaR*; Syriac *'aBaR*; Mandaic *'BR*; Arabic *'aBaRa*; Soq. *'BR*. 1. "to pass" vb.

a) *L'PT' BḤDR ḤŠK 'BR*
"O fliers, from the underworld (?) pass"
(Ph. Arslan Tash: BASOR 197 [1970] p. 46, col. B, line 1)

b) *MN' ḤMŠ PRṢM L'BR BN' Y'BR*
"he counted five *PRṢM* to pass, (?) his (?) will pass"
(N.Pu. Tripolitania: Or 33 [1964] p. 4, line 5)

Bibl. DISO 202; KAI/II 43; BASOR 197 (1970) 46, esp. note 23a; Or 33 (1964) 12.

*'*BR* III Heb. *'aBūR* "yield"; Akk. *eBūRu* "harvest"; Emp.Aram. *'BR*; Syriac *'aBuRa'* "corn"; J.Aram. *'eBūRa'* "grain, bread stuff"; Mandaic *'BuRia'*. 1. "field produce" n.m.

a) *T HMZBḤ ŠHMQNT Š'BR'*
"and the altar for cattle (and for) field produce"
(N.Pu. Bir Tlesa: KAI/I p. 26, ins. #138, line 3)

Bibl. DISO 202; LS I 98-99; KAI/II 138; JNES 8 (1949) 249-51; Bib 48 (1967) 551, 555.

'G' Heb. *'ūGā* "cake of bread". 1. "bread cake" n.f.

a) *Š'G' ŠBŠM*
"for bread cake (?), for spice (?)"
(N.Pu. Bir Tlesa: KAI/I p. 26, ins. #138, line 4)

Bibl. KAI/II 137; DISO 202; LS I 99.

'GL Heb. *'eGeL* "young bull"; Ug. *'GL;* Anc.Aram. *'GL;* Syriac *'eGLa';* J.Aram. *'iGLa';* Arabic *'iJLuN;* Akk. *'aGaLu* "an equid". 1. "calf" n.m.

a) *B'GL 'Š QRNY LMBMḤSR*
"for a calf whose horns are wanting"
(Pu. Marseilles: CIS I, ins. #165, line 5)

Bibl. DISO 202; Harris 131; Amadasi 169; KAI/II 83; Slouszch 144.

'GLT Heb. *'aGāLā* "chariot, cart"; J.Aram. *'aGaLTa';* Syriac *'aGaLTa';* Arabic *'aJaLaTuN.* 1. "cart" n.f.

a) *ḤRŠ 'GLT*
"the wagon craftsman"
(Ph. Kition: NSI p. 72, ins. #22, line 2)

b) *'Š NDR MGN BN ḤMLK BN ḤMLKT 'GLT 'Ṣ*
"that which *MGN*, son of *ḤMLK* son of *ḤMLKT* (the maker) of wooden wagons vowed"
(Pu. Carthage: Slouszch p. 296, ins. #430, lines 2-3)

Bibl. DISO 202; Slouszch 296; Harris 131; NSI 72-73.

'D I Heb. *'aD* "until, while, even"; Ug. *'D;* Akk. *'aDi;* Mandaic *'aD;* Syriac *'aD;* J.Aram. *'aD;* ESArab. *'D;* Soq. *'aD* "again, not again"; Arabic *'aTa(y)* "until". 1. "until" preposition 2. "even" 3. in combinations

1 a) *LMMṢ' ŠMŠ W'D MB'Y*
"from the rising of the sun (east) and until its setting (west)"
(Ph. Karatepe: KAI/I p. 5, ins. #26, lines A I,4-5)

2 a) *'DRNM W'D Ṣ'RN[M]*
"the greatest of them even unto the least of [them]"
(Pu. Sardinia: KAI/I p. 14, ins. #65, line 2)

3 a) *YRḤ MD YRḤ 'D 'LM*
"month by month for eternity"
(Ph. Larnaka: KAI/I p. 10, ins. #43, line 12)

b) *YBRKY WYŠM' QL 'D 'LM*
"bless him and hear (his) voice for eternity"
(Pu. Carthage: KAI/I p. 17, ins. #78, line 1)

c) *ʿD PʿMT BRBM*
"exceedingly often (?)"
(Pu. Sardinia: KAI/I p. 15, ins. #68, line 5)

Bibl. DISO 203; PPG 125; KAI/II 36, 60, 80, 82, 96; Amadasi 115; ANET 653; Harris 131; Slouszch 159, 176.

ʿD II — Heb. *ʿōD* "still, yet, besides"; Emp.Aram. *ʿD*, *ʿWD*; B.Aram. *ʿōD*. 1. "moreover" adv. 2. "yet"

1 a) *WʿD YTN LN ʾDN MLKM ʾYT DʾR WYPY*
"and moreover, the lord of kingdoms gave us *DʾR* and *YPY*"
(Ph. Sidon: KAI/I p. 3, ins. #14, lines 18-19)

b) *WʿD KSP*
"and moreover (?) silver"
(Ph. Tyre: NSI p. 43, ins. #8, line 2)

2 a) *ʿD PʿMT BRBM*
"yet most exceedingly" (see *ʿD* I for another possible translation of this line)
(Pu. Sardinia: KAI/I p. 15, ins. #68, line 5)

Bibl. Harris 127; NSI 43; KAI/II 19, 82; ANET 662; Slouszch 27, 35; DISO 203; PPG 124; Amadasi 115.

ʿDL — Arabic *ʿaDDaLa* "to pronounce someone to be good or righteous"; Mandaic *ʿiDaLaT* "justice"; N.Syr. *ʿaDaLaT*; Syriac *ʿeDaL* "to find fault". 1. "to justify" vb.

a) *ʾLNM ŠM[Š] ʿDL ʾTY*
"the divine Su[n] (?) justified me"
(Pu. Carthage: ESE I p. 169, line 5)

Bibl. DISO 204; Slouszch 182.

ʿDR — Heb. *ʿeDeR* "flock, herd"; J.Aram. *ʿaDRaʾ*. 1. "herd" n.m.

a) *ŠTY BʿL ʿDR*
"I established him (as) the possessor of a herd"
(Ph. Zinjirli: KAI/I p. 4, ins. #24, line 11)

Bibl. DISO 205; KAI/II 31; ANET 654; Harris 131.

ʿ*WR* Heb. ʿ*iWWeR* "to be blind"; Ug. ʿ*WR* "to be blind in one eye"; Emp.Aram. ʿ*WYR* "to be blind"; Amh. *TaWWaRa*; Syriac ʿ*eWeR* "to put out one or both eyes"; J.Aram. ʿ*aWWeR* "to be blind"; Mandaic ʿ*aWR* "to be blind"; Arabic ʿ*aWiRa* "to be or become blind in one eye"; Soq. ʿ*eR* "to be blind".
1. "blind" adj. m.

a) *SḤR* ʿ*WR*
"the blind (?) merchant"
(Pu. Carthage: Slouszch p. 190, ins. #174, line 1)

Bibl. Slouszch 290.

ʿ*Z* I Heb. ʿ*oZ* "strength"; Ug. ʿ*Z*; J.Aram. ʿ*aZaZ* "to be strong"; Syriac ʿ*aZ* "to be powerful"; Mandaic ʿ*iZ* "power"; Emp.Aram. ʿ*ZYZ* "strong"; ESArab. ʿ*ZT* "glory"; Arabic ʿ*iZZuN* "power". 1. "strength" n.m.

a) *L*ʿ*NT* ʿ*Z ḤYM* (KAI reads *M*ʿ*Z ḤYM*)
"to ʿ*NT*, (who is) the strength of life" (or "strength of mortals")
(Ph. Larnaka: KAI/I p. 10, ins. #42, line 1)

b) *W*ʿ*Z* ʾ*DR* ʿ*L KL MLK*
"and awesome strength over all kings"
(Ph. Karatepe: KAI/I p. 6, ins. #26, line A III,4)

Bibl. DISO 205-6; ANET 653; KAI/II 36; Harris 131; Benz 374-75; Slouszch 106-7; JNES 31 (1971) 90; AJSL 41 (1925) 82.

ʿ*Z* II Heb. ʿ*āZaZ* "to be strong"; Ug. ʿ*Z*; Emp.Aram. ʿ*ZYZ* "strong"; J.Aram. ʿ*aZaZ* "to be strong"; Syriac ʿ*aZ*; Arabic ʿ*aZZa*; Soq. ʿ*ZZ*. 1. "mighty" adj. f.

a) *WBN* ʾ*NK ḤMYT* ʿ*ZT*
"and I built mighty fortresses"
(Ph. Karatepe: KAI/I p. 5, ins. #26, lines A I,13-14)

Bibl. ANET 653; KAI/II 36.

ʿ*Z* III C.S. 1. "goat" n.f.

a) *BYBL* ʾ*M B*ʿ*Z*
"for a ram or for a goat"
(Pu. Marseilles: KAI/I p. 15, ins. #69, line 7)

b) ʿ*RT H*ʿ*ZM*
"the skins of the goats"
(Pu. Carthage: KAI/I p. 16, ins. #74, line 4)

Bibl. Amadasi 169; ANET 656; DISO 206; Harris 134; Slouszch 144-45, 167; NE 344.

'ZZ for etymology, see under *'Z* adj.
1. "mighty" n.m.

a) *L'DN L'ZZ MLK'ŠTRT*
"to the lord, to the mighty one *MLK'ŠTRT*"
(Pu. Spain: Amadasi p. 146, ins. #12, lines 1-2)

Bibl. Amadasi 146; KAI/II 87; Or 26 (1957) 340; Benz 374-75.

'ZR Heb. *'āZaR* "to help"; Akk. *'aZāRu, ḪāZīRu* "helper"; Ug. *'ḎR*; J.Aram. *'aDaR* "to help, assist"; Mandaic *'uZaRa'* "helper"; Syriac *'aDaR*; Palm. *'DR*; Arabic *'aZZaRa* "to assist"; [*'aḎaRa* "to excuse or clear some one"]; ESArab. *'ḎR* "to give help". 1. "to help" vb.

a) *NṢḤT 'T [ ]Y HYṢ'M W'ZRNM*
"I conquered the (?) of the attackers and their helpers"
(Ph. Idalion: CIS I, ins. #91, line 2)

b) *K ŠM' QL' BRK' 'ZR'*
"because he heard his voice, he blessed him, he helped him"
(N.Pu. Constantine: JA Series 11 vol. 10 [1917] p. 65, ins. # Costa 92, lines 3-4)

c) *QL' ŠL' 'ZR*
"his voice helped (?)"
(N.Pu. Maktar: KAI/I p. 28, ins. #147, line 4)

Bibl. DISO 206; KAI/II 144; Harris 131-32; Slouszch 101; Benz 375-76.

'ṬPT B.Heb. *Ma'aṬāPā* "overtunic"; N.Heb. *M'aṬePeT* "wrap"; Syriac *'aṬaPa'*; Arabic *Mi'aṬaFuN*; Soq. *'aṬaF* "to cover".
1. "wrapping" n.f.

a) *KST W'ṬPT*
"coverings (?) and wrappings (?)"
(Pu. Carthage: Slouszch p. 162, ins. #140, line 1)

Bibl. Harris 132; Slouszch 162; DISO 206.

'ṬR Heb. *'āṬaR* "to crown, surround"; J.Aram. *'aṬaR*. 1. "to crown" vb.

a) *L'ṬR 'YT ŠM'B'L BN MGN*
"to crown *ŠM'B'L*, son of *MGN*"
(Ph. Piraeus: KAI/I p. 13, ins. #60, lines 1-2)

Bibl. KAI/II 73; DISO 206; Harris 132; Slouszch 117.

'ṬRT B.Heb. *'aṬāRā* "crown, wreath"; N.Heb. *'aṬāRa* "protection, brickwork, moulding". 1. "crown" n.f. 2. "cornice work" 3. figurative, meaning "glory"

1 a) *'ṬRT ḤRṢ*
"a gold crown"
(Ph. Piraeus: KAI/I p. 13, ins. #60, line 3)

2 a) *'ṬRT 'DR'T*
"glorious cornice(work)"
(N.Pu. Maktar: KAI/I p. 27, ins. #145, line 3)

3 a) *DL 'ṬRT WDL ŠM T'ṢMT*
"the possessor of glory (?) and the possessor of honor (?)"
(N.Pu. Guelaat Bou-Sba: KAI/I p. 30, ins. #165, lines 6-7)

Bibl. Harris 132; KAI/II 73, 141, 154; DISO 207; Slouszch 117.

'KSNDR' Gk. *Excedra* "a covered place in front of the house"; J.Aram. *'aKSaDRa'*; Palm. *'KSDR'*, *'KSDR'*; Q.Heb. *'KSDRN*.
1. "excedra" n.m.

a) *T 'KSNDR' WT 'RPT ST*
"the excedra and this portico"
(N.Pu. Leptis Magna: KAI/I p. 25, ins. #129, line 2)

Bibl. DISO 13; KAI/II 133.

'KR B.Heb. *'āKaR* "to stir up, disturb" (Josh. 7:27); N.Heb. *'āKaR* "to make turbid, ban" (Mish. Sanhedrin 6:2); Syriac *'aKaR* "to hinder, obstruct"; Q.Aram. *'KYR* "stirred"; J.Aram. *'aKaR* "make turbid"; Mandaic *'aKR* "to detain, obstruct"; Chr.Pal.Aram. *'KR* "to disquiet, confuse". 1. "to ban" vb.

a) *WL'KR WLŠBT Y'ML YD*[']
"and to ban (?) and to put an end to [that] which enfeebles [his] hand"
(Pu. Carthage: CIS I, ins. #5510, line 3)

Bibl. DISO 208.

'L I C.S. 1. "for, for the sake of" 2. "over, in charge of" 3. "against" 4. in combinations

1 a) *'L BN BNY*
"for the sake of her grandsons"
(Ph. Idalion: KAI/I p. 9, ins. #40, line 4)

b) *LSKR 'L M'SPT 'ṢMY*
"in memory of the gathering (place) of my bones"
(Pu. Carthage: Slouszch p. 178, ins. #155, line 4)

c) *'Š NDR MGN 'L 'DNB'L*
"that which *MGN* vowed for the sake of *'DNB'L*"
(Pu. Carthage: Slouszch p. 296, ins. #433, lines 3-4)

2 a) *MṬ'NM 'L HMLKT Z*
"appointed over this work"
(Pu. Dougga: KAI/I p. 19, ins. #96, line 5)

b) *H'ŠM 'Š 'L HMQDŠM*
"the men who are (appointed) over the sanctuaries"
(Pu. Carthage: KAI/I p. 17, ins. #80, line 1)

c) *'L BT 'LM*
"in charge of the temple"
(Ph. Piraeus: KAI/I p. 13, ins. #60, line 2)

d) *KL' 'L MLKT HBN'*
"they were (appointed) over the building work"
(N.Pu. Bir Bou-Rekba: KAI/I p. 26, ins. #137, line 2)

e) *MMLKT 'L GBL*
"ruler over *GBL*"
(Ph. Byblos: KAI/I p. 2, ins. #10, line 2)

f) *MLK GRB 'L Y'DY WBL P['L]*
"*GBR* ruled over *Y'DY* but he was in[effective]"
(Ph. Zinjirli: KAI/I p. 4, ins. #24, line 2)

g) *W'Z 'DR 'L KL MLK*
"and awesome strength over all kings"
(Ph. Karatepe: KAI/I p. 5, ins. #26, line A III,4)

3 a) *WŠKR 'NK 'LY MLK 'ŠR*
"and I hired against him the king of *'ŠR*"
(Ph. Zinjirli: KAI/I p. 4, ins. #24, lines 7-8)

4 a) *'L PN PTḤY Z*
"over against this engraved work of mine"
(Ph. Byblos: KAI/I p. 2, ins. #10, line 5)

b) *WDL H'LM 'Š 'L PN HMQDŠ[M 'L]*
"and with the stairs (?) which are set against [these sanc]-tuaries"
(Pu. Carthage: KAI/I p. 17, ins. #81, line 3)

c) *'L KN P'L[T]*
"on this account I made"
(Ph. Byblos: KAI/I p. 2, ins. #9, line A 2)

Bibl. ANET 656, 662; Harris 132-33; DISO 207-9; PPG 23, 124, 125, 126, 128; KAI/II 10, 12, 31, 36, 58, 73, 98, 136; Slouszch 181, 296; Branden 117.

'L II 1. "from" preposition (Ps. 81:6)

a) *WNḤT TBRḤ 'L GBL*
"may calm depart from *GBL*"
(Ph. Byblos: KAI/I p. 1, ins. #1, line 2)

'L III B.Heb. *'ōLā* "ascent, stairway," *Ma'aLeh* "ascent". 1. "stair" n.m.

a) *WDL H'LM 'Š 'L PN HMQDŠ[M 'L]*
"and with the stairs (?) which are set against [these sanc]-tuaries"
(Pu. Carthage: KAI/I p. 17, ins. #81, line 3)

Bibl. DISO 201; KAI/II 98; Harris 133.

'LY C.S. 1. "to rise" 2. "to offer" (sacrifice" vb. 3. in legal context

1 a) *WTM' MḤNT 'LY GBL*
"or an army commander rises (against) *GBL*"
(Ph. Byblos: KAI/I p. 1, ins. #1, line 1)

2 a) *'Š H'L' [K]' 'LT*
"those who [her]e offered holocaust(s)"
(N.Pu. Henschir Medina: KAI/I p. 29, ins. #159, line 8)

3 a) *QMD' 'Š 'L' BBN*
"*QMD'*, who was adopted (?) as a son"
(N.Pu. Leptis Magna: KAI/I p. 23, ins. #124, line 3)

Bibl. KAI/II 2, 130, 148; DISO 211; PPG 23, 82, 84; Harris 133.

'LM I C.S. (except Akk.) Ph., Pu. *'LM* (N.Pu. *'WLM*, *'LM*). 1. "tomb" n.m. 2. "eternity" 3. "ancient" adj. m.

1 a) *L'ḤRM 'BH KŠTḤ B'LM*
"for *'ḤRM* his father, when he placed him in the tomb"
(Ph. Byblos: KAI/I p. 1, ins. #1, line 1)

b) *ḤDR BT 'LM*
"the chamber of the tomb"
(Pu. Malta: Slouszch p. 126, ins. #109, line 1)

c) *MŠB' [B]'LM*
"his dwelling place (?) (in) the tomb"
(N.Pu. Ksar Toual Zouameul: BAC [1947] p. 253, line 3)

2 a) *YRḤ MD YRḤ 'D 'LM*
"month by month for eternity"
(Ph. Larnaka: KAI/I p. 10, ins. #43, line 12)

b) *L'LM YBRKN*
"may he bless me for eternity"
(Ph. Umm el-Awamid: KAI/I p. 4, ins. #18, line 8)

c) *[SK]R DR' L'WLM*
"[a memori]al of his family, for eternity"
(N.Pu. Leptis Magna: KAI/I p. 25, ins. #128, line 2)

d) *SK'R DR' L'LM*
"a memorial of his family, for eternity"
(N.Pu. Guelaat Bou-Sba: KAI/I p. 30, ins. #165, lines 7-8)

e) *NDR L'WLMM*
"his vow for eternity"
(N.Pu. Carthage: Sainte-Marie, p. 120, line 3)

3 a) *B'LT ŠMM W'RṢ 'LM*
"with the oaths of heaven and ancient earth"
(Ph. Arslan Tash: BASOR 197 [1970] p. 44, rev. lines 13-14)

Bibl. BASOR 197 (1970) 44-45; PPG 8; KAI/II 2, 26, 43, 60, 132, 154; Harris 133; DISO 213-14; IEJ 21 (1971) 50; ANET 656; Slouszch 3, 126; Amadasi 18; JNES 31 (1971) 353.

'LM II — Heb. *'eLeM* "young man"; Ug. *ĜLM* "boy"; Syriac *'aLiMa'* "youth"; J.Aram. *'uLeMa'*; Mandaic *'LiMaNa'*; ESArab. *ĜLM*; Arabic *ĜuLāMuN*; Q.Aram. *'LYM*; Anc.Aram. *'LM*.
1. "youth" n.m.

a) *LZKR H'LM*
"in memory of the youth"
(Pu. Carthage: Slouszch p. 208, ins. #209, line 1)

Bibl. Slouszch 208.

'LMT — Heb. *'aLMā* "young woman"; Ug. *ĜLMT*; Syriac *'aLiMTa'*; J.Aram. *'aLiMTa'*; Palm. *'LYMT'* "prostitute"; Nab. *'LYM* "servant".
1. "maid" n.f.]. "singer" 3. "prostitute"

1 a) *'LMT YTN BŠ*
"(who) gave a maid for a sheep"
(Ph. Zinjirli: KAI/I p. 4, ins. #24, line 8)

2 a) *L'LMT W L'LMT 22 BZBH*
"for the prostitutes (?) and the twenty-two singers (?) at the sacrifice"
(Ph. Kition: Or 37 [1968] p. 305, line B 9)

3 a) *L'LMT WL'LMT 22 BZBḤ*
"for the prostitutes (?) and the twenty-two singers (?) at the sacrifice"
(Ph. Kition: Or 37 [1968] p. 305, line B 9)

Bibl. DISO 214; Harris 133; ANET 654; KAI/II 30; Or 37 (1968) 323, esp. note 4.

'LṢ — Heb. *'āLaṢ* "to rejoice, exalt"; Akk. *eLēṢu*; ESArab. *M'LṢ* "joy". 1. "to exalt" vb.

a) *K' 'LṢ' 'LTY BKSP*
"for she exalted (?) over me in the matter of the silver"
(Pu. Carthage: KAI/I p. 18, ins. #89, lines 4-5)

b) *KL 'DM 'Š 'LṢ 'LTY*
"any man who exalts (?) over me"
(Pu. Carthage: KAI/I p. 18, ins. #89, line 5)

Bibl. PPG 59-60; DISO 214; KAI/II 102; Harris 133; Slouszch 202; MUSJ 45 (1969) 315.

'LŠ meaning and etymology unknown; perhaps related to *Ḥalaš*, B.Heb. "to be weak, feeble" with dissimilation of the *Ḥ* to *'ayin*

a) *'LŠ WTMK*
"meekly (?)"
(Pu. Carthage: CIS I, ins. #5510, line 10)

Bibl. DISO 215.

'LT I Heb. *'ōLā* "burnt offering"; B.Aram. *'*aLaT*
1. "holocaust" n.f.

a) *'Š H'L' [K]' 'LT*
"those who [her]e offered holocaust(s)"
(N.Pu. Henschir Medina: KAI/I p. 29, ins. #159, line 8)

Bibl. KAI/II 148; DISO 211.

'LT II etymology and meaning unknown; perhaps a phonetic variant of *ḤLT*. 1. "sarcophagus" n.f. (also see *ḤLT* II)

a) *'L 'L TPTḤ 'LTY*
"do not, do not open my sarcophagus (?)"
(Ph. Sidon: KAI/I p. 2, ins. #13, lines 3-4)

b) *'LT MGN MQM 'LM MLT*
"the sarcophagus of *MGN* the awakener of the god(s) *MLT*"
(Pu. Carthage: Slouszch p. 193, ins. #181, lines 1-2)

c) *W'M PTḤ TPTḤ 'LTY*
"and if you open my sarcophagus"
(Ph. Sidon: KAI/I p. 2, ins. #13, lines 6-7)

Bibl. ANET 662; KAI/II 17; Sem 5 (1955) 59-62; Slouszch 193; Harris 133; DISO 215; JAOS 94 (1974) 268.

'LT III Heb. *'aLiā* "upper chamber, upper story"; Akk. *eLāTu* "upper part"; J.Aram. *'aLiYūTa'* "height, heaven"; B.Aram. *'iLLi* "attic"; Syriac *'eLiTa'* "an upper room, upper story"; Mandaic *'LaYa'* "high"; Arabic *'iLaWaTuN* "upper part". 1. "lid" (of a sarcophagus) n.f. (also see *ḤLT* II)

a) *'LT 'RN*
"the lid (?) of the sarcophagus"
(Ph. Byblos: KAI/I p. 3, ins. #9, line A 2)

b) *'RN W'LT 'RN*
"the sarcophagus and the lid of the sarcophagus"
(Ph. Byblos: KAI/I p. 2, ins. #9, line B 4)

c) *KL 'DM 'Š YPTḤ 'LT MŠKB Z*
"any man who shall open the lid (?) of this resting place"
(Ph. Sidon: KAI/I p. 3, ins. #14, line 7)

Bibl. ANET 662; KAI/II 10, 19; Slouszch 22; JAOS 94 (1974) 268.

'LT IV Akk. *'eLaT* "besides, in addition to, beyond". 1. "upon" preposition 2. "over" 3. "into" 4. "besides"

1 a) *'LT MQM Z*
"upon this sacred place"
(Ph. Byblos: KAI/I p. 2, ins. #10, line 14)

b) *WP'LT 'NK 'LT*
"and I made upon"
(Ph. Larnaka: KAI/I p. 10, ins. #43, line 13)

c) *'LT MṢBT ḤRṢ*
"upon a golden monument"
(Ph. Piraeus: KAI/I p. 13, ins. #60, line 5)

d) *WP'L 'YT KL 'Š 'LTY MŠRT*
"and he performed all the service which was incumbent upon him"
(Ph. Piraeus: KAI/I p. 13, ins. #60, lines 3-4)

e) *LŠT 'LT HḤDRT NPT*
"to set upon the chamber honey (?)"
(Pu. Carthage: KAI/I p. 16, ins. #76, line B 8)

2 a) *NSMRN BN 'T W'YSPN 'LT MQDŠM*
"*NSMRN* son of *'T* (?) and *'YSPN* (who) are over the sanctuaries"
(N.Pu. Henschir Medina: KAI/I p. 29, ins. #159, line 5)

3 a) *'L 'LT HMQDŠM 'L*
"into these sanctuaries"
(N.Pu. Bir Bou-Rekba: KAI/I p. 26, ins. #137, lines 4-5)

4 a) *'LT PN HMŠ'T Z*
"besides this payment"
(Pu. Marseilles: KAI/I p. 15, ins. #69, line 3)

Bibl. KAI/II 12, 60, 83, 93, 136, 148; DISO 215; Amadasi 169; ANET 655; Branden 117; PPG 125-26, 128, 284; Harris 133; NE 340.

'M Heb. *'aM* "people, kinsman"; Ug. *'M*; Anc.Aram. *'M*; J.Aram. *'aMa'*; Syriac *'aMa'*; Nab. *'M* "grandfather"; Mandaic *'aMa'* "aunt", *'aMa* "uncle"; ESArab. *'M* "paternal uncle"; Arabic *'aMuN*, *'āMaTuN* "common people". 1. "people" n.m. 2. "community" (i.e., "people bearing arms" 3. "temple personnel"

1 a) *W'M Z 'Š YŠB BN*
"and may this people which dwells there in"
(Ph. Karatepe: KAI/I p. 5, ins. #26, lines A III,7-8)

b) *ŠLŠ ḤMŠM ŠT L'M [ṢR]*
"the fifty-third year of the people of [*ṢR*]"
(Ph. Ma'ṣub: KAI/I p. 4, ins. #19, line 8)

c) *BŠT 14 L'M ṢDN*
"in the fourteenth year of the people of *ṢDN*"
(Ph. Greece: Slouszch p. 116, ins. #99, line 1)

d) *'M QRTḤDŠT*
"the people of *QRTḤDŠT*"
(Pu. Carthage: CIS I, ins. #269, line 5)

e) *'Š P'L KL 'M BYT'N*
"are (those) which all the people of *BYT'N* made"
(N.Pu. Sardinia: KAI/I p. 31, ins. #173, line 1)

2 a) *'M HMḤNT*
"the community (?) of the army (camp)"
(Pu. Sardinia: Slouszch p. 131, ins. #113, line 1)

3 a) *'Š B'M BT MLQRT*
"who is among the personnel of the temple of *MLQRT*"
(Pu. Carthage: KAI/I p. 18, ins. #86, line 4)

Bibl. DISO 216; Slouszch 116, 131; Harris 133; KAI/II 27, 36, 101, 157; ANET 653; Amadasi 133; Benz 379; JBL 79 (1960) 157-63.

'MD Heb. *'aMūD* "pillar, column"; Syriac *'eMuDa'*; Akk. *eMDu*; J.Aram. *'aMūDa'*; Emp.Aram. *'MuD*; Arabic *'aMūDuN*.
1. "pillar" n.m.

a) *WH'RPT Z' W'MDH*
"and this portico and its pillars"
(Ph. Byblos: KAI/I p. 2, ins. #10, line 6)

b) *T 'MDM WT HM'Q'M*
"the pillars and the sanctuary"
(N.Pu. Leptis Magna: KAI/I p. 23, ins. #124, lines 1-2)

Bibl. DISO 216-17; Harris 133; Slouszch 12; KAI/II 12, 130; ANET 656.

'MS Heb. *'āMaS* "to load, carry"; Ug. *'MS*; [J.Aram. *'aMaS* "to press the teeth together"]. 1. "to carry" vb.
2. "to be set" (N)

1 a) *'M 'Š Y'MSN BMŠKB Z*
"or if he shall carry me from this resting place"
(Ph. Sidon: KAI/I p. 3, ins. #14, lines 7-8)

b) *W'L Y'MSN BMŠKB Z*
"and may he not carry me from this resting place"
(Ph. Sidon: KAI/I p. 3, ins. #14, line 21)

2 a) *'Š Y'MS PNT 'LM*
"which will be set before the gods"
(Pu. Marseilles: KAI/I p. 15, ins. #69, line 13)

Bibl. DISO 217; PPG 61, 65, 88; Harris 134; ANET 662; KAI/II 19, 83; Amadasi 180; Benz 379-80.

'MQ Heb. *'eMeQ* "valley, plain"; Ug. *'MQ*; Akk. *ḫaMQu*; Syriac *'aMiQTa'* "a profound abyss"; Mandaic *'uMQa'* "depth"; J.Aram. *'iMQa'* "valley"; Arabic *'aMQuN* "the bottom of a well or a valley"; Soq. *'MQ* "middle".
1. "plain" n.m. 2. "valley"

1 a) *YRḤB 'NK 'RṢ 'MQ 'DN*
"I widened the land of the plain of *'DN*"
(Ph. Karatepe: KAI/I p. 5, ins. #26, line A I,4)

b) *BKL GBL 'MQ 'DN*
"in the entire territory of the plain of *'DN*"
(Ph. Karatepe: KAI/I p. 5, ins. #26, lines A II,1-2)

2 a) *B'MQT ŠHT'M'R*
"in the valley of the date palm"
(N.Pu. Tripolitania: Or 33 [1964] p. 4, line 4)

Bibl. ANET 653; KAI/II 36; Or 33 (1964) 11; DISO 217.

'MT I   Heb. *'ūMā* "junction, corresponding".
1. "beside" preposition

a) *ŠT'T 'L 'MT 'ṬRT 'DR'T*
"at the side of the glorious cornice (work)"
(N.Pu. Maktar: KAI/I p. 27, ins. #145, lines 2-3)

Bibl. DISO 217; KAI/II 141.

'MT II   Heb. *'āMīT* "associate, community".
1. "associate" n.f.

a) *'Š B'MT 'Š 'ŠTRT*
"who is among (?) the associates (?) of worshippers (?) of *'ŠTRT*"
(Pu. Carthage: Slouszch p. 235, ins. #258, lines 3-4)

Bibl. Slouszch 235; Harris 133; DISO 217.

'MT III   Heb. *'āMīT* "associate, fellow"; J.Aram. *'aMiTa'*. 1. "servant" n.f.

a) *'Š NDR 'RŠTB'L BT 'MTMLQRT BT 'BDMLQRT 'MT Š 'ŠTRT 'RK*
"that which *'RŠTB'L* daughter of *'MTMLQRT* daughter of *'BDMLQRT* the servant (?) of *'ŠTRT 'RK* vowed"
(Pu. Carthage: Slouszch p. 249, ins. #296, lines 3-4)

Bibl. Slouszch 250; Benz 270; Harris 79; DISO 16.

'N I   B.Heb. *'ōYeN* "to see, perceive"; Akk. *īNu*; Ug. *'N*. 1. "to cast the evil eye" vb.
2. "glance" n.m.

1 a) *BRḤ 'YN*
"flee O caster of the evil eye"
(Ph. Arslan Tash: BASOR 209 [1973] p. 19, rev. line 2)

2 a) *'N YTM 'NK*
"the evil glance shall be ended, yea your evil glance"
(Ph. Arslan Tash: BASOR 209 [1973] p. 19, rev. lines 5-6)

Bibl. BASOR 209 (1973) 25-26; Syria 48 (1971) 405.

'N II C.S. 1. "spring" n.m.

a) *B'N YDL*
"at the spring of *YDL*"
(Ph. Sidon: BMB 18 [1965] p. 106, line 1)

b) *'N YDLL*
"spring of *YDLL*"
(Ph. Sidon: KAI/I p. 3, ins. #14, line 17)

Bibl. ANET 662; KAI/I 19; Slouszch 25.

'N III C.S. 1. "sight" n.f.

a) *[WY]TN LM ḤN WḤẎM L'N 'LNM WBN 'DM*
"[may he gr]ant them favor and life in the sight of the gods and man"
(Ph. Memphis: Slouszch p. 52, ins. #35, line 4)

b) *L'N 'LNM WL'N 'M 'RṢ Z*
"in the sight of the gods and in the sight of this people"
(Ph. Byblos: KAI/I p. 3, ins. #10, lines 10-11)

c) *'N 'Š*
"in the sight of man"
(Ph. Piraeus: KAI/I p. 13, ins. #60, line 5)

Bibl. Slouszch 13, 53; ANET 656; KAI/II 12, 64, 73; Harris 132; DISO 207.

'N IV for etymology, see *'T*. 1. "now" adv.

a) *WK'N ŠLK SP 50*
"and now, he paid fifty cents (?) for the basin"
(Pu. Carthage: Syria 9 [1930] p. 202, line 1)

Bibl. Syria 9 (1930) 202.

*'*NY* Heb. *'iNNā* "to humble". 1. "to humble" vb.

a) *W'N 'NK 'RṢT 'ZT*
"and I humbled mighty lands"
(Ph. Karatepe: KAI/I p. 5, ins. #26, line A I,18)

b) *'Š BL 'N KL HMLKM 'Š KN LPNY*
"which all the kings who were before me did not humble"
(Ph. Karatepe: KAI/I p. 5, ins. #26, line A I,19)

Bibl. KAI/II 36; ANET 653; DISO 218.

'NŠ I — Heb. *'oNeŠ* "punishment, penalty".
1. "tax" n.m.

a) *YŠBM 'RB' P'L' B'NŠM 'RKT*
"they made the four seats out of their tax assessment"
(N.Pu. Leptis Magna: KAI/I p. 25, ins. #130, line 5)

b) *WKT/NDRM TŠ' LMB'NŠM*
"and nine *KT/NDRM* as their tax"
(N.Pu. Leptis Magna: KAI/I p. 25, ins. #130, line 2)

Bibl. KAI/II 130; DISO 219; PPG 127.

'NŠ II — Heb. *'āNaŠ* "to punish, fine"; J.Aram. *'aNaŠ*. 1. "to be fined" vb. (N)
2. "to fine"

1 a) *KL KHN 'Š YQḤ MŠ'T BDṢ L'Š ŠT BPS Z WN'N[Š]*
"all priests who would take payment other than (?) which is set down on this tablet shall be fin[ed]"
(Pu. Marseilles: KAI/I p. 15, ins. #69, line 20)

2 a) *W'NŠ HMḤŠBM 'Š LN*
"may our accountants impose a fine"
(Pu. Carthage: CRAI [1968] p. 117, line 7)

Bibl. DISO 219; Harris 134; Slouszch 150; Amadasi 169; KAI/II 83; ANET 656; CRAI (1968) 131.

'SR — C.S. Ph., Pu., N.Pu. *'SR* (N.Pu. *'SR*, *'SR*, *'ŠR*, *'Š'R*, *'Ṣ'[R]*. 1. "ten" num.

a) *BŠNT 'SR W'RB'*
"in the fourteenth year"
(Ph. Sidon: KAI/I p. 3, ins. #14, line 1)

b) *B'SR WŠMN LYRḤ MRP'M*
"on the eighteenth day of the month of *MRP'M*"
(Pu. Constantine: Berthier/Charlier p. 53, ins. #58, lines 2-3)

c) *B'SR W'ḤD LZYB*
"on the eleventh day of the (month) of *ZYB*"
(Pu. Constantine: ESE I p. 41, Villefosse 69, line 4)

d) *'SR WŠB' LYRḤ MP'*
"the seventeenth day of the month of *MP'*"
(N.Pu. Tunisia: ESE III p. 58, line 5)

e) *W'W' Š'NT 'SR WŠ'LŠ*
"and he lived thirteen years"
(N.Pu. Henschir Guergour: KAI/I p. 27, ins. #144, lines 3-4)

f) *'Ṣ'[R] WḤMŠ*
"[fi]fteen"
(N.Pu. Uzappa: JA Series 11 vol. 11 [1918] p. 255, ins. #4, line 3)

Bibl. Harris 135; DISO 223; Berthier/Charlier 53; PPG 18-19, 120; KAI/II 140; Branden 7, 38-40.

'SRM C.S. N.Pu. *'SRM* (N.Pu. *'SRM*, *'ŠRM*, *HSRM*). 1. "twenty" num.

a) *BŠṬ 'SRM W'ḤT*
"in the twenty-first year"
(N.Pu. Dschebel Massoudj: KAI/I p. 26, ins. #141, line 3)

b) *'W' Š'NT 'SRM W'MŠ*
"she lived twenty-five years"
(N.Pu. Tunisia: KAI/I p. 25, ins. #135, lines 3-4)

c) *W'W' 'ŠRM WHMŠ*
"and she lived twenty-five years"
(N.Pu. Henschir Brigitta: NE p. 436, ins. #67, lines 3-4)

d) *BT Š'NT HSRM WŠB '*
"twenty-seven years of age"
(N.Pu. Maktar: KAI/I p. 28, ins. #148, lines 2-3)

Bibl. PPG 120; Branden 38-40; NE 346-47; KAI/II 135, 139, 145; DISO 223; Harris 135.

'PT Heb. *'ōP* "flying creature"; Ug. *'P* "to fly"; Syriac *'oPa'* "fowl"; J.Aram. *'oPa'*; Chr.Pal.Aram. *'oP'* "bird"; Arabic *'aFa* "to hover (bird)". 1. "flier" n.f. 2. "bird" (type of engraved object)

1 a) *L'PT' 'LT*
"O fliers, goddesses"
(Ph. Arslan Tash: BASOR 197 [1970] p. 44, obv. line 1)

2 a) *WH'ṖT ḪRṢ*
"and the birds (?) of gold"
(Ph. Byblos: KAI/I p. 2, ins. #10, line 5)

Bibl. DISO 219; KAI/II 12, 44; ANET 656, 658; BASOR 197 (1970) 44, esp. note 5; LS I 55-56.

'Ṣ C.S. 1. "wood" n.m.

a) *'GLT 'Ṣ*
"wooden wagons"
(Pu. Carthage: Slouszch p. 296, ins. #430, line 3)

Bibl. Slouszch 296; Harris 134; DISO 219.

'ṢM Heb. *'eṢeM* "bone"; Akk. *eṢiMTu*; J.Aram. *'iṬMa'*; Chr.Pal.Aram. *'ṬM'* "thigh"; Syriac *'aṬMa'*; Arabic *'aẒuMuN* "bone".
1. "gone" n.m.

a) *LRGZ 'ṢMY*
"to disturb my bones"
(Ph. Byblos: KAI/I p. 2, ins. #9, line A 5)

b) *WLRGZ 'ṢMY*
"and to disturb my bones"
(Ph. Byblos: MUSJ 45 [1969] p. 262, line 2)

c) *'ṢM' MTMLQRT BT ḪMLKT*
"the bones of *MTMLQRT*, daughter of *ḪMLKT*"
(Pu. Sousse: Slouszch p. 213, ins. #214, lines 1-2)

d) *LSKR 'L M'SPT 'ṢMY*
"in memory of the gathering (place) of my bones"
(Pu. Carthage: Slouszch p. 180, ins. #155, line 4)

Bibl. DISO 220; PPG 105, 111; Slouszch 181, 213; Harris 134; NE 345; MUSJ 45 (1969) 264.

'ṢMT B.Heb. *'oṢMā* "might"; Te. *'əSṢuM* "strong".
1. "mighty" adj. f.

a) *LMDT 'ṢMT 'Š P'LT*
"in accordance with the mighty deeds which I performed"
(Ph. Sidon: KAI/I p. 3, ins. #14, line 19)

Bibl. ANET 662; KAI/II 19; DISO 220; PPG 154; Harris 135; Slouszch 27.

'QB Heb. *'eQeB* "rear, in consequence"; Syriac *'eQaBa'* "succession"; J.Aram. *'eQBa'* "consequence"; Mandaic *'aQBa'* "after"; ESArab. *'QB*; Arabic *'aQiBuN* "anything that is a sequent to, or of another thing". 1. "continuation" n.m.

a) *'QB BḤDŠ YRḤ P'LT*
"continuation: on the new moon of the month of *P'LT*"
(Ph. Kition: KAI/I p. 8, ins. #37, lines B 1-2)

Bibl. DISO 220; KAI/II 54; Harris 135; Slouszch 80; NE 345; Or 37 (1968) 318, esp. note 1.

'QRT etymology unknown. 1. "storehouse" n.f. (from context)

a) *WML' 'NK 'QRT P'R*
"and I filled the storehouse (?) of *P'R*"
(Ph. Karatepe: KAI/I p. 5, ins. #26, line A I,6)

Bibl. KAI/II 36; ANET 653; DISO 220; LS I 75.

'R I Heb. *'iR* "city, town"; Ug. *'R*; ESArab *'R* "mountain". 1. "town" n.f. 2. "city"

1 a) *B'R 'Š ŠKNY LMLKT QDŠT*
"in the town where the holy queen had her dwelling"
(Ph. Kition: Or 37 [1968] p. 305, line A 7)

2 a) *QRN 'R D ŠT 60*
"*QRN* the city of (?), the year 60"
(Ph. Carne: Slouszch p. 50, ins. #33, lines 1-3)

b) *W'LT 'R SHRW*
"and I went up against the city of *SHRW*"
(Ph. Abu Simbel: CIS I, ins. #113, line 1)

Bibl. DISO 221; Or 37 (1968) 311, esp. note 2; KAI/II 54.

'R II Heb. *'ōR* "skin, hide". 1. "skin" n.f.

a) *H'RT WHŠLBM WHP'MM*
"the skins and the joints and the feet"
(Pu. Marseilles: KAI/I p. 15, ins. #69, line 4)

b) *WKN 'RT H'ZM LKHNM*
"and the skins of the goats shall be for the priests"
(Pu. Carthage: KAI/I p. 16, ins. #74, line 4)

Bibl. KAI/II 83, 92; DISO 221; Harris 127; Slouszch 144; Amadasi 169; NE 346.

'RB B.Heb. *'eRāBōN* "pledge"; Ug. *'RBN*; Akk. *uRBaNu*; Syriac *'aRBa'*; J.Aram. *'aRBa'*; ESArab. *'RBT*; Amh. *'aRaBoN*.
1. "exchange" n.m. 2. "surety"

1 a) *'L 'RB MLKT HMQM*
"in exchange for labor (furnished) for the temple"
(N.Pu. Leptis Magna: KAI/I p. 22, ins. #119, line 7)

2 a) *'Š LKNT GW 'RB*
"that the community be designated as surety (for it)"
(Ph. Piraeus: KAI/I p. 13, ins. #60, lines 5-6)

Bibl. KAI/II 73; DISO 221; Harris 135; Slouszch 118.

**'RY* B.Heb. *'eRā* "to be naked, bare"; Akk. *uRRu* "to make bare"; J.Aram. *'a'aRe* "to pour out"; Arabic *'aRi* "to be naked". 1. "to lay bare" vb.

a) *W'L Y'R 'LTY*
"and may he not lay bare my sarcophagus (?)"
(Ph. Sidon: KAI/I p. 3, ins. #14, line 21)

Bibl. KAI/II 19; ANET 662; PPG 83, 85; Harris 135; DISO 221; Slouszch 29.

'RK Heb. *'eReK* "estimate, order, equivalent".
1. "estimation" n.m.

a) *LPY KL 'RK' ML'Ṫ*
"in conformity with all his estimation of the (?)"
(N.Pu. Leptis Magna: KAI/I p. 22, ins. #119, line 5)

Bibl. DISO 222; KAI/II 124; LS I 55.

'RKT Heb. *'eReK* "estimate, order," *Ma'aRāKā* "battle line"; Arabic *Ma'RaKaTuN*.
1. "estimate, value" n.m. 2. "battle array, possibly troops"

1 a) *YŠBM 'RB' P'L' B'NŠM 'RKT*
"they made the four seats out of their tax assessment"
(N.Pu. Leptis Magna: KAI/I p. 25, ins. #130, line 5)

2 a) *B'T R 'DR 'RKT 'RŠ BN Y'L[ ]*
"at the time of the chief of the crack troops, *'RŠ* son of *Y'L*[ ]"
(Pu. Malta: Amadasi p. 23, ins. #6, line 4)

Bibl. Amadasi 25; KAI/II 78, 133; DISO 222; Harris 135; Or 38 (1969) 159; Slouszch 129.

'RPT Heb. *'oReP* "upper part of the neck"; Arabic *ĠuRFaTuN* "an uppermost chamber".
1. "portico" n.f.

a) *'RPT Z' W'MDH*
"this portico and its pillars"
(Ph. Byblos: KAI/I p. 2, ins. #10, line 6)

b) *W'LT 'RPT Z'*
"and upon this portico"
(Ph. Byblos: KAI/I p. 2, ins. #10, line 12)

c) *'RPT KBRT MṢ' HŠMŠ*
"the portico in the direction (?) of sunrise"
(Ph. Ma'ṣub: KAI/I p. 4, ins. #19, line 1)

d) *[H]ṢRT HMQDŠ W'RP'T*
"the [co]urtyard of the sanctuary and the porticos"
(N.Pu. Leptis Magna: KAI/I p. 23, ins. #122, line 2)

Bibl. PPG 101, 107-8; DISO 222; Harris 135; Slouszch 12; ANET 656; KAI/II 12, 27, 128.

'ŠQ meaning and etymology unknown

a) *'Š[Y]Q BHL'L'T Q'M BB'T*
(N.Pu. Tripolitania: Or 33 [1964] p. 4, line 3)

Bibl. Or 33 (1964) 9-10.

'ŠRT C.S. 1. "ten" num.

a) *LKHNM KSP 'ŠRT 10 B'ḤD*
"the priests shall have ten silver (shekels) for each"
(Pu. Marseilles: CIS I, ins. #165, line 3)

b) *'ŠRT H'ŠM 'Š 'L HMQDŠM*
"the ten men who are (appointed) over the sanctuaries"
(Pu. Carthage: CIS I, ins. #175, line 1)

Bibl. KAI/II 83, 98; Amadasi 169; Slouszch 143; ANET 655; Harris 135; PPG 120; DISO 223.

'T Heb. *'eT* "time"; Ug. *'NT* "now"; N.Heb. *'ōNā* "set period of time"; B.Aram. *Ke'aN*, *Ke'eNeT* "and now"; J.Aram. *Ke'aN*; Akk. *eTTu* "time"; Ph., Pu., N.Pu. *'T* (N.Pu. *Ḥ'T* [?]). 1. "time" n.f.

a) *NGZLT BL 'TY*
"I have been snatched away before my time"
(Ph. Sidon: KAI/I p. 3, ins. #14, lines 2-3)

b) *B'T R 'DR 'RKT*
"at the time of the chief of the crack troops"
(Pu. Malta: Amadasi p. 23, ins. #6, line 4)

c) *YTN' L 'BD BṢP'T KL Ḥ'T*
"they allowed him to use (?) the tunic (?) at all times"
(N.Pu. Leptis Magna: KAI/I p. 24, ins. #126, line 9)

d) *'T R 'DNB'L*
"(at) the time of the chief *'DNB'L*"
(Pu. Carthage: CRAI [1968] p. 117, line 2)

Bibl. ANET 662; KAI/II 19, 78, 131; Harris 134; PPG 53; DISO 224; Slouszch 19, 128-29; KAR 12 (1963-64) 52; CRAI (1968) 123; LS I 79.

P

P I — meaning and etymology uncertain; perhaps related to Ug. *P* "and"; Arabic *Fa*; ESArab. *F* "so, then"; Eg. *PW* copulative particle; Emp.Aram. *P* "and"; Nab. *P*. 1. "also" conj. 2. "and"

1 a) *MQDŠ ḤṢRT PḤNT QDŠM*
"sanctuary, courts also (?) the arches (?) of the temples"
(N.Pu. Maktar: KAI/I p. 27, ins. #145, lines 1-2)

2 a) *'Š NDR PSN'M Š ŠPṬ PḤLM*
"that which *PSN'M* vowed. (He) who judged and (?) dreamed (?)"
(Pu. Carthage: Slouszch p. 327, ins. #525, lines 2-3)

Bibl. Slouszch 327; Harris 136; NE 350; KAI/II 141; Leš 14 (1947-48) 8; PPG 13; Bib 38 (1957) 419-27; DISO 225; JAOS 62 (1942) 235, also n. 32.

**P* II — Heb. *Pe* "mouth"; Ug. *P*; Akk. *Pū*; Anc.Aram. *PM*; Emp.Aram. *PM*; J.Aram. *PūMa'*; Syriac *PuMa'*; Mandaic *PuMa'*; ESArab. *P*; Arabic *FuMuN*, *FuHuN*; Geez *'aF*. 1. "mouth" n.m. 2. "word" 3. in combinations

1 a) *WMḤSM ḤRṢ LPY*
"and a muzzle of gold upon my mouth"
(Ph. Byblos: KAI/I p. 2, ins. #11, line 1)

2 a) *'Š TM PY*
"whose word is true"
(Ph. Arslan Tash: KAI/I p. 6, ins. #27, rev. line 16)

b) *BY PY 'NK WBY 'DM BŠMY*
"without my word or without the word of a man (speaking) in my name"
(Pu. Carthage: KAI/I p. 17, ins. #79, lines 8-9)

3 a) *LPY M'S' 'BTY*
"according to the deeds of his fathers"
(N.Pu. Leptis Magna: KAI/I p. 24, ins. #126, line 8)

b) *LPY KL 'RK'*
"in conformity with all his estimation (?)"
(N.Pu. Leptis Magna: KAI/I p. 22, ins. #119, line 5)

Bibl. BASOR 197 (1970) 44-45; KAI/II 15-16, 43, 97, 124, 131; DISO 227; Harris 136; ANET 658; Branden 19; PPG 117, 127.

P' B.Heb. *PYM* "type of weight". 1. type of coin n.m.

a) *LKLBM WLGRM QR 3 WP' 3*
"for the dogs and the lions, three *QR* and three *P'*"
(Ph. Kition: KAI/I p. 8, ins. #37, line B 10)

Bibl. Harris 136; DISO 225; NE 365; BASOR 77 (1940) 15-20; BASOR 164 (1961) 21-23.

P'DY Lat. *podium*. 1. "podium" n.m.

a) *MZBḤ WP'DY*
"altar and podium"
(N.Pu. Leptis Magna: KAI/I p. 24, ins. #126, line 10)

Bibl. DISO 225; KAI/II 131; PPG 43, 99.

PG' Heb. *PāGa'* "to meet, fall upon"; Emp.Aram. *PG'*; J.Aram. *PeGa'*; Syriac *PeGa'*; Mandaic *BG'*, *PG'*; Arabic *FaJa'a* "to pain"; Ph. *PG*['] (N.Pu. *PG'*, *PG*). 1. "to supplicate" vb. 2. "to discharge a vow"

1 a) *WYP[G' BRBT 'Š]TRT*
"and he supplicated [to the lady *'Š]TRT*"
(Ph. Kition: CRAI [1968] p. 15, line 1)

2 a) *PG' 'ŠRM H'Š*
"he discharged (?) this *'ŠRM* sacrifice"
(N.Pu. Guelma: JA Series 11 vol. 8 [1916] p. 516, line 3)

b) *PG 'T ND'RM*
"he discharged his vow"
(N.Pu. Guelma: JA Series 11 vol. 8 [1916] p. 518, ins. #38, line 3)

Bibl. CRAI (1968) 17; DISO 225; Harris 136; LS I 106-7, note 3; JA Series 11 vol. 8 (1916) 519.

**PD* Heb. *PīD* "ruin, disaster"; Syriac *PeDa'* "to stray, miss, fail"; Arabic *FaDa* "to die". 1. "to bring ruin" vb.

a) *HN YPD LK*
"behold, you shall come to ruin"
(Ph. Byblos: KAI/I p. 1, ins. #2, lines 1-2)

Bibl. DISO 225; KAI/II 4.

PḤM Heb. *PeḤaM* "coal"; Akk. *PeMu*; Ug. *PḤM*; Syriac *PaḤMa'*; Arabic *FaḤMuN*. 1. "coal" n.m.

a) *Š 'BN PḤMT*
"which is of coal stones"
(Pu. Carthage: BAC 214 [1915-16] p. ccxiv, line 1)

PṬBḤ meaning and etymology unknown

a) *'ZRB'L HPṬBḤ*
"*'ZRB'L* the (?)"
(Pu. Constantine: Berthier/Charlier p. 74, ins. #85, lines 52-53)

PṬRT [N.Heb. *NiPṬāR* "dead, deceased," *PeṬiRā* "dead"; Akk. *PaṬāRu* "to loosen, draw out"; Emp.Aram. *PṬR* "to detach"; J.Aram. *PeṬRa'* "farewell," *PeṬaR* "to dismiss, free"; Syriac *PeṬuRuTa'* "passing away, dying," *PeṬaR* "to leave, quit"; Mandaic *PiṬiaRuTa'* "opening," *PṬR* "to open up, separate"; Chr.Pal.Aram. *PṬR* "to dismiss"; Arabic *FaṬaRa* "to cleave, to split a thing"; Geez *FaṬaRa* "to create"]. 1. "dismissal" n.f.

a) *BPṬRT 'BDMLQRT*
"at the dismissal (?) of *'BDMLQRT*" (or "death of")
(Ph. Abydos: KAI/I p. 11, ins. #49, line 34)

Bibl. KAI/II 65; Slouszch 56-57; Harris 137; DISO 227; AJSL 34 (1918) 229.

PYTR' [Heb. *PāTaR* "to solve, interpret"; J.Aram. *PeTaR* "to interpret," *PaTōRa'* "interpreter"]; Nab. *PTWR'* "seer"; N.Pu. *PYTR* (N.Pu. *PYTR'*, Pu. *PTR*). 1. "interpreter" n.m.

a) *B'LN' HPYTR'*
"*B'LN'* the interpreter (?)"
(N.Pu. Maktar: JA Series 11 vol. 10 [1917] p. 22, ins. #2, line 2)

b) *PRNṬ' 'PYTR*
"*PRNṬ'* the interpreter (?)"
(N.Pu. Maktar: JA Series 11 vol. 10 [1917] p. 21, ins. #4, line 3)

c) *B'LHN' [H]PTR*
"*B'LHN'* [the] interpreter (?)"
(Pu. Carthage: RES ins. #1535, line 2)

Bibl. DISO 240.

PL

Heb. *PōL* "beans"; Akk. *PuLiLu*; J.Aram. *PōLa'*; Geez *FL*; Arabic *FūLuN*; Ph. *P'L* (Pu. *PL*). 1. "beans" coll. n.

a) *BṢL PLN' WP'L*
"onion (?) and beans"
(Ph. Egypt: KAI/I p. 12, ins. #51, line 4)

b) *ZYBQ MKR HPL*
"*ZYBQ* the seller of beans (or elephants)"
(Pu. Carthage: Slouszch p. 349, ins. #578, lines 2-3)

Bibl. Slouszch 349; KAI/II 69.

PLG

N.Heb. *PeLeK* "district"; Akk. *PiLKu*; J.Aram. *PiLKa'*; Syriac *PeLūGTa'* "part, division, portion"; Emp.Aram. *PLG'* "canal"; Mandaic *PLuGTa'*; Palm. *PLGH* "part"; Nab. *PLG'*; Geez *FaLoG* "valley"; Arabic *FaLGuN* "division, half"; Soq. *FiLiGoh* "way, road". 1. "district" n.m.

a) *BPLG L'DK*
"in the district of *L'DK*"
(Ph. Umm el-Awamid: KAI/I p. 13, ins. #18, line 3)

Bibl. KAI/II 26; Harris 137; Slouszch 39-40; NE 35; DISO 228; Branden 7.

PLK

B.Heb. *PeLeK* "spindle, support"; Sum. *BiLa* / the genitive (= *aK*); Akk. *PiLaKKu*; Ug. *PLK*; Arabic *FiLKaTuN* "whirl of a spindle". 1. "support" n.m.

a) *'ŠT TK LḤDY DL PLKM*
"a woman walked by herself without supports"
(Ph. Karatepe: KAI/I p. 5, ins. #26, lines A II,5-6)

Bibl. ANET 653; KAI/II 36; DISO 229; MUSJ 45 (1969) 262; LS I 77-78.

PLS

B.Heb. *PāLaS* "to weigh, make level," *PeLeS* "balance"; Akk. *PaLāSU* "to look towards, to watch"; J.Aram. *PeLaS* "to split"; Soq. *FLS* "to reveal, uncover"; [Geez *FaLaSa* "to emigrate"].
1. "architect" n.m.

a) *'KBRM HPLS*
"*'KBRM* the architect"
(Pu. Carthage: Slouszch p. 166, ins. #137, line 9)

b) *HPLS BN*
"the architect, son of"
(Ph. Kition: Slouszch p. 86, ins. #70, line 1)

c) *MTN [H]PLS*
"*MTN* [the] architect"
(Pu. Carthage: ESE I p. 174, line 5)

d) *BDMLQRT PLS*
"*BDMLQRT* the architect"
(Pu. Carthage: CRAI [1968] p. 117, line 4)

Bibl. DISO 229; ESE I 174; Harris 137; Benz 391; Slouszch 87, 160; CRAI (1968) 125; JAOS 45 (1925) 271.

PN Heb. *PāNīM* "face, front side"; Ug. *PNM*; Akk. *PāNu*; Moab. *PN*; Emp.Aram. *PN*; J.Aram. *PaNYa'* "afternoon, sunset"; Syriac *PeNiTa'* "region, quarter"; Mandaic *PaiNa'* "evening"; ESArab. *FNWT* "before, towards"; Soq. *FáNe* "way"; [Arabic *PaNāNuN* "courtyard"]. 1. "face" n.m. 2. "side" 3. in combinations

1 a) *WMY BL ḤZ PN Š*
"and whoever had never seen the face of a sheep"
(Ph. Zinjirli: KAI/I p. 4, ins. #24, line 11)

2 a) *PNY MB' HŠMŠ*
"its front side, facing west"
(Pu. Carthage: KAI/I p. 17, ins. #78, lines 5-6)

3 a) *'LT PN HMŠ'T Z*
"besides this payment"
(Pu. Marseilles: KAI/I p. 15, ins. #69, line 3)

b) *'Š 'L PN PTḤY Z*
"which is over against this engraved work of mine"
(Ph. Byblos: KAI/I p. 2, ins. #10, line 5)

c) *'T PN KL 'LN G[BL]*
"before all the gods of *G[BL]*"
(Ph. Byblos: KAI/I p. 2, ins. #10, line 16)

d) *'T PN GW*
"before the community"
(Ph. Piraeus: KAI/I p. 13, ins. #60, line 8)

e) *'L PN ŠMŠ*
"before the face of the sun"
(Pu. Carthage: CIS I, ins. #5510, line 5)

Bibl. DISO 229-30; ANET 654, 656; Amadasi 169; Harris 137; Branden 6, 32; PPG 124; NE 352; Benz 392; Albright 113, 117-18; Slouszch 317, 319; JNES 8 (1949) 292, note 178; NSI 132-33; ZDMG 91 (1937) 347.

PNT for etymology, see under *PN*. "before" preposition

a) *'Š Y'MS PNT 'LM*
"which will be set before the gods"
(Pu. Marseilles: KAI/I p. 15, ins. #69, line 13)

Bibl. Harris 138; DISO 230; Amadasi 169; ANET 656; Branden 4; Slouszch 147; PPG 125.

PS B.Heb. *PaS* "stripe"; N.Heb. *PaS* "board"; [Akk. *PaSSu* "doll, puppet";] J.Aram. *PaSSa'* "spade"; Syriac *PaSTa'* "palm of the hand"; Mandaic *PaSa'*, *PaSaNTa'*; Pu. *PS* (N.Pu. *P'S*). 1. "tablet" n.m.

a) *'Š 'YBL ŠT BPS Z*
"which is not set down on this tablet"
(Pu. Marseilles: KAI/I p. 15, ins. #69, line 18)

b) *ẆQR' T P'S*
"and read the tablet"
(N.Pu. Guelaat Bou-Sba: KAI/I p. 30, ins. #165, lines 1-2)

Bibl. DISO 230; Harris 138; NE 352; KAI/II 83, 154; Slouszch 149; ANET 656-57.

PSLT I Heb. *PeSeL* "idol"; Ug. *PSL*; Emp.Aram. *PSYLH* "hewn stone"; J.Aram. *PeSiLa'* "idol"; Syriac *PeSuLa'* "a stone cutter, axe"; Nab. *PSL'* "sculptor". 1. "hewn" p.p. f.

a) *MNṢBT PSLT*
"the hewn pillars"
(Pu. Carthage: KAI/I p. 17, ins. #78, line 4)

Bibl. KAI/II 96; Harris 138; Slouszch 176; DISO 231; PPG 64.

PSLT II — for etymology, see *PSLT* I. 1. "hewn stone" n.f.

a) *BN'M BPSLT*
"he built it with hewn stone"
(or "the builder with hewn stone")
(Pu. Sardinia: Amadasi p. 117, ins. #36, line 1)

Bibl. Amadasi 118.

P'L — Heb. *Pā'aL* "to do, make"; Ug. *B'L* ; J.Aram. *Pea'L*; Syriac *Pe'aL*; ESArab. *F'L*; Arabic *Fa'aLa*; Ph., Pu., N.Pu. *P'L* (N.Pu. *PHL*, *PL*). 1. "to do, make, add" vb. 2. "was made" (N)

1 a) *'RN Z P'L [']TB'L BN 'ḤRM*
"the sarcophagus which [']*TB'L* son of *'ḤRM* made"
(Ph. Byblos: KAI/I p. 1, ins. #1, line 1)

b) *P'LT LY HMŠKB ZN*
"I made for myself this resting place"
(Ph. Byblos: KAI/I p. 2, ins. #9, line A 1)

c) *'Š P'LTN HRBT B'LT GBL*
"whom the lady, the Mistress of *GBL* made"
(Ph. Byblos: KAI/I p. 2, ins. #10, line 2)

d) *P'L N'M*
"the doer of good"
(Ph. Ma'ṣub: KAI/I p. 4, ins. #19, line 6)

e) *WY'MR 'P'L SML ZR*
"and he would say, let me make a hated (?) image"
(Ph. Karatepe: KAI/I p. 5, ins. #26, lines C IV,17-18)

f) *WP'L 'NK SS 'L SS*
"and I added horse upon horse"
(Ph. Karatepe: KAI/I p. 5, ins. #26, lines A I,6-7)

g) *P'L HMGRDM*
"maker of files"
(Pu. Carthage: Slouszch p. 241, ins. #272, lines 3-4)

h) *ŠPṬ P'L KL*
"*ŠPṬ*, the general contractor"
(Pu. Carthage: Slouszch p. 315, ins. #489, line 4)

i) *ḤMLKT P'L HŠM*
"*ḤMLKT*, the plant merchant"
(Pu. Constantine: Berthier/Charlier p. 83, ins. #101, line 3)

j) *ḤN' P'L HŠḤM*
"*ḤN'*, the plant merchant"
(N.Pu. Leptis Magna: KAI/I p. 22, ins. #120, line 2)

k) *PHL' L'B'NHM*
"they made it for their father"
(N.Pu. Henschir Brigitta: KAI/I p. 26, ins. #142, line 4)

l) *PL MGN*
"*MGN* made"
(N.Pu. Spain: Amadasi p. 152, line 1)

2 a) *NP'L NBL NSKT 'RB'*
"there were made four molten metal goblets"
(N.Pu. Bir Bou-Rekba: KAI/I p. 26, ins. #137, lines 5-6)

b) *NP'L' ŠŠ HYŠBM 'L'*
"there were made these six seats"
(N.Pu. Leptis Magna: KAI/I p. 25, ins. #130, line 1)

c) *NP'L' HMNṢBT Š'*
"this pillar was made"
(N.Pu. Tripolitania: LibAnt 1 [1964] p. 64, line 1)

Bibl. Harris 138; NE 352; Berthier/Charlier 83; ClassFol 22 (1968) 172; Amadasi 152; Benz 393; DISO 231; Branden 16; PPG 13, 41, 57-60, 87-88; KAI/II 2, 11, 12, 27, 36, 126, 133, 136, 139.

P'LT I   Heb. *Pe'ūLā*; J.Aram. *Pe'ūLTa* "work, recompense, deeds"; Ph., N.Pu. *P'LT* (N.Pu. *P'LT*). 1. "deed" n.f. 2. type of work

1 a) *'L P'LT M'ŠRT*
"for honest deeds"
(N.Pu. Leptis Magna: KAI/I p. 23, ins. #123, lines 4-5)

2 a) *KM P'LT M'ṢRT*
"as a work of walled enclosure (?)" (or "as a fortified construction")
(N.Pu. Maktar: KAR 12 [1963-64] p. 51, col. III, line 2)

b) *WP'LT '[T]*
"and work (?) [with it]"
(Ph. Cyprus: Slouszch p. 95, ins. #85, line 2)

Bibl. KAR 12 (1963-64) 52; Slouszch 96; DISO 232; KAI/II 130.

P'LT II etymology unknown. 1. "name of a month"

a) *WBYRḤ P'LT*
"and in the month of *P'LT*"
(Ph. Larnaka: KAI/I p. 10, ins. #43, lines 7-8)

b) *BḤMŠ LYRḤ P'LT*
"on the fifth (day) of the month of *P'LT*"
(Pu. Constantine: Berthier/Charlier p. 52, ins. #57, line 3)

c) *BYMM 17 LYRḤ P'L[T]*
"on the seventeenth day of the month of *P'L[T]*"
(Ph. Tamassos: Slouszch p. 114, ins. #98, line 1)

Bibl. KAI/II 60; Berthier/Charlier 53; NSI 69; Harris 138; Slouszch 114.

P'M I Heb. *Pa'aM* "foot, step"; Shauri *Fa'aM*; Ug. *P'N*; Akk. *PēNū* "ankle"; Meh. *FaM* "foot". 1. "foot" n.f.

1 a) *W'NK 'ZTWD ŠTNM TḤT P'MY*
"and I *'ZTWD* set them under my feet"
(Ph. Karatepe: KAI/I p. 5, ins. #26, lines A I,16-17)

b) *TḤT P'M 'DNY*
"under the feet of my lord"
(Ph. Umm el-Awamid: KAI/I p. 3, ins. #18, line 7)

2 a) *HMTBḤ Z DL P'MM*
"this slaughtering place deficient with regard to feet"
(Pu. Carthage: KAI/I p. 17, ins. #80, line 1)

3 a) *H'RT WHŠLBM WHP'MM*
"the skins and the joints and the feet"
(Pu. Marseilles: KAI/I p. 15, ins. #69, line 4)

Bibl. DISO 232; Branden 29; Harris 138; NE 353; KAI/II 26, 36, 83, 98; ANET 652, 656; Amadasi 169; NSI 47; Slouszch 144; LS I 479.

P'M II — Heb. *Pa'aM* "time, occurrence".
1. "time" n.f.

a) *BḤDR ḤŠK 'BR P'M P'M LLYN*
"from the underworld, pass, pass (at once) (?) O night demons"
(Ph. Arslan Tash: BASOR 197 [1970] col. B, lines 1-2)

b) *'D P'MT BRBM*
"exceedingly often (?)" (or "yet most exceedingly")
(Pu. Sardinia: KAI/I p. 15, ins. #68, line 5)

c) *RB MḤNT P'M'T 'SR W'ḤT*
"army commander for the eleventh time"
(N.Pu. Leptis Magna: KAI/I p. 22, ins. #120, line 1)

Bibl. DISO 232; KAI/II 43, 82, 126; ANET 658; Harris 138; Amadasi 115; BASOR 197 (1970) 46; LS I 62-63; PPG 108, 124; Slouszch 225; JAOS 94 (1974) 269.

P'R — etymology unknown; perhaps related to Sum. *BaḪaR* "potter"; Akk. *PaḪḪaRu*; B.Aram. *PeḪaR*; J. Aram. *PaḤāRa'*, *PaḤRa'* "fragment of a clay vessel"; Syriac *PaḤaRa'*, *PaḤaRaiia'* "of earthenware"; Arabic *FaḪḪāRuN* "potter"; Mandaic *PaHaRa'* "potter," *PaHRa'* "clay, pottery"; N.Syr. *PaḪaRa'* "pottery," *PiḪaRa'* "an earthen vessel," with disassimilation of *Ḥet* to *'Ayin*. 1. "pottery" n.m. (?)

a) *M'Š 'LM ŠP'R ST*
"this divine (?) statue (fashioned from) pottery (?)"
(N.Pu. Ras el-Haddiga: KAI/I p. 22, ins. #118, line 1)

PṢ' — B.Heb. *Pāṣā* "to open (the mouth)"; J.Aram. *Peṣa'*; Syriac *Peṣa'* "to rescue, set free"; Mandaic *PṢ'*; Chr.Pal.Aram. *PṢ'* "to deliver". 1. "to offer" vb.

a) *PṢ' 'T NDR Z RMK'Ṭ LB'L*
"RMK'Ṭ offered (?) this vow to B'L"
(N.Pu. Constantine: Slouszch p. 227, ins. #240, lines 1-2)

Bibl. Slouszch 227; Tarbiz 19 (1948) 53-55.

PQD Heb. *PāQaD* "to visit, muster, appoint"; Akk. *PaQāDu* "to hand over, order, tend, entrust"; J.Aram. *PeQaD* "to visit, muster, appoint"; Syriac *PeQaD*; Mandaic *PQD*; Nab. *PQD*; Palm. *PQD*; Arabic *FaQaDa* "to lose, miss, give attention to"; Geez *FaQaDa* "to examine, research"; Soq. *FoQaD* "not to find". 1. "to commission" vb.

a) *PQD HMPQD Z WHSLMT 'Š LMPQD ['Z]*
"this tower, and the steps which belong to (this) tower were commissioned" (or "he commissioned...")
(Ph. Idalion: NSI p. 73, ins. #23, line 4)

b) *'Š YPQD '[DN]Š[MŠ] BN RŠP[YTN]*
"that which '[DN]Š[MŠ] son of RŠP[YTN] commissioned"
(Ph. Idalion: NSI p. 73, ins. #23, line 4)

Bibl. NSI 74-75; Harris 139; NE 353; Slouszch 98-99; DISO 233-34.

PQT meaning and etymology uncertain. 1. "profit" n.f. (from context)

a) *PQT WN'M YKN LY WLZR'Y*
"may profit (?) and goodness be mine and my offsprings"
(Ph. Larnaka: KAI/I p. 10, ins. #43, line 15)

Bibl. Harris 139; KAI/II 60; DISO 234; Slouszch 113.

PR Heb. *PeRi* "fruit, branches"; Akk. *PiRu* "offshoot"; Ug. *PR*; J.Aram. *PeRa'*; Syriac *PeRYa'* "offspring"; Mandaic *PeRa'*; Geez *FoRe* "fruit". 1. "branches" n.m. 2. "fruit"

1 a) *'L YKN LM ŠRŠ LMṬ 'WPR LM'L*
"may they have no stock downwards or branches upwards"
(Ph. Sidon: KAI/I p. 3, ins. #14, lines 11-12)

2 a) *ŠḤ PR Y'*
"plants of fair fruit"
(Pu. Carthage: KAI/I p. 16, ins. #76, line B 2)

b) *YLK HTM 'T HPRY*
"the total (?) will produce (?) fruit"
(N.Pu. Tripolitania: Or 33 [1964] p. 4, line 6)

Bibl. Or 33 (1964) 13; ANET 662; Harris 139; DISO 234; Driver-Fs 73-75; Albright-Fs 265.

PRṬ [B.Heb. *PāRaṬ* "to pluck" (Amos. 6:5); N.Heb. *PāRaṬ* "to unlock, split"; J.Aram. *PeRaṬ*; Syriac *PeRaṬ*; Mandaic *PRṬ*; Amh. *FaRRaṬa* "to burst"; Arabic *FaRiṬuN* "improvisor"]. 1. "provider" n.m. (meaning doubtful)

a) *ḤMLKT HPRṬ 'L MYṬB 'RŠ' HSLKY* "*ḤMLKT*, the provider (?) for the best wishes of the [senators] of *SKLY*" (N.Pu. Sardinia: Amadasi p. 130, ins. #5, lines 1-2)

Bibl. KAI/II 172; DISO 235; Amadasi 130.

PR(D)KRML meaning and etymology unknown. 1. title or function n.m.

a) *'BD'ŠTRT BN GR'ŠTRT RB 'RṢ PR(D)KRML* "*'BD'ŠTRT* son of *GR'ŠTRT*, the district chief (?) *PR(D)KRML*" (Ph. Larnaka: KAI/I p. 10, ins. #43, lines 5-6)

Bibl. DISO 235; KAI/II 60; Slouszch 108; Harris 139.

PRṢ meaning and etymology unknown. 1. type of coin n.m.

a) *MN' ḤMŠ PRṢM* "he counted five *PRṢM*" (N.Pu. Tripolitania: Or 33 [1964] p. 4, line 5)

Bibl. Or 33 (1964) 12.

PŠT B.Heb. *PeŠeT* "flax"; N.Heb. *PiŠTāN*; Akk. *PiŠTu*, *PiLTu*. 1. "flax" n.m.

a) *B'LYTN BN M... MKR HPŠT* "*B'LYTN* son of *M...*, seller of flax" (Pu. Carthage: CIS I, ins. #4874, lines 1-2)

Bibl. DISO 238; LS I 48.

PT' Heb. *PeTi* "simpleton, fool, youth"; J.Aram. *PaTYa'*; ESArab. *FTYN*; Arabic *FaTaN*. 1. "youth" n.m.

a) *'Š N[DR B]DMLQRT BN 'BD'ŠMN HPT'* "that which [*B*]*DMLQRT* son of *'BD'ŠMN* the youth [vowed]" (Pu. Carthage: CIS I, ins. #357, lines 3-5)

Bibl. Slouszch 256; DISO 238; Harris 138; NE 355.

PTḤ I Heb. *PiTTūaḤ* "incision," *PaTTāḤ* "engraver"; Akk. *PaTāḪu* "to bore"; ESArab. *FTḤ*; [Arabic *FuTuḪuN* "claws of a lion," *FaTaḪa* "to bend and stretch (the fingers and toes)"].
1. "engraving" n.m. 2. engraved work n.m.

1 a) *WHPTḤ ḤRṢ ZN*
"and this gold engraving"
(Ph. Byblos: KAI/I p. 2, ins. #10, line 4)

2 a) *'Š 'L PN PTḤY Z*
"which is over against this engraved work of mine"
(Ph. Byblos: KAI/I p. 2, ins. #10, lines 4-5)

Bibl. Harris 139; KAI/II 12; ANET 656; DISO 238-39.

PTḤ II C.S. 1. "to open" vb.

a) *'L YPTḤ 'YT MŠKB Z*
"may he not open this resting place"
(Ph. Sidon: KAI/I p. 3, ins. #14, line 4)

b) *'L 'L TPTḤ 'LTY*
"do not, do not open my sarcophagus (?)"
(Ph. Sidon: KAI/I p. 2, ins. #13, lines 3-4)

c) *'L ẎPTḤ LY*
"let it not be opened to him" (reading of line uncertain)
(Ph. Arslan Tash: BASOR 197 [1970] p. 46, lines 1-3)

d) *PTḤ' Š'M' ḤR'B K'*
"the drying sheds (?) were set open (?) here"
(N.Pu. Tripolitania: Or 33 [1964] p. 4, line 1)

Bibl. BASOR 197 (1970) 46-47; DISO 238-39; Or 33 (1964) 7; ANET 662, 668; Harris 139; Benz 396-97; PPG 60; NE 355.

Ṣ

Ṣ'N Heb. *Ṣ'oN*; Akk. *Ṣēnu*; Amar.Akk. *Ṣūnu*; Ug. *Ṣ'iN*; Moab. *Ṣ'N*; Emp.Aram. *QN'*; J.Aram. *'āNa'*; Syriac *'aNa'*; Mandaic *'aQNa'*, *'aNa'*; Palm. *'N'*; ESArab. *Ḍ'N*; Arabic *Ḍa'aNuN*. 1. "sheep" coll. n.

a) *B'L Ṣ'N*
"possessor of sheep"
(Ph. Karatepe: KAI/I p. 5, ins. #26, lines A III,8-9)

Bibl. KAI/II 36; ANET 653; DISO 240.

ṢB' Heb. *Ṣāba'* "army, warfare, host"; Akk. *Ṣabū* "group of people, troop of soldiers"; Ug. *ṢB'*; ESArab. *ḌB'* "war, fighting"; Geez *ḌB'* "to wage war"; Amh. *Ṭab* "quarrel". 1. "force" n.m. 2. "workers"

1 a) *ŠLM ṢB'*
"his forces found refuge"
(Ph. Nora: Or 41 [1972] p. 459, lines 4-5)

2 a) *'Š NDR PMYŠ[M']BN 'ŠMNŠLK 'L '[B]Y WṢB'*
"that which *PMYŠ[M']* son of *'ŠMNŠLK* vowed on behalf of his [fat]her and his workers (?)"
(Pu. Carthage: Slouszch p. 327, ins. #524, lines 3-5)

Bibl. Or 41 (1972) 464; BASOR 208 (1972) 16; Slouszch 327; DISO 241; Harris 139; NE 356; Benz 397.

ṢBT B.Heb. *Ṣābaṭ* "to hold out, reach"; N.Heb. *Ṣābat* "to bind, untie"; Akk. *Ṣabātu* "to grasp, take"; Ug. *MṢBṬM* "tongs"; J.Aram. *Ṣebat* "to join"; Mandaic *'abṬ*; Geez *Ḍabaṭa* "to seize"; Arabic *Ḍabaṭa* "to hold, keep guard". 1. "to hold" vb.

a) *ṢBT N' HQŠ[B]*
"hold now, pay atten[tion]" (?)
(reading of entire line uncertain)
(N.Pu. Sicily: RSO 40 [1965] p. 205, line 1)

Bibl. RSO 40 (1965) 205-6.

ṢD I Heb. *Ṣad* "side"; B.Aram. *LeṢad* "against"; J.Aram. *Ṣedad'* "side"; Mandaic *Ṣida'*; Arabic *Ṣadad* "in front of". 1. "side" n.m. 2. "besides" adv.

1 a) *WṢD' MṢ' HŠMŠ*
"and its side, facing east"
(Pu. Carthage: KAI/I p. 17, ins. #78, line 6)

2 a) *'Š BṢD 'L HMḤZM*
"besides that which is (incumbent) upon the market officers"
(N.Pu. Leptis Magna: KAI/I p. 25 ins. #130, lines 2-3)

Bibl. Harris 140; DISO 242; Slouszch 177; KAI/II 96, 133, 139; PPG 124-25, 128.

ṢD II — Heb. *ṢūD* "to lie in wait, watch"; Akk. *ṢāDu* "to prowl, make one's rounds"; Anc.Aram. *ṢYD* "hunting"; J.Aram. *ṢūD* "to hunt"; Syriac *ṢuD*; Mandaic *ṢuD*; Arabic *ṢāDa*. 1. "sacrifice of game" n.m.

a) *'M ZBḤ ṢD*
"or a sacrifice of game"
(Pu. Marseilles: KAI/I p. 15, ins. #69, line 12)

b) *W'L ZBḤ ṢD*
"and for a sacrifice of game"
(Pu. Carthage: KAI/I p. 16, ins. #74, line 9)

Bibl. Harris 139; Amadasi 169; ANET 656-57; DISO 244; Slouszch 147; KAI/II 83, 92.

ṢD III — etymology unknown. 1. "payment" n.m.

a) *B'N ṢDN*
"without payment (?)"
(Pu. Carthage: CIS I, ins. #5522, line 9)

Bibl. DISO 242-43.

**ṢDQ* I — Heb. *ṢaDiQ* "just, correct, righteous"; N.Heb. *ṢaDeQeT*; J.Aram. *ṢaDiQa'*, *ṢaDiQTa'*. 1. "pious" n.f.

a) *PWLY' HṢDYQ'*
"*PWLY'* the pious (one)"
(N.Pu. Henschir Meded: KAI/I p. 28, ins. #154, lines 2-3)

Bibl. KAI/II 147; Harris 140; Branden 26; PPG 101, 107; Benz 398-99.

ṢDQ II — Heb. *ṢeDeQ* "just, right"; Ug. *ṢDQ*; Akk. *ṢaDuQu*; Anc.Aram. *ṢDQ*; Emp.Aram. *ṢDQ*; J.Aram. *ṢiDQa'*; Syriac *ZeDQa'* "right, law, rule"; Mandaic *ZaDiQa'* "righteous"; Palm. *ZDQT*; ESArab. *ṢDQ* "perfect"; Arabic *ṢiDQuN* "truth, veracity". 1. "just" adj. 2. "legitimate"

1 a) *K MLK ṢDQ WMLK YŠR*
"for he is a just and upright king"
(Ph. Byblos: KAI/I p. 1, ins. #4, lines 6-7)

b) *K MLK ṢDQ H'*
"for he is a just king"
(Ph. Byblos: KAI/I p. 2, ins. #10, line 9)

2 a) *WBN ṢDQ YTNMLK*
"and the legitimate heir, *YTNMLK*"
(Ph. Sidon: KAI/I p. 3, ins. #16, line 1)

b) *WLṢMḤ ṢDQ*
"and for the legitimate offspring"
(Ph. Larnaka: KAI/I p. 10, ins. #43, line 11)

Bibl. DISO 243; Harris 140; Benz 398-99; Slouszch 30, 111; NE 357; ANET 653, 656; KAI/II 6, 12, 25, 60; Bib 46 (1965) 29-40; VT 4 (1954) 164-76.

ṢDQ III for etymology, see under *ṢDQ* II.
1. "righteousness" n.

a) *BṢDQY WBḤKMTY*
"because of my righteousness and my wisdom"
(Ph. Karatepe: KAI/I p. 5, ins. #26, lines A I,12-13)

Bibl. KAI/II 36; ANET 653.

ṢW'T etymology and meaning unknown.
1. "type of sacrifice" n.f.

a) *B'LP KLL 'M ṢW'T*
"for an ox, whole offering or *ṢW'T* offering"
(Pu. Marseilles: KAI/I p. 15, ins. #69, line 3)

b) *'M ŠRB 'YL KLL 'M ṢW'T*
"or the young of a hart whole offering or *ṢW'T* offering"
(Pu. Marseilles: KAI/I p. 15, ins. #69, line 9)

Bibl. Harris 141; AJSL 47 (1930-31) 52-53; PEQ 80 (1948-49) 67-71; NSI 117; DISO 244; Slouszch 143; NE 357; ANET 656; KAI/II 83; Amadasi 175-76.

ṢLB N.Heb. *ṢāLaB* "to hang, impale"; J.Aram. *ṢeLaB*; Syriac *ṢeLaB*; Mandaic *ṢLB*; Chr.Pal.Aram. *ṢLB*; Arabic *ṢaLaBa*.
1. "to hang" vb.

a) *Š ṢLB 'B[D]B'L BN 'ZR*
"that which *'B[D]B'L* son of *'ZR* hung"
(Pu. Carthage: Slouszch p. 204, ins. #199, line 1)

Bibl. Slouszch 204; Harris 141; DISO 245.

ṢLL [N.Heb. *NāṢaL* "to be cleared"; Akk. *ṢaLāLu* "to be light, to shine"; J.Aram. *ṢeLaL* "to be clear, to clarify"; Syriac *ṢeL* "to clear away," *ṢeLaLa* "pure condition"; Mandaic *ṢLL* "to be purified (?)"; Arabic *ṢaLLa* "to filter, to cleanse"]. 1. "to be clean" vb. (meaning doubtful)

a) *ŠḤT MWṢL*
"a clean (?) knife (?)"
(N.Pu. Spain: Amadasi p. 153, ins. #3, line 1)

Bibl. Amadasi 153; DISO 245; ClassFol 22 (1968) 173.

ṢMḤ Heb. *ṢeMaḤ* "sprout, growth"; J.Aram. *ṢiMHa'*; Syriac *ṢeMḤa'*; Mandaic *ṢiHMa'* "shining, light". 1. "offspring" n.m.

a) *ṢMḤ ṢDQ*
"legitimate offspring"
(Ph. Larnaka: KAI/I p. 10, ins. #43, line 11)

b) *ḂṢMḤ Š'RM*
"from (?) the offspring (?) of his flesh (?)"
(N.Pu. Constantine: KAI/I p. 30, ins. #163, line 3)

c) *BṢMḤ T-SPT ḂŠ'ṘM*
"for the additional (?) offspring of his flesh"
(N.Pu. Constantine: KAI/I p. 30, ins. #162, line 2)

Bibl. KAI/II 60, 152-53; Harris 141; DISO 246.

ṢMQ N.Heb. *ṢiMūQ* "raisin, dried olive"; Ug. *ṢMQ*; J.Aram. *ṢiMūQa'*. 1. "raisin" n.m.

a) *'SR KKR' ṢMQ*
"ten talents of raisins"
(N.Pu. Tripolitania: Or 33 [1964] p. 41, line 2)

Bibl. Or 33 (1964) 8-9; PPG 105.

Ṣ'R Heb. *Ṣā'iR* "little, young"; Akk. *ṣeḪRu* "small"; Ug. *ṢĠR*; J.Aram. *Ze'eRa'*; Syriac *Ze'oRa'*; [Mandaic *Ṣ'aR* "to maltreat, dishonor"]; ESArab. *ṢĠR* "little, small"; Arabic *ṢaĠiRuN*. 1. "least" n.m.

a) *'DRNM W'D Ṣ'RN[M]*
"the greatest of them, even unto the least of [them]"
(Pu. Sardinia: KAI/I p. 14, ins. #65, line 2)

b) *'DRNM W'D Ṣ'RNM*
"the greatest of them, even unto the least of them"
(Pu. Carthage: KAI/I p. 17, ins. #81, line 5)

Bibl. Harris 141; KAI/II 80, 98; DISO 246; Slouszch 159, 345; Amadasi 118.

ṢP' Heb. *ṢāPā* "to look, watch out for"; Ug. *ṢPY* (?) "view"; J.Aram. *ṢaPPe* "to look out, wait"; Chr.Pal.Aram. *ṢPWY* "custodian". 1. "seer" n.m.

a) *MBYW HṢP'*
"*MBYW* the seer"
(N.Pu. Henschir Medina: KAI/I p. 29, ins. #159, line 6)

Bibl. KAI/II 198.

ṢP'T [Heb. *ṢiPūi* "plating"; J.Aram. *ṢaPiTa'* "lamp"]. 1. "tunic" n.f. (etymology doubtful)

a) *YTN' L 'BD BṢP'T KL Ḥ'T*
"they allowed him to use (?) the tunic (?) at all times"
(N.Pu. Leptis Magna: KAI/I p. 24, ins. #126, line 9)

Bibl. KAI/II 131; DISO 246.

ṢPL Heb. *ṢāPōN* "north"; Ug. *ṢPN* name of a holy mountain in the heights of heaven; J.Aram. *ṢiPPōN* "north". 1. "north" n.m.

a) *'RPT KBRT MṢ' ŠMŠ WṢPLY*
"the portico in the direction (?) of sunrise and the north (side) of it"
(Ph. Ma'ṣub: KAI/I p. 4, ins. #19, lines 1-2)

Bibl. KAI/II 27; Benz 205, 401; NE 359; DISO 246; Harris 141; Slouszch 44; Branden 8; PPG 22.

ṢPR Heb. *ṢIPPōR* "bird"; [Akk. *ṢaBāRu* "to twitter"]; Emp.Aram. *ṢNPR*; B.Aram. *ṢiPPaR* "bird"; J.Aram. *ṢiPPaRa'*, *ṢiPPōR*; Syriac *ṢePRa'*; Mandaic *ṢiPRa'*; N.Syr. *ṢiPRa'*; Arabic *ṢāFiRuN* "yellow bird"; Pu. *ṢPR* (N.Pu. *ṢYPR*). 1. "bird" n.f. 2. name of a god

1 a) *'M DL ṢPR*
"or deficient with regard to birds"
(Pu. Marseilles: KAI/I p. 15, ins. #69, line 15)

b) [']*L ṢPR*
"for a bird"
(Pu. Marseilles: KAI/I p. 15, ins. #69, line 12)

c) *ṢYPRM 'RRM*
"calling birds"
(N.Pu. Tripolitania: Or 33 [1964] p. 4, line 7)

2 a) *K B'L WRŠP ṢPRM ŠLḤN*
"because *B'L* and *RŠP ṢPRM* sent me"
(Ph. Karatepe: KAI/I p. 5, ins. #26, line A II,10-11)

Bibl. Harris 141; Amadasi 169; Benz 411-12; NE 359; Slouszch 146; ANET 653, 656; DISO 246; LS I 78-79; Tur-Sinai 92-93; Or 33 (1964) 13; PPG 42.

ṢṢ J.Aram. *ṢīṢa'* type of a bird of prey; Sam.Aram. *ṢūṢ* "young bird". 1. "type of bird" n.f.

a) *'M ṢṢ*
"or a *ṢṢ* bird"
(Pu. Marseilles: KAI/I p. 15, ins. #69, line 11)

b) *BṢṢ*
"for a *ṢṢ* bird"
(Pu. Carthage: KAI/I p. 16, ins. #74, line 7)

Bibl. Amadasi 179; KAI/II 83, 92; ANET 656, 657; Harris 139; Slouszch 146.

ṢRB J.Aram. *ṢoRBa'* "student"; Syriac *'aRBa'* "sheep"; Chr.Pal.Aram. *'RB'*. 1. "young stag" n.m. (found only in combinations)

a) *BṢRB 'YL KLL*
"for a young stag, whole offering"
(Pu. Marseilles: KAI/I p. 15, ins. #69, line 9)

b) *[B]ṢRB 'YL KLLM*
"[for] a young stag, whole offerings"
(Pu. Carthage: KAI/I p. 16, ins. #74, line 5)

Bibl. ZDMG 40 (1896) 737; Benz 402-3; DISO 247; Harris 142; Amadasi 179; Slouszch 145-46; ANET 656-57.

ṢRT B.Heb. *ṢāRā* "rival wife"; Syriac *'aRTa'*; Arabic *ḌaRRaTuN*. 1. "fellow wife" n.f.

a) *WŠB' ṢRTY*
"and his seven fellow wives"
(Ph. Arslan Tash: KAI/I p. 6, ins. #27, rev. line 17)

Bibl. BASOR 197 (1970) 45; ANET 658; DISO 247; KAI/II 43; Driver, Sam. 9; PPG 113.

Q

**QBB* B.Heb. *QāBaB* "to curse"; Akk. *QaBū* "to speak"; N.Heb. *QaBBā* "curse". 1. "to curse" vb.

a) *WQBT TNT PN B'L*
"may *TNT PN B'L* curse"
(Pu. Carthage: CIS I, ins. #4945, lines 5-6)

Bibl. DISO 245.

QB' B.Heb. *QuBa'aT* "goblet" (Is. 51:17); Arabic *Qa'aBuN*; Akk. *QuBūTu*; Ug. *QB'T*; [Eg. *QBḤW*]. 1. "goblet" n.f.

a) *QB'M ŠLKSP*
"goblets of silver"
(Ph. Larnaka: Mus 51 [1938] p. 286, line 4)

Bibl. DISO 248; Mus 51 (1938) 292.

QBR I C.S. 1. "to be buried" vb. (N) 2. in religious context

1 a) *W'L YQBR BQBR*
"may he not be buried in a grave"
(Ph. Sidon: KAI/I p. 3, ins. #14, line 8)

b) *QYBR TḤT 'BN ZT 'BNT*
"under this stone he has been buried (?)"
(N.Pu. Maktar: KAI/I p. 28, ins. #152, lines 2-3)

2 a) *BYM QBR 'LM*
"on the day of the burial of the god(s)"
(Pu. Pyrgi: KAI/I p. 53, ins. #277, lines 8-9)

Bibl. Mus 84 (1971) 534-35; Harris 142; NE 360; ANET 662; DISO 250; VT 11 (1961) 344-48, esp. p. 346; NSI 142; KAI/II 19, 146; Amadasi 167; PPG 66.

QBR II C.S. Ph., Pu., N.Pu. *QBR* (Pu., N.Pu. *QB'R*, *QB'R*). 1. "grave" n.m.

a) *WBQBR Z*
"and in this grave"
(Ph. Sidon: KAI/I p. 3, ins. #14, line 3)

b) *QBR B'L'ZBL 'ŠT 'ZRB'L*
"the grave of *B'L'ZBL*, the wife of *'ZRB'L*"
(Pu. Tharros: KAI/I p. 15, ins. #67, lines 1-4)

c) *QBR ZYBQT HKHNT*
"the grave of *ZYBQT*, the priestess"
(Pu. Avignon: KAI/I p. 16, ins. #70, line 1)

d) *QB'R ṢPNB'L HKHNT*
"the grave of *ṢPNB'L* the priestess"
(Pu. Carthage: KAI/I p. 19, ins. #93, line 1)

e) *QB'R Ṭ[N']*
"a grave [set up]"
(N.Pu. Leptis Magna: KAI/I p. 25, ins. #128, line 2)

f) *W'ḤDR DL 'QBR'*
"and the chamber with its grave"
(N.Pu. Cherchel: KAI/I p. 29, ins. #161, line 3)

g) *[Q]B'R MQN'T 'TM'*
"[a gr]ave, the completed property"
(N.Pu. Tripolitania: LibAnt 1 [1964] p. 57, line 1)

Bibl. DISO 250; Harris 142; NE 360; ANET 662; Amadasi 103, 183; KAI/II 19, 82, 87, 104, 132, 150; LibAnt 1 (1964) 58; LS II 342-43.

QDḤ

B.Heb. *QāDaḤ* "to be kindled"; [N.Heb. *QaDaḤ* "to bore, perforate"; J.Aram. *QeDaḤ* "to bore, perforate"]; Syriac *QeDaḤ* ["to tear the hair,] to catch fire, blaze up"; Arabic *QaDaḤa* "to strike fire"; Mandaic *QD'* ["to bore], inflame"; Soq. *QaDaḤ* ["to bore,] to catch fire"; [Geez *DaQaḤa* "to bore"]. 1. "to light" vb.

a) *MGN HMQDḤ*
"*MGN* the lamp lighter"
(Pu. Carthage: CIS I, ins. #352, line 3)

Bibl. Slouszch 296; DISO 250; NE 360; Harris 143.

QDM

Heb. *QeDeM* "aforetime"; Ug. *QDM* "in front of"; Akk. *QaDMiŠ* "earlier"; J.Aram. *QeDōMa'* "antiquity"; Syriac *QaDMiTa'* "primitive, ancient"; Mandaic *QDiMa'* "former, primeval". 1. "aforetime" n.m.

a) *YRḤ MD YRḤ 'D 'LM KQDM*
"month by month, forever, as
aforetime"
(Ph. Larnaka: KAI/I p. 10,
ins. #43, line 12)

Bibl. KAI/II 60; DISO 251; Harris 143.

QDMT   C.S. rt. 1. "first fruits" n.f. (Lev.
27:30)

a) *'M QDMT QDŠ*
"or first fruits"
(Pu. Marseilles: KAI/I p. 15,
ins. #69, line 12)

b) *WQDMT*
"and first fruits"
(Pu. Carthage: KAI/I p. 16,
ins. #76, line A 7)

Bibl. Harris 143; KAI/II 83, 93; DISO 252;
NE 361; ANET 656; Amadasi 169;
Slouszch 146.

QDŠ I   C.S. 1. "to consecrate" vb. (Y) 2. "to
consecrate oneself" (Hith.)

1 a) *B'LŠLM BN [S]SMY YQDŠ [']T MŻBḤ*
"B'LŠLM son of [S]SMY consecrated
(this) altar"
(Ph. Larnaka: KAI/I p. 10,
ins. #42, lines 3-4)

b) *YTT WYQDŠT ḤYT ŠĠYT*
"I offered and consecrated many
animals"
(Ph. Larnaka: KAI/I p. 10,
ins. #43, line 9)

c) *WḤ[']ṚP'Ṭ 'Š B'N' W'YQ̇DŠ*
"the porticos which they built
and consecrated"
(N.Pu. Ras el-Haddagia: KAI/I
p. 22, ins. #118, line 1)

d) *BTM P'L W'YQDŠ*
"completely of his own cost, he
made and consecrated"
(N.Pu. Leptis Magna: KAI/I p.
26, ins. #121, line 2)

2 a) *LB'L 'DR HTQDŠ B'LŠYLK*
"to B'L'DR, B'LŠYLK...consecrated
himself"
(N.Pu. Bir Tlesa: KAI/I p. 26,
ins. #138, lines 1-2)

Bibl. KAI/II 59-60, 123, 128, 137; Harris
143; NE 361; DISO 253; LS I 98-100;
Branden 81; PPG 69; Slouszch 106,

QDŠ II C.S. 1. "holy" n.m. 2. "holy" adj. m. 3. in combinations

1 a) *WMPḤRT 'L GBL QDŠM*
"and the assembly of the gods of *GBL*, the holy ones"
(Ph. Byblos: KAI/I p. 1, ins. #4, lines 4-5)

b) *L'DN LB'L HQDŠ*
"to the lord, to *B'L*, the holy one"
(Pu. Constantine: Berthier/Charlier p. 61, ins. #64, lines 1-2)

2 a) *L'ŠMN ŠR QDŠ*
"for *'ŠMN* the holy prince (?)"
(Ph. Sidon: KAI/I p. 3, ins. #15, line 2)

b) *L'DN L'LN HQDŠ B'L ḤMN*
"to the lord, to the holy god, *B'L ḤMN*"
(Pu. Constantine: KAI/I p. 20, ins. #104, line 1)

c) *WYSGRNM H'LNM HQDŠM*
"may the holy gods deliver them up"
(Ph. Sidon: KAI/I p. 3, ins. #14, line 9)

d) [*B*]*'ŠR HQDŠ*
"[in] the holy place"
(Pu. Carthage: Slouszch p. 351, ins. #584, line 6)

e) *'BD BT SKN B'L QDŠ*
"servant of the temple of *SKN B'L*, the holy one"
(Pu. Carthage: CIS I, ins. #4841, lines 6-8)

3 a) *'M QDMT QDŠ*
"or first fruits"
(Pu. Marseilles: KAI/I p. 15, ins. #69, line 12)

Bibl. Harris 143; DISO 253-54; NE 361; KAI/II 6, 19, 23, 114; Slouszch 352; Berthier/Charlier 62; Amadasi 162; Bib 38 (1957) 253, note 2; Bib 46 (1965) 412-14.

QDŠ III B.Heb. *QoDeŠ* "inner sanctuary"; Ph., N.Pu. *QDŠ* (Pu. *KDŠ*). 1. "sanctuary" n.m. 2. "temple"

1 a) *LRBTY L'ŠTRT 'Š BGW HQDŠ 'Š LY 'NK*
"for my lady, for *'ŠTRT* who is in the midst of the sanctuary which is mine"
(Ph. Tyre: KAI/I p. 3, ins. #17, lines 1-2)

b) *BKDŠ B'L ḤMN*
"in the sanctuary of *B'L ḤMN*"
(Pu. Carthage: KAI/I p. 17,
ins. #78, line 5)

2 a) *PḤNT QDŠM*
"also (?) the arches (?) of the temples"
(N.Pu. Maktar: KAI/I p. 27,
ins. #145, line 2)

Bibl. DISO 253; KAI/II 25, 96, 141; Harris 143; PPG 17.

QDŠT C.S. rt. 1. "holy" adj. f. 2. in combinations

1 a) *LGBL QDŠT*
"to holy *GBL*"
(Ph. Byblos: Slouszch p. 15,
ins. #8, line 1)

b) *LMLKT QDŠT*
"to the holy queen"
(Ph. Kition: KAI/I p. 8,
ins. #37, line A 7)

2 a) *'M QDMT QDŠT*
"or first fruits"
(Pu. Marseilles: KAI/I p. 15,
ins. #69, line 12)

Bibl. Harris 143; Amadasi 180; ANET 656; KAI/II 54, 83; Or 37 (1968) 311-12; Slouszch 15, 78, 146.

QṬN Heb. *QāṬōN* "to be small"; Akk. *QaTāNu* "to be thin," *QaTNu* "young"; J.Aram. *QaṬNūTa'* "youth"; Mandaic *GṬN* "to be fine, thin"; Syriac *QeṬaN* "to be harrowed, grow thin"; [Geez *QaṬiN* "servant"; Arabic *QaṬiNuN* "servant,"] *QaTiNuN* "starved"; Soq. *QeṬeHoN* "thin, slender". 1. "small" n.m.

a) *'Š NDR 'ZRB'L BN GR'ŠTRT ŠM' QL' BRK' 'QṬN*
"that which *'ZRB'L* son of *GR'ŠTRT* the small (?) vowed. He heard his voice and blessed him"
(N.Pu. Constantine: JA Series 11 vol. 10 [1917] p. 58, costa 38,
lines 2-3)

Bibl. Harris 143; DISO 257.

QṬRT Heb. *QeṬōReT* "incense"; Q.Heb. *MQṬRT*; Ug. *QṬR*; Akk. *QaTāRu* "to smoke," *QuTRu* "smoke"; J.Aram. *'aQṬaR* "to let incense rise"; ESArab. *MQṬR* "censor"; Arabic *QuṬRuN* "smoke"; [Soq. *QaṬRaN* "tar, pitch"]; Pu. *QṬRT* (N.Pu. *KTRT*). 1. "incense" n.f.

a) [*'BD'*]*LM MKR 'QṬRT*
"[*'BD'*]*LM*, the seller of incense"
(Pu. Carthage: Slouszch p. 336, ins. #555, lines 2-3)

b) *WQṬRT LBNT DQT*
"and incense, fine frankincense"
(Pu. Carthage: KAI/I p. 16, ins. #76, line B 6)

c) *'KTRT B'YM ŠK'RNM*
"the incense (?) from his (?) earnings (?)"
(N.Pu. Henschir Medina: KAI/I p. 29, ins. #160, line 1)

Bibl. DISO 130, 257; Harris 143; NE 362; Slouszch 168, 337; KAI/II 93, 149; Branden 7.

QL Heb. *QōL* "sound, voice"; Ug. *QL*; [Akk. *QūLu* "silence"]; Anc.Aram. *QL*; Emp.Aram. *QL*; J.Aram. *QāLa'*; Mandaic *QaLa'*; Syriac *QāLa'*; Palm. *QL*; ESArab. *QL*; Geez *QL*; Arabic *QūLuN*; Ph., Pu., N.Pu. *QL* (N.Pu. *QWL*, *Q'L*).
1. "voice" n.m.

a) *K ŠM' QL YBRK*
"because he heard (his) voice, may he bless (him)"
(Ph. Idalion: KAI/I p. 8, ins. #38, line 2)

b) *K ŠM' QLM YBRKM*
"because he heard the sound of their words, may he bless them"
(Ph. Malta: KAI/I p. 11, ins. #47, lines 3-4)

c) *K ŠM' QL DBRY*
"because he heard the sound of his words"
(Pu. Malta: KAI/I p. 14, ins. #61, lines A 5-6)

d) *K ŠM' QL' YBRK'*
"because he heard his voice, may he bless him"
(Pu. Sicily: KAI/I p. 14, ins. #63, line 3)

e) *YBRKY WYŠM' QL 'D 'LM*
"may he bless him and hear his voice forever"
(Pu. Carthage: KAI/I p. 17, ins. #78, line 1)

f) *BḤRK' WŠMḤ QLH*
"he blessed him and heard his voice"
(N.Pu. Constantine: Slouszch p. 224, ins. #232, lines 2-3)

g) *WŠ'M' 'T QWL'*
"and he heard his voice"
(N.Pu. Guelma: JA Series 11 vol. 8 [1916] p. 500, ins. #19, lines 3-4)

h) *Š'M['] 'T Q'L[']*
"he heard his voice"
(N.Pu. Guelma: JA Series 11 vol. 8 [1916] p. 499, ins. #18, line 3)

Bibl. Harris 143; DISO 258; NE 361; Berthier/Charlier 111, 134; PPG 14, 44, 94, 109-10; KAI/II 56, 64, 76, 79, 96, 133.

QLL N.Heb. *QaLaL* "a vessel"; J.Aram. *QeLaLa'*. 1. type of vessel n.m.

a) *QLLṀ W* _____
"*QLLṀ* vessels and (?)"
(Ph. Egypt: KAI/I p. 12, ins. #51, obv. line 3)

Bibl. KAI/II 69.

QL' B.Heb. *QaLLā'* "slinger"; Heb. *QāLa'* "to sling"; Ug. *QL'* "sling"; Syriac *QeL'a'*; J.Aram. *QiL'a'*; Geez *MaQLa'* "sling"; Arabic *MaQLa'uN*; Soq. *QaLaḤ* "to throw, fling". 1. "slinger" n.m.

a) *'ŠMNḤLṢ HQL'*
"*'ŠMNḤLS* the slinger"
(Ph. Cyprus: RES ins. #1214, line 2)

Bibl. Harris 143; DISO 259; Syria 45 (1968) 296-99.

QN' Heb. *QāNe* "reed"; Ug. *QN*; Akk. *QaNū*; J.Aram. *QaNYa'*; Syriac *QaNYa'*; Mandaic *QaiNa'*; Arabic *QaNāTuN* "pipe, conduit for a canal". 1. "reed" n.m.

a) *PTR' MKR HQN' ZK'*
"*PTR'*, the seller of pure reed"
(Pu. Carthage: Slouszch p. 337, ins. #557, lines 1-2)

Bibl. DISO 259; Harris 143; Slouszch 337.

**QNY I* B.Heb. *QāNā* "to create"; Ug. *QNY*; Arabic *QaNa*; Soq. *QeNe* "to take care of, attend to". 1. "to create" vb. 2. "to fashion"

1 a) *'L QN 'RṢ*
"*'L*, the Creator of earth"
(Ph. Karatepe: KAI/I p. 5, ins. #26, line A III,18)

b) *L'DN L'L QN 'RṢ*
"to the lord, to *'L*, the Creator of earth"
(N.Pu. Leptis Magna: KAI/I p. 25, ins. #129, line 1)

2 a) *SMR Z QN KLMW BR ḤY*
"the scepter (?) which (?) *KLMW* son of *ḤY* fashioned"
(Ph. Zinjirli: KAI/I p. 5, ins. #25, lines 1-3)

Bibl. KAI/II 35, 36, 133; DISO 260; ANET 653, 655; VT 11 (1960) 143, note 4; PPG 23, 83-84; JBL 80 (1961) 137; BASOR 98 (1945) 22, note 68; BASOR 94 (1944) 34, note 21.

**QNY* II — Heb. *QāNā* "to get, acquire"; Akk. *QaNū*; J.Aram. *QeNa'*; Syriac *QeNa'*; B.Aram. *QeNa'*; Mandaic *QN'*; ESArab. *QNY*; Geez *QeNy*; Arabic *QaNa*; [Soq. *QeNe* "to take care of, to nurse"]. 1. "to acquire" vb. 2. "to sell" (Y)

1 a) *'QN' 'GN*
"I acquired a bowl"
(Ph. Byblos: MUSJ 45 [1969] p. 262, line 4)

2 a) *ḤNB'L MQNY HTRŠM*
"*ḤNB'L*, the seller (?) of wines (?)"
(Pu. Carthage: CIS I, ins. #5522, line 2)

Bibl. DISO 335-36; MUSJ 45 (1969) 270; CRST 38-39.

QNM — Chr.Pal.Aram. *QNWM* reflexive pr.; Syriac *QeNoM* "person"; Ph. *QNM* (N.Pu. *QN'M*). 1. reflexive pr.

a) *QNMY 'T KL MMLKT WKL 'DM*
"whoever you are, any prince and any man"
(Ph. Sidon: KAI/I p. 3, ins. #14, line 4)

b) *MYQDŠ QN'M*
"(my) sanctuary, whoever (you) are (?)"
(N.Pu. Cherchel: KAI/I p. 29, ins. #161, line 1)

Bibl. ANET 662; ESE II 164; DISO 260-61; KAI/I 19, 150; PPG 55; Branden 62; NSI 148.

Q'YSR Latin *Caesar*; J.Aram. *QeSaR*; Nab. *QYSR*.
1. "Caesar" n.m.

a) *WDR'SS Q'[Y]ṢṘ*
"and Drusus Caesar"
(N.Pu. Leptis Magna: KAI/I p. 23, ins. #122, line 1)

b) *MYNKD Q'YSR 'WGSṬS*
"the emperor Caesar Augustus"
(N.Pu. Leptis Magna: KAI/I p. 22, ins. #120, line 1)

c) *Q'YSR M'RQH 'WRHLY*
"Caesar Marcus Aurelius"
(N.Pu. Bitia: KAI/I p. 31, ins. #173, line 2)

Bibl. KAI/II 126, 128, 157; Amadasi 133; PPG 16, 44.

QP' etymology unknown. 1. type of coin n.m. (from context)

a) *L'LN ḤDŠ QP' 2*
"for the gods of the new moon, two *QP'*"
(Ph. Kition: KAI/I p. 8, ins. #37, line A 3)

Bibl. Or 37 (1968) 309, note 1; DISO 261; KAI/II 54.

QṢY I B.Heb. *Qāṣe* "end, extremity"; Ph. *QṢ* (N.Pu. *QṢ'*). 1. "edge" n.m.

a) *BKL QṢYT*
"at all the edges"
(Ph. Karatepe: KAI/I p. 5, ins. #26, line A I,14)

b) *BQṢT GBLY*
"at the edge(s) of my border"
(Ph. Karatepe: KAI/I p. 5, ins. #26, line A I,21)

c) *HQṢ'H ŠHBHRM*
"the edge of the wells"
(N.Pu. Sardinia: KAI/I p. 31, ins. #173, line 3)

Bibl. KAI/II 36; ANET 653; DISO 262; PPG 98; Amadasi 135.

**QṢY* II B.Heb. *QāṣaṢ* "to cut off, exterminate"; Akk. *KaṢāṢu* "to shorten, cut short"; J.Aram. *Qeṣa'* "to break off"; Syriac *Qeṣa'*; Mandaic *QṢṢ*; Arabic *QaṢṢa* "to cut off, chip off".
1. "to exterminate" vb.

a) *'Š MŠL BNM LQṢTNM*
"who shall rule over them, to exterminate them" (or "that they may perish")
(Ph. Sidon: KAI/I p. 3, ins. #14, lines 9-10)

b) *WYQṢN HMMLKT H'*
"and exterminate that ruler"
(Ph. Sidon: KAI/I p. 3, ins. #14, line 22)

c) *B'L ḤMN YQṢY'*
"(may) *B'L ḤMN* exterminate him"
(Pu. Carthage: Slouszch p. 347, ins. #574, lines 2-3)

Bibl. KAI/II 19; DISO 262; ANET 662; Harris 144; Slouszch 23, 348; PPG 62, 83, 85, 89; Gaster-Fs 143.

QṢR Heb. *QāṢiR* "harvest"; Akk. *KaṢaRu* "to bind together"; Emp.Aram. *KṢYR*. 1. "harvest" n.m.

a) *WB'T QṢR Š*
"and the time of harvest, a sheep"
(Ph. Karatepe: KAI/I p. 5, ins. #26, line A III,2)

Bibl. KAI/II 36; DISO 262; ANET 653.

QṢRT N.Heb. *QiṢRā* "short board at the head and at the foot of a bed"; Akk. *KiṢRu* "elbow"; Arabic *MaQṢiRuN* "extremity"; Mandaic "to shorten"; Soq. *QaṢeRHeR*. 1. "rib" n.f.

a) *QṢRT WYṢLT*
"ribs and joints"
(Pu. Marseilles: KAI/I p. 15, ins. #69, line 4)

b) *YKN LKHNM QṢRT WYṢLT*
"the priests shall have the ribs and the joints"
(Pu. Marseilles: KAI/I p. 15, ins. #69, line 13)

Bibl. Harris 144; ANET 656; DISO 262; Slouszch 143-44; KAI/II 83; Amadasi 176-77; Levine 118f.; ZA 42 (1934) 158.

QR I Heb. *QīR* "wall"; Moab. *QR* "city". 1. "wall" n.m.

a) *QR Z BNY ŠPṬB'L*
"the wall which *ŠPṬB'L*...built"
(Ph. Byblos: KAI/I p. 1, ins. #7, line 1)

Bibl. KAI/II 9; DISO 263.

QR II — etymology unknown. 1. "type of small coin" n.m. (from context)

a) *LKLBM WLGRM QR 3 WP' 3*
"for the dogs and for the lions three *QR* and three *P'*"
(Ph. Kition: KAI/I p. 8, ins. #37, line B 10)

Bibl. Or 37 (1968) 309, note 1; DISO 263; KAI/II 54.

QR' — C.S. (except Akk. and Geez). 1. "to invoke" vb. 2. "to read"

1 a) *WQR' 'NK 'T RBTY B'LT GBL*
"and I invoked my lady, the Mistress of *GBL*"
(Ph. Byblos: KAI/I p. 2, ins. #10, lines 2-3)

b) *KM 'Š QR'T*
"when I invoked"
(Ph. Byblos: KAI/I p. 2, ins. #10, line 7)

c) *QR' LMLQRT*
"(who) invokes *MLQRT*"
(Pu. Carthage: CIS I, ins. #5510, line 6)

d) *'ZMLK 'QR'*
"*'ZMLK*, the invoker"
(Pu. Carthage: CIS I, ins. #4883, line 4)

2 a) *QR' T P'S*
"read the tablet"
(N.Pu. Guelaat Bou-Sba: KAI/I p. 30, ins. #165, lines 1-2)

b) *QR' LMM'L' MT'*
"read from upwards downwards"
(N.Pu. Maktar: KAI/I p. 27, ins. #145, line 14)

Bibl. KAI/II 12, 141, 154; DISO 263-64; Harris 144; Slouszch 11; ANET 656.

QRB — C.S. 1. "to offer in sacrifice" vb. (Hith. [?])

a) *WYTQR[B ']YT*
"and he offered (?) (in sacrifice)"
(Ph. Kition: CRAI [1968] p. 15, line 2)

Bibl. CRAI (1968) 20-22.

QRYN J.Aram. *QaRYāNa'* "one able to read scripture". 1. "proof reader" n.m.

a) *BD'ŠTRT QRYN*
"*BD'ŠTRT* (the) proof reader (?)"
(Pu. Constantine: Berthier/Charlier p. 94, line 3)

Bibl. Berthier/Charlier 94; Benz 407.

QRN C.S. 1. "horn" n.m.

a) *B'GL 'Š QRNY LMBMḤSR*
"for a calf whose horns are wanting"
(Pu. Marseilles: KAI/I p. 15, ins. #69, line 5)

Bibl. DISO 266; Harris 144; Amadasi 169; ANET 656.

QRŠ [N.Heb. *QāRaŠ* "to coagulate, to be joined, made solid"; Akk. *QaRāŠu* "to carve, cut up"; J.Aram. *QeRaŠ* "to be joined"; Syriac *QeRaŠ* "to become chilled, frozen"; Mandaic *QRŠ*; Arabic *QaRaSa*]. 1. "to become frozen" vb.

a) *QRŠ*
"become as a frozen mass (?)"
(Ph. Arslan Tash: BASOR [1973] p. 18, line 6)

Bibl. Syria 48 (1971) 403.

QRT Heb. *QeReT*, *QiRYā* "town, city"; Ug. *QYRT*; Anc.Aram. *QRYH*; Emp.Aram. *QRYT'*; B.Aram. *QiRYa'*, *QiRYah*; Syriac *QiRYa'*; J.Aram. *QiRYa'*, *QiRYah*; Mandaic *QiRYaTa'*; Palm. *QYR'*; Arabic *QiRYaTuN*; Soq. *QeRYeh*. 1. "city" n.f.

a) *WBN 'NK HQRT Z*
"and I built this city"
(Ph. Karatepe: KAI/I p. 5, ins. #26, line A II,9)

b) *WKL 'LN QRT*
"and all the gods of the city"
(Ph. Karatepe: KAI/I p. 5, ins. #26, line A III,5)

c) *QBR ŠBLT SḤRT ḤQRT*
"the grave of *ŠBLT*, the merchant of the city"
(Pu. Carthage: KAI/I p. 18, ins. #92, line 1)

Bibl. Slouszch 198; Harris 144; Benz 407; DISO 267; ANET 653; KAI/II 36, 104.

QŠḤT etymology and meaning unknown.

a) *QŠḤT*
(Pu. Carthage: Slouszch p. 204, ins. #200, line 1)

Bibl. DISO 267.

QŠT Heb. *QeŠeT* "bow, rainbow," *QaŠŠāT* "bowman"; Ug. *QŠT*; Akk. *QaŠTu*; Emp.Aram. *QŠT*; J.Aram. *QaŠTa'*, *QaŠŠāTa'* "bowman"; Syriac *QaŠTa'*, *QaŠaTa'*; Palm. *QaŠT'*, *QaŠT'*; Mandaic *QaŠTa'*; Arabic *QuSuN* "bow". 1. "bow" n.f.

a) *ḤN' P'L HQŠT*
"*ḤN'*, the maker of bows"
(Pu. Constantine: Berthier/Charlier p. 82, ins. #100, line 3)

Bibl. DISO 268; Berthier/Charlier 82; LS I 474.

R

R'Y Heb. *Rā'ā* "to see," *Rō'i* "sight, seeing"; Moab. *R'Y* "to see"; ESArab. *R'Y*; Arabic *Ra'a*; J.Aram. *ReWa'* "features".
1. "eyesight" n.f.

a) *LYŠ' R'Y*
"for the preservation of his eyesight"
(Ph. Site not known: JAOS 16 [1907] p. 353, line 3)

R'Š C.S. Ph., N.Pu. *R'Š* (Pu. *RŠ*; N.Pu. *RŠ*, *R'Š*). 1. "leader" n.m. 2. "head" 3. "promontory" 4. in combinations

1 a) *'Y MPT WR'Š*
"there is no dignitary (?) or leader"
(Ph. Cyprus: KAI/I p. 7, ins. #30, line 1)

b) *R'Š 'MŠ'ṘT*
"chief gatekeeper" (or "chief singer")
(N.Pu. Tunisia: KAI/I p. 25, ins. #136, lines 5-6)

2 a) *YŠḤT R'Š B'L ṢMD*
"may his head be smashed by *B'L ṢMD*"
(Ph. Zinjirli: KAI/I p. 4, ins. #24, line 15)

3 a) *RŠ 'DR*
"Rusadir"
(N.Pu. Rusadir: Harris p. 145, sub. *RŠ 'DR*)

b) *B'M RŠ MLQRT*
"among the people of *RŠ MLQRT*"
(Pu. Carthage: Harris p. 145, sub. *RŠ MLQRT*)

4 a) *BDD BR'Š MGMR BNT*
"separate at once (?) O destroyer of intelligence (?)"
(Ph. Arslan Tash: BASOR 209 [1973] p. 19, rev. lines 3-4)

Bibl. EHO 19; Harris 145; ANET 654; DISO 269-70; KAI/II 31, 48, 135; NE 366; PPG 19, 13, 48, 109; Branden 20; BASOR 109 (1973) 25; Syria 48 (1971) 404-5.

R'ŠT Heb. *Re'ŠiT* "beginning, chief"; Akk. *ReŠTu* "first"; Syriac *ReŠiTa'*; J.Aram. *ReŠiTa'*; Q.Heb. *RŠT*; Ph. *R'ŠT* (N.Pu. *RŠT*). 1. "choicest" n.f. 2. "first fruits"

1 a) *BR'ŠT NḤŠT*
"of the choicest bronze"
(Ph. Limassol: KAI/I p. 7, ins. #31, line 1)

2 a) *'BDMLQRT BN ḤNB'L B'L ŠLM HRŠT/N*
"*'BDMLQRT* son of *ḤNB'L*, donor (?) of a *SLM* offering of first fruits"
(N.Pu. Leptis Magna: KAI/I p. 22, ins. #120, line 2)

Bibl. Harris 54; Slouszch 66; KAI/II 49, 126; DISO 270.

RB I C.S. 1. "chief" n.m. 2. "in divine titles" 3. in combinations 4. in abbreviations

1 a) *B'LŠLK HRB*
"*B'LŠLK* the chief"
(Pu. Carthage: Slouszch p. 187, ins. #166, line A 1)

b) *'ZRB'L HRB*
"*'ZRB'L* the chief"
(Pu. Carthage: Slouszch p. 234, ins. #254, line 5)

2 a) *LRBY LT[NT P]N B'L*
"to my lord, to *T[NT P]N B'L*"
(Pu. Carthage: Slouszch p. 338, ins. #560, line 1)

3 a) *'RŠ RB SRSRM*
"*'RŠ*, the chief broker"
(Ph. Kition: KAI/I p. 8, ins. #34, line 2)

b) *YTNB'L RB 'RṢ*
"*YTNB'L*, the district chief"
(Ph. Larnaka: KAI/I p. 10, ins. #43, line 2)

c) *[B]DB'L RB ḤRM*
"*[B]DB'L*, the chief fisherman"
(Ph. Egypt: KAI/I p. 12, ins. #51, rev. line 2)

d) *'BDBL'L RB M'T*
"*'BDB'L*, the centurion"
(Ph. Tyre: Slouszch p. 42, ins. #25, line 1)

e) *BDMSKR RB 'BR LSPT RB ŠNY*
"*BDMSKR*, the chief of *'BR LSPT*, the lieutenant"
(Ph. Tyre: Slouszch p. 42, ins. #26, lines 1-2)

f) *ḤN' R[B] ŠLŠ'*
"*ḤN'*, the troop lea[der]" (or "chi[ef] shield bearer")
(Pu. Carthage: Slouszch p. 207, ins. #207, lines 1-2)

g) *MLKYTN RB ḤRŠ*
"*MLKYTN*, the chief craftsman"
(Ph. Kition: Slouszch p. 95, ins. #84, lines 2-3)

h) *Ḥ[L]D RB KHNT*
"*Ḥ[L]D*, the chief priestess"
(Pu. Carthage: Slouszch p. 189, ins. #172, line 1)

i) *RB T'ḤT RB MḤNT*
"proconsul"
(N.Pu. Ras el-Haddagia: KAI/I p. 22, ins. #118, line 2)

j) *GRSKN RB KHNM*
"*GRSKN*, the chief priest"
(Pu. Carthage: KAI/I p. 19, ins. #96, line 8)

k) *'BD'ŠMN RB SPRM*
"*'BD'ŠMN*, the chief scribe"
(Ph. Kition: KAI/I p. 8, ins. #37, line A 15)

l) *RB MZRḤ SHLKNY*
"the chief of the association (or "citizens council"), *SHLKNY*"
(N.Pu. Maktar: KAI/I p. 27, ins. #145, line 16)

m) *B'LŠLK RB HMŠṬRT*
"*B'LŠLK*, the overseer of the officers"
(Pu. Constantine: Berthier/Charlier p. 68, ins. #75, lines 1-3)

n) *'DNB'L RB HMṪRṀ*
"*'DNB'L*, the chief of the reserves"
(N.Pu. Constantine: Berthier/Charlier p. 73, ins. #84, lines 2-3)

o) *'ZR RB ḤZ'NM*
"*'ZR*, the chief inspector (?)"
(Ph. Kition: KAI/I p. 8, ins. #34, lines 4-5)

p) *QMMḤ RB HŠPṬM*
"*QMMḤ*, the chief magistrate"
(N.Pu. Maktar: KAR 12 [1963-64] p. 46, line 2)

4 a) *R 'DR 'RKT*
"chief of the crack troops"
(Pu. Malta: KAI/I p. 14, ins. #62, line 4)

Bibl. DISO 271-72; Harris 145-46; NE 366-67; Amadasi 117; PPG 117; KAI/II 52, 54, 60, 69, 78, 105, 123, 141.

RB II

Heb. *RaB* "chief, lord"; Ug. *RB*; Anc.Aram. *RB*; Emp.Aram. *RB*; Moab. *RB*; Akk. *RaBBu*; J.Aram. *RaBBa'*; Syriac *RaBa'*; Nab. *RB'*; Palm. *RB'*; Mandaic *RaBa'*. 1. "great" n.m. 2. "great" adj. f.

1 a) *WRB DR KL QDŠṀ* (or *QDŠṄ*)
"and the great of the assembly of all the holy ones"
(Ph. Arslan Tash: KAI/I p. 6, ins. #27, rev. line 12)

2 a) *MYŠR 'RṢT RBT*
"the bringer of prosperity to the great lands"
(N.Pu. Cherchel: KAI/I p. 29, ins. #161, line 2)

Bibl. DISO 270-72; Harris 145-46; ANET 658; BASOR 197 (1970) 44-45; KAI/II 43, 150; ZA 35 (1927) 227f.

RB III

Heb. *RōB* "multitude, abundance". 1. "many" adj. 2. "greatly" adv. 3. in combinations

1 a) *'RK YMM WRB ŠNT*
"length of days and many years"
(Ph. Karatepe: KAI/I p. 5, ins. #26, lines A III,5-6)

2 a) *WBRBM YLḊ WBRḂM [Y]'DR WR[B]RM Y'BD L'ZTWD*
"and may they greatly multiply and may they greatly fear and may they greatly serve *'ZTWD*"
(Ph. Karatepe: KAI/I p. 5, ins. #26, lines C IV,10-11)

3 a) *K ŠM' QL' 'D P'MT BRBM*
"because he has heard his voice exceedingly often (?)"
(Pu. Sardinia: KAI/I p. 15, ins. #68, line 5)

Bibl. DISO 270-72; ANET 653; KAI/II 36, 82; Harris 145; ESE III 281-82; Amadasi 113; JAOS 94 (1974) 269.

RBD

B.Heb. *RāBaD* "to be spread," *MaRBaD* "coverlet"; Ug. *MRBD* "bedcover"; N.Heb. *RōBeD* "pavement"; J.Aram. *ReBDa'*, *RoBeDa'* "pavement". 1. "to pave" vb.

a) *WT HMḤZ RBD*
"and the forum, he paved"
(N.Pu. Leptis Magna: KAI/I p. 23, ins. #124, line 2)

Bibl. KAI/II 130; DISO 272.

RB' C.S. rt. 1. "quarter" n.m.

a) *KSP RB' ŠLŠT*
"three-quarters of a silver (shekel)"
(Pu. Marseilles: KAI/I p. 15, ins. #69, line 11)

Bibl. DISO 23.

RB'N precise meaning unknown. 1. "large eyed" adj. m. (from context)

a) *RB'N 'TY 'LŠYY YṢ'*
"a large eyed *'LŠYY* has attacked with him"
(Ph. Arslan Tash: BASOR 209 [1973] p. 18, obv. lines 2-3)

Bibl. BASOR 209 (1973) 21-22; Syria 48 (1971) 399-400.

RBT Ug. *RBT* "lady"; Akk. *RaBiTu* "queen"; Mandaic *RaBiTa'* "young girl"; Ph., Pu., N.Pu. *RBT* (Pu. *RB'T*, *RBBT*; N.Pu. *RB'T*). 1. in divine titles only, "lady" n.f.

a) *HRBT B'LT GBL*
"the lady, the Mistress of *GBL*"
(Ph. Byblos: KAI/I p. 2, ins. #10, line 2)

b) *RBTY B'LT GBL*
"my lady, Mistress of *GBL*"
(Ph. Byblos: KAI/I p. 2, ins. #10, line 3)

c) *LRBBTN LTNT 'DRT*
"for our lady, for *TNT* the Mighty"
(Pu. Ibiza: KAI/I p. 16 ins. #72, line B 3)

d) *LRBT LTNT PN B'L*
"for the lady, for *TNT PN B'L*"
(Pu. Carthage: KAI/I p. 17, ins. #79, line 1)

e) *L'RBT LTNT PN' <B>'L*
"for the lady, for *TNT PN B'L*"
(Pu. Carthage: KAI/I p. 19, ins. #94, line 1)

f) *LRB'TN TNT P'N'* [*B*]*'L*
"for our lady, for *TNT P'N' B'L*"
(Pu. Constantine: Berthier/Charlier p. 111, ins. #153, lines 2-3)

g) *RB'T TẎNT PN'* [*B'L*]
"the lady, *TNT PN* [*B'L*]
(N.Pu. Constantine: KAI/I p. 30, ins. #164, line 1)

h) *RBT 'LPQY*
"lady of *'LPQY*"
(N.Pu. Leptis Magna: KAI/I p. 22, ins. #119, line 1)

i) *LHRBT L'LT*
"for the lady, for the goddess" (or "for *'LT*")
(N.Pu. Sardinia: KAI/I p. 31, ins. #172, line 3)

Bibl. DISO 270-71; Harris 146; NE 366-67; Benz 408; Amadasi 130, 143, 159-60; Slouszch 173, 188; ANET 656, 662; PPG 113, 117; Berthier/Charlier 112; KAI/II 12, 88, 97, 104, 124, 153, 156; Bib 49 (1968) 29-31 (discusses the possibility of *RBT* in B.Heb.).

RGZ Heb. *RāGaZ* "to be agitated, disturbed"; Anc.Aram. *RGZ*; J.Aram. *ReGaZ*; Syriac *ReGaZ*; Mandaic *RGZ*; Arabic *RiGZun* "anger"; [Soq. *ReQoZ* "to dance"; Amh. *RaGGaDa* "shake with fear"]. 1. "to disturb" vb. (Y)

a) *WLRGZ 'ṢMY*
"and to disturb my bones"
(Ph. Byblos: KAI/I p. 2, ins. #9, line A 5)

b) *W'L TRGZN*
"and do not disturb me"
(Ph. Sidon: KAI/I p. 2, ins. #13, line 4)

c) *WRGZ TRGZN*
"and if you shall disturb me"
(Ph. Sidon: KAI/I p. 2, ins. #13, line 7)

d) *W'Š YRGZ T MTNT Z*
"and who disturbs this present"
(Pu. Carthage: CIS I, ins. #3945, lines 4-5)

Bibl. KAI/II 10, 17; Slouszch 16; NE 367; Harris 146; DISO 274; PPG 68, 90; ANET 662; MUSJ 45 (1969) 264; LS I 398-99.

*RWḤ B.Heb. *ReWaḤ* "to be wide, spacious"; N.Heb. *HiRWîaḤ* "to be relieved, make profit"; J.Aram. *ReWaḤ*; Syriac *RaWWaḤ* "to enlarge, widen"; Arabic *RaWiḤa* "to widen"; Saftaitic *'RḤ* "to give rest".
1. "prosperity" n.m.

a) *YSP 'LTY LŠLM WLYRWḤY*
"(may *MLQRT*) increase (his) well being and (his) prosperity"
(Pu. Carthage: CIS I, ins. #5510, line 6)

Bibl. DISO 275.

RZN Heb. *RoZeN* "high official"; Arabic *RaZuNa* "to be grave, firm of judgment"; Shauri *ReZiN* "serious"; Q.Heb. *RWZN* "lord (?)".
1. type of high official n.m.

a) *WRZN BRZNM*
"and any high official"
(Ph. Karatepe: KAI/I p. 5, ins. #26, line A III,12)

b) *MLK ḤṬR MYSKR RZN YMM*
"king *ḤṬR MYSKR*, high official of the days (?)"
(N.Pu. Maktar: KAI/I p. 22, ins. #145, line 5)

Bibl. KAI/II 36, 141; DISO 276; ANET 653; Leš 14 (1947-48) 9.

RḤ C.S. 1. "spirit" n.f.

a) *WŠPṬ TNT PN B'L BRḤ 'DM H'*
"may *TNT PN B'L* judge the spirit of that man"
(Pu. Carthage: KAI/I p. 17, ins. #79, lines 10-11)

b) *K RḤ DL QDŠM*
"because (my) spirit glorified (?) the holy ones"
(Pu. Carthage: Slouszch p. 180, ins. #155, line 4)

c) *WBRḤT 'ZRTNM*
"and with the spirits of their clans (?)"
(Pu. Carthage: CIS I, ins. #5510, line 2)

Bibl. DISO 276; Slouszch 181; Harris 145; KAI/II 97.

RḤB Heb. *RāḤaB* "to be or to grow large or wide"; Ug. *RḤBT* type of a large vessel; J.Aram. *ReḤaB* "ambitious, greedy"; Mandaic *RḤB* "to be wide, extend"; ESArab. *RḤB* "spacious, wide"; Arabic *RaḤuBa* "to be wide or spacious"; Geez *RəḤBa* "to be large". 1. "to widen" vb. (Y)

a) *YRḤB 'NK 'RṢ 'MQ 'DN*
"I widened the land of the plain of *'DN*"
(Ph. Karatepe: KAI/I p. 5, ins. #26, line A I,4)

Bibl. ANET 653; KAI/II 36; Slouszch 276; PPG 68.

RḤMT [Arabic *RuH̱aMuN* "marble, alabaster"; Soq. *RaḤMaM* "of the color ash"]. 1. "marble" n.f.

a) *MLMN P'L HRḤMT*
"*MLMN*, the worker of marble (?)" (i.e., "marble craftsman")
(Pu. Carthage: Slouszch p. 298, ins. #439, line 2)

Bibl. Slouszch 298; DISO 278.

RM Heb. *RūM* "to be high, exalted"; Ug. *R(W/Y)M; Anc.Aram. *HRM* "to make high"; Emp.Aram. *'TRWM* "to elevate"; J.Aram. *RūM* "to be high, exalted"; Syriac *RuM*; ESArab. *RYM*; Soq. *RYM* "to be long"; Geez *'aRYaM* "heaven". 1. "highest" adj. m.

a) *MLK ṢDNM BSDN YM ŠMM RMM*
"king of the *ṢDNM*, in *ṢDN* of the sea, the high heavens"
(Ph. Sidon: KAI/I p. 3, ins. #15, line 1)

Bibl. NSI 402; Harris 145; Benz 408-9; Slouszch 28; KAI/II 23; DISO 280.

R' I Heb. *Rā'a* "to pasture, tend"; Akk. *Rē'u*; Ug. *R'Y*; Emp.Aram. *R'Y*; J.Aram. *Re'a'*; Syriac *Re'a'*; Mandaic *RA''*; Geez *Rə'Y*; Soq. *Re'e*; Arabic *Ra'a*; ESArab *MR'Y* "pasture". 1. "shepherd" n.m.

a) LR'M 'Š BD ŠP* LKD QR 2
"for the shepherds who caught by means of traps (?) two *QR*"
(Ph. Kition: Or 37 [1969] p. 305, line B 8)

*Reading uncertain.

Bibl. Or 37 (1968) 323; Harris 147; DISO 281; KAI/II 54.

R' II   Heb. *Ra'* "bad, evil". 1. "evil" adj. m. 2. "evil" n.m.

1 a) *BMQMM B'Š KN 'ŠM R'M*
"in the places where there were evil men"
(Ph. Karatepe: KAI/I p. 5, ins. #26, lines A I,14-15)

2 a) *'M BŠN'T WBR'*
"or with hatred or with evil (intention)"
(Ph. Karatepe: KAI/I p. 5, ins. #26, line A III,17)

Bibl. ANET 653; DISO 281.

R'Š   Heb. *Ra'aŠ* "to quake, shake"; J.Aram. *Re'aŠ* "to trample"; Arabic *Ra'aSa* "to quake, shake," *Ra'aŠa* "to tremble". 1. "earthquake" n.m. (only in place names)

a) *BYR'Š*
"(who is) on the Island of Earthquakes (?)"
(Pu. Carthage: Slouszch p. 278, ins. #379, line 4)

R'T   Heb. *Re'ūT* "desire"; J.Aram. *Ra'ūTa'*; Syriac *TaR'iTa'* "meditation". 1. "intention" n.f.

a) *'YT R'T Z*
"with this (our) intention"
(Pu. Piraeus: KAI/I p. 13, ins. #60, line 4)

Bibl. Harris 147; DISO 281; KAI/II 73; PPG 99, 106; JAOS 89 (1969) 694.

RP'   Heb. *RiPPe'* "to heal"; Emp.Aram. *RP'*; ESArab. *RF'*; Amar.Akk. *RiPūTi* "healing"; Soq. *TeRoF* "to be cured"; Arabic *RaFa'* "to mend"; Pu., N.Pu. *RP'* (N.Pu. *RP, R'B'*). 1. "doctor" n.m. 2. "to cure" vb. 3. in divine titles (Q)

1 a) *B'LḤN' HRP'*
"*B'LḤN'* the doctor"
(Pu. Constantine: Berthier/Charlier p. 79, ins. #92, line 2)

b) *B'LYTN HRP'*
"*B'LYTN* the doctor"
(Pu. Carthage: Slouszch p. 297, ins. #434, lines 4-5)

c) *'DRB'L HR'B'*
"*'DRB'L* the doctor"
(N.Pu. Leptis Magna: KAI/I p. 25, ins. #131, line 1)

d) *QYNṬ' M'RQY PRṬ[MQ' H]RP'*
"*QYNṬ' M'RQY PRṬ[MQ'* the] doctor"
(N.Pu. Henschir Aleouin: Slouszch p. 15, ins. #218, lines 1-2)

e) *YKNŠLM BN B'DŠ HRP*
"*YKNŠLM* son of *B'DŠ* the doctor"
(N.Pu. Constantine: JA Series 11 vol. 10 [1917] p. 42, ins. #15, line 2)

2 a) *SM[' Q]L RPY'*
"he hea[rd] his [vo]ice (and) healed him"
(Pu. Sardinia: KAI/I p. 14, ins. #66, lines 1-2)

3 a) *B'L MRP'*
"*B'L* the healer"
(Ph. Cyprus: CIS I, ins. #41, line 3)

Bibl. DISO 282; Harris 88, 147; Benz 410-11; Amadasi 91; NE 369; KAI/II 81, 134; PPG 24, 44, 84, 91; Branden 6, 100; VT 6 (1956) 190-98.

RP'M exact meaning and etymology unknown.
1. "shades" n.m.

a) *MŠKB 'T RP'M*
"resting place with the shades"
(Ph. Sidon: KAI/I p. 2, ins. #13, line 8)

b) *L'L[NM] 'R'P'M*
"to the gods, the shades"
(N.Pu. Libya: KAI/I p. 22, ins. #117, line 1)

Bibl. KAI/II 17, 122; ANET 662; DISO 282; PEQ 84 (1949) 127-29; Harris 147; Slouszch 17, 216; MUSJ 45 (1969) 265-66.

RQḤ I Heb. *RōQeaḤ* "perfumer," *RaQQaḤ*; Ug. *RQḤ*; Akk. *RuQQu* "compound ointment"; J.Aram. *MeRQaḤTa'* "ointment"; Ph., Pu. *RQḤ* (N.Pu. *RQ'*). 1. "perfumer" n.m.

a) *'RMY HRQḤ* (reading uncertain)
"*'RMY* the perfumer"
(Ph. Abydos: Slouszch p. 61, ins. #50, line 1)

b) *B'L'ZR HRQḤ*
"*B'L'ZR* the perfumer"
(Pu. Carthage: Slouszch p. 348, ins. #574, line 6)

c) *B'LŠLK HRQ'*
"*B'LŠLK* the perfumer"
(Pu. Carthage: Slouszch p. 240, ins. #271, lines 3-4)

d) *MGNM RQ'*
"*MGNM* (the) perfumer"
(Pu. Carthage: Slouszch p. 224, ins. #281, lines 5-6)

Bibl. DISO 282; Harris 147; NE 370; Slouszch 241.

RQḤ II   for etymology, see *RQḤ* I; "perfumer"

a) *ḤMLKT BN BN KNT MRQḤ*
"*ḤMLKT* grandson of *KNT* (the) perfumer"
(N.Pu. Constantine: Berthier/Charlier p. 158, ins. #263, line 2)

Bibl. Berthier/Charlier 158.

RQM   Heb. *RāQaM* "to varigate cloth"; J.Aram. *RiQMaTa'* "varigated cloth"; Arabic *RaQaMa* "to varigate"; Syriac *TaRQiMaTa'* "freckles". 1. "embroider" n.m.

a) *'BDMLQRT HRQM*
"*'BDMLQRT* the embroiderer"
(Pu. Carthage: CIS I, ins. #4912, line 2)

Bibl. DISO 283.

**RQ'*   B.Heb. *RāQia'* "extended surface". 1. "foundation" n.m.

a) *HYKRT R'QYM*
"he hewed (?) the foundations (?)"
(N.Pu. Maktar: KAR 12 [1963-64] p. 50, col. I, line 2)

Bibl. KAR 12 (1963-64) 50; LS III 195-96.

RŠ'T   N.Heb. *RiŠYōN* "permission," *HiRŠā* "to empower"; Akk. *RaŠū* "to receive, to have," *RaŠūTu* "credit, balance"; J.Aram. *ReŠi* "to empower," *RaŠūTa'* "power, authority"; Mandaic *RŠ'* "to lend, bribe"; Nab. *RŠY* "having right". 1. "rule" n.f.

a) *'RK YMM RB ŠNT WRŠ'T N'MT*
"length of days, many years and favorable rule
(Ph. Karatepe: KAI/I p. 5, ins. #26, lines A III,5-6)

Bibl. KAI/II 36; ANET 653; Benz 411; DISO 283; LS I 80.

Š

Š I — Heb. *Śe* "sheep, one of a flock"; Ug. *Š*; Akk. *Šu'u*; Arabic *ŠaTuN*; ESArab. *ŠHW* "lamb"; Ph. *Š* (Ph. *Š'*). 1. "sheep" n.m.

a) *WMY BL ḤZ PN Š*
"and whoever had never seen the face of a sheep"
(Ph. Zinjirli: KAI/I p. 4, ins. #24, line 11)

b) *WB'T QṢR Š*
"and at the time of harvest a sheep"
(Ph. Karatepe: KAI/I p. 5, ins. #26, line A III,2)

c) *'LMT YTN BŠ*
"(who) gave a maid for a sheep"
(Ph. Zinjirli: KAI/I p. 4, ins. #24, line 8)

d) *Š DD*
"a sheep (?) *DD*"
(Ph. Kition: CRAI [1968] p. 15, line 3)

Bibl. ANET 653-54; EHO 17; CRAI (1968) 21-22; JNES 28 (1969) 263; Harris 148; KAI/II 30, 36; DISO 286; PPG 19; Levine 133; Fitzmyer 41.

Š II — Heb. *Še* rel. part.; Akk. *Ša*; Emp.Aram. *Š*; [Soq. *Š* "with"; Ph., Pu., N.Pu. *Š* (N.Pu. *Š'*; Berthier/Charlier #11, lines 2-3, p. 18 [?]). 1. rel. particle 2. with suffix.

1 a) *W'L PN 'Š Š LḤR[M]*
"and in addition to the fisher-[men] (i.e., men of the ne[t])"
(Ph. Egypt: KAI/I p. 12, ins. #51, rev. line 2)

b) *Š 'ZRB'L BN MṢLḤ*
"that which belongs to *'ZRB'L* son of *MṢLḤ*"
(Pu. Sicily: Slouszch p. 130, ins. #111, line 1)

c) *KHN Š B'L ŠMM*
"priest of *B'L ŠMM*"
(Pu. Carthage: Slouszch p. 284, ins. #397, lines 1-2)

d) *QBR GRTMLQRT HKHNT Š RBTN*
"the grave of *GRTMLQRT* the priestess of our lady"
(Pu. Carthage: Slouszch p. 188, ins. #170, lines 1-2)

e) *'RŠ BN Š MGNM*
"*'RŠ* son of *MGNM*"
(Pu. Carthage: Slouszch p. 244, ins. #281, lines 4-5)

f) *-ḤSGN Š HMQM*
"the overseer (?) of the sacred place"
(N.Pu. Maktar: KAI/I p. 28, ins. #146, line 4)

g) *S'LWL BT BRKB'L 'ŠTM Š B'LYN*
"*S'LWL* daughter of *BRKB'L*, the wife of *B'LYN*"
(N.Pu. Kef Bezioun: KAI/I p. 31, ins. #171, lines 1-3)

2 a) *LB'L LTNT B'LM ŠL'*
"to *B'L*, to *TNT*, his masters"
(N.Pu. Constantine: JA Series 11 vol. 10 [1917] p. 42, ins. #15, lines 2-3)

b) *GWMZ'L H'S SL'*
"*GWMZ'L* her husband"
(N.Pu. Ksiba Mapou: JA Series 11 vol. 10 [1917] p. 12, ins. #1, line 3)

c) *DR' KN' ŠLM*
"they have named their family (?)"
(N.Pu. Maktar: KAR 12 [1963-64] p. 54, col. V, line 1)

Bibl. Amadasi 101; DISO 285-86; Harris 148; NE 227-28; Benz 412; PPG 54-55, 156; Branden 34, 60; KAI/II 69, 144, 156; KAR 12 (1963-64) 54; on the possibility of *Š* in Ug., see Bib 53 (1972) 401.

Š'K etymology and meaning unknown.
1. "pit" n.m. (from context)

a) *KR' HŠ'KM*
"digger of pits"
(N.Pu. Tripolitania: Libya 3 [1927] p. 110, line 2)

Bibl. DISO 299.

Š'R I Ug. *T̲'R* "kinsman"; B.Heb. *Še'eR* "flesh (blood) relation" (Lev 18:12); ESArab. *T̲'R* "blood revenge"; Arabic *T̲aa'RuN*.
I. "kinsman" n.m.

a) *[BN 'BDML]QRT BS'RY YBRKY*
"[son of *'BDML*]*QRT*, (who is) among my kinsmen (?), may he bless me" (or "bless him")
(Pu. Carthage: Slouszch p. 313, ins. #484, lines 2-3)

Bibl. Slouszch 313 (also see *ŠR* I, p. 331).

Š'R II Heb. *Še'eR* "flesh"; Ug. *Š'R*; Akk. *ŠīRu*; Soq. *SiRHi* "skin". 1. "flesh" n.m.

a) *W'ḤRY HŠ'R*
"and the remainder of the flesh"
(Pu. Marseilles: KAI/I p. 15, ins. #69, line 4)

b) *Š'R MŠQL M'T WḤMŠM*
"flesh, in weight one hundred and fifty (shekels)"
(Pu. Marseilles: KAI/I p. 15, ins. #69, line 6)

Bibl. Slouszch 143; DISO 288; Amadasi 169; Harris 148; NE 371; ANET 656; KAI/II 83.

Š'T for possible etymology, see *NŠ'* I.

a) *'BDMLKT KL T Š'T'*
"*'BDMLKT* completed his offering (?)
(Pu. Carthage: Slouszch p. 205, ins. #203, lines 1-2)

ŠB' I Heb. *ŚoB'a* "abundance, satiety, corn" (Prov. 3:10); Ug. *ŠB'*; Akk. *ŠeBū* "to be satisfied"; J.Aram. *SiB'a'* "plenty"; Syriac *SaB'a'*; ESArab. *ŠB'* "to be satisfied"; Arabic *ŠaB'uN* "plenty"; [Geez *ŠaBḤa* "to grow fat"]. 1. "corn" n.m.

a) *ŠB' WTRŠ*
"corn and wine"
(Ph. Karatepe: KAI/I p. 5, ins. #26, line C IV,7)

b) *ŠB' WMN'M*
"corn and well being"
(Ph. Karatepe: KAI/I p. 5, ins. #26, line A I,6)

c) *B'L ŠB' WTRŠ*
"possessor of corn and wine"
(Ph. Karatepe: KAI/I p. 5, ins. #26, line A III,9)

Bibl. ANET 653; KAI/II 36; DISO 289; BMB 8 (1946-48) 32; Bib 53 (1972) 397.

ŠB' II C.S. 1. "seven" num.

a) *WŠB' ṢRTY*
"and his seven fellow wives"
(Ph. Arslan Tash: KAI/I p. 6, ins. #27, rev. line 17)

b) *BŠB'T 'RB'M [Š]T*
"in the forty-seventh [ye]ar"
(Pu. Constantine: Berthier/Charlier p. 56, ins. #60, lines 4-5)

c) *BT Š'NT ŠB'M WŠB'*
"seventy-seven years of age"
(N.Pu. Tunisia: KAI/I p. 25, ins. #136, lines 2-3)

d) *B'SR WŠB' LYRḤ MP'*
"on the seventeenth of the month of *MP'*"
(N.Pu. Tunisia: KAI/I p. 26, ins. #137, line 5)

Bibl. KAI/II 43, 135-36; DISO 289; Harris 148; ANET 658; BASOR 197 (1970) 45-46; PPG 120-21; Berthier/Charlier 56.

ŠB'M C.S. num. 1. "seventy" (reading uncertain)

a) *BN Š'NT ŠB'M*
"seventy years of age"
(N.Pu. Tunisia: KAI/I p. 25, ins. #133, line 3)

b) *BT ŠB'M WŠB'*
"seventy-seven years of age"
(N.Pu. Tunisia: KAI/I p. 25, ins. #136, lines 2-3)

c) *'W' ŠNT ŠB'M W'MŠ* (J. Friedrich reads a Samach not a Shin)
"she lived seventy-five years"
(N.Pu. Guelma: NE p. 437, ins. #1, lines 3-4)

Bibl. DISO 289; Harris 148; KAI/II 135; PPG 121.

ŠB'T Heb. *ŠeBū'a*; J.Aram. *ŠeBū'āTa'*.
1. "oath" n.f.

a) *W'L KY HMZR' 'Š Y'TN' T 'ŠB'T*
"and because the association (?) which has given the oath (?)"
(N.Pu. Maktar: KAR 12 [1963-64] p. 53, col. III, line 2)

b) *W'N' ŠM'TM 'Š Y'TN' T 'ŠB'T*
"and here are their names (of those) who gave the oath (?)"
(N.Pu. Maktar: KAR 12 [1963-64] p. 54, col. IV, line 2)

c) *YTNṪẎ ŠB'T*
"I gave my oath (?)"
(N.Pu. Maktar: KAI/I p. 27, ins. #145, line 6)

d) *ṬN'T HMNṢBT BŠB'T* * *'BD'ŠMN BN 'ZRB'L*
"the monument was erected because of the oath of *'BD'ŠMN* son of *'ZRB'L*"
(N.Pu. Cherchel: NSI p. 147, ins. #58, lines 1-2)

*I read *BŠB'T* rather than *RŠ B'T* as do Cooke and Lidzbarski.

Bibl. KAI/II 141; DISO 289; KAR 12 (1963-64) 50-51.

ŠBRT [B.Heb. *ŠeBeR* (Jud. 7:15) "breaking of a dream" (i.e., its interpretation), Akk. *ŠuBRu* "to show, reveal"]. 1. "report" n.f.

a) *ŠBRT MLṢM*
"report(s) of the messengers"
(Ph. Karatepe: KAI/I p. 5, ins. #26, line A I,8)

Bibl. LS I 75-76; Tur-Sinai 269-70; ANET 653; KAI/II 36; DISO 290; PPG 58; EI IX 152.

ŠBT I B.Heb. *ŠāBaT* "to cease, desist". 1. "to cease" vb. 2. "to put an end to" (Y)

1 a) *TŠ'M ŠLM SG NŠBT*
"if you seek peace, we shall cease strife"
(Ph. Byblos: JAOS 81 [1961] p. 32, lines 2-3)

2 a) *L'KR WLŠBT Y'ML YD*[']
"and to ban (?) and to put an end to [that] which enfeebles [his] hand"
(Pu. Carthage: CIS I, ins. #5510, line 3)

Bibl. DISO 290; BASOR 212 (1973) 20.

ŠBT II Heb. *ŠeBeT* "inaction, sitting". 1. "situation" n.f.

a) *ŠBT N'MT*
"favorable situation"
(Ph. Karatepe: KAI/I p. 5, ins. #26, lines A II,7-8)

Bibl. KAI/II 36; ANET 653; DISO 290; PPG 73.

ŠGY Heb. *ŚaGGī'* "great"; Emp.Aram. *ŠGY* "multitude"; Palm. *SGY'* "many"; J.Aram. *SaGGi'*; Syriac *SaGGi'*; B.Aram. *ŚaGGi'*; Mandaic *SG'* "to be many, large".
1. "many" adj. f.

a) *ḤYT ŠĠYT*
"many animals"
(Ph. Larnaka: KAI/I p. 10, ins. #43, line 9)

Bibl. Harris 148; Slouszch 110; KAI/II 60; PPG 10-11; Branden 4.

ŠD Heb. *ŚāDe* "field, country, acre"; Ug. *ŠD* (?); Akk. *ŠaDū* "steppe" (?); Amar.Akk. *ŠaTe*; Ph. *ŠD* (Ph. *ŠDH*). 1. "field" n.m. 2. "territory" 3. "cemetery" 4. "mainland"

1 a) *BGBL ŠD NRNK*
"from the territory of the fields of *NRNK*"
(Ph. Larnaka: KAI/I p. 10, ins. #43, line 9)

b) *ŠD ŠRN*
"the fields of *ŠRN*"
(Ph. Sidon: KAI/I p. 3, ins. #14, line 19)

c) *GRHKL BM ḤLM 'Š 'L ŠḊ KŠ*
"*GRHKL* son of *ḤLM* who is over the fields of *KŠ*"
(Ph. Abu Simbel: Slouszch p. 62, ins. #54, line 2)

d) *'Š BŠDH*
"one who is (at home) in the field (?)"
(Ph. Arslan Tash: BASOR 209 [1973] p. 18, obv. line 4)

2 a) *ŠD LWBYM*
"territory of (the) *LWBYM*"
(N.Pu. Ras el-Haddigia: KAI/I p. 22, ins. #118, line 2)

3 a) *ŠD 'LNM*
"cemetery"
(Ph. Egypt: ESE III p. 126, line 1)

4 a) *ṢDN ŠD/R*
"mainland (?) *ṢDN*"
(Pu. Sidon: KAI/I p. 3, ins. #15, line 2)

Bibl. Harris 149; DISO 291; ESE III 126; ANET 662; Slouszch 169; KAI/II 19, 60, 123; PPG 19; JNES 8 (1949) 233-35; BASOR 109 (1973) 18, note 1; Syria 48 (1971) 400-401; Bib 48 (1967) 575, note 6; HTR 55 (1962) 244-50.

SḤ Heb. *Śiaḥ* "plant, tree"; Syriac *Šiḥa'* "Ortemisa"; Pu., N.Pu. *ŠḤ* (Pu. *ŠM*--only in pl.). 1. "plant" n.m.

a) *SḤ PR Y'*
"plants of fine fruit"
(Pu. Carthage: KAI/I p. 16, ins. #76, line B 2)

b) *GR'ŠTRT BN ḤMLK' P'L HŠM*
"*GR'ŠTRT* son of *ḤMLK'*, the plant merchant (?)"
(Pu. Constantine: Berthier/Charlier p. 83, ins. #101, lines 2-3)

c) *MTN BN ḤN' P'L HŠḤM*
"*MTN* son of *ḤN'*, the plant merchant (?)"
(N.Pu. Leptis Magna: KAI/I p. 22, ins. #120, line 2)

Bibl. Harris 148; DISO 299; KAI/II 93, 126; Berthier/Charlier 83.

ŠḤṬ I [Heb. *Šāḥaṭ* "to slaughter"; J.Aram. *Šeḥaṭ*; Arabic *Saḥaṭa*]. 1. "knife" n.m. (meaning doubtful)

a) *ŠḤṬ MWṢL*
"a clean knife (?)"
(N.Pu. Spain: Amadasi p. 153, ins. #3, line 1)

Bibl. Amadasi 153.

ŠḤT II Heb. *ŠiḥeT* "to spoil, ruin"; Anc.Aram. *ŠḤT* "to destroy"; B.Aram. *ŠeḥaT* "to be corrupt"; J.Aram. *ŠeḥaT* "to be mutilated"; [Syriac *ŠaḥeT* "to contract, rust"]. 1. "to ruin" vb. (Y)

a) *WMY YŠḤT HSPR Z*
"he who ruins this inscription"
(Ph. Zinjirli: KAI/I p. 4, ins. #24, line 15)

b) *YŠḤT R'Š B'L ṢMD*
"may his head be smashed by *B'L ṢMD*"
(Ph. Zinjirli: KAI/I p. 4, ins. #24, line 15)

c) *WYŠḤT R'Š B'L ḤMN*
"and may his head be smashed by *B'L ḤMN*"
(Ph. Zinjirli: KAI/I p. 4, ins. #24, line 16)

Bibl. ANET 654; KAI/II 30; Harris 149; DISO 295; PPG 12, 68.

ŠY Heb. *Šai* "gift, tribute"; Ug. *Ṯ̲Y*; P.S. *Ṯ̲Y*. 1. "gift" n.m.

a) *'BRGD NT<N> ŠY NMḤL*
"*'BRGD* offered a gift to *ḤMN*"
(Ph. Site not known: IEJ 16 [1966] p. 243, lines 1-3)

Bibl. IEJ 16 (1966) 245; EI VIII (English section) 16, note 48; LS I 483-84, also notes 1, 2.

ŠKB Heb. *ŠāKaB* "to lie down"; Ug. *ŠKB*; Akk. *ŠaKāPu*; J.Aram. *ŠeKaB*; Syriac *ŠeKaB*; Mandaic *ŠKB*; Geez *ŠKB*. 1. "to lie down" vb. 2. "to be laid to rest" (N)

1 a) *ŠKB B'RN Z*
"lie in this sarcophagus"
(Ph. Sidon: KAI/I p. 2, ins. #13, lines 2-3)

b) *BLT NK ŠKB B RN Z*
"only I lie in this sarcophagus"
(Ph. Sidon: KAI/I p. 2, ins. #13, line 5)

c) *ŠKBT BSWT*
"lie in a burial robe"
(Ph. Byblos: KAI/I p. 2, ins. #11, line 1)

2 a) *HNŠKBT BT ŠMNM ŠT*
"she who is laid to rest (at) eighty years of age"
(N.Pu. Cherchel: NE p. 438, line 6)

Bibl. Harris 149; ANET 662; DISO 299; Slouszch 340; NSI 198.

ŠKN C.S. 1. "dwelling" n.m.

a) *LŠRM B'R 'Š ŠKNY LMLKT QDŠT*
"for the singers, in the town where the holy queen had her dwelling"
(Ph. Kition: Or 37 [1968] p. 305, line A 7)

Bibl. Or 37 (1968) 311-12, esp. note 1 p. 312; KAI/II 54; Slouszch 76; Harris 149; DISO 299.

ŠKR Heb. *ŚāKaR* "to hire, rent"; Ug. *ŠKR*; Palm. *ŠKR* "to give a reward"; Arabic *ŠaKaRa*; Geez *ŠoKuR* "hired"; Amh. *'aŠKuR* "servant"; [ESArab. *ŠKR* "to defeat"]; Emp.Aram. *ŠKR* "wages". 1. "wages" vb.

a) *WŠKR 'NK 'LY MLK 'ŠR*
"and I hired against him the king of *'ŠR*"
(Ph. Zinjirli: KAI/I p. 4, ins. #24, lines 7-8)

Bibl. KAI/II 30; ANET 654; DISO 299-300; Harris 150; JAOS 74 (1954) 227-28.

ŠLB Heb. *ŠeLaBBiM* "steps of a ladder"; N.Heb. *ŠeLaBBiōT* "wedges"; [Akk. *ŠaBuLu* "leg, thigh"; Syriac *ŠuLBa'* "bird fat"].
1. "joint" n.m.

a) *H'RT WHŠLBM*
"the skins and the joints"
(Pu. Marseilles: KAI/I p. 15, ins. #69, line 4)

b) *H'ŠL[BM]*
"the join[ts]"
(Pu. Carthage: KAI/I p. 16, ins. #74, line 4)

Bibl. Levine 118f.; KAI/II 83, 92; DISO 300; Amadasi 177-78; Slouszch 144.

ŠLḤ Heb. *ŠāLaḤ* "to send"; Ug. *ŠLḤ*; Anc.Aram. *ŠLḤ*; Emp.Aram. *ŠLḤ*; J.Aram. *ŠeLaḤ*; Syriac *ŠeLaḤ*; Mandaic *ŠLH*, *ŠLa*; [Akk. *ŠaLū* "to shoot, cast up"; Eg. *Ŝ3Ḥ* "to reach"].
1. "to send" vb.

a) *'Š ŠLḤT LY*
"which you sent me"
(Ph. Saqqara: KAI/I p. 12, ins. #50, line 3)

b) *K B'L WRŠP ṢPRM ŠLḤN*
"because *B'L* and *RŠP ṢPRM* sent me"
(Ph. Karatepe: KAI/I p. 5, ins. #26, lines A II,10-11)

c) *WKL ŠLḤ YD*
"and everybody sent forth his hand"
(Ph. Zinjirli: KAI/I p. 4, ins. #24, line 6)

Bibl. ANET 653-54; DISO 300-302; Harris 150; Benz 416; KAI/II 30, 36, 54; PPG 58, 88; Leš 38 (1973-74) 11-32.

ŠLK etymology unknown. 1. "to provide" vb.
2. "to pay" vb.

1 a) *M[Š]LK BN' 'M*
"the pr[ovid]er of the common people"
(N.Pu. Leptis Magna: KAI/I p. 24, ins. #126, line 6)

2 a) *WK'N ŠLK SP 50*
"and now, he paid fifty cents (?) for the basin"
(Pu. Carthage: Syria 9 [1930] p. 202, line 1)

Bibl. Benz 416; P.S. II 37-38, 80; Harris 150; NE 326; KAI/II 131; Syria 9 (1930) 202.

ŠLM I — Heb. *ŠeLāMiM* "gift of greeting, present"; Ug. *ŠLMM*. 1. type of offering n.m.

a) *'M ŠLM KLL*
"or the *ŠLM* of the *KLL* offering"
(Pu. Marseilles: KAI/I p. 15, ins. #69, line 3)

b) *BRKTMLQRT ŠLMM 3*
"*BRKTMLQRT*, three *ŠLMM* offerings"
(Ph. Egypt: KAI/I p. 12, ins. #51, obv. lines 5-6)

c) *'BDMLQRT BN ḤNB'L B'L ŠLM HRŠT/N*
"*'BDMLQRT* son of *ḤNB'L*, donor (?) of a *ŠLM* offering of first fruits"
(N.Pu. Tripolitania: KAI/I p. 22, ins. #120, line 2)

Bibl. PEQ 80 (1948-49) 67-71; Harris 150; ANET 156; KAI/II 69, 83, 126; DISO 305; Amadasi 174-76; Slouszch 143; Levine 10, 118f.; JAOS 94 (1974) 269.

ŠLM II — C.S. 1. "peace" n.m. (in a political sense) 2. "refuge" 3. "well being" 4. "peace of the grave" 5. "completion, soundness"

1 a) *WBRK B'L KR[N]TRYŠ 'YT 'ZTWD ḤYM WŠLM*
"and may *B'L KR[N]TRYŠ* bless *'ZTWD* with life and with peace"
(Ph. Karatepe: KAI/I p. 5, ins. #26, lines A III,2-3)

b) *WŠT 'NK ŠLM 'T KL MLK*
"and I established peace with all kings"
(Ph. Karatepe: KAI/I p. 5, ins. #26, lines A I,11-12)

2 a) *BŠRDN ŠLM H' ŠLM ṢB'*
"in *ŠRDN* he found refuge, his forces found refuge"
(Ph. Nora: Or 41 [1972] p. 459, lines 3-5)

3 a) *WŠLM 'T 'P 'NK ŠLM*
"is it well with you, even (as) I am well"
(Ph. Saqqara: KAI/I p. 12, ins. #50, line 2)

b) *WLKL 'L TḤPNṢ YP'L̇K ŠLM*
"and may all the gods of *TḤPNṢ* give you peace"
(N.Pu. Tunisia: KAI/I p. 26, ins. #142, line 7)

4 a) *'QBR BŠLM*
"the grave, in peace"
(N.Pu. Tunisia: KAI/I p. 26, ins. #142, line 7)

Bibl. Or 41 (1972) 463-64; BASOR 208 (1972) 16; ANET 653; DISO 303-4; KAI/II 36, 63, 67, 139; Harris 150; Benz 417-18; JAOS 93 (1973) 191-93.

ŠLM III C.S. 1. "to fulfill (a vow)" vb.

a) *ŠLM BD'ŠTRT BN ḂD'ŠMN 'YT NDRM*
"*BD'ŠTRT* son of *BD'ŠMN* fulfilled his vow"
(Pu. Constantine: Berthier/Charlier p. 28, ins. #27, lines 1-2)

b) *ŠLM 'T NDRM*
"he fulfilled his vow"
(Pu. Constantine: Berthier/Charlier p. 96, ins. #121, line 3)

c) *ŠLMTY 'T NDRY 'NK ḤN' B<N> MLYKT*
"I *ḤN'* s[on] of *MLẎKT* fulfilled my vow"
(Pu. Constantine: JA Series 11 vol. 10 [1917] p. 45, ins. #31, lines 3-4)

Bibl. Benz 417-18; Harris 150; DISO 303; Berthier/Charlier 28, 96; JA Series 11 vol. 10 (1917) 45.

ŠLŠ' B.Heb. *ŠāLiŠ* type of officer; Akk. *TaŠLīŠu* "driver's mate"; B.Aram. *TaLTi* type of official. 1. military title n.m.

a) *R[B] ŠLŠ'*
"the chi[ef] shield bearer" (or "troop lea[der]")
(Pu. Carthage: Slouszch p. 207, ins. #207, line 2)

Bibl. DISO 306; Harris 151; Slouszch 207; RB 65 (1958) 342.

ŠLŠ(T) C.S. Ph., Pu., N.Pu. *ŠLŠ* (N.Pu. *Š'LŠ*). 1. "three" num.

a) *'ŠMN'DN WŠLM W'BDRŠP ŠLŠT BN MRYḤY*
"*'ŠMN'DN* and *ŠLM* and *'BDRŠP*, the three sons of *MRYḤY*"
(Ph. Idalion: KAI/I p. 9, ins. #40, line 4)

b) *ŠLŠ WḤMŠM ŠT L'M [ṢR]*
"(in the) fifty-third year of the people of [*ṢR*]"
(Ph. Ma'ṣub: KAI/I p. 4, ins. #19, line 8)

c) *KSP RB' ŠLŠT ZR 2 B'ḤD*
"three-quarters of a silver (shekel), two *ZR* for each"
(Pu. Marseilles: KAI/I p. 15, ins. #69, line 11)

d) *BN ŠŠM ŠT WŠLŠ*
"sixty-three years old"
(N.Pu. Constantine: KAI/I p. 28, ins. #152, line 3)

e) *W'W' Š'NT 'SR WŠ'LŠ*
"and he lived thirteen years"
(N.Pu. Henschir Guergour: KAI/I p. 27, ins. #144, lines 2-3)

Bibl. Amadasi 169; DISO 305-6; Harris 150; PPG 8, 119; Branden 37; KAI/II 27, 57, 83, 140, 146.

ŠLŠM C.S. 1. "thirty num.

a) *BŠNT ŠLŠM LMLK MLKYTN*
"in the thirtieth year of king *MLKYTN*"
(Ph. Tamassos: KAI/I p. 9, ins. #41, lines 4-5)

b) *DN'RY' M'T WŠLŠM WŠLŠ*
"one hundred and thirty-three *DN'RY'*"
(N.Pu. Leptis Magna: KAI/I p. 25, ins. #130, lines 1-2)

Bibl. DISO 306; Harris 150; KAI/II 58, 133; PPG 119.

ŠM I Heb. *ŠāM* "there"; Ug. *ṮM*; Anc.Aram. *ŠM*; Emp.Aram. *TMH*; B.Aram. *TaMā*; Syriac *TaMaN*; J.Aram. *TaMMāN*; N.Syr. *TeMạ*; Arabic *ṮaMMa*; Mandaic *HaTaM*; Ph. *ŠM* (N.Pu. *Š'M*).
I. "there" adv.

a) *WDNNYM YŠBT ŠM*
"and I established the *DNNYM* there"
(Ph. Karatepe: KAI/I p. 5, ins. #26, lines A I,21-II,1)

b) *W'T' DN'Ṭ' B'T 'T' Š'M*
"and *DN'Ṭ'* came during the time in which he came there"
(N.Pu. Tripolitania: Or 33 [1969] p. 4, line 2)

Bibl. Or 33 (1969) 9; KAI/II 36; ANET 653; PPG 124.

ŠM II C.S. Ph., Pu. *ŠM* (N.Pu. *Š'M*). 1. "name" n.m. (in royal inscriptions) 2. in general inscriptions

1 a) *ŠM 'NK YḤWMLK MLK GBL*
"my name, *YḤWMLK*, king of *GBL*"
(Ph. Byblos: KAI/I p. 2, ins. #10, lines 12-13)

b) *W'M 'BL TŠT ŠM 'TK*
"and if you place my name with yours"
(Ph. Byblos: KAI/I p. 2, ins. #10, line 13)

c) *'S YMḤ ŠM 'ZTWD*
"who shall erase the name of *'ZTWD*"
(Ph. Karatepe: KAI/I p. 5, ins. #26, lines A III,13-14)

d) *WŠT ŠM 'LY*
"and place his name upon it"
(Ph. Karatepe: KAI/I p. 5, ins. #26, lines A III,16-17)

e) *KM ŠM ŠMŠ WYRḤ*
"as the name of the Sun and the Moon"
(Ph. Karatepe: KAI/I p. 5, ins. #20, lines A IV,2-3)

2 a) *DL ŠM N'M*
"the possessor of a good name"
(N.Pu. Guelma: JA Series 11 vol. 9 [1917] p. 162, ins. #29, line 3)

b) *DL ŠM T'ṢMT*
"the possessor of honor"
(N.Pu. Guelaat Bou-Sba: KAI/I p. 30, ins. #165, lines 6-7)

3 a) *WBY PY 'DM BŠMY*
"or without the word of a man (speaking) in my name"
(Pu. Carthage: KAI/I p. 17, ins. #79, lines 9-10)

b) *'N' ŠM'TM*
"here are the names"
(N.Pu. Maktar: KAR 12 [1963-64] p. 54, col. IV, line 2)

c) *Š'M' NYMR'N BN ŠN'T*
"his name (is) *NYMR'N* son of *ŠN'T*"
(N.Pu. Tripolitania: LibAnt 1 [1964] p. 62, line 4)

Bibl. Harris 151; DISO 306-7; JA Series 11 vol. 9 (1917) 162; Benz 419; NSI 24; PPG 153; Branden 31; KAI/II 12, 36, 97, 154; ANET 653, 656; AJSL 41 (1929) 93.

*Š*M III — Heb. *ŚīM* "to put, set"; Akk. *ŠāMu* "to fix, determine"; Emp.Aram. *ŠYM* "to put, set"; B.Aram. *ŠīM*; J.Aram. *ŠūM*, *SūM*; Syriac *SiM*; Mandaic *SuM*; ESArab. *ŠYM* "to hide, conceal"; Arabic *ŠāMa* "to hide or conceal a thing". 1. "to place, set up" vb.

a) *K 'Y ŠM BN MNM*
"because there is nothing placed in it"
(Ph. Sidon: KAI/I p. 3, ins. #14, line 5)

b) *'Š ŠM NḤM LB'L ḤMN*
"which *NḤM* set up to *B'L ḤMN*"
(Pu. Malta: KAI/I p. 14, ins. #61A, lines 2-4)

c) *PTḤ' Š'M' ḤR'B*
"the drying sheds (?) were set open (?)"
(N.Pu. Tripolitania: Or 33 [1964] p. 9, line 1)

Bibl. Or 33 (1964) 7-8; KAI/II 19, 76; Harris 148; ANET 662; Amadasi 20; Slouszch 21; JBL 56 (1937) 140; PPG 19.

ŠMM — C.S. 1. "heaven" n.m. 2. in place names 3. in religious context

1 a) *B'LT ŠMM W'RṢ 'LM*
"with oaths of heaven and ancient earth"
(Ph. Arslan Tash: BASOR 197 [1970] p. 44, rev. lines 13-14)

2 a) *BSDN YM ŠMM RMM*
"in *ṢDN* (land) of the sea, the high heavens"
(Ph. Sidon: KAI/I p. 3, ins. #15, line 1)

b) *WYŠRN* 'YT 'ŠTRT ŠMM 'DRM*
"and we established *'ŠTRT* (in) the mighty heavens"
(Ph. Sidon: KAI/I p. 3, ins. #14, line 16)

*Probably an error for *YŠBN*.

3 a) *GD HŠMM*
"*GD* of the heavens"
(N.Pu. Maktar: KAI/I p. 28, ins. #147, line 2)

Bibl. DISO 308; Harris 151; BASOR 197 (1970) 44-45; ANET 658, 662; KAI/II 19, 43, 144.

ŠMN I   C.S. 1. "oil" n.m.

a) *ZBḤ ŠMN*
"sacrifice of oil"
(Pu. Marseilles: KAI/I p. 1, ins. #69, line 12)

Bibl. KAI/II 83; Amadasi 169; DISO 309.

ŠMN II   C.S. Ph., Pu., N.Pu. *ŠMN* (Ph. *ŠMNH*, N.Pu. *ŠMN'*). 1. "eight" num.

a) *WŠMNH 'ŠT B'L QDŠ*
"and the eight wives of *B'L*, the holy one"
(Ph. Arslan Tash: KAI/I p. 6, ins. #27, rev. lines 17-18)

b) *BŠNT ŠMN LMLKY*
"in the eighth year of his rule"
(Ph. Idalion: Slouszch p. 102, ins. #92, line 2)

c) *B SR WŠMN LYRḤ MRP'M*
"on the eighteenth of the month of *MRP'M*"
(Pu. Constantine: KAI/I p. 21, ins. #111, lines 2-3)

d) *'W' ŠNT ŠMN'*
"she lived eight years"
(N.Pu. Bou Aftan: JA Series 11 vol. 7 [1916] p. 465, ins. #1, lines 4-5)

Bibl. Slouszch 103; JA Series 11 vol. 7 (1916) 465; Harris 151; DISO 309; PPG 120; Branden 38; ANET 658; BASOR 197 (1970) 44-45; JAOS 94 (1974) 268.

ŠMNM   C.S. 1. "eighty" num.

a) *ŠMN ŠŠ*
"eighty-six"
(N.Pu. Leptis Magna: KAI/I p. 25, ins. #128, line 3)

b) *DN'RY' ŠMNM*
"eighty *DN'RY'*"
(N.Pu. Leptis Magna: KAI/I p. 25, ins. #130, line 2)

Bibl. DISO 309; Harris 151; PPG 39, 121.

ŠM'   C.S. Ph., Pu., N.Pu. *ŠM'* (Pu. *ŠMḤ*, *ŠM'*, *Š'*; N.Pu. *ŠM'*, *ŠMW*). 1. "to hear" vb.

a) *K ŠM' QL YBRK*
"because he heard (his) voice, may he bless him"
(Ph. Tamassos: KAI/I p. 9, ins. #41, line 6)

b) *K Š̌M' QLM YBRKM*
"because he heard their voice, may he bless them"
(Ph. Malta: KAI/I p. 11, ins. #47, lines 3-4)

c) *ŠMḤ QL' BRK'*
"he heard his voice and blessed him"
(Pu. Constantine: Berthier/Charlier p. 106, ins. #141, line 3)

d) *KY Š' QL' BRK'*
"because he heard his voice and blessed him"
(Pu. Constantine: Berthier/Charlier p. 103, ins. #135, line 3)

e) *K ŠM' QL' YBRK'*
"because they heard her voice, may they bless her"
(Pu. Carthage: KAI/I p. 18, ins. #88, lines 5-6)

f) *ŠM QL' BR[K']*
"he heard his voice and bles[sed him]"
(Pu. Constantine: KAI/I p. 21, ins. #114, line 3)

g) *K ŠM' QL' BRK'*
"because he heard his voice and blessed him"
(Pu. Constantine: KAI/I p. 21, ins. #110, line 4)

h) *BḤRK' WŠMḤ QLH*
"he blessed him and heard his voice"
(N.Pu. Constantine: Slouszch p. 224, ins. #232, lines 2-3)

i) *ŠM' QLM*
"(and) heard their voice"
(N.Pu. Maktar: KAI/I p. 28, ins. #146, line 6)

j) *ŠM' 'T QWL'*
"he heard his voice"
(N.Pu. Guelma: JA Series 11 vol. 8 [1910] p. 505, ins. #26, line 4)

k) *BR'K' WŠMW QL'*
"he blessed him and heard his voice"
(N.Pu. Guelma: JA Series 11 vol. 8 [1916] p. 508, ins. #31, lines 3-4)

Bibl. Benz 421; Harris 151: NE 378; Amadasi 15-16; DISO 309-10; KAI/II 58, 64, 102, 116, 144; PPG 15, 59, 60, 88, 92; JA Series 11 vol. 8 (1916) 505, 508.

ŠMR Heb. *ŠāMaR* "to keep watch"; Akk. *ŠaMāRu*; J.Aram. *SeMaR* "to guard oneself"; Mandaic *SMR* "to heed, observe". 1. "to guard" vb.

a) [*'L '*]*DT ŠMR N'LKY*
"[becaus]e of the guarding of my way"
(Ph. Memphis: KAI/I p. 11, ins. #48, line 2)

b) *BL' BN KLM BN Y'ZR ŠMR MḤṢB*
"*BL'*, son of *KLM*, son of *Y'ZR*, guardian of the quarry"
(Pu. Malta: KAI/I p. 14, ins. #62, line 7)

c) *ŠMR WNṢR ḤLṢB'L BN 'ŠY*
"*ḤLṢB'L* son of *'ŠY* guarded and watched"
(Pu. Carthage: Slouszch p. 205, ins. #207, lines 1-2)

d) *NṢR WŠMR ḤLṢB'L BN 'RŠTB'L*
"*ḤLṢB'L* son of *'RŠTB'L* watched and guarded"
(Pu. Carthage: Slouszch p. 205, ins. #201, lines 1-2)

e) *TŠ'MRN' ḂĠẆD*
"may you guard him in (?)"
(Pu. Morocco: BAC [1955] p. 31, line 2)

Bibl. Slouszch 205; KAI/II 64, 78; DISO 310; Harris 151-52; Benz 421-22; Amadasi 23; BAC (1955) 31-32; JAOS 93 (1973) 193-96.

ŠMRT N.Heb. *ŠōMeRā* "watchman's hut". 1. "wall" n.f.

a) *ḤGR HŠMRT*
"the protective wall"
(Pu. Carthage: KAI/I p. 17, ins. #81, line 4)

Bibl. KAI/II 98; Harris 152; DISO 310; Slouszch 158; Bib 48 (1967) 564.

ŠMŠ C.S. 1. "sun" n.f. (m) 2. as a god

1 a) *TḤT HŠMŠ*
"under the sun"
(Ph. Sidon: KAI/I p. 2, ins. #13, lines 7-8)

b) *LMMṢ' ŠMŠ W'D MB'Y*
"from the rising of the sun (east) until its setting (west)"
(Ph. Karatepe: KAI/I p. 5, ins. #26, lines A I,4-5)

c) *'RPT KBRT MṢ' ŠMŠ WṢPLY*
"the portico in the direction (?) of sunrise and the north (side) of it"
(Ph. Ma'ṣub: KAI/I p. 4, ins. #19, lines 1-2)

2 a) *'L QN 'RṢ WŠMŠ 'LM*
"*'L* the Creator of earth and the Eternal sun"
(Ph. Karatepe: KAI/I p. 5, ins. #26, lines A III,18-19)

b) *'BD BT ŠMŠ*
"the servant of the temple of the Sun"
(Pu. Carthage: Slouszch p. 306, ins. #462, line 4)

Bibl. ESE I 168; ANET 653, 662; Benz 422; Harris 152; KAI/II 17; DISO 30; Slouszch 306; JNES 31 (1972) 355.

ŠN' Heb. *ŠāNā* "to repeat, study, teach"; Ug. *ṮNY*; Akk. *ŠaNū*; Emp.Aram. *ŠNY*; J.Aram. *ṮeNa'*; Syriac *TeNa'*; Mandaic *TN'*; Nab. *ŠN'*; Arabic *ṮaNa* "to fold, double".
1. "teacher" n.m.

a) *'ZRB'L HŠN'*
"*'ZRB'L* the teacher (?)"
(Pu. Carthage: Slouszch p. 191, ins. #176, line 1)

b) *'ŠMN'MS HŠN'*
"*'ŠMN'MS* the teacher (?)"
(Pu. Carthage: Slouszch p. 191, ins. #176, lines 1-2)

Bibl. Harris 152; Slouszch 191, 259.

ŠN'T Heb. *ŚiN'ā* "hatred"; Ug. *ŠN'*; Moab. *ŠN'* "enemy"; Emp.Aram. *ŠN'H*; ESArab. *ŠN'* "to hate"; B.Aram. *ŚeNa'*; J.Aram. *SeNa'*; Syriac *SeNa'*; Mandaic *SiNa'* "hatred"; [Eg. *ŠN'* "to ward off";] Arabic *ŠaNaa'* "to hate"; [Geez *Ta-SaNaNa* "to quarrel, dispute"]. 1. "hatred" n.f.

a) *'M BŠN'T WBR'*
"or with hatred and with evil (intention)"
(Ph. Karatepe: KAI/I p. 5, ins. #26, line A III,17)

Bibl. DISO 311; KAI/II 36; ANET 653.

Š NY C.S. num. 1. "second" 2. in military titles

1 a) *MŠKB ŠNY*
"a second resting place"
(Ph. Sidon: KAI/I p. 3, ins. #14, line 6)

2 a) *'BDMSKR RB 'BR LSPT RB ŠNY*
"*'BDMSKR* chief of *'BR LSPT*, lieutenant"
(Ph. Tyre: Slouszch p. 42, ins. #26, lines 1-2)

Bibl. ANET 662; Slouszch 43; PPG 98, 123; DISO 314; Harris 152; KAI/II 19.

ŠNM C.S. Ph., Pu., N.Pu. *ŠNM* (Ph. *'ŠNM*). 1. "two" num.

a) *W'RWM 'ŠNM*
"and the two lions"
(Ph. Kition: KAI/I p. 7, ins. #32, line 3)

b) *'BDK 'BD'SR W'ḤY 'SRŠMR ŠN BN 'SRŠMR*
"your servant *'BD'SR* and his brother *'SRŠMR*, the two sons of *'SRŠMR*"
(Ph. Malta: KAI/I p. 11, ins. #47, lines 2-3)

c) *SMLM ŠNM 'L*
"these two images"
(Ph. Sidon: Slouszch p. 341, ins. #566, line 1)

d) *ẆḤNẆTM ŠNM*
"and two statues (?)"
(Pu. Malta: KAI/I p. 14, ins. #64, line 1)

e) *DN'RY' ḤMŠM WŠNM*
"fifty-two *DN'RY'*"
(N.Pu. Leptis Magna: KAI/I p. 25, ins. #130, line 3)

f) *ŠṢP WŠṢPT 'ŠN BN' MHRB'L*
"*ŠṢP* and *ŠṢPT*, the two sons of *MHRB'L*"
(Pu. Carthage: CIS I, ins. #4596, lines 2-3)

Bibl. DISO 314; Harris 152; Amadasi 16, 101; Slouszch 341; PPG 37, 119, 122; Branden 37, 43; KAI/II 50, 64, 79, 133.

*Š'Y — Heb. *Šā'ā* "to look for, to seek"; Akk. *Še'u* "to look for"; Soq. *Š'ii* "to listen, to remark, to observe". 1. "to seek" vb.

a) *L'ZṘB'L TŠ'M ŠLM*
"to *'ZṘB'L*, if you seek peace"
(Ph. Byblos: KAI/I p. 1, ins. #3, lines 1-3)

Bibl. KAI/II 5; BASOR 212 (1973) 19; JAOS 81 (1961) 27-34; LS I 35-43; DISO 336; PPG 121; JCS 5 (1951) 123-28.

Š'R — Heb. *Ša'aR* "gate"; Ug. *ṮĠR*; B.Aram. *TaR'a'*; J.Aram. *TaR'a'*; Syriac *T̄aR'a'*; Mandaic *ṮYRa'*; Nab. *TR''*; Palm. *TR''*; Amar.Akk. *ŠaḪRi*; Arabic *ṮuĠRuN* "crevice"; Soq. *THeR* "entrance". 1. "gate" n.m.

a) *HŠ'R Z WHDLHT*
"this gate and the doors"
(Ph. Umm el-Awamid: KAI/I p. 3, ins. #18, line 3)

b) *BŠ'R Z*
"from this gate"
(Ph. Karatepe: KAI/I p. 5, ins. #26, line A III,14)

c) *Š'R HḤDS*
"the new gate"
(Pu. Carthage: CRAI [1968] p. 117, line 1)

d) *LŠ'R ZR*
"a hated (?) gate"
(Ph. Karatepe: KAI/I p. 5, ins. #26, line A III,16)

Bibl. ANET 653; Harris 153; DISO 315; KAI/II 26, 36; CRAI (1968) 122.

ŠP — [Heb. *ŠūP* "to bruise"; J.Aram. *ŠūP*; Syriac *ŠaP* "to rub off, grind"; Mandaic *ŠuP*]. 1. "trap" n.m. (connection with above doubtful)

a) *LR'M 'Š BD ŠP* LKD*
"for the shepherds who caught by means of trap(s) (?)"
(Ph. Kition: Or 37 [1968] p. 305, line B 8)

*Reading uncertain.

Bibl. Or 37 (1968) 323, esp. note 3.

ŠPḤ Heb. *MiŠPāḤā* "family," "clan"; Ug. *ŠPḤ*; Pu. *ŠPḤ* (N.Pu. *ŠP'T*). 1. "clan" n.m.

a) *WKL ŠPḤ*
"and every clan"
(Pu. Marseilles: KAI/I p. 15, ins. #69, line 16)

b) *'DR ŠPḤ*
"the chief of the clan (?)"
(Pu. Carthage: Slouszch p. 182, ins. #155, line 7)

c) *ZR' WŠP'T*
"(and as) offspring and (as) a clan (?)"
(N.Pu. Maktar: KAR 12 [1963-64] p. 54, col. V, line 1)

Bibl. DISO 316; Amadasi 181-82; ANET 656; Harris 153; Slouszch 148, 183; KAI/II 83; KAR 12 (1963-64) 54.

ŠPṬ Heb. *ŠāPaṬ* "to judge, rule," *ŠōPeṬ* "judge, magistrate"; Ug. *ṮPṬ* "to judge"; Akk. *ŠaPāṬu* "to reprimand"; ESArab. *ṮPṬ* "a trial". 1. "magistrate" n.m. 2. "to judge" vb.

1 a) *'BD'ŠMN HŠPṬ*
"*'BD'ŠMN* the magistrate"
(Ph. Kition: KAI/I p. 8, ins. #36, lines 1-2)

b) *B'LYTN HŠPṬ*
"*B'LYTN* the magistrate"
(Ph. Piraeus: KAI/I p. 13, ins. #58, line 1)

c) *PNP' HŠPṬ*
"*PNP'* the magistrate"
(Pu. Carthage: KAI/I p. 17, ins. #78, line 8)

d) [*ḤLṢB'L*] *HŠPṬ BN BD'ŠMN*
"[*ḤLṢB'L*] the magistrate, son of *BD'ŠMN*"
(Pu. Marseilles: KAI/I p. 15, ins. #69, lines 1-2)

e) *BŠT ŠPṬM ḤMLK WḤMLK BN 'NKN*
"in the year of the magistrates *ḤMLK* and *ḤMLK* son of *'NKN*"
(N.Pu. Bir Bou-Rekba: KAI/I p. 26, ins. #137, lines 1-2)

2 a) *WŠPṬ TNT PN B'L*
"may *TNT PN B'L* judge"
(Pu. Carthage: KAI/I p. 17, ins. #79, lines 10-11)

Bibl. Benz 423-24; Harris 153; DISO 316; Amadasi 169; NE 381; ANET 656; KAI/II 53, 72, 83, 97, 136; JAOS 89 (1969) 694, 697; Leš (1968-69) 3-6; JNES 30 (1971) 186ff.; ZAW 77 (1965) 40ff.

ŠṢP etymology unknown. 1. type of sacrifice n.m.

a) *'M ŠṢP*
"or a *ŠṢP* sacrifice"
(Pu. Marseilles: KAI/I p. 15, ins. #69, line 11)

Bibl. PEQ 80 (1948-49) 70; DISO 317; KAI/II 83; Amadasi 179-80; Slouszch 146; ANET 656; Harris 153.

**SQD* I Heb. *ŠāQaD* "to watch, wait"; J.Aram. *ŠeQaD* "to be mindful". 1. "to be mindful" vb.

a) *WTYN Y' LBN LQḤT TŠQD*
"and figs, fair (and) white, be mindful to fetch"
(Pu. Carthage: KAI/I p. 16, ins. #76, line B 5)

Bibl. Harris 153; KAI/II 93; DISO 318; Slouszch 166.

ŠQD II Heb. *ŠāQeD* "almond tree"; Akk. *ŠiQDu*; J.Aram. *ŠiGDa'*; Syriac *ŠeGDa'*; Mandaic *ŠiGDa'*. 1. "almond" n.m.

a) *ŠQḊM WKMN*
"almonds and cumin"
(Ph. Egypt: KAI/I p. 12, ins. #51, obv. lines 6-7)

Bibl. KAI/II 69.

ŠQL I Heb. *ŠāQaL* "to weigh"; Akk. *ŠaQāLu*; B.Aram. *TeQaL*; J.Aram. *TeQaL*; Syriac *TeQaL*; Mandaic *TeQaL*; Arabic *ṮaQaLa* "to be heavy". 1. "weigher" n.m. 2. "to examine" vb.

1 a) *'BDB'L ŠQL*
"*'BDB'L* (the) weigher"
(Pu. Carthage: Slouszch p. 203, ins. #196, line 1)

b) *ŠQL MḤTT*
"the weighers of the coal pans (?)"
(Pu. Carthage: CRAI [1968] p. 117, line 5)

2 a) *PTḤ' Š'M' ḤR'B K' WYŠQL*
"the drying sheds (?) were set open (?) here and examined (?)"
(N.Pu. Tripolitania: Or 33 [1964] p. 4, line 1)

Bibl. Harris 153; DISO 318; Slouszch 203; CRAI (1968) 128; RSO (1968) 13.

ŠQL II Heb. *ŠeQeL* special weight; Ug. *ṮQL*; Akk. *ŠiQLu*; Anc.Aram. *ŠQL*; Emp.Aram. *ŠQL*, *TQL*; B.Aram. *TiQLa'*; J.Aram. *TiQLa'*; Syriac *TaQLuTa'*; Arabic *ṮiQLuN'*. 1. special weight n.m.

a) *LKHNM KSP ŠQL 1*
"the priests (shall have) one silver *ŠQL*"
(Pu. Marseilles: KAI/I p. 15, ins. #69, line 7)

Bibl. KAI/II 83; Harris 153; ANET 656; DISO 318-19.

ŠQL III [J.Aram. *ŠeQaL* "to carry"; Syriac *'aŠQel* "to lead forth"; Mandaic *ŠaŠQiL* "to raise (sails)"]. 1. "to lead" vb. (Y)

a) *ḤNB'L MYŠQL 'RṢ*
"*ḤNB'L*, the leader (?) of the land"
(N.Pu. Leptis Magna: KAI/I p. 23, ins. #121, line 1)

Bibl. KAI/II 126; DISO 150.

ŠR I for possible etymology, see under *Š'R* I. 1. "kin" n.m.

a) *'YT 'RŠT ŠRY*
"*'RŠT* his kin (?)"
(Pu. Carthage: CIS I, ins. #5689, lines 4-5)

ŠR II Heb. *ŚaR* "official, leader, prince"; Akk. *ŠaRRu* "king"; Palm. *ŠR* "prince". 1. "prince" n.m.

1 a) *L'LY L'ŠMN ŠR QDŠ*
"for his god, for *'ŠMN* the holy prince (?)"
(Ph. Sidon: KAI/I p. 3, ins. #16, line 2)

Bibl. DISO 319; Harris 154; KAI/II 24-25.

Š R III

Heb. *ŠiR* "to sing"; Ug. *ŠR*; Akk. *ŠēRu*; Sum. *SiR*; Arabic *Ši'RuN* "poem".
1. "to sing" vb.

a) *LŠRM B'R*
"for the singers in the town"
(Ph. Kition: Or 37 [1968] p. 305, line A 7)

b) *R'Š MŠ'ṘT*
"chief singer" (or "chief gatekeeper")
(N.Pu. Tunisia: KAI/I p. 25, ins. #136, lines 5-6)

Bibl. KAI/II 135; JNES 9 (1950) 110; LS I 456.

ŠRŠ

Heb. *ŠoReš* "root, root stock"; Ug. *ŠRŠ*; Akk. *ŠuRŠu*; Anc.Aram. *ŠRŠ*; J.Aram. *ŠiRŠa'*; Syriac *ŠeRŠa'*; Mandaic *ŠiRŠa'*; Chr.Palm.Aram. *ŠuRŠ'*; ESArab. *ŠRŠ*; Arabic *ŠiRSuN*.
1. "stock" n.m. 2. "root"

1 a) *'L YKN LM ŠRŠ LMṬ*
"may they have no stock downwards"
(Ph. Sidon: KAI/I p. 3, ins. #14, line 11)

b) *MLQRT ŠRŠ YBRK*
"may *MLQRT* bless my stock"
(Ph. Larnaka: Mus 51 [1958] p. 286, line 3)

2 a) *WP'L 'NK LŠRŠ 'DNY N'M*
"and I acted kindly to the root(s) of my royalty (?)"
(Ph. Karatepe: KAI/I p. 5, ins. #26, line A I,10)

Bibl. Albright-Fs 265; Slouszch 23; KAI/II 19, 36; DISO 321; Mus 51 (1938) 291-92; ANET 653, 662.

ŠRT

B.Heb. *ŠāRaT* "to minister, serve".
1. "to serve" vb.

a) *[WKL ']DM 'Š 'YBL MŠRT*
"[and all m]en who do not serve"
(Pu. Carthage: CIS I, ins. #5510, line 4)

b) *LŠRT ŠNT ḤMŠM*
"to serve (?) fifty years"
(N.Pu. Cherchel: NSI p. 147, ins. #58, line 4)

Bibl. DISO 321; NSI 147-48.

ŠŠ C.S. Pu., N.Pu. *ŠŠ* (N.Pu. *Š'Š*).
1. "six" num.

a) *ŠŠ HYSBM 'L'*
"these six seats"
(N.Pu. Leptis Magna: KAI/I p. 25, ins. #130, line 1)

b) *BŠŠT WḤMŠM ŠT LMLKNM*
"in the fifty-sixth year of their rule"
(Pu. Constantine: KAI/I p. 21, ins. #112, lines 4-5)

c) *'WH Š'N'[T] Š['Š]M WŠ'Š*
"he lived si[xy]y-six yea[rs]"
(N.Pu. Henschir Brigitta: KAI/I p. 26, ins. #142, line 2)

Bibl. Harris 149; DISO 321; PPG 121; KAI/II 117, 133, 139.

ŠŠM C.S. N.Pu. *ŠŠM* (N.Pu. *ŠYŠM*). 1. "sixty" num.

a) *'W' Š'NT ŠŠM*
"she lived sixty years"
(N.Pu. Maktar: KAI/I p. 28, ins. #149, line 4)

b) *BN ŠŠM ŠT WŠLŠ*
"sixty-three years of age"
(N.Pu. Maktar: KAI/I p. 28, ins. #152, line 3)

c) *ŠYŠM W'MŠ*
"sixty-five"
(N.Pu. Henschir Meded: KAI/I p. 29, ins. #157, line 3)

Bibl. PPG 121; Harris 149; DISO 321; KAI/II 145-46, 148.

ŠT I C.S. Ph. *ŠNT* (N.Pu. *Š'N'T*, *Š'NT*, *ŠN'T*)-- all pl. forms. 1. "year" n.f.

a) *YMT ŠPṬB'L WŠNTW*
"the days of *ŠPṬB'L* and his years"
(Ph. Byblos: KAI/I p. 1, ins. #7, line 5)

b) *'RK YMM WRB ŠNT*
"length of days and many years"
(Ph. Karatepe: KAI/I p. 5, ins. #26, lines A III,5-6)

c) *BŠNT 37 LMLK PNYYTN*
"in the thirty-seventh year of king *PNYYTN*"
(Ph. Kition: KAI/I p. 7, ins. #33, line 1)

d) *BŠNT 4 LMLK MLKYTN*
"in the fourth year of king *MLKYTN*"
(Ph. Idalion: Slouszch p. 98, ins. #89, line 1)

e) *BŠT 180 L'DN MLKM*
"in the one hundred and eightieth year of the lords of the kingdoms"
(Ph. Umm el-Awamid: KAI/I p. 3, ins. #18, lines 4-5)

f) *BŠT ŠPṬ HMMLKT BN 'PŠN*
"in the year of *ŠPṬ* the ruler, son of *'PŠN*"
(Pu. Dougga: KAI/I p. 20, ins. #101, line 2)

g) *'WH Š'NT 'SRM W'D*
"he lived twenty-one years"
(N.Pu. Henschir Meded: KAI/I p. 29, ins. #158, lines 2-3)

h) *'W' Š'N'T 'SR WḤMŠ*
"he lived twenty-five years"
(N.Pu. Masculula: JA Series 11 vol. 7 [1916] p. 454, ins. #3, lines 2-3)

i) *'W' Š'NWT ŠMNM WḤMŠ*
"she lived eighty-five years"
(N.Pu. Ksiba Mraou: JA Series 11 vol. 10 [1917] p. 13, ins. #3, lines 2-3)

j) *'W' ŠNWT W'ḤD*
"he lived (?) years and one"
(N.Pu. Ksiba Mraou: JA Series 11 vol. 10 [1917] p. 15, ins. #4, lines 2-3)

Bibl. JA Series 11 vol. 7 (1916) 954; JA Series 11 vol. 10 (1917) 13, 15; Harris 152; NE 379-80; DISO 312-13; Slouszch 96; ANET 653; PPG 22, 101, 118, 158; Branden 10, 44; KAI/II 9, 26, 36, 51, 110, 148.

ŠT II   Heb. *ŠīT* "to place, set"; Ug. *ŠT*.
1. "to place, set" vb.

a) *KŠTḢ B'LM*
"when he placed him in the tomb"
(Ph. Byblos: KAI/I p. 1, ins. #1, line 1)

b) *ŠTY B'L 'DR*
"I established him (as) the possessor of a herd"
(Ph. Zinjirli: KAI/I p. 4, ins. #24, line 11)

c) *WHMT ŠT NBŠ*
"and as for them (each) placed himself"
(Ph. Zinjirli: KAI/I p. 4, ins. #24, line 13)

d) *WŠT ŠM 'LY*
"and place his name upon it"
(Ph. Karatepe: KAI/I p. 5, ins. #26, line A III,16)

e) *WŠT 'NK ŠLM 'T 'KL MLK*
"and I established peace with all kings"
(Ph. Karatepe: KAI/I p. 5, ins. #26, lines A I,11-12)

f) *LŠT 'LT ḤḤDRT NPT*
"to set upon the chamber honey (?)"
(Pu. Carthage: KAI/I p. 16, ins. #76, line B 8)

g) *'Š 'YBL ŠT*
"which is not set down"
(Pu. Marseilles: KAI/I p. 15, ins. #69, line 18)

Bibl. Harris 148; DISO 298; Amadasi 169; Slouszch 199, 242; NE 375; PPG 49, 76, 87-88, 91; Branden 95; KAI/II 2, 30, 36, 83, 93; ANET 653-54, 656, 661.

ŠT' B.Heb. *ŠaT'a* "to fear"; Ug. *T̲T̲'*; Amm. *ŠT'*; ESArab *T̲T̲'T* "fear". 1. "to fear" vb.

a) *'Š YŠT' 'DM LLKT DRK*
"where a man was afraid to walk on the road"
(Ph. Karatepe: KAI/I p. 5, ins. #26, lines A II,4-5)

Bibl. ANET 653; DISO 322; PPG 61; Gaster-Fs 134.

T

T'R I N.Heb. *Tā'aR* "to give a fine appearance"; Chr.Pal.Aram. *T'R* "to gaze at"; Arabic *'aTāRa* "to stare at". 1. "to be famous" vb.

a) *WT'RṪ W[ ]T Š̌MY*
"and I became famous and I[ ]my name"
(Pu. Carthage: Slouszch p. 182, ins. #155, line 6)

Bibl. Slouszch 182; Harris 154; ESE I 166.

T'R II Heb. *To'aR* "outline, form". 1. "fame" n.m. 2. "type"

1 a) *WT'R BḤYM TḤT ŠMŠ*
"and fame (?) among the living under the sun"
(Ph. Sidon: KAI/I p. 3, ins. #14, line 12)

2 a) *BT'R YḤNM*
"according to the type (?) of *YḤNM*"
(Pu. Carthage: Slouszch p. 169, ins. #144, line 4)

Bibl. DISO 323; KAI/II 19; Slouszch 18, 169; ANET 662; Harris 154; Benz 426-27.

T'R III for possibly etymology, see under *Š'R* I. 1. "kin" n.m.

a) *'T 'BTM W'T T'RM*
"his forefathers (?) and his kin (?)"
(N.Pu. Leptis Magna: KAI/I p. 22, ins. #119, line 7)

b) *BT'RM BTM*
"with his kin (?) intact"
(N.Pu. Bir Tlesa: KAI/I p. 26, ins. #138, line 5)

Bibl. LS I 99; KAI/II 124, 137.

TBRT etymology unknown; perhaps related to the B.Heb. *BāRi'* "to be fat". 1. "fat" n.f.

a) *WTBRT LB'L HZBḤ*
"and the fat to the owner of the sacrifice"
(Pu. Carthage: KAI/I p. 16, ins. #74, line 3)

Bibl. DISO 324; KAI/II 92; Harris 155; Slouszch 166; ANET 657.

TḤT Heb. *TaḤaT* "under, at, instead of"; Ug. *TḤT*; Anc.Aram. *TḤT*; Emp.Aram. *TḤT*; ESArab. *TḤT*; B.Aram. *TeḤōT*; J.Aram. *TeḤōT*; Syriac *TeḤoT*; Mandaic *TiT*; Arabic *TaḤT*; Amh. *TaHaTa* "to be humble"; Ph., N.Pu. *TḤT* (N.Pu. *T'ḤT*, *T'T*). 1. "under" preposition 2. in combinations

1 a) *W'NK 'ZTWD ŠTNM TḤT P'MY*
"and I *'ZTWD* set them under my feet"
(Ph. Karatepe: KAI/I p. 5, ins. #26, lines A I,16-17)

b) *TḤT ŠMŠ*
"under the sun"
(Ph. Sidon: KAI/I p. 3, ins. #14, line 12)

c) *W'L YKN LM BN WZR' TḤTNM*
"may they have no son or offspring in their place"
(Ph. Sidon: KAI/I p. 3, ins. #14, lines 8-9)

2 a) *BŠT RB T'ḤT RB MḤNT*
"in the year of the proconsul"
(N.Pu. Ras el-Haddagia: KAI/I p. 22, ins. #118, line 2)

b) *TḤT 'BN ZT*
"under this (grave)stone"
(N.Pu. Maktar: KAI/I p. 28, ins. #152, line 2)

c) *T'T HBNT ST*
"under this stone"
(N.Pu. Maktar: JA Series 11 vol. 7 [1916] p. 93, ins. #7, lines 4-5)

Bibl. Harris 155; ANET 653, 662; EHO 18; Slouszch 14, 38; NE 385; KAI/II 19, 36, 146; DISO 326-27; PPG 12, 126, 128, 145.

TYL Heb. *TeL* "mound"; Akk. *TiLLu* "ruin, heap"; Emp.Aram. *TL*; J.Aram. *TiLLa'*; Syriac *TeLa'*; Arabic *TiLLuN*. 1. "ruin" n.m.

a) *['L]T TYL HYKRT R'QYM*
"upon its ruin he hewed the foundations"
(N.Pu. Maktar: KAR 12 [1963-64] p. 50, col. I, line 2)

Bibl. KAR 12 (1963-64) 50; DISO 328.

TYN Heb. *Te'eNā*; Akk. *TiTTu*; J.Aram. *Te'aNTa'*; Syriac *TiTa'*; Mandaic *TiNa'*; Arabic *TiNNuN*.
1. "fig" n.f.

a) *WTYN Y' LBN*
"and figs, fair (and) white"
(Pu. Carthage: KAI/I p. 16, ins. #76, line B 5)

Bibl. Harris 155; Slouszch 166; KAI/II 93; DISO 327.

**TKD* meaning and etymology unknown. 1. "to decide" vb. (from context)

a) *W'TKD YKRY 'T HŠD*
"and he decided (?) to purchase the field"
(N.Pu. Tripolitania: Or 33 [1964] p. 4, line 3)

b) *'YTKD' 'DR' 'LPQY WKL 'M'[L]Ṗ[QY]*
"the nobles and all the people of '[*L*]*P*[*QY*] decided (?)"
(N.Pu. Leptis Magna: KAI/I p. 22, ins. #119, line 4)

Bibl. KAI/II 124; DISO 328; Or 33 (1964) 10-11.

TKLT etymology unknown; perhaps related to B.Heb. *KūL* "to contain"; Q.Heb. *TKLT* "perfection"; Heb. *KiLKeL* "to supply," *TaKLīT* "end, object". Ph., N.Pu. *TKLT* (N.Pu. *TKL'T*).
1. "account" n.f. 2. "completion"
3. "communal" adj. f.

1 a) *ṪḲLT YRḤ 'TNM*
"accounts (?) of the month of '*TNM*"
(Ph. Kition: Or 37 [1968] p. 305, line A 1)

2 a) *BTKLT MQM*
"the completion of the temple"
(N.Pu. Leptis Magna: KAI/I p. 22, ins. #119, line 5)

b) *'S P'L KL 'M BYT'N BTṢ'T WTKL'T*
"which all the people of *BYT'N* made, totally (at their own) expense"
(N.Pu. Bitia: KAI/I p. 31, ins. #173, line 1)

3 a) *'DR TKLT*
"a communal (?) burial chamber"
(N.Pu. Bitia: OrAnt 4 [1965] p. 69, line 1)

Bibl. Amadasi 134; DISO 328; Or 37 (1968) 307, esp. note 1; PPG 97; Harris 111; Slouszch 76; KAI/II 54, 124, 157; OrAnt 4 (1965) 70.

TKT for etymology, see under *MTKT*. 1. "midst" n.f.

a) *'Š BTKT 'BN*
"which is in the midst of a (semiprecious) stone"
(Ph. Byblos: KAI/I p. 2, ins. #10, line 5)

Bibl. ANET 656; Slouszch 8; KAI/II 12; Harris 155.

TL N.Heb. *TeL* "lock, curl," *TaLTaL* "curl," *TiLTūL* "wart". 1. "wart" n.m.

a) *'BDMLQRT HRQM B'L HTLM*
"*'BDMLQRT* the embroiderer, the possessor of warts"
(Pu. Carthage: CIS I, ins. #4912, line 2)

(see Talmud Babli, *Bekōrōt* p. 2, side 2)

TM I Heb. *ToM* "completeness, integrity"; Syriac *TaMiMa'* "perfect"; J.Aram. *TeMiMa'*. 1. "true" adj. m. 2. in combinations 3. "complete" adj. f.

1 a) *'Š TM PY*
"whose word is true"
(Ph. Arslan Tash: BASOR 192 [1970] p. 44, rev. line 16)

2 a) *BN' W'YQDŠ T 'KNSDR' WT 'RPT ST BTS'TM BTM*
"he built and consecrated the excedra and this portico totally at his own expense"
(N.Pu. Leptis Magna: KAI/I p. 25, ins. #129, lines 1-3)

b) *WB'L ḤRŠ H' BTM*
"and he (himself) was the master craftsman at his own expense"
(Pu. Spain: KAI/I p. 16, ins. #72, line B 4)

c) *BTM P'L W'YQDŠ*
"at his own expense he made and consecrated"
(N.Pu. Leptis Magna: KAI/I p. 23, ins. #121, line 2)

d) *LMBMLKTM BTM*
"his work at his own expense"
(N.Pu. Leptis Magna: KAI/I p. 23, ins. #124, line 2)

e) *MZBḤ WP'DY P'L LMBMLKTM BTM*
"he made the altar and podium, his work at his own expense"
(N.Pu. Leptis Magna: KAI/I p. 24, ins. #126, lines 10-11)

f) *BŠRM BTM*
"(whose) flesh is intact"
(Pu. Carthage: KAI/I p. 20, ins. #104, lines 2-3)

g) *TM BḤYM*
"upright in life"
(N.Pu. Maktar: KAI/I p. 28, ins. #152, line 3)

3 a) *[Q]B'R MQN'T 'TM'*
"a [gr]ave, the complete property"
(N.Pu. Tripolitania: LibAnt 1 [1964] p. 57, line 1)

Bibl. DISO 329; BASOR 197 (1970) 44-45; KAI/II 43, 88, 114, 146; Benz 429; Amadasi 145; Slouszch 222-23; ClassFol 22 (1968) 170-71; LibAnt 1 (1964) 58.

TM II — for etymology, see *TMM*. 1. "total" n.m.

a) *TMNM DN'RY' M'T WŠLŠM WŠLŠ*
"their total (cost), one hundred and thirty-three *DN'RY'*"
(N.Pu. Leptis Magna: KAI/I p. 25, ins. #130, lines 1-2)

Bibl. KAI/II 133; PPG 111.

TM' — etymology unknown. Ph. *TM'* (N.Pu. *TMY'*). 1. type of military officer n.m. (from context)

a) *WTM' MḤNT*
"and an army commander"
(Ph. Byblos: KAI/I p. 1, ins. #1, line 2)

b) *NDR 'Š NDR ŠPṬ ḤTMY'*
"the vow which *ŠPṬ* the military commander vowed"
(N.Pu. Constantine: Berthier/Charlier p. 85, ins. #104, lines 1-2)

Bibl. DISO 330; Harris 155; JNES 16 (1967) 15-16; Berthier/Charlier 105; KAI/II 1; Slouszch 3.

TMK I — Heb. *TāMaK* "to grasp, hold fast"; Akk. *TaMāKu*; J.Aram. *TeMaK*. 1. "to support" vb.

a) *W'NK TMKT MŠKBM LYD*
"and I supported the *MŠKBM* by the hand"
(Ph. Zinjirli: KAI/I p. 4, ins. #24, line 13)

b) *'LŠ WTMK HMT*
"(?) and supporting them (?)"
(see *TMK* II)
(Pu. Carthage: CIS I, ins. #5510, line 10)

Bibl. KAI/II 30; PPG 58; Harris 155; EHO 18; DISO 330; ANET 654; Benz 429.

TMK II — meaning and etymology uncertain; perhaps related to B.Heb. *MōK* "to be low"

a) *'LŠ WTMK*
"meekly (?)"
(Pu. Carthage: CIS I, ins. #5510, line 10)

TMM — Heb. *TāMaM* "to be complete, finished"; Ug. *TM*; Syriac *TaM* "to be innocent, harmless"; Mandaic *TMM* "to stay, remain"; Soq. *TeM(M)* "to be complete"; Arabic *TaMMa*. 1. "to decide" vb. 2. "to cause to cease"

1 a) *TM BD ṢDNYM*
"it was decided on behalf of the *ṢDNYM*"
(Ph. Piraeus: KAI/I p. 13, ins. #60, line 1)

2 a) *'N YTM 'NK*
"the evil glance shall be ended, yea your evil glance"
(Ph. Arslan Tash: BASOR 209 [1973] p. 19, rev. lines 5-6)

Bibl. KAI/II 73; Harris 155; Slouszch 116; DISO 331; PPG 75-76; BASOR 209 (1973) 25-26; Syria 48 (1971) 405.

TMR — Heb. *TāMāR* "date palm"; ESArab. *TMR*; J.Aram. *TaMRa'*; Syriac *TeMaRTa'*; Mandaic *TuMaRTa'*; Arabic *TaMeRuN*; Meh. *ToMeR*. 1. "date palm" n.f.

a) *B'MQT ŠHT'M'R*
"in the valley of the date palm"
(N.Pu. Tripolitania: Or 33 [1964] p. 4, line 4)

Bibl. Or 33 (1964) 14; PPG 43.

TMT Heb. *ToM* "simplicity, integrity"; B.Heb. *TūMā*; J.Aram. *TūMa'* "simplicity".
1. "harmony" n.f.

a) *MḤB D'T HTMT*
"(he who is) the lover of the knowledge of harmony (?)"
(N.Pu. Leptis Magna: KAI/I p. 23, ins. #121, line 1)

Bibl. KAI/II 128; DISO 330.

TN B.Heb. *TaN* "jackal"; Arabic *TiNaNuN*.
1. "jackal" n.m. (only in place names)

a) *'Š B'M 'YTNM*
"who is among the people of the Island of Jackals"
(Pu. Sousse: KAI/I p. 19, ins. #99, line 5)

Bibl. KAI/II 107.

T'BT Heb. *Tō'eBā* "abomination"; Eg. *W'B* "to clean"; Arabic *Wa'aBa* "to be intact".
1. "abomination" n.f.

a) *K T'BT 'ŠTRT HDBR H'*
"because that thing is an abomination to *'ŠTRT*"
(Ph. Sidon: KAI/I p. 2, ins. #13, line 6)

Bibl. DISO 332; KAI/II 17; Harris 156; ANET 662; Slouszch 14.

T'LBT etymology and meaning obscure; perhaps composed of two words, *T'L* and *BT*, meaning frames of a house. 1. "frames of a house" n.f.

a) *'BDMLQRT P'L HT'LBT*
"*'BDMLQRT*, the maker of house frames (?)"
(Pu. Carthage: CIS I, ins. #5952, lines 1-2)

Bibl. DISO 332.

**T'LT* Heb. *Te'āLā* "grove, channel, water course".
1. "water course" n.f.

a) *QBR 'BDMLQRT P'L HT'LẎT*
"the grave of *'BDMLQRT*, the maker of water courses (?)"
(Pu. Carthage: Slouszch p. 194, ins. #185, lines 1-2)

Bibl. Slouszch 195; Harris 156; DISO 332.

T'SMT B.Heb. *Ta'aṢūMā* "might". 1. "mighty" n.f. (idiom, meaning honor)

a) *WDL Š̌M T'ṢMT*
"and the possessor of honor (?)"
(N.Pu. Guelaat Bou-Sba: KAI/I p. 30, ins. #165, lines 6-7)

Bibl. KAI/II 154; DISO 332.

TPP Heb. *TāPaP* "to strike the timbrel, to beat"; J.Aram. *TuPPa'* "drum". 1. "to sound the drum" vb.

a) *PSR BN B'LYTN HMTPP*
"*PSR* son of *B'LYTN* the drummer"
(Ph. Egypt: KAI/I p. 11, ins. #49, line 7)

Bibl. KAI/II 65; Slouszch 60; DISO 332; Harris 156.

TṢ'T B.Heb. *ToṢā'ā* "extremity, escape"; N.Heb. *TōṢạ'ā* "issue, made". 1. "expense" n.f.

a) *BTṢ'TM BTM*
"totally at his own expense"
(N.Pu. Leptis Magna: KAI/I p. 25, ins. #129, line 3)

b) *'Š̌ P'L KL 'M BYT'N BTṢ'T WTKL'T*
"which all the people of *BYT'N* made, totally (at their own) expense"
(N.Pu. Bitia: KAI/I p. 31, ins. #173, line 1)

c) *NLQḤ' BTṢ'T MQM N'TR*
"(these) were bought at the expense of the remaining temple"
(N.Pu. Leptis Magna: KAI/I p. 23, ins. #122, line 2)

Bibl. Amadasi 134; DISO 333; KAI/II 123, 128, 133, 157; PPG 97, 107.

TRN Heb. *ToReN* "mast"; J.Aram. *TuRNa'*. 1. "shaft" n.m.

a) *'TRNM WT 'KHNYM*
"the shafts (?) and the bases"
(N.Pu. Cherchel: KAI/I p. 29, ins. #161, lines 5-6)

Bibl. KAI/II 150.

TRQ etymology unknown; perhaps *TaQTeL* of *RWQ*. 1. "to remove" vb.

a) *WTRQ 'NK KL HR' 'Š̌ KN B'RṢ*
"and I removed (?) all the evil which was in the land"
(Ph. Karatepe: KAI/I p. 5, ins. #26, line A I,9)

Bibl. DISO 335; KAI/II 36; ANET 653.

TRŠ Heb. *TiRōŠ* "wine"; Ug. *TRŠ*. 1. "wine" n.m.

a) *ḤNB'L MQNY HTRŠM*
"*ḤNB'L*, the seller (?) of wines (?)"
(Pu. Carthage: CIS I, ins. #5522, line 2)

b) *ŠB' WTRŠ*
"corn and wine"
(Ph. Karatepe: KAI/I p. 5, ins. #26, line C IV,7)

Bibl. DISO 335-36; KAI/II 36; ANET 653; Amadasi 432.

TŠ' etymology and meaning unknown.

a) *'RŠ BN 'RŠM HTŠ' LQḤ*
"*'RŠ* son of *'RŠM* the (?)"
(Pu. Constantine: Berthier/Charlier p. 84, ins. #103, lines 2-3)

Bibl. DISO 336; Berthier/Charlier 85.

TŠ' C.S. 1. "nine" num.

a) *[B'SR W]TŠ' LYRḤ 'YR*
"on the nine[teenth] of the month of *'YR*"
(Pu. Constantine: Berthier/Charlier p. 57, ins. #61, lines 3-4)

Bibl. DISO 336; Berthier/Charlier 57.

TŠ'M C.S. 1. "ninety" num.

a) *'W' ŠNT TŠM WḤD*
"she lived ninety-one years"
(N.Pu. Uzappa: JA Series 11 vol. 2 [1918] p. 252, line 5)

b) *[W]'W' Š[']NT ṬYŠM [W]ŠB'*
"[and] lived ninety-seven years"
(N.Pu. Mididi: JA Series 11 vol. 7 [1916] p. 107, ins. #4, lines 1-2)

Bibl. DISO 336; Harris 156; PPG 13, 121; Branden 6; JA Series 11 vol. 11 (1918) 253; JA Series 11 vol. 7 (1916) 108.

BIBLIOGRAPHY

A. BIBLIOGRAPHIES

1. For the best bibliography of North Semitic materials to 1898, see Mark Lidzbarski, *Handbuch der nordsemitischen Epigraphik* (Hildesheim: Georg Olms, 1962), pp. 5-83, 492-98.

2. There is an important bibliography of Phoenician materials down to 1936 in Zellig Harris's *Grammar of the Phoenician Language* (New Haven: American Oriental Society, 1936), pp. 157-72.

3. For a fine bibliography of North Semitic material up to 1952, see Frank Moore Cross, Jr., and David Noel Freedman, *Early Hebrew Orthography* (New Haven: American Oriental Society, 1952), pp. 71-77.

4. For a specialized bibliography of Phoenician and Punic inscriptions, see Frank Benz, *Personal Names in the Phoenician and Punic Inscriptions*, Studia Pohl 8 (Rome: Biblical Institute Press, 1972), pp. 14-45.

5. A recent general bibliography of North Semitic materials down to 1971 may be found in John C. L. Gibson, *A Textbook of Syrian Semitic Inscriptions*, Vol. I (Oxford: Oxford University Press, 1971), pp. 90-99.

6. For the most up-to-date report of findings in the study of North Semitic epigraphy, see J. Teixidor, *Bulletin d'Épigraphie Sémitique* (Syria 44, 1967, fasc. 1-2; Syria 45, 1968, fasc. 3-4; Syria 45, 1969, fasc. 3-4; Syria 47, 1970, fasc. 3-4) Libraire Orientaliste, Paul Guethner, Paris.

B. BOOKS

Albright, William F. *Yahweh and the Gods of Canaan: A Historical Analysis of Two Contrasting Faiths.* Garden City: Doubleday & Co., 1968.

Aruch Completum. Sive Lexicon Vocabula et res, quae in Libris Targumicus, Talmuddicis et Midrashicis continentur Explicans Auctore Nathane filio Jechielis. 9 vols. New York: Pardes Publishing House, 1955.

The Assyrian Dictionary of the University of Chicago. Editorial Board: I. J. Gelb, Th. Jacobsen, B. Landsberger, A. L. Oppenheim. Chicago/Glückstadt: Oriental Institute/J. J. Augustin, 1956-.

Baramki, Dimitri. *Phoenicia and the Phoenicians.* Beirut: Khayats, 1961.

Bauer, Hans, and Leander, Pontus. *Historische Grammatik der hebräischen Sprache des Alten Testaments*. Vol. I: Einleitung, Schriftlehre, Laut- und Formlehre. Halle: Georg Olms, 1922.

Ben-David, Abba. *Lešōn Miqra' WeLešōn Ḥakhāmim* ["Biblical Hebrew and Mishnaic Hebrew"]. 2 vols. Tel Aviv: Dvir, 1967-71.

Barr, James. *Comparative Philology and the Text of the Old Testament*. Oxford: Oxford University Press, 1968.

Barth, Jacob. *Die Pronominalbildung in den semitischen Sprachen*. Hildesheim: Georg Olms, 1967.

________. *Die Nominalbildung in den semitischen Sprachen*. Hildesheim: Georg Olms, 1967.

Ben-Ḥayyim, Zev. *'Ivrit We'Aramit Nūsaḥ Šōmrōn* ["The Literary and Oral Tradition of Hebrew and Aramaic Amongst the Samaritans"]. 3 vols. Jerusalem: The Academy of the Hebrew Language, 1957-67.

________. *Studies in the Traditions of the Hebrew Language*. Madrid/Barcelona: Instituto Arias Montano, 1954.

Benz, F. L. *Personal Names in the Phoenician and Punic Inscriptions*, Studia Pohl 8 (Rome: Pontifical Biblical Institute, 1972).

Berthier, A., and Charlier, R. *Le santuaire punique d'El Hofra à Constantine*. Paris: Arts et Metiers Graphiques, 1955.

Bloch, A. *Phönizisches Glossar*. Berlin: Mayer-Müller, 1890.

Branden, A. van den. *Grammaire phénicienne*. Beirut: Libraire du Liban, 1969.

Brown, Francis; Driver, S. R.; and Briggs, Charles. *A Hebrew and English Lexicon of the Old Testament*. Oxford: Oxford University Press, 1952.

Clifford, Richard J. *The Cosmic Mountain in Canaan and the Old Testament*. Harvard Semitic Monographs, vol. 4. Cambridge, MA: Harvard University Press, 1972.

Cooke, George A. *A Text-Book of North-Semitic Inscriptions*. Oxford: Oxford University Press, 1903.

Corpus Inscriptionum Semiticarum. Pars Prima, Inscriptiones Phoeniciae. Paris: C. Klincksieck, 1881-.

Cross, Frank Moore, Jr. *Canaanite Myth and Hebrew Epic: Essays in the History of the Religion of Israel*. Cambridge, MA: Harvard University Press, 1973.

Cross, Frank Moore, Jr., and Freedman, David Noel. *Early Hebrew Orthography: A Study of the Epigraphic Evidence.* American Oriental Series, vol. 36. New Haven: American Oriental Society, 1952.

Dahood, Mitchell. *Psalms I: 1-50.* The Anchor Bible, vol. 16. Edited by W. F. Albright and D. N. Freedman. Garden City, NY: Doubleday, 1966.

________. *Psalms II: 51-100.* The Anchor Bible, vol. 17. Garden City, NY: Doubleday, 1968.

________. *Psalms III: 101-150.* The Anchor Bible, vol. 17a. Garden City, NY: Doubleday, 1970.

Dalman, Gustaf H. *Aramäisch-neuhebräisches Handwörterbuch zu Targum, Talmud und Midrasch.* Hildesheim: Georg Olms, 1968.

DeBeer, Gavin. *Hannibal Challenging Rome's Supremacy.* New York: The Viking Press, 1969.

Degen, Rainer; Müller, Walter; and Röllig, Wolfgang. *Neue Ephemeris für semitische Epigraphik.* Wiesbaden: Otto Harrassowitz, 1972.

de Vaux, Roland. *Studies in Old Testament Sacrifice.* Cardiff: University of Wales Press, 1964.

Dietrich, Albert. *Phönizische Ortsnamen in Spanien.* Abhandlungen für die Kunde des Morgenländes, vol. 21, no. 2. Leipzig: Deutsche Morgenländische Gesellschaft, 1936.

Donner, H., and Röllig, W. *Kanaanäische und aramäische Inschriften.* Wiesbaden: Otto Harrassowitz, 1966-69.

Driver, S. R. *Notes on the Hebrew Text and the Topography of the Books of Samuel.* 2nd ed. Oxford: Oxford University Press, 1913.

Drower, E. S., and Macuch, R. A. *A Mandaic Dictionary.* Oxford: Oxford University Press, 1963.

Du Mesnil du Buisson, Robert. *Études sur les dieux phéniciens hérités par l'Empire romain.* Leiden: E. J. Brill, 1970.

Dunand, M., and Duru, R. *Oumm el-Amed.* Paris: A. Maisonneuve, 1962.

Epstein, Ya'akov. *Mavō LeNusaḥ HaMMišnā* ["Introduction to the Versions of the Mishnah"]. 2 vols. Jerusalem/Tel Aviv: Magnes and Dvir Presses, 1964.

Ferron, Jean. *Mélanges de Carthage offertes à Charles Saumagne, Louis Poinssot, Maurice Pinard.* Paris: Paul Geuthner, 1964-65.

Fisher, L. R. *The Claremont Ras Shamra Tablets*. Analecta Orientalia, vol. 48. In collaboration with M. C. Astour, M. Dahood, and P. D. Miller, Jr. Rome: Pontifical Biblical Institute, 1971.

Fitzmyer, J. A. *The Aramaic Inscriptions of Sefîre*. Rome: Pontifical Biblical Institute, 1967.

Fleisch, H. *Introduction à l'étude des langues sémitiques*. Paris, 1947.

Frankel, Siegmund. *Die aramäischen Fremdwörter im Arabischen*. Hildesheim: Georg Olms, 1962.

Friedrich, Johannes, and Röllig, Wolfgang. *Phönizisch-punische Grammatik*. Analecta Orientalia, vol. 46. Rome: Pontifical Biblical Institute, 1970.

Garbini, G. *Il Semitico di Nord-Ovest*. Napoli: Istituto Universitario Orientale di Napoli, 1960.

Gesenius' Hebrew Grammar. Edited and enlarged by E. Kautzsch, revised by A. E. Cowley. 2nd English ed. Oxford: Oxford University Press, 1910.

Gibson, John C. L. *Textbook of Syrian Semitic Inscriptions*. Vol. I. Oxford: Oxford University Press, 1971.

Goedicke, Hans, ed. *Near Eastern Studies in Honor of William Foxwell Albright*. Baltimore: Johns Hopkins University, 1971.

Gordon, Cyrus H. *Ugaritic Textbook*. Analecta Orientalia, vol. 38. Rome: Pontifical Biblical Institute, 1967.

Gray, George. *Sacrifice in the Old Testament, Its Theory and Its Practice*. New York: Ktav Publishing House, 1971.

Grotta Regina-I Studi Semitici, vol. 33. Universita di Roma: Istituto di Studi del Vicino Oriente, 1969.

Guzzo Amadasi, M. G. *Le iscrizioni fenicie e puniche delle colonie in occidente*. Studi Semitici 28. Rome: University of Rome, 1967.

Harden, Donald. *The Phoenicians*. Ancient Peoples and Places, vol. 26. New York: Frederick Praeger, 1962.

Harris, Zellig. *A Grammar of the Phoenician Language*. American Oriental Series, vol. 8. New Haven: American Oriental Society, 1936.

________. *Development of the Canaanite Dialects*. American Oriental Series, vol. 16. New Haven: American Oriental Society, 1939.

Har-Zāhāv, Zvi. *Diqdūq Lešōn Hā'ivrit* ["Grammar of the Hebrew Language"]. 6 vols. Tel Aviv: Maḥberet LaSSifrūt, 1951-56.

Hillers, Delbert. *Lamentations*. The Anchor Bible, vol. 7a. Garden City, NY: Doubleday, 1972.

Horowitz, Avi. *Ben Lāšōn LeLāšōn. LeTōldōt Lešōn HaMMiqrā' Bimey Bayit Šeni* ["The Transition Period in Biblical Hebrew. A Study in Post-Exilic Hebrew and Its Implications for the Dating of Psalms"]. Jerusalem: Bialik Institute, 1964.

Ibn Janaḥ, Yonah. *Sefer HāRiqmā* ["Book of Embroidery"]. Translated from the Arabic by Rabbi Judah Ibn Tibbon. Edited by M. Wilensky. 2 vols. Jerusalem: Academy of the Hebrew Language, 1964.

Jamme, Albert. *Sabaean Inscriptions from Maḥram Bilqis* (Marib). Baltimore: Johns Hopkins Press, 1962.

Jastrow, Marcus. *Dictionary of the Talmud Babli, Yerushalmi, Midrashic Literature and Targumim*. 2 vols. New York: Pardes Publishing House, 1950.

Jean, Ch.-F., and Hoftijzer, J. *Dictionnaire des inscriptions sémitiques de l'ouest*. Leiden: E. J. Brill, 1965.

Joüon, Paul P. *Grammaire de l'hébreu biblique*. Rome: Institut Biblique Pontifical, 1923.

Kassovsky, Benjamin. *Otzar Lešōn HaTTannāim* ["Concordance of the Sifra' or Tōrat Kōhanim"]. 9 vols. Jerusalem: Jewish Theological Seminary, 1967.

Kassovsky, Yehošu'a Chaim. *Otzar Lešōn HaMMišnah* ["Thesaurus of the Mišnah"]. 4 vols. Tel Aviv: Massadah Publishing Co., 1967.

Koehler, L., and Baumgartner, W. *Lexicon in Veteris Testamenti Libros*. Leiden: E. J. Brill, 1953.

Knudtzon, J. A.; Weber, Otto; and Ebeling, Erich. *Die El-Amarna Tafeln*. 2 vols. Leipzig: Vorderasiatische Bibliothek, Vol. 2, 1915.

Kutscher, Yehezkel. *HaLLašōn WeHāReqa' HaLLišōni šel Migilat Yeš'ayahu Haššlemah MeMigilat Yam HaMMelaḥ* ["The Language and Linguistic Background of the Isaiah Scroll"]. Jerusalem: Magnes Press, 1959.

________. *Millim WeTōldōtehen* ["Words and their History"]. Jerusalem: Kiryath Sefer, 1961.

Leslau, Wolf. *Lexique Soqotri. (Sudarabique moderne)*. Paris: Klincksieck, 1938.

Levine, Baruch Abraham. *In the Presence of the Lord*. Leiden: E. J. Brill, 1974.

Levy, Jacob. *Neuhebräisches und chaldäisches Wörterbuch*. 4 vols. Leipzig, 1876-89.

Levy, M. A. *Siegel und Gemmen mit aramäischen, phönizischen, althebräischen, himjarischen, nabathäischen und altsyrischen Inschriften erklärt*. Breslau: [publisher not cited], 1869.

Lidzbarski, Mark. *Phönizische und aramäische Krugaufschriften aus Elephantine*. Anhang zu den Abhandlungen der Königlich Preussischen Akademie der Wissenschaften, Philosophisch-historische Klasse. Berlin: Der Königl., 1912.

________. *Ephemeris für semitische Epigraphik*. 3 vols. Giessen: Ricker and Töpelmann, 1900-1915.

________. *Handbuch der nordsemitischen Epigraphik*. Hildesheim: Georg Olms, 1962.

MacLean, Arthur John. *Dictionary of the Dialects of Vernacular Syriac*. Amsterdam: Philo Press, 1972.

Mandelkern, Solomon, ed. *Veteris Testamenti Concordantiae*. 2 vols. Jerusalem/Tel Aviv: 1959.

Margoliouth, G. P. *Supplement to the Thesaurus Syriacus of R. Payne Smith*. Oxford: Oxford University Press, 1927.

Mazar, Benjamin, ed. *Hā'Avōt WeHaššōftim* ["The Patriarchs and the Judges"]. Vol. 2 of *The World History of the Jewish People*. Tel Aviv: Massadah, 1967.

Mentz, Arthur. *Beiträge zur Deutung der phönizischen Inschriften*. Abhandlungen für die Kunde des Morgenländes, vol. 29, no. 2. Leipzig: Deutsche Morgenländische Gesellschaft, 1944.

Meyer, Rudolf D. *Hebräische Grammatik*. 4 vols. Berlin: Walter de Gruyter and Co., 1966-72.

Miller, Patrick D., Jr. *The Divine Warrior in Early Israel*. Harvard Semitic Monographs, vol. 5. Cambridge, MA: Harvard University Press, 1973.

Morag, Šlomo. *Hā'Ivrit ŠeBeFi Yehūdei Temān* ["The Hebrew Language Tradition of the Yemenite Jews"]. Jerusalem: The Academy of the Hebrew Language, 1963.

Moscati, Sabatino. *The World of the Phoenicians*. New York: Praeger Inc., Publishers, 1968.

Moscati, S., ed.; Spitaler, A.; Ullendorff, E.; and von Soden, W. *An Introduction to the Comparative Grammar of the Semitic Languages: Phonology and Morphology*. Porta Linguarum Semiticarum, NS VI. Wiesbaden: Otto Harrassowitz, 1964.

Netanyahu, B., ed. *At the Dawn of Civilization*. Vol. 1 of *The World History of the Jewish People*. Rutgers: Rutgers University Press, 1964.

Oldenburg, Ulf. *The Conflict Between El and Baal in the Canaanite Religion*. Supplementa ad Numen, Altera Series vol. 3. Leiden: E. J. Brill, 1969.

Payne, Smith J. A. *Compendious Syriac Dictionary*. Oxford: Oxford University Press, 1967.

Peckham, J. Brian. *The Development of the Late Phoenician Scripts*. Harvard Semitic Series, vol. 20. Cambridge, MA: Harvard University Press, 1968.

Picard, Gilbert. *Carthage*. London: Elek Books, 1964.

Pope, Marvin. *El in the Ugaritic Texts*. Supplements to Vetus Testamentum, vol. 2. Leiden: E. J. Brill, 1955.

Pritchard, J. B. *Ancient Near Eastern Texts Relating to the Old Testament*. 3rd ed. Princeton: Princeton University Press, 1969.

Qimhi, David. *Mikhlōl* ["Hebrew Grammar"]. Systematically Presented and Critically Annotated by William Chomsky. New York: Bloch Publishing Co., 1952.

Reifenberg, A. *Ancient Jewish Coins*. Jerusalem: Rubin Mass, 1969.

Répertoire d'épigraphie sémitique. Vols. 1-5. Edited by Ch. Clermont-Ganneau and Jean Baptiste Chabot. Paris: Paul Geuthner, 1920-29.

Ricerche Puniche ad Antas. Studi Semitici, vol. 30. Universita di Roma: Istituto di Studi del Vicino Oriente, 1969.

Rin, Zvi. *'Alilōt Hā'Elim* ["Acts of the Gods"]. Jerusalem: Israel Society for Biblical Research, 1968.

Sainte-Marie, E. de. *Mission à Carthage*. Paris: Ernest Leroux, 1884.

Selms, A. van. *Marriage and Family Life in Ugaritic Literature*. Pretoria Oriental Series I. London: Luzac and Company, 1954.

Slouszch, Naḥum. *Otzar HaKKitōbōt HaPPinikiyōt* ["Thesaurus of Phoenician Inscriptions"]. Tel Aviv: Dvir, 1942.

Soden, W. von. *Akkadisches Handwörterbuch*. Wiesbaden: Otto Harrassowitz, 1959-.

Speiser, E. A. *Genesis*. The Anchor Bible, vol. 1. Edited by W. F. Albright and D. N. Freedman. Garden City, NY: Doubleday, 1964.

Sznycer, Maurice. *Les passages puniques en transcription latine.* Paris: C. Klincksieck, 1967.

Tallqvist, Knut. *Assyrian Names.* Hildesheim: Georg Olms, 1966.

Thomas, D. W., and McHardy, W. D., eds. *Hebrew and Semitic Studies Presented to G. R. Driver.* Oxford: Oxford University Press, 1963.

Tur-Sinai, N. H. *The Book of Job: A New Commentary.* Jerusalem: Kiryath Sepher, 1967.

Ugarit-Forschungen. Editorial Board: K. Bergerhof, M. Dietrich, Otto Loretz, J. C. Moor. Neukirchen-Vluyn: Butzon and Bercker, 1969-.

Yalon, Hanoch. *Mavō LeNiqqūd HaMMišnā* ["Introduction to the Vocalization of the Mishnah"]. Jerusalem: Bialik Institute, 1964.

________. *Perqey Lašōn* ["Studies in the Hebrew Language"]. Jerusalem: Bialik Institute, 1971.

________. *Quntrasim Le'Inyeney HaLLašōn Hā'Ivrit* ["Bulletin of Hebrew Language Studies"]. Jerusalem: Wahrman Books, 1963.

Yellin, David. *Diqdūq HaLLašōn Hā'Ivrit* ["Hebrew Grammar"]. 3rd ed. Jerusalem: Rubin Mass, 1963.

C. ARTICLES

Albright, William F. "Northwest Semitic Names in a List of Egyptian Slaves from the Eighteenth Century, B.C.," *JAOS* 74 (1954) 222-33.

________. "The Old Testament and Canaanite Literature," *CBQ* 7 (1945) 5-31.

Ap-Thomas, D. R. "The Phoenicians," in *Peoples of Old Testament Times.* Edited by D. J. Wiseman. Oxford: Oxford University Press, 1973.

Blau, Yeḥosu'a. "*Diqdūq Mešawweh Ḥādāš šel HaLLišōnōt HaŠŠmiyōt*" ["A New Comparative Semitic Grammar"], *Leš* 30 (1966) 136-56.

Branden, A. van den. "Levitique 1-7 et le tariff de Marseilles CIS I, 165," *RSO* (1965) 107-30.

Cooke, Stanley. "North Semitic Epigraphy," *JQR* (OS) 16 (1904) 258-89.

Cross, Frank Moore, Jr. "The Old Phoenician Inscription from Spain Dedicated to Hurrian Astarte," *HTR* 64 (1971) 189-95.

________. "Jar Inscriptions from Shiqmona," *IEJ* 18 (1968) 226-33.

________. "Yahweh and the God of the Patriarchs," *HTR* 55 (1962) 229-59.

________. "An Interpretation of the Nora Stone," *BASOR* 208 (1972) 13-19.

Dahood, Mitchell. Review of *Le iscrizioni fenice e puniche delle colonie in occidente*, by Maria Gulia Guzzo Amadasi, in *Or* 38 (1969) 158-60.

Delekat, L. "Ein Papyrusbrief in einer phönizisch gefärbten Konsekutivetempus-Sprache aus Ägypten (KAI/50)," *Or* 40 (1971) 401-9.

Demsky, Aharon. "*THTPK KS' MLKH-Gilgileha Šel Qelālā Nimreṣet*" ["The Evolution of a Vehement Curse"], *Leš* 34 (1970) 185-86.

Driver, G. R. "Note on a Phoenician Inscription of a Ptolemaic Date," *JEA* 36 (1950) 82.

Du Mesnil du Buisson, Robert, and Caquot, André. "La Seconde Tablette ou Petite Amulette d'Arslan Tash," *Syria* 48 (1971) 391-406.

Dunand, Maurice. "Nouvelles inscriptions phénicienes du Temple d'Echmoun à Bostan Ech-Cheikh près Sidon," *BMB* 18 (1965) 105-9.

Eissfeldt, Otto. "Etymologische und archäologische Erklärung alttestamentlicher Wörter," *OrAnt* 6 (1966) 165-76.

Ešel, Ben-Zion. "*Mōsek, Nōsek-Yōsek (Mateket)*" ["The Caster of Metals"], *Leš* 33 (1968-69) 72-73.

Ferron, Jean. "La Inscription Cartaginesa en el Apocrates Madrileño," *TrabPre* 28 (1971) 359-84.

________. "Chaton de Bague punique inscrit," *Mus* 34 (1971) 537-52.

________. "Inscription néopunique à Malta," *ZDMG* 117 (1967) 17-21.

________. "L'Inscription carthaginoise peinte sur l'urne cinéraine d'Almuñécar," *Mus* 83 (1970) 249-65.

________. "Epigraphie funeraire punique," *OrAnt* 5 (1966) 197-201.

Fevrier, Jean. "Rémarques sur l'épigraphie néopunique," *OrAnt* 2 (1963) 256-67.

________. "Sur le mot *'LT* en phénicien et en punique," *Sem* 5 (1955) 60-64.

________. "Paralipomena punica V--Une formule funeraire néopunique," *CB* 8 (1958-59) 25-29.

________. "Paralipomena punica VIII--Le mot *MĀQŌM* en phénicien-punique," *CB* 9 (1960-61) 33-36.

________. "Remarques sur l'épigraphie néopunique," *OrAnt* 2 (1963) 257-67.

________. "Le vocabulaire sacrificiel punique," *JA* 243 (1955) 49-63.

Fitzmyer, Joseph A. "The Aramaic Letter of King 'Adon to the Egyptian Pharaoh," *Bib* 46 (1965) 41-59.

Gevirtz, Stanley. "A Spindle Whorl with a Phoenician Inscription," *JNES* 26 (1967) 13-16.

Ginsberg, H. L. "Review of a *Grammar of the Phoenician Language*, by Zellig Harris," in *JBL* 57 (1937) 138-43.

________. "King of Kings and Lord of Kingdoms," *AJSL* 57 (1940) 71-74.

________. "Roots Below and Fruits Above and Related Matters," in *Hebrew and Semitic Studies Presented to G. R. Driver*. Edited by D. Winton Thomas and W. D. McHardy. Oxford: Oxford University Press, 1963, 72-76.

________. "Ugaritica-Phoenicia," in the *Gaster Festschrift, Journal of the Ancient Near East Society of Columbia University*, Vol. 5, New York, NY: Ancient Near East Society, 1973, 131-48.

Krahmalkov, C. R. "Comments on the Vocalization of the Suffix Pronoun of the Third Feminine Singular in Phoenician and Punic," *JSS* 17 (1972) 68-75.

________. "Studies in Phoenician and Punic Grammar," *JSS* 15 (1970) 181-88.

________. "Observations on the Affixing of Possessive Pronouns in Punic," *RSO* 44 (1970) 181-86.

________. "The Punic Speech of Hanno," *Or* 39 (1970) 52-74.

Kutscher, Yehezkel. "*Lešōnan Šel Hā'Iegarōt Hā'Ivriōt WeHā'Aramiōt Šel Bar Kōsbā uViney Dōrō*" ["The Language of the Hebrew and Aramaic Letters of Bar Kosbah and of his Generation"], *Leš* 25 (1961) 117-33.

Kutscher, Yehezkel. "*Lešonan Šel Ha'Iegarōt Ha'Ivriōt WeHa'Aramiōt Šel Bar Kōsbā uViney Dōrō*" ["The Language of the Hebrew and Aramaic Letters of Bar Kosbah and of his Generation"], *Leš* 26 (1962) 7-23.

________. "*BeŠuley HaMMilōn HaMMiqra'i*" ["Marginal notes on the Hebrew Dictionary of the Bible"], *Leš* 27 (1963) 186-88.

________. "*Meḥqar HaŠŠemit HaṢṢipōnit Ma'aravit BeYāmenū*" ["Contemporary North-West Semitic Studies"], *Leš* 29 (1965) 115-28.

________. "*Meḥqar HaŠŠemit HaṢṢipōnit Ma'aravit BeYāmenū*" ["Contemporary North-West Semitic Studies"], *Leš* 29 (1965) 47-58.

________. "*BeŠuley HaMMilōn HaMMiqra'i*" ["Marginal notes on the Hebrew Dictionary of the Bible"], *Leš* 30 (1965) 23.

________. "*BeŠuley HaMMilōn HaMMiqra'i*" ["Marginal notes on the Hebrew Dictionary of the Bible"], *Leš* 32 (1968) 345-46.

________. "*BeŠuley Ma'amarah Šel S. Yafet*" ["Marginal Notes on the Article by S. Yafet"], *Leš* 31 (1967) 28-32.

________. "*Kena'anit, 'Ivrit, Piniqit, 'Aramit, Lešōn Ḥazal, Punit*" ["Canaanite, Hebrew, Phoenician, Aramaic, Neo-Hebrew and Punic"], *Leš* 33 (1968-69) 83-110.

Landgraf, John. "The Maḥanat Inscription," *Levant* 3 (1971) 92-95.

Lane, William R. "The Phoenician Dialect of Larnex Tes Lapethou," *BASOR* 194 (1969) 39-45.

Lambdin, Thomas O. "The Junctural Origin of the West Semitic Definite Article," in *Near Eastern Studies in Honor of William Foxwell Albright*. Edited by Hans Goedicke. Baltimore: Johns Hopkins Press, 1971, 305-31.

Levi Della Vida, Giorgio. "Parerga neopunica," *OrAnt* 4 (1965) 59-70.

________. "Note di epigrafia punica-I," *RSO* 40 (1965) 205-13.

________. "Ostracon neopunica dalla Tripolitania," *Or* 33 (1964) 1-14.

________. "Le iscrizioni neopuniche di Wadi El-Amud," *LibAnt* 1 (1964) 57-63.

Lieberman, Saul. "*Hōraōt Niškaḥōt*" ["Forgotten Meanings"], *Leš* 33 (1968-69) 90-92.

Levine, B. A. "Notes on a Hebrew Ostracon from Arad," *IEJ* 19 (1969) 49-51.

Loewenstamm, S. E. "The Hebrew Root *ḤRŠ* in Light of the Ugaritic Texts," *JSS* 10 (1959) 63-65.

Marcus, David. "The Verb 'To Live' in Ugaritic," *JSS* 17 (1972) 76-82.

Martin, M. "A Preliminary Report After Re-Examination of the Byblian Inscriptions," *Or* (1961) 46-78.

Morag, Šelomo. "*Meša'*" in *Eretz Israel Archaeological, Historical and Geographical Studies*, Book 5. Jerusalem: Central Press, 1958, 138-44.

McKenzie, D. A. "The Judge of Israel," *VT* 17 (1967) 118-21.

McKenzie, J. L. "The Elders in the Old Testament," *Bib* 40 (1959) 522-40.

Moran, William L. "Does Amarna Bear on Karatepe?," *JCS* 6 (1952) 76-80.

________. "The Use of the Canaanite Infinitive Absolute as a Finite Verb in the Amarna Letters," *JCS* 4 (1950) 169-72.

________. "The Hebrew Language in its Northwest Semitic Background," in *The Bible and the Ancient Near East*. (Essays in Honor of W. F. Albright). Edited by G. E. Wright. Garden City, NY: Doubleday, 1961, 54-72.

Naveh, Joseph. "The Scripts of Two Ostraca From Elath," *BASOR* 183 (1966) 27-28.

________. "*Ketōbōt Piniqiyōt uFūniyōt*" ["Phoenician and Punic Inscriptions"], *Leš* 30 (1966) 232-39.

Neiman, David. "Phoenician Place-Names," *JNES* 24 (1965) 113-15.

Neuberg, Frank J. "An Unrecognized Meaning of the Hebrew *Dōr*," *JNES* 9 (1950) 215-17.

Obermann, Julian. "Does Amarna Bear on Karatepe?," *JCS* 5 (1951) 58-61.

Peckham, Brian. "The Nora Inscription," *Or* 41 (1972) 457-68.

Sarfatti, G. "*HaQQeta'im HaPPūniyim ŠeBeFornulus*" ["The Punic Fragments in Pornulus"], *Leš* 33 (1968-69) 48-59.

________. "*HaKKitōbōt HaPPiniqiyōt WeHaPPuniyōt Šel Mōšvōt HaMMa'arāv*" ["The Phoenician and Punic Inscriptions of the West"], *Leš* 34 (1969-70) 137-40.

Solá-Solé, Joseph M. "Inscriptions From Ibiza," *ClassFol* 22 (1968) 167-79.

Starky, Jean. "Une inscription phénicienne de Byblos," *MUSJ* 15 (1969) 259-73.

Slouszch, Naḥum. "*HaPPūnit HaḤadašah BeYaḥas Le 'Ivrit. Pi'nūaḥ Ketōbet LeDūgmā*" ["Neo-Punic in Relation to Hebrew. A Translation as an Example"], *Leš* 12 (1947-48) 3-11.

_______. "*LeŠemōt Ha'Umanim WeHa'Umamiyōt BiŚifat Kena'an*" ["Art and Artisans in the Language of Canaan"], *Leš* 2 (1937) 351-54.

Szyncer, Maurice. "Une inscription punique trouvée à Monte Sirai, (Sardaigne)," *Sem* 15 (1965) 35-43.

_______. "Rémarques sur le grafitto phénicien en characteres grecs de la Grotto de Wasta," *Sem* 8 (1958) 5-10.

_______. "Quelques observations sur la grande inscription dedicatoire de Mactar," *Sem* 22 (1972) 25-44.

Tawil, Hayyim. "*He'ārā LeKetōbet Aḥiram*" ["A Suggestion for the Aḥiram Inscription"], *Leš* 37 (1973) 99-101.

Thomas, D. Winton. "A Consideration of Some Unusual Ways of Expressing the Superlative in Hebrew," *VT* 3 (1953) 209-24.

Urie, D. M. L. "Sacrifice Among the West Semites," *PEQ* 8 (1948-49) 67-71.

Yeivin, Shmuel. "*He'arōt Balšāniyōt*" ["Philological Suggestions"], *Leš* 36 (1972) 245-56.

_______. "*He'arōt LeKetōbot HaPPiniqit MeKaratape*" ["Suggestions for the Phoenician Karatepe Inscription"], *Leš* 16 (1951) 265-69.

Young, D. W. "Notes on the Root *NTN* in Biblical Hebrew," *VT* 10 (1960) 457-59.

D. UNPUBLISHED MATERIAL

Lane, William R. "A Handbook of Phoenician Inscriptions." Unpublished Ph.D. dissertation, The Johns Hopkins University, 1962.

Moran, W. L. "A Syntactical Study of the Dialect of Byblos as Reflected in Amarna." Unpublished Ph.D. dissertation, The Johns Hopkins University, 1950.

ADDENDA TO BIBLIOGRAPHY

Brin, Geršōn. "'*al HaTTo'ar Ben HaMMelek*" ["On the Title *Ben HaMMelek*"], *Leš* 31 (1967) 85-96.

Gelb, I. J. "The Early History of the West Semitic Peoples," *JCS* 15 (1961) 43.

Goshen-Gottstein, M. H. "'*al HaBBerākā*" ["*BRK* in Ugaritic and Hebrew"], *Leš* 32 (1967/68) 59-62.

Levine, B. A. "The Language of the Magical Bowls." Pp. 344-47 in *A History of the Jews in Babylonia* by Jacob Neusner. Leiden: E. J. Brill, 1970.

Nicholson, E. H. "Review of *A History of Old Testament Priesthood* (Analecta Biblica 35), by A. Cody," in *JSS* 18 (1973) 282-85.

Porten, Bezalel. *Archives From Elephantine*. Los Angeles: University of California Press, 1968.

Ṣarfatti, G. "'*Iyūnīm BeSimantiqā šel Lešōn Ḥazal UVeDeršotehem*" ["Semantics of Mishnaic Hebrew and Interpretation of the Bible by the *Tanna'im*"], *Leš* 30 (1965) 34-40.

Silverman, M. H. "Review of *Kanaanäische und aramäische Inschriften*, by H. Donner and W. Röllig," in *JAOS* 94 (1974) 268-69.

Slouszch, Nahum. "*Meḥqārīm 'Ivrim-Kena'anim*" ["Hebrew-Canaanite Studies"], *Leš* 4 (1932) 115-18.

Printed in the USA
CPSIA information can be obtained
at www.ICGtesting.com
LVHW050719261023
761976LV00005B/133

9 781532 6909